" POLITICIANS ARE LIKE ~~DINOSAURS~~.

— BIG HEARTS

&

— SMALL BRAINS "

SEN. RAND PAUL 2017

"Finally someone has written a comprehensive history of America's efforts to help worthy groups of Americans: the elderly, the veteran, the less fortunate and the very young. It is a history of ever more generous help to ever larger groups of people. You can agree or disagree with the merit of all these programs, but the cost is clear, and John Cogan shows why that cost has been either ignored or passed to future generations. The first step in fixing our entitlements is knowing their history. Cogan has now given us that history."
—Bill Bradley, former U.S. Senator

"John Cogan thoroughly reviews one of the greatest challenges facing our country: the unsustainable growth of entitlement spending. He provides a comprehensive view of the issue by looking at the history, the evolution, and the daunting numbers. Cogan brings his extraordinary knowledge and background in economics, fiscal policy, health care, and Social Security to bear in this book to give the reader a full understanding of the roots and the extent of this growing problem that must be tackled."
—Paul D. Ryan, Speaker of the U.S. House of Representatives

THE HIGH COST
OF GOOD INTENTIONS

THE HIGH COST
OF GOOD INTENTIONS

*A History of U.S. Federal
Entitlement Programs*

John F. Cogan

Stanford University Press
Stanford, California

Stanford University Press
Stanford, California

Printed in the United States of America on acid-free, archival-quality paper

Library of Congress Cataloging-in-Publication Data

Names: Cogan, John F., author.
Title: The high cost of good intentions : a history of U.S. federal entitlement programs / John F. Cogan.
Description: Stanford, California : Stanford University Press, 2017. | Includes bibliographical references and index.
Identifiers: LCCN 2017009793 (print) | LCCN 2017022252 (ebook) | ISBN 9781503604254 | ISBN 9781503603547 (cloth : alk. paper)
Subjects: LCSH: Entitlement spending—United States—History. | Public welfare—United States—History. | Social security—United States—History.
Classification: LCC HJ7543 (ebook) | LCC HJ7543 .C64 2017 (print) | DDC 361.60973—dc23
LC record available at https://lccn.loc.gov/2017009793

For
Thomas Paul
and
Nicholas Lee

Acknowledgments

I OWE AN ESPECIALLY DEEP DEBT OF GRATITUDE TO two friends and colleagues, David Koitz and David Brady. The two Davids have been invaluable colleagues and active contributors to the development of this work from the time the ideas presented here were merely a collection of hazy, unconnected thoughts to the manuscript's completion. I have had the good fortune to be able to draw on David Koitz's encyclopedic knowledge of federal programs, his keen understanding of Congress, and his remarkable understanding of the dynamics of entitlement legislation that he gained from a lifetime of public service. I have likewise benefited from David Brady's deep knowledge of Congress, how it works (and sometimes doesn't), and the influence of politics on policymaking. He has been a source of continuing encouragement.

I have benefited greatly from the expert research assistance of Daniel Heil. From collecting and collating statistical data and performing computer runs on large complex data sets, to unearthing obscure nineteenth-century government documents, to providing substantive comments on various drafts. Daniel diligently contributed to every aspect of this manuscript. Tom Church, Chris Castellanos, Sarah Jarman, and Griffin Weir also provided expert research assistance that greatly improved the quality of the manuscript. I thank Maria Sanchez for her assistance in gathering data and library work and Barbara Egbert for editorial assistance.

I am indebted to Michael Boskin, Barry Clendenin, Tim Muris, Charles Palm, John Taylor, Tom Saving, and George Shultz for providing valuable comments on earlier versions of the entire manuscript; to Joe Antos, Scott Atlas, and Daniel Kessler for contributions to sections on health care entitlements; to Chuck Blahous for comments on Social Security issues; to Richard Epstein and Sai Prakash for guidance on legal issues; and to Barry Anderson for help on budget process matters.

I owe a unique debt to my long-time friend and former Hoover Institution director John Raisian for his support and encouragement of this work. I thank John and director Tom Gilligan for maintaining Hoover's unique research environment that has allowed me the intellectual freedom and the time to pursue my research

Last and certainly not least, I thank my wife, Dupi, for putting up with me throughout the duration of my research. Dupi has been a true partner on this project in every sense of the word. She has discussed and debated many of my ideas, edited the manuscript, and has been an invaluable source of support and encouragement. It is fair to say that without Dupi, this manuscript would not have been possible.

Contents

1 Introduction

Many of these programs may have come from a good heart, but not all
have come from a clear head—and the costs have been staggering. We can
be compassionate about human needs without being complacent about
budget extravagance.

Ronald Reagan, 1981[1]

THROUGHOUT U.S. HISTORY, FEDERAL ENTITLE-
ment programs have sprung from the noble intention of
providing assistance to people who are destitute through no fault of
their own. Veterans' entitlements, dating back to the Revolutionary
War, were created to provide assistance to soldiers disabled by injuries
and illness suffered during wartime service. The New Deal and Great
Society social insurance and welfare entitlements were created with the
lofty goal of providing a safety net of assistance to the elderly, single
mothers, the disabled, the unemployed, and people suffering from ill
health. These programs kept disabled veterans of nineteenth-century
wars out of almshouses, enabled millions of senior citizens to live out
their retirement years without poverty, and provided needed assistance
to countless Americans who faced economic destitution.

But over time, entitlements have become a complex system that now
transfers hundreds of billions of dollars *each month* from one group in
society to another, most often regardless of individual need. The scale
of federal entitlement assistance today is unmatched in human history.

Fifty-five percent of all U.S. households receive cash or in-kind assistance from at least one major federal entitlement program. Among all households headed by a person under age 65, over 40 percent receive entitlement program benefits. Eighty percent of all people living in households headed by single mothers receive entitlement benefits, and nearly six out of every ten children in the United States (58 percent) are growing up in a family on the entitlement rolls.

The labyrinth of overlapping entitlement programs, each with its own eligibility rules, allows 120 million people, two-thirds of all entitlement recipients, to simultaneously collect benefits from at least two programs. Forty-six million people, nearly one-third of all recipients, collect benefits from three or more federal entitlement programs simultaneously.

As well-meaning and beneficial as many entitlements may be, they have come at a high cost. They have undermined the natural human desire for self-sufficiency and self-improvement. Social Security and Medicare have reduced the perceived need by young workers to save for their retirement and have induced senior citizens to forgo years of productive and rewarding employment. The welfare system's high marginal tax rates have discouraged work and penalized investments in human capital. The system has created incentives for young women to bear children out of wedlock and remain unmarried. It has discouraged fathers of young children from meeting their parental responsibilities.

This high human cost has been matched by large fiscal costs and monumental inefficiency. The $2.4 trillion the federal government currently spends annually on entitlements equals $7,500 for every man, woman, and child living in the United States, an amount that is five times the money necessary to lift every poor person out of poverty. Only about half of all entitlement assistance (48 percent) goes to the poor. The other half, amounting to over $1 trillion annually, is spread widely across households located over all parts of the U.S. income distribution. While the massive expenditure has significantly reduced poverty among senior citizens, poverty rates for all other adults and for children are no lower today than they were a half century ago.

Since World War II, total federal spending as a share of the nation's output of goods and services has increased from 15 to 21 percent.

The growth in entitlement spending accounts for all of this increase. Federal spending as a percent of U.S. gross domestic product on all other federal activities combined, including national defense, foreign affairs, and the broad array of nonentitlement domestic programs, has declined. Neither revenues generated by the growing national economy nor those extracted from individuals through taxation have kept pace with rising entitlement spending. As a consequence, the national debt now stands at a record peacetime high.

Entitlements have created a fiscal challenge unlike any other in the nation's history. The baby boom generation's retirement, coming on the heels of eight decades of entitlement liberalizations, has put the nation's budget on a dangerous financial trajectory. Previous periods of high federal expenditures and increasing debt have been due mainly to wars and have been temporary. Today, the nation faces a prolonged period of permanently high federal expenditures that will impose a crippling debt burden on future generations if they are left unchecked.

How did America arrive at this point? How were noble and well-intentioned ideals distorted into unaffordable programs that now threaten U.S. economic prosperity and harm many of those individuals whom entitlement programs seek to help? How did we end up transferring billions of dollars to well-off and moderately well-off senior citizens, most of whom are able to provide for their own retirement needs and, at the same time, leave 16 million children in poverty? How long can we rationalize providing more than $50,000 a year in Social Security and Medicare benefits to retired middle-income couples when nearly half of all U.S. households headed by people under age 65 are living on less than that? And how, in the name of helping destitute younger members of society, can we justify erecting barriers to their efforts to climb up from poverty? How did the simple idea of assisting people in need evolve into compulsory laws that require citizens to sacrifice their individual liberties?

This book examines how and why entitlement programs have grown so large and have become so far removed from the ideals on which they were founded. It presents a history of major federal entitlement programs from the beginning of the Republic to today, showing how they evolved and explaining the forces that caused their evolution.

The book's central theme is that the creation of entitlements brings forth relentless forces that cause them to inexorably expand. These liberalizing forces are inevitable and inseparable from the entitlements themselves. They originate from a well-meaning human impulse to treat all similarly situated people equally under the law. When first enacted, entitlement laws, for policy or fiscal reasons, confine benefits to a group of individuals who are deemed to be particularly worthy of assistance. As time passes, groups of excluded individuals come forth claiming that they are no less deserving of aid. Pressure is brought by, or on behalf of, excluded groups to relax eligibility rules. The ever-present pressure is magnified during periods of budget surpluses and by public officials' imperative to be elected and reelected. Eventually the government acquiesces and additional claimants deemed worthy are allowed to join the benefit rolls. That very broadening of eligibility rules inevitably brings another group of claimants closer to the eligibility boundary line, and the pressure to relax qualifying rules begins again. The process of liberalization repeats itself until benefits are extended to a point where the program's purposes bear only a faint resemblance to its original noble intentions.[2]

As this book will show, these forces are evident in the early histories of nineteenth-century entitlements, and they continue to drive entitlement policy today. They cause entitlements to follow a common evolutionary path of nearly continual liberalization that is interrupted only rarely by legislative retrenchments. Each step along the path establishes a new base on which future expansions are built.

The nation's first major federal entitlements were benefit programs for disabled wartime veterans. Enacted at the outset of each major war, these programs were originally established to compensate soldiers who were disabled in wartime service and widows of soldiers killed in action. Revolutionary War pensions were initially confined to members of the Continental Army and Navy. Congress then extended pensions to members of state militias, then to disabled wartime veterans regardless of whether their disability was related to wartime service, and finally, in 1832, to virtually all remaining Revolutionary War veterans. These laws effectively transformed the original disability program for Continental Army soldiers and seamen into a general retirement program for all remaining War of Independence veterans.

Civil War and World War I pensions repeated this pattern, but on a far grander scale. What began as an entitlement to Union veterans disabled during the Civil War grew to cover all Union veterans who reached old age, transforming the initial disability program into the nation's first large-scale federal retirement program. An extreme instance of just how broadly Congress is willing to extend the class of worthy entitlement recipients occurred nearly one hundred years after the Civil War began when in 1956, Congress extended pensions to a few remaining widows of Confederate soldiers. During World War I, Congress took steps to prevent a repeat of the Civil War pension experience. However, despite these precautionary measures, Congress quickly extended pensions to all disabled veterans regardless of whether their disability was war related.

All of the major Revolutionary War pension expansions were enacted during years of large budget surpluses. The 1890 Dependent Pension Act for Civil War veterans, at the time the single costliest entitlement expansion in U.S. history, was enacted following twenty-four consecutive years of annual budget surpluses. The magnitude of these surpluses was, according to historian Davis Dewey, "without parallel in the history of any nation."[3] World War I veterans' pension liberalizations came amid a decade of large annual budget surpluses. The last of these occurred in 1930, just before the Great Depression plunged the federal budget into deep deficit.

The navy pension fund, the federal government's first trust fund, foreshadows the road the nation is traveling down with Social Security. The navy fund was financed by prize money, or "booty," from the sale of the captured contents of enemy and pirate ships. Temporary trust fund surpluses during the 1830s gave rise to sweeping expansions of navy pensions. The last of these awarded retroactive lump-sum benefits in excess of $100,000 (in today's dollars) to 9 percent of the program's new beneficiaries. The largesse quickly bankrupted the trust fund, and Congress turned to general revenues to finance future navy pensions, all the while maintaining the fiction of trust fund financing.

In dispensing Civil War pensions, Congress discovered the power of entitlements as an efficient vehicle for gaining electoral advantage. During the late 1800s and early 1900s, the Republican Party used Civil War pensions as a tool to help realign the American electorate and secure unified control over Congress and the presidency for fourteen consecutive years. Their efforts were aided by the Grand Army of the Republic (GAR), the country's first large national lobbying organization, which rose to prominence only after Civil War pensions were firmly established. The GAR joined with the Pension Bureau and the congressional Veterans Committees to form the nineteenth century's most powerful iron triangle to protect and extend veterans' pensions.

The fiscal consequences of these liberalizations were, for the most part, limited. The ultimate size of the group that Congress could consider to be worthy of pensions was restricted to wartime veterans and their survivors. Consequently, for most of the nineteenth century, entitlement expenditures remained a light burden on the nation's income. Even these burdens were temporary as time exacted its inevitable toll on wartime veteran populations.

The New Deal broke new ground by extending entitlements to people in the general population who had performed no particular service to the federal government. The nation's experience with nineteenth-century veterans' entitlements should have served as a warning about the fiscal and societal consequences of extending entitlements. Policymakers should have foreseen that the same forces that had caused them to continually liberalize veterans' entitlements would have an even stronger effect on broader entitlement programs. By 1935, the tendency to continually expand entitlements, born of a desire to help the destitute and reinforced by more than a century of legislative precedent, had already been firmly embedded in Congress's collective DNA. Policymakers should have also recognized that broader entitlements made the potential class of people deemed worthy of government aid open-ended. Since one cohort of retirees or low-income people immediately replaces its predecessor, entitlements for the general population would continue ad infinitum. There is no starting over, as in the cases of the veterans' pensions. Moreover, each legislative expansion would establish a new permanent base on which future liberalizations would be added.

The nineteenth-century entitlement lessons went unheeded, and the entitlements arising out of the New Deal marched along the same liberalizing path as the earlier veterans' programs, but with far more vigor and far larger consequences. The flagship Social Security program initially covered only 50 percent of the workforce and was designed to provide a safety net of assistance to retired workers. But the "large reserve" of surplus payroll tax revenues created by the Roosevelt administration in order to finance future benefits tempted Congress in 1939 into extending benefits to wives and surviving children of qualifying workers and raising benefits significantly.

The pattern of expanding Social Security when program surpluses emerged was repeated over and over again following World War II. Every Congress, save one, and every president during the years from 1950 to 1972 took action to expand the program. By the mid-1950s, Congress had made coverage nearly universal. Disability benefits for older workers with permanent disabilities were established in 1956. Within a decade, Congress extended the class of worthy disability recipients to temporarily disabled and younger workers. Medicare benefits were added, first for senior citizens and then for disabled workers. Numerous increases in retirement benefits tripled the inflation-adjusted value of the typical new retiree's monthly Social Security check. By the mid-1970s, these expansions had transformed the original safety net program into one that padded the already comfortable lifestyles of millions of middle-class retirees. But the high cost of these liberalizations brought the program to the brink of bankruptcy in 1980, just as liberalizations had done with the navy pension fund 140 years earlier.

In the process of enacting these expansions, Congress, led this time by Democrats, raised the practice of using entitlements for electoral gain to a finely honed skill. From the end of World War II through 1975, seven of the ten legislative increases in Social Security monthly benefits took effect during an election year; four of these increases first appeared in retirees' October Social Security checks—one month before national elections. The election-year bidding war in 1972 between Democratic party presidential contenders and President Richard Nixon produced an across-the-board, permanent, 20 percent increase in monthly benefit levels for the 28 million recipients.

The New Deal public assistance programs initially provided financial assistance to supplement state government support only of people who were unable to provide for themselves: the poor elderly, blind people, and poor children in need of assistance due to the father's death or desertion. Under this policy, states retained primary authority to determine which individuals in each of these groups were worthy of welfare assistance.

Following World War II, the federal government progressively expanded its authority over welfare entitlements. Executive branch officials began by using federal financial assistance as leverage to force states into expanding the universe of worthy claims. From 1965 to 1975, the desire by federal authorities to ensure that all worthy welfare claimants receive assistance produced a bipartisan executive, legislative, and judicial blitzkrieg of liberalizations that is unmatched in all of U.S. history. The barrage included establishing new entitlements for Medicaid, food stamps, Supplemental Security Income, child nutrition programs, social service benefits, and earned income tax credits. It included Supreme Court decisions that embraced novel interpretations of the law and the U.S. Constitution to declare that long-standing state and local government public assistance rules and regulations were violations of welfare claimants' statutory and constitutional rights. And it included congressional acts that wrote into the federal statute books new public assistance requirements on state governments.

By the late 1960s, the federal government had established primary control over welfare entitlements. Federal authorities now played a central role in determining who were worthy claimants. State governments were reduced to acting mainly as administrative agents for these federal programs. The New Deal policy of allowing states to determine welfare eligibility had become a dead letter.

By the mid-1970s, the network of federal entitlement programs that constitutes today's welfare state was fully in place. All of today's major federal entitlement programs, except for the Affordable Care Act's health insurance entitlements, had been written into the statute books. Entitlement spending accounted for over half of all federal program expenditures.

Ronald Reagan's election in 1980 brought an attempt to slow the juggernaut. The attempt, however, achieved only modest success in restraining the growth in entitlement spending and in putting Social Security temporarily on a sound financial footing.

By the 1990s, there was widespread recognition in Washington that decades of liberalizing entitlements and demographic trends had put the federal government's finances on an unsustainable path. A storm was brewing on the fiscal horizon. Yet all three branches of government acted as if they were in a collective state of denial. Despite knowledge that without legislative action, Social Security was destined to become insolvent, no Social Security reforms were enacted or implemented. Congress and the executive branch, despite the same knowledge about Medicare's poor financial future, were not only unable to restrain the existing program's expenditures, they extended Medicare coverage to include prescription drugs.

Knowing full well the dimensions of the coming fiscal storm, Congresses and various presidents of the past twenty-five years continued a steady stream of legislation extending the class of worthy welfare claimants higher up the income ladder. The Congress and the executive branch capped off this remarkable period by mandating universal health insurance coverage and subsidizing its purchase for households with incomes far in excess of the national median. The Supreme Court added to the profligacy with decisions in the 1990s liberalizing disability and welfare programs and later by straining to uphold the Affordable Care Act.

Post–World War II Congresses and presidents have transformed programs whose original purpose was to alleviate poverty among well-identified worthy groups into a vast network of programs designed to redistribute income across a broad spectrum of American society. In recent years the percentage of the U.S. population living in households that receive benefits from at least one major federal entitlement program has reached an all-time record high for nonrecessionary years.

The book covers major programs that are commonly understood to be entitlements, including veterans' pensions and compensation programs, the Social Security retirement and disability insurance

programs, Medicare, unemployment insurance, Medicaid, the Temporary Assistance to Needy Families program, the food stamp program,
child nutrition programs, Supplemental Security Income, the earned
income tax credit, and the Affordable Care Act's health insurance subsidies. Although histories of each of these individual programs have
been written, to date no other written work has provided a comprehensive treatment. This book draws heavily on these prior works to trace
the common history and evolution of major federal entitlement programs. No previous work has sought to systematically identify similari-
ties in the evolution of these programs or the common forces that have
shaped their expansion. This book is a first step to filling this void.

The book's coverage is not exhaustive. The federal government officially defines an entitlement as a "statutory mandate or requirement of
the United States to incur a financial obligation unless that obligation
is explicitly conditioned on the appropriation in subsequent legislation
of sufficient funds for that purpose."[4] However, federal authorities do
not apply this definition to classify individual programs into entitlements and nonentitlements. For our purposes, this definition, is, on
one hand, too restrictive in that it might exclude such programs as veterans' compensation and pension payments, food stamps, Medicaid,
Supplemental Security Income, the Temporary Assistance for Needy
Families program, and Medicare physician and prescription drug
reimbursements. The payment of a financial obligation under each of
these programs is, at least in part, conditional on subsequent annual
appropriations. On the other hand, the definition might also include a
wide array of business, agriculture, and individual loan guarantee and
insurance programs, farm price and income support payments, payments to Indian Nations, and payments to current and former federal
government employees. The entitlement definition might be even more
expansively interpreted to include various tax deductions, such as the
mortgage interest deduction and the employer-sponsored health insurance exclusion. A treatment of these programs and so-called tax expenditures is beyond the scope of this work.[5]

2 Creating Legislative Precedents

Revolutionary War Pensions

Pensions in all countries begin on a small scale, and are at first generally granted on proper consideration, and that they increase till at last they are granted as often on whim or caprice as for proper considerations.

Senator Nathaniel Macon, 1818[1]

REVOLUTIONARY WAR PENSIONS WERE THE NATION'S first entitlement program. Through a series of laws enacted between 1789 and 1793, the federal government agreed to pay annual pensions to Continental Army soldiers and seamen who became disabled as a result of wartime injuries or illness. The laws also provided pensions to widows of soldiers and seamen killed in action. For forty years, Congress enlarged and expanded these benefits until, by the 1830s, they covered virtually all Revolutionary War seamen and soldiers, including volunteers and members of the state militia and their widows, regardless of disability or income.

From the beginning, Congress regarded entitlements differently from other government programs, conferring a degree of permanence that it did not bestow on other programs. Congress never reduced monthly Revolutionary War pensions, and only twice, under extraordinary circumstances, restricted pension eligibility. Liberalizations were enacted with regularity and were usually justified on the basis that previously uncovered soldiers were as equally worthy to receive benefits as those already on the pension rolls. Pension liberalizations coincided with large federal budget surpluses when pressure for expansion invariably overwhelmed congressional resistance.

This legislative record provides the first glimpse of the explosive budgetary cost of entitlements and the government's tendency to underestimate their cost. The pension laws of 1818 and 1832 caused tenfold and threefold unanticipated increases in pension expenditures, respectively. These underestimates resulted primarily from ignorance about the number of veterans still living. But as the quotation at this chapter's beginning indicates, the underestimates were also due to the failure to account for how potential recipients would modify their circumstances to qualify for pensions.

The Early Years: 1789–1816

Since colonial times, military pensions were provided to soldiers wounded during combat and to the widows of soldiers killed in battle. When the colonies declared their independence in 1776, the Continental Congress established pensions for officers and soldiers of the Continental Army. In 1789, the new national government quickly assumed responsibility for these pensions. During its inaugural session, Congress authorized the federal government to temporarily continue to pay Revolutionary War pensions. Congress extended the temporary law in 1790 and made the pension program permanent in 1792. The laws granted pensions to regular army officers, soldiers, and seamen who had suffered injuries in battle and were impoverished as a result. The benefit structure was progressive. For privates and noncommissioned officers, benefit levels were a higher proportion of their monthly pay than they were for commissioned officers. The laws limited coverage to the Continental Army and Navy, thus excluding others who had fought, most notably members of the state militias.[2]

The first major expansion came in 1806 as the expanding economy, fueled by growing international trade, increased government revenues.[3] The years 1803 to 1806 were bountiful ones for the U.S. Treasury. Federal revenues, mostly from tariffs, rose from $11 million in 1803 to nearly $16 million in 1806. Annual expenditures, despite the Louisiana Purchase and a rapid naval buildup, remained equal to or less than $10 million annually.[4] The surplus was more than enough to continue reducing the national debt.

The surpluses provided an opportunity to extend pensions to members of state militias. Advocates argued that militia veterans were no less worthy of disability pensions than Continental Army veterans. New York congressman John C. Smith observed "that the wounds received by . . . [militia soldiers] . . . had been as serious to them, and as important to their country, as those received in the actual service of the United States."[5] Opponents said it was improper for the federal government to pay pensions to soldiers who had "acted under the authority of the States."[6] The potent moral force of the equally worthy claim in combination with a large surplus of revenues overwhelmed the opposition. Congress voted in 1806 to extend pensions to all classes of the military, including volunteers, members of the militia, and state troops.

Congress's response to a precipitous drop in tax revenue in 1809 provided an early indication that it regarded entitlements as a special class of federal programs. That year, the embargo of British and French vessels caused federal revenue to plummet by 50 percent. Congress reduced total appropriations by 22 percent. The broad-based reductions applied to most government functions and remained in place for two years until revenues returned to their pre-embargo level in 1811. Congress exempted veterans' pensions from any reductions.[7]

Pensions remained a small part of total federal spending during the years preceding the War of 1812. From 1800 to 1811, annual pension outlays were only 1 percent of annual federal spending. The War of 1812 added new pensioners to the rolls, but pension outlays still constituted less than 1 percent of total federal spending in 1816, the year after the war ended.[8]

Strong economic growth following the War of 1812 produced a large budget surplus in 1816, and with it came general support for legislation to expand veterans' pensions. Since the enactment of the original pension law, prices of consumer goods had risen 45 percent, eroding the purchasing power of monthly pensions.[9] Congress responded by substantially raising monthly benefits paid to disabled Revolutionary War and War of 1812 soldiers, scaled so that those on the benefit ladder's lowest rung received the largest increases. Privates and noncommissioned officers received a 60 percent increase, and officers received an increase of around 30 percent.[10] Future entitlement programs, particularly Social Security, would follow this pattern.

The Service Pension Law of 1818

Continuing economic prosperity caused revenues to exceed expenditures by more than 50 percent in both 1816 and 1817. The newly elected president, James Monroe, proposed in his first Annual Message to Congress that the large surpluses be used to expand pension benefits. In his words, Revolutionary War veterans "have a claim on the gratitude of the country, and it will do honor to their country to provide for them."[11] The American public shared President Monroe's sentiment. Many of the few soldiers who were still alive were infirmed or unable to work.

Congress expressed the nation's gratitude with the landmark pension law of March 18, 1818, which entitled all veterans who had served in the Continental Army for at least nine months and were "in reduced circumstances" to a lifetime pension.[12] No longer did those veterans have to prove that they had been disabled as a result of wartime service. A Continental Army veteran merely had to be "in need of assistance from his country for support."[13]

The 1818 law was extensively debated in Congress. Supporters emphasized the country's debt to Revolutionary War veterans. Congressman Edward Colston of Virginia reminded his fellow congressmen, "Let not the soldier, by whose bravery and sufferings we are entitled to hold seats on this floor, be required to expose his poverty to the world."[14] The emotional argument that veterans had an earned right to assistance was compelling. This earned-right concept was a powerful force, then and in the future. President Franklin Delano Roosevelt recognized its power and used it as the foundation of his Social Security program, which by virtue of the payment of payroll taxes created an earned right to government benefits.

Opponents of the 1818 law predicted that granting lifetime pensions to Revolutionary War veterans who were "in reduced circumstances" would be costly. Senator Nathaniel Macon of North Carolina observed, "Pensions in all countries begin on a small scale and are at first generally granted on proper consideration, and that they increase till at last they are granted as often on whim or caprice as for proper considerations." He warned that this path would eventually require higher taxes: "To provide for those who will not provide for themselves, will, on experiment, be found an endless task. It will drain any treasury, no matter how full."[15]

Opponents also argued that establishing an entitlement to veterans merely for their service amounted to elevating a particular group in society above all others. They believed that military service to defend the nation was a citizen's duty that did not warrant any special preference. This belief, widely held at the time of the Revolutionary War, prompted John Adams's well-known 1776 declaration, "We must all be soldiers." Much later, President Franklin Roosevelt would apply the same belief in opposing veterans' benefit extension to those who had not been disabled in wartime service.

Supporters stressed that the bill was designed primarily to assist needy veterans. Failure to pass the bill, according to Senator Robert Goldsborough of Maryland, would abandon veterans "in the advanced age and infirmities, to the precarious offerings of charity; to the protection of the almshouse and such receptacles of human wretchedness whilst the treasury of the country is ample to relieve them."[16] But the cold reality of limiting benefits to needy veterans meant the law would require them to prove their indigence. Many members regarded such a means test as degrading. After defeating an amendment to impose a means test, Congress settled the issue in a way that it would so often settle difficult issues in the future: It adopted the purposely vague wording that to qualify for assistance, the veteran must be "in need of assistance from his country for support"[17] but without requiring the veteran to demonstrate that need. Congress approved the law by overwhelming margins.

Significantly, the law did not apply to Revolutionary War soldiers who had served in the state militia or to War of 1812 veterans. Efforts were made during the House debate to include militia members on the grounds that they were no less worthy. Congressman James Johnson of Kentucky pressed the case for the militia by arguing that "whatever sentiment may prevail as to their inefficiency, experience confirms the opinion that they were equally useful, and equally important in their place, with the gallant soldiers of the Continental line."[18]

This argument ran up against the need to keep the bill's cost within limits. Senator Goldsborough put the dilemma succinctly: "If we discriminate we shall do injustice; and if we include all, . . . the finances of the country will be exhausted in the undertaking."[19]

Ultimately cost considerations prevailed and members of the militia were excluded from the law's liberalizing disability provisions[20]—but only temporarily. A decade and a half later, when federal revenues were far more plentiful, the "equally worthy" argument won the day for veterans of the militia.

The law produced a massive surge in applications and an unexpected and unprecedented cost to the Treasury. The law's proponents had estimated that fewer than two thousand veterans would qualify and that the annual cost might reach $115,000. But by the end of 1819, more than twenty-eight thousand individuals had applied, and over sixteen thousand applicants had been approved. Astoundingly, the number of applicants exceeded the entire number of Continental Army veterans who were thought to be still alive. The 1818 law's annual cost to the Treasury had ballooned from $300,000 to a staggering $1.8 million. That year, pensions accounted for 11 percent of federal program expenditures.[21] Two years later, the 1818 law cost more than the entire amount spent on Revolutionary War disability pensions from 1791 to 1817.[22] The surge of applications was accompanied by widespread charges of pension fraud and corruption. A law designed to assist destitute veterans was providing pensions to many financially well-off veterans, and even many who had never fought for the nation's independence.

The highly public scandal put considerable pressure on Congress to reform the program. Additional pressure came from a severe economic contraction that produced the first peacetime deficit in more than a decade.[23] Congress slashed total government appropriations by 46 percent in 1820 but rejected proposals to reduce monthly pension benefits. It did, however, respond to the pension scandal with the Act of May 1, 1820, which required all pensioners who had been permitted under the 1818 law to reapply for benefits, sign an oath of poverty, and submit a complete schedule of income and property; in other words, the law established a means test. The War Department was authorized to review and approve any applicant who was "in such indigent circumstances as to be unable to support himself without the assistance of his country."

The law's enactment was followed by numerous reports of veterans gathering to march, rank and file, accompanied by patriotic music, to local courthouses to reapply for benefits. The old Revolutionary War soldiers were marching, as one New Hampshire newspaper wrote, to the "pensioners' court in this town to prove their poverty."[24] According to a later recollection by Congressman Dudley Marvin of New York, "In the villages in his part of the country, when the semi-annual pay day arrived, they were in the habit of forming themselves into companies, then forming a column, and thus marching to receive their quota of the public bounty."[25]

This spectacle served as an early hint of the sense of entitlement that can affect groups of recipients of public assistance. Once they have received such assistance, such groups can develop an expectation that society owes them benefits that initially were bestowed out of gratitude for military service or a desire to alleviate the hardship. We will observe this expectation and the sometimes remarkable behavior it generates in later chapters on twentieth-century entitlements.

This pension belt tightening was only temporary. Two years later, the War Department reported that 80 percent of veterans who had originally been approved for pensions had reapplied, and 83 percent of those had been approved.[26] Once federal revenues returned to their prerecession level, Congress immediately restored benefits to the reapplicants who had been denied.[27] For the next decade, pension expenditures averaged 10 percent of total federal spending.

The 1818 pension law is a good example of how small changes in benefits or eligibility can cause program costs to spiral upward at surprising rates. Congress's underestimate of the cost was only the first of many underestimates. These miscalculations are invariably due to Congress's failure to appreciate how an offer of entitlement assistance can cause individuals to change their circumstances to qualify for aid they have previously managed to live without.

Retirement Pensions for Officers in 1828 and the Universal Service Act of 1832

The 1820s were years of extraordinary prosperity, leading to large federal budget surpluses that again were accompanied by calls to expand veterans' pensions. With federal revenues consistently exceeding expenditures by 50 percent, Congress focused on larger pensions for Revolutionary War officers. The Continental Army officers had a long-standing, but questionably meritorious, claim on the U.S. Treasury. In 1783, they had been given the option of exchanging their one-half-pay-for-life retirement pensions for a lump-sum payment, equal to full pay for five years and payable in stock certificates that yielded 6 percent interest. Those who opted for the certificates soon found that the nation's weak finances caused the certificates to lose considerable value.[28] In 1790, the inaugural Congress agreed to exchange U.S. Treasury securities for the certificates and to pay accrued interest. By that time, however, many officers already had sold their certificates, often at a deep discount.

The officers felt shortchanged and for the next thirty years repeatedly petitioned Congress for compensation. Congress repeatedly rejected their petitions, mainly on the ground that the losses the officers had suffered resulted from choices they had made.[29]

In 1828, Congressman Phineas Tracy of New York initiated a successful effort to secure higher retirement pensions for the officers with the declaration, "Our government is rich, its Treasury overflowing, and we are amply able to meet every just demand; and we are bound to compensate these claims, justly incurred in achieving that independence."[30] Under the guise of providing "justly incurred" claims, Congress granted the 235 Revolutionary War officers who were still alive in 1828 a pension bonanza they had no right to expect or receive: full monthly pay pensions for the remainder of their natural lives plus two years of arrears payments.[31] For officers who had opted for the lump-sum five-year payments as part of a voluntary election forty-five years earlier, the law's grant of lifetime pension was more than adequate compensation for any loss they might have incurred in the value of their certificates. For officers who in 1783 had opted to receive half pay for life, the law doubled their annual pensions going forward. The two years of arrears pensions at half-pay added another year's worth of benefits pension in a lump sum.

The economic prosperity of the 1820s continued into the 1830s. The U.S. Treasury recorded a dozen consecutive years of annual budget surpluses from 1823 to 1835. Revenues in 1832, fueled by the proceeds from land sales, were nearly three times that year's federal expenditures. So bright were the future revenue prospects that the Jackson administration announced that it expected to extinguish the national debt within three years. As had happened in 1806, 1818, and 1828, a strong economy created a favorable climate for further expanding pension benefits.

Advocates for broader pensions seized on the opportunity the surpluses provided to remove the glaring inequity in the 1818 law: its pensions for Continental Army veterans but not veterans of the state militia. They also sought to eliminate the 1820 law's means test, which advocates regarded as degrading.

On June 7, 1832, Congress passed the third and last of the large liberalizations of Revolutionary War pensions, extending lifetime service pensions to militia veterans of the Revolutionary War and eliminating the means test.[32] Aptly named the Universal Service Act, the law completed the transition of the Revolutionary War pension program from one that awarded benefits solely to veterans disabled in the line of duty and impoverished as a result to one that granted benefits to all veterans who met the law's minimum length-of-service requirement.

Advocates for granting service pensions to former members of the state militia made their case on the now familiar ground that these veterans were equally worthy to Continental Army veterans. Congressman Warren Davis of Massachusetts asked and answered the question of the militia's role in the War of Independence:

> Who, sir, moved by the great impulses of patriotism and an ardent love of liberty, opened the great avenue of the revolution at Lexington? The militia. Who were they that volunteered their services against oppression, left the peaceful occupations of private life, and marched under the standard of freedom to Bunker's hill, and offered up their lives in the great cause of liberty, when you had no Government to raise or pay an army . . . The militia.[33]

Congressman Henry Hubbard of New Hampshire, the law's chief sponsor, took the moral high ground, declaring it was time "to extend equal justice to all . . . to place them all on an equal and impartial footing."[34] The prospect that the budget surpluses would extinguish the national debt made the force of the equally worthy claim stronger. The case for using the surplus to meet the claim was best expressed by Representative Hubbard:

> And while we contemplate the universal prosperity and happiness which pervades our land, can we fail to take a retrospect, and bring to mind by whose efforts and energies, by whose services and sacrifices, these invaluable blessings have been secured? . . . Let us then unite with one mind and with one heart to effect a satisfactory payment of this debt; a debt which we should most willingly admit; a debt which our country is now well able . . . to discharge.[35]

Pension advocates attacked the means test as degrading and unworthy of a nation whose very existence was due to the sacrifices of the brave soldiers. The debate record is strewn with references to the requirement as "odious" and "repugnant." In Congressman Tracy's view, the proof of poverty requirement in the 1818 law was "a foul blot upon our statute book."[36] Congressman Hubbard stated flatly that many veterans had chosen to forgo benefits to which they were rightfully entitled rather than "make the humiliating, the mortifying declaration of their abject poverty."[37]

Opposition came primarily from representatives of western and southern states. Some saw the legislation as a product of the large surplus, not a means to fulfill an unmet need. Senator Robert Hayne of South Carolina concluded that the bill was not an "old soldiers' bill." Instead, it was "a safety valve of the high pressure engine" that the surplus fueled.[38] Others opposed the bill because it would require maintaining the high tariffs that had been put in place by the 1828 Tariff of Abominations law. Congressman James Trezvant of Virginia declared that the expansion "would fasten upon the people, for an indefinite period, a system of taxation under which, even now, they are justly restless and dissatisfied."[39] Congressman Warren Davis of South Carolina argued that when tariffs are used to finance liberal pensions, we unfairly "tax the poor for the support of those who were much wealthier than themselves."[40] In the end, the potency of the "equally worthy" claim combined with large budget surpluses overwhelmed congressional opposition, and the universal service bill passed by large margins in both houses. The law proved costly. In January 1833, a scant seven months after the law's enactment, Secretary of War Lewis Cass reported to Congress that 24,260 Revolutionary War veterans had applied for benefits, more than double the 10,000 the Senate had estimated would become eligible.[41] By June, the pension rolls had swelled to 33,354, up from fewer than 11,000 three years earlier. Forty-nine years had elapsed since the Revolutionary War's end, and the average age of surviving veterans was 77. The life expectancy of adults at the time was between 60 and 70. The unexpected surge of Revolutionary War pensioners, coming so long after the war's end, led former president John Quincy Adams to observe: "Uriah Tracy, thirty years ago, used to say that the soldiers of the Revolution never died—that they were immortal. Had he lived to this time, he would have seen that they multiply with the lapse of time."[42]

The rapid surge in the pension rolls was no doubt due to the arrears provision of the law, which allowed veterans to collect a benefit retroactive to March 4, 1831. This lump-sum payment amounted to more than a year's worth of benefits.

The Senate report estimated that the bill's first-year cost would be in the neighborhood of $450,000 and would decline rapidly as aging veterans passed away.[43] Before the law, pension spending totaled around $1.2 million, about 7 percent of total federal spending. The surge of pensioners and the lump-sum arrears payments pushed the law's first-year cost to $4.6 million, ten times the congressional estimate. The surge drove total pension expenditures to an extraordinary 29 percent of total federal spending.[44] Similarly, arrears payments, which totaled $1.8 million in 1833, were four times the congressional estimate.

The universal service pension law, like the 1818 pension law, did not apply to War of 1812 veterans. They would have to wait a very long time, until 1871, for Congress to grant them service pensions. There is no indication from the congressional debates that the differential treatment between the two groups was based on a view that Revolutionary

War veterans were more deserving than War of 1812 veterans. Instead, it appears that Congress based its differential treatment on age. In 1832, the typical Revolutionary War veteran was in his 70s, an age when infirmities were widespread. In an economy in which the overwhelming type of employment required manual labor, such people were not expected to be able to provide for their own subsistence through labor. The typical War of 1812 veteran, however, was in his late 30s or early 40s and, unless disabled, was fully expected to provide for his own subsistence. The distinction is important because it suggests that as early as 1832, Congress embraced the idea of an entitlement to old-age assistance. But the idea was limited: Congress did not grant an entitlement to all elderly people, only to those who had earned a right to it by their service during the Revolutionary War.

In 1835, even with the large pension expenditure, the federal government achieved a most remarkable feat: It extinguished the national debt. This accomplishment, which made the United States unique among the world's governments, was announced by President Jackson in a widely heralded message to Congress in December 1834. The state of fiscal bliss, however, was short-lived. The panic of 1837 and a long economic recession stood just over the horizon.

From the late 1830s to the 1850s, Congress incrementally liberalized pensions to Revolutionary War widows and survivors. The original pension laws granted lifetime pensions to widows and survivors of Continental Army soldiers and seamen killed in the line of duty. In 1836, Congress extended the same benefit to widows and survivors of the state militia and volunteers. These laws required the widow to have been married to the soldier during the war. Two years later, Congress approved half-pay pensions for five years to widows who had married after the war but before 1794. In 1843, rather than allow the five-year pensions to expire, Congress granted these widows an additional year of pensions. A year later, it extended the duration of their pensions once again, for another four years. In 1848, it allowed widows who had married Revolutionary War soldiers before 1800 to collect pensions. In 1853, Congress granted pensions to widows regardless of when they married.

Aside from the Revolutionary War widows laws, the years from the 1830s to the Civil War were relatively quiet ones for pension legislation. Congress followed its own precedent in granting pensions to veterans of the Mexican-American War: first, to soldiers injured in battle and to widows of soldiers killed in combat;[45] then to widows and survivors of Mexican-American War soldiers who died subsequently from injuries or illness incurred during the war. In 1853, Congress finally extended pensions to widows of veterans of the War of 1812. As death from old age gradually reduced the pension rolls, the burden of pensions on the Treasury gradually declined from 4 percent of federal spending in the late 1840s to just 2 percent in the late 1850s.[46]

By the late 1850s, the Revolutionary War pension program had run its course. But the process by which Congress created and extended pensions revealed patterns of behavior that would be important for future Congresses. First, there was a clear tendency to regularly and incrementally extend an existing entitlement and a corresponding deep reluctance to restrict it. Each legislative expansion established a new base from which subsequent Congresses would consider further liberalizations, based on the equally worthy claim. The liberalizations broadened eligibility far beyond the good intentions of the original program. Second, there was a strong tendency for Congress to enact liberalizations when the federal government was experiencing large budget surpluses. Third, through either ignorance or other less flattering reasons (e.g., to minimize a bill's apparent cost), Congress would invariably underestimate the cost of its legislative expansions, often by staggeringly large amounts.

3 An Experiment with Government Trust Funds

Navy Pensions

> The fund is their property, and not that of the nation, and why shall they not have the benefit of it?
>
> *Congressman Benjamin Crowninshield on the navy pension fund, 1823*[1]

NOT LONG AFTER CONGRESS ASSUMED RESPON-sibility for Revolutionary War pensions, it created a separate pension program for sailors and seamen that occupies a unique place in nineteenth-century entitlement history. The navy pension program was financed by a single, dedicated, source of revenue: prize money from the sale of captured enemy and pirate ships and their contents, commonly called "booty." The special fund Congress established to receive prize money and disburse funds for pensions was the federal government's first trust fund.[2]

Congress set much the same pattern for the navy pensions as it did for the army where benefit and eligibility expansions, with rare exceptions, were permanent. Each expansion established a new base from which Congress considered subsequent liberalizations, and these liberalizations generally occurred when surplus revenues were available. However, in the case of navy pensions, it was surpluses of prize money in the trust fund, rather than overall federal budget surpluses, that led to the expansions.

Congress established unfortunate precedents by bailing out an insolvent navy fund with an annual infusion of general revenues and by using creative accounting procedures to mask the use of general revenues to finance pensions rather than earnings on trust fund assets. The latter action serves as a forerunner to similar accounting procedures used in twentieth-century entitlements funded through trust funds, such as Social Security and Medicare.

Surpluses and Incremental Expansions: 1799–1830s

Laws passed in 1799 and 1800 established a separate navy pension program that provided annual cash benefits to naval officers and seamen who had suffered disabilities in the line of duty. These laws also established the navy pension trust fund to hold the prize money that would finance these pensions. The trust fund was administered by a commission consisting of the secretaries of the Navy, Treasury, and War departments, who could invest surplus receipts in U.S. government and nongovernment securities.[3]

Trouble on the high seas with France, and later with England, provided the navy with the opportunity to increase the fund's receipts. The large inflow of prize money helped the fund run annual surpluses throughout its first decade. The fund's asset balance, which stood at $56,000 in 1801, rose to $193,000 in 1810. Pension expenditures remained small, less than $8,000 per year, and accounted for less than 1 percent of all navy expenditures throughout the decade. They were financed entirely by interest on the fund's balance.[4]

The War of 1812 was a boon to the trust fund, albeit a temporary one. Prize money flowed into the fund in record amounts. By the end of 1814, fund assets had grown to $449,000. Its outlays of $14,000 could be covered entirely by its investment income.[5]

Congress responded to the growing fund in 1813 by granting pensions to widows and children of seamen who were killed or died from wounds received in the line of duty. In 1814, Congress extended these pensions to widows and children of seamen who died in the line of duty since the start of the War of 1812.[6] It further liberalized eligibility in 1817 by extending pensions to widows and children of seamen who died after the start of the War of 1812 "in consequence of disease contracted or of casualties or injuries received, while in the line of duty."[7] Each law granted widows pensions for five years. Under the law's new eligibility rule in 1817, a survivor need only to show that the seaman's death was connected to injury or disease incurred *during his time* in the navy. The new standard opened up the rolls to many new survivors. Between 1817 and 1824, the number of navy pensioners increased by 50 percent from 358 to 524. Pension benefit payments rose correspondingly.

An increasing prevalence of dubious claims by War of 1812 widows prompted Congress in 1824 to repeal the 1817 provision that granted pensions to widows whose husbands had died "in consequence of disease . . . or injuries received in the line of his duty." But this change in eligibility applied only to future applicants, not to those already on the pension rolls, demonstrating Congress's unwillingness to remove entitled individuals once they were on the pension rolls.[8]

From 1818 to 1837, Congress showed its tendency for incremental legislation and a further unwillingness to allow recipients to lose entitlement benefits. The pre-1818 laws had granted five-year pensions to widows and children of seamen who died of wounds received in the line of duty since the start of the War of 1812. Congress extended these pensions to ten years in 1818, fifteen years in 1828, twenty years in 1832, and finally thirty years in 1834. It subsequently extended pensions to survivors of seamen who died in the line of duty prior to the War of 1812 to ten years in 1819, fifteen years in 1824, and twenty years in 1828. Finally, in 1837, in a law that is discussed in more detail below, Congress granted lifetime pensions to all widows whose husbands had died while in the navy.[9]

Bailout and Bankruptcy

In the early 1830s, Congress first displayed its tendency to use general revenues to finance trust fund benefits whenever an opportunity presented itself. Until 1809, annual surplus funds had been invested exclusively in U.S. government securities. That year, the fund made its first purchase of non-U.S. government securities when it bought $48,523 of common stock issued by the Bank of Columbia, a District of Columbia Bank. Over the next decade, the fund more than doubled its stake in the bank. The fund also made smaller purchases of common stock of two other newly chartered Washington, D.C., banks: Union Bank and the Bank of Washington. With these purchases, the share of the fund's assets invested in nongovernment securities totaled 44 percent in 1814, an imprudent portion by investment standards because of the risk associated with these securities.[10]

The reason for the fund's large investment in bank stocks is not entirely clear. Certainly the high returns that the stocks promised played a central role. The bank stocks paid dividends in the 10 to 12 percent range, much higher than the 3 to 6 percent return on U.S. government securities.[11] The prominent positions held by the bank's senior officials and stockholders suggest that cronyism might have also been at work. The bank's second president, Benjamin Stoddard, had stepped down in 1798 to become the navy's first secretary. He was instrumental in setting up the navy trust fund prior to his retirement from the navy in 1801. The bank's president in 1809 was John Mason, son of founding father George Mason. The bank's board of directors in 1809 included Henry Foxhall, the former mayor of Georgetown, and William Marbury, of *Marbury v. Madison* fame. Later, Francis Scott Key joined the board. The bank's shareholders included George Washington and war hero Henry "Light Horse Harry" Lee, father of Robert E. Lee.[12]

For all practical purposes, the Columbia Bank discontinued operations in 1823, and its failure was followed by the collapse of the two other banks in which the fund had invested.[13] The fund's losses were substantial. Congress responded in the early 1830s by appropriating $167,164 from the general fund to reimburse the pension fund for its losses—the first government bailout of a trust fund.[14] Congress felt it had "an obligation to repair a loss which . . . operates so materially against the most unprotected class of society, the widows and orphans of the brave men who have perished in the service of the country."[15] The large revenue surplus in the rest of the federal budget provided Congress with the means to meet this obligation.

Prize money continued to flow, and the fund's assets remained over $1 million at the beginning of 1837. Revolutionary War seamen were in their 70s and War of 1812 veterans were in their 30s and 40s, so pension commitments were expected to gradually decline.[16] But the pension fund was irreversibly damaged when Congress passed the 1837 Jarvis bill, a sweeping expansion of eligibility rules to survivors of navy men who died while in military service regardless of the cause of their death. Thus, the law's beneficiaries included widows and the adult children of navy seamen who had died decades before from natural causes. The benefits granted were retroactive to the date of the seaman's death.

The fiscal dangers of such a sweeping retroactive eligibility expansion should have been well known to Congress, which had seen the results of the 1832 universal pension bill that ballooned army pension expenditures to 29 percent of the federal budget. Despite this recent history, the Jarvis bill generated little debate.

As with the army pensions, the promise of large lump-sum payments attracted a large number of claims, causing outlays to more than triple in 1839 compared to 1836. In the two years between the Jarvis bill's enactment and June 30, 1839, the navy pension fund paid out $600,000 in retroactive benefits. The benefits distributed to pensioners during this period exceeded the entire amount spent on navy pensions during the prior forty years.

The individual retroactive awards were often astonishingly large. One example among many was the payment to Sarah Fletcher, the widow of navy captain Patrick Fletcher, who died in 1800. Mrs. Fletcher's lump-sum retroactive benefit of $22,133 is equal to $628,373 in today's dollars. If there were a hall of fame for entitlement recipients, Sarah Fletcher would certainly have earned a prominent place in it. But she was only one of many recipients of the 1837 law's largesse; 9 percent of the law's 847 recipients of retroactive beneficiaries received lump-sum awards that exceed $100,000 in today's dollars.[17] The increased outlays required the fund to sell 75 percent of its assets between 1837 and the end of 1839. The Jarvis bill had put the fund on an inescapable path to insolvency. By 1841, the trust fund was unable to pay the full benefits. The Jarvis act had bankrupted it.

The fund's bankruptcy and reports of the extravagant retroactive payments generated two extraordinary legislative responses. First, Congress repealed the Jarvis bill in 1842. Second, it bailed out the navy fund with a $140,000 infusion of general fund revenues. The appropriation was the first of two decades of appropriations that would be annually required. The bailout had, in the words of former president John Quincy Adams, "saddled [the U.S. government] with a permanent national debt . . . as permanent as the lives of any of the persons described in the bill as entitled to call upon the Treasury for the money."[18]

The Origin of Modern Trust Funds

With the beginning of the Civil War, sizable amounts of prize money flowed into the U.S. Treasury once again. This new flow of funds induced Congress to reestablish the navy trust fund in 1862. Having learned from the experience of the 1820s, it restricted all trust fund investments to "registered securities of the United States."[19]

The trust fund had built up a large asset balance by 1867, when Navy Secretary Gideon Welles proposed that Congress use the large surplus to finance a substantial increase in monthly navy pension benefits and liberalize pension eligibility rules. Welles's proposal generated considerable debate in Congress. Congressman Benjamin Butler of Massachusetts, its leading critic, declared that passage of the Welles proposal would mean that "the pension list is not to be guided by what they ought to have, but by the amount of the fund."[20] Whenever the federal government had attempted to build a surplus in a particular fund, Mr. Butler observed, Congress had spent it:

> Whenever there is any sinking fund or other fund remaining in the Treasury, there are always being devised ways and means to get it out. That has been the universal history of all sinking funds. Every Administration that could not get through a proposition to tax the people to raise money always plunged at the sinking fund, when there was one.[21]

In Congressman Butler's view, the large navy trust fund balance, like sinking funds in prior years, was a pot of gold waiting to be raided. Secretary Welles's proposal, the congressman argued, was just another example of this long-standing behavior. His alternative was to transfer the trust fund's securities to the Treasury's general fund and thereby eliminate the principal source of pressure to liberalize pensions. Henceforth, all navy pensions would be financed by annual transfers of general fund revenues to the trust fund in an amount equal to the 6 percent interest that would have been paid on the securities. Mr. Butler's proposal passed the House.

In the Senate, the Butler plan's opponents argued that Congress had created the trust fund to make good on its commitment to disabled navy veterans. The plan would violate this sacred promise. Senator James Wilson Grimes of Iowa made this point by saying that "this is a trust fund dedicated to a particular purpose, and . . . [Butler's plan] . . . would violate a faith pledged" to the veterans.[22]

Congress eventually passed an amended version of the Butler plan, reducing the annual 6 percent general fund transfer to the trust fund to 3 percent.[23] The reduction brought the trust fund's annual revenues in line with its projected annual pension outlays. Thus, the reduction would avoid building up future surpluses and, with them, the inevitable pressures for benefit liberalizations.

The Act of July 28, 1868, was an important compromise measure that preserved the trust fund as a symbol of a navy pensioner's special claim on the Treasury and removed the large trust fund balance, mitigating concerns that such a balance would lead to an unwarranted expansion of pension benefits. However, the compromise came at a price: General tax revenues became the permanent means of financing navy pensions, and the trust fund became an accounting fiction. The annual transfer, equal to 3 percent of the trust fund's former assets, was designed to make the fund appear to earn money on behalf of disabled sailors and seamen. But in fact, it would make no investments and earn no returns. The act created the model for Social Security and most of the other large twentieth-century trust funds. The modern trust funds, like the revised navy fund, hold special-issue nonmarketable Treasury securities. As their name implies, these securities are created exclusively for the purpose of representing hypothetical trust fund deposits. They cannot be purchased or sold. Their interest rate is set by administrative fiat according to Treasury Department rules rather than by marketplace supply and demand.

4   The First Great Entitlement

Civil War Pensions

I will drive a six-mule team through the Treasury.

God help the surplus when I get at it.

James Tanner, Commission of Pensions, 1889[1]

T HE CIVIL WAR PENSION PROGRAM BEGAN WITH the same high-minded, noble, and limited goal as Revolutionary War pensions: to compensate soldiers for the loss of life and limb suffered in wartime service to their country. Pensions were a just reward and a measure of the country's debt of gratitude owed to these men and women who fought to preserve the nation. A half-century later, the program evolved into a general disability and retirement program for virtually all Union soldiers that provided entitlement benefits on a scale unparalleled in prior U.S. history. Congress also eventually stretched eligibility for pensions to virtually all widows and survivors of Union soldiers, even those who had married many decades after the war had ended and, nearly 100 years after the war, even to the few remaining widows of Confederate soldiers.

The Civil War pension expenditures proved to be every bit as rapid as Revolutionary War pensions, but because the Civil War program was far larger, its consequences for the federal budget were much greater.

Figure 1 displays the trend in veterans' pensions from the end of the War of Rebellion to the year prior to the start of World War I. The figure shows annual veterans' pension expenditures as a percent of total federal spending (left axis) and annual number of Civil War pensioners (right axis).[2]

At its peak in 1896, the Civil War program provided pensions to nearly 1 million Union soldiers and their survivors. By 1900, thirty-five years after General Lee surrendered at Appomattox, 75 percent of Union veterans, representing 21 percent of white males in the United States age 55 and older, were still receiving disability benefits.[3] The Civil War program made veterans' pension expenditures the federal government's single largest annual program expenditure from 1880 to the Spanish-American War. Annual pension expenditures reached an extraordinary 40 percent of federal budget expenditures in 1896.[4] Today, in comparison, Social Security and Medicare combine to account for 39 percent of total federal spending. Although Civil War pensions constituted a large share of federal expenditures, the program's burden on the general public was light. Total government spending in the 1890s, excluding 1899 when the Spanish American War arrived, ranged between 2 and 3 percent of gross national product. Pension expenditures, at their peak, reached just 1 percent of GNP.[5] Nevertheless, the size and reach of Civil War pensions make it the nation's first great entitlement program.

Two major laws drove these trends. The 1879 Arrears Act allowed disabled veterans and widows to claim benefits retroactive to the date of the soldier's war injury. The Dependent Pension Act of 1890 eliminated the requirement that a veteran's disability must have been incurred during the war and granted pensions to disabled veterans and widows regardless of the soldiers' income. These two laws raised the pension rolls and pension expenditures to their peaks in the 1890s. Eligibility liberalizations enacted after the turn of the century, including granting automatic eligibility at age 62, temporarily maintained the pension rolls until the natural decline from old age took its toll.

The Civil War pension program had profound and lasting effects on American electoral politics and political institutions. Distributing lavish cash benefits, providing constituent service for pension applicants, and using the federal Pension Office for political advantage became

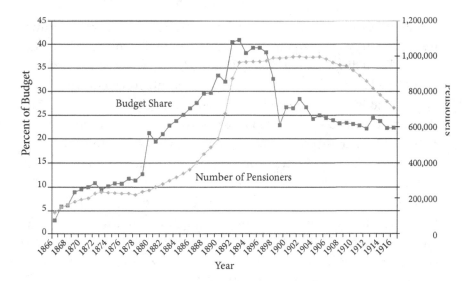

Figure 1. Civil War Pensions, 1866–1916. Source: *Annual Report of the Commissioner of Pensions, 1917*, pp. 319–320; *Annual Report of the Secretary of the Treasury*, Statistical Appendix, 1980, Table 2.

commonplace as a means of securing and maintaining electoral office. The Republican Party, calling itself the "party of the Union," used pensions to align the American electorate behind it in the 1890s. The pension program also spawned America's first national, single-issue, lobby, the Grand Army of the Republic, which exerted a powerful influence on pension legislation and served as a forerunner to large twentieth-century lobbying organizations.

The Civil War Pension Program Origins: 1861–1873

At the outbreak of the Civil War, the Union had no standing army of any consequence. An army of 500,000 had to be raised immediately, and the government, without a draft law in effect, had no legal ability to compel men to fight.[6] A pension program that guaranteed assistance to soldiers injured in battle and to widows of soldiers killed in battle was an essential instrument for building a fighting force. Congress hastily enacted an initial pension law on July 22, 1861. A more comprehensive law enacted a year later was patterned after the initial Revolutionary War pension program and granted pensions to soldiers who suffered disabling injuries or illness while in wartime military service. [7] The law covered all military branches and every rank, provided pensions to widows and children of soldiers killed in action, and took the unprecedented step of extending pensions to mothers and sisters of deceased soldiers—though not, of course, members of the Confederate military. The law's extraordinary generosity did not go unnoticed. Commissioner of Pensions Joseph Barrett warned that the law was "by far the most liberal pension law ever enacted by this government" and noted that it would result in "an extravagant, if not unsupportable, annual burden."[8] But in Congress, the large expenditure generated no controversy. The nation faced disunion and more servicemen had to be attracted to the Union's preservation.

The sheer size of the Union army (2.6 million soldiers) the war's human devastation, and the generous Civil War pension law guaranteed that the budgetary costs would be large. When the war began, 10,709 soldiers and widows were receiving pensions. In 1866, a year after the war ended, 126,722 pensioners were on the rolls.[9] The country had never experienced anything remotely close to this number of veterans receiving government aid. The prior record had been set in 1833, when the universal service bill temporarily increased the pension rolls to 33,354. But, the pension program in 1866 paled in comparison to the mammoth program it would become two decades later.

In the war's immediate aftermath, Congress made numerous enhancements to the pension program. From 1865 to 1873, it enacted no fewer than six laws making mostly minor program liberalizations.[10] By 1873, the flurry of laws had created an unnecessarily complex system that caused much confusion, great uncertainty about eligibility and benefits, and considerable inequities. In response, Congress passed the Consolidation Act of 1873, bringing the various pension statutes together under a single statutory authority that created more uniform administrative procedures. These laws caused the pension rolls to nearly double to 238,411 by 1873, with one pensioner for every seven Union soldiers.[11]

By the early 1870s, most knowledgeable observers believed that the number of pensioners would gradually decline as old age, disease, and complications from injuries took their toll.[12] The number of applicants had already slowed to a trickle, and the number of recipients removed from the rolls by death had already begun to rise. By 1878, there were about 9,000 fewer pensioners than in 1872. Pension outlays were 10 percent lower and constituted only 11 percent of noninterest federal spending.[13]

The Arrears Law of 1879

As the pension rolls declined, pension advocates pushed for eliminating the deadline for veterans to file disability claims. The original 1862 law had permitted soldiers a year from the date of discharge. Those who qualified received benefits retroactively to the date of their discharge. Those who applied after the one-year time period had elapsed still qualified, but benefits were retroactive only to the date of their application. In all cases, claimants had to prove that their disabilities were a result of injuries or illness incurred during wartime service. The Act of July 27, 1868, extended the allowable time period to five years, a sufficient amount of time, Congress believed, to allow any disease or complication from wartime injuries to become manifest.[14]

Pension advocates argued that many "worthy" veterans were not receiving pensions because they couldn't adequately document that their disability was connected to wartime service. Years had elapsed since the war's end, important paperwork had been lost or misplaced, and memories had faded. According to pension advocates, these disabled veterans who were often poorly educated or woefully ignorant of the law suffered from wartime injuries and illness that were no less debilitating than those suffered by pension recipients. They were, the advocates argued, no less worthy than those who were receiving pensions.[15]

The "equally worthy claim" struck a responsive chord. By the mid-1870s, petitions calling for elimination of the five-year time period had been submitted to Congress by every state except those that had joined the Confederacy.[16] In Congress, the pressure that accompanied the petitions was magnified by large budget surpluses. Since the end of the panic of 1873, a growing economy had generated sizable annual federal budget surpluses. By 1877, the $40 million surplus was large enough to finance a 40 percent increase in the number of pensioners. With these surpluses available, the argument that "equally worthy" veterans should be given their due proved irresistible.

Congress passed the arrears bill in 1879. The votes on the bill clearly delineated party positions in Congress—positions that would remain fixed for the remainder of the century. Republicans overwhelmingly supported pension liberalizations, 115–1 in the House. The House Democratic vote reflected a heavily conflicted party. Northern Democrats, much like their Republican counterparts, supported pension expansions, 46–4, with 23 abstentions. Southern Democrats, no doubt reflecting the fact that Confederate soldiers were not eligible for federal pensions, voted 5–56 against the House bill.[17] The Senate vote tells an identical story.[18]

The law extended the allowable time limit for filing disability claims and permitted veterans who qualified for benefits to receive a lump sum arrears payment retroactive to the date of their discharge.[19] This could be an extraordinary sum. A veteran who had been discharged in 1862 and filed a successful claim in 1879 could expect an arrears payment check of about $3,900, an amount equal to nine years of wages for an average manufacturing worker and $92,000 in today's dollars.[20]

Newspapers around the country called on President Hayes to veto the bill. The *New York Tribune*, for example, wrote, "Nothing but a presidential veto could prevent a grand scramble by a horde of claimants to get their hands upon vast unearned portions of the national treasure."[21] President Hayes, however, declared that the inability of the government to protect the Treasury was no reason for denying claims to "worthy" veterans. He said, "The failure of the Government to protect itself against frauds is no reason for evading just obligations,"[22] and signed the bill into law on January 25, 1879.

The law produced an extraordinary rush among veterans to file claims for arrears payments. Within three weeks of the law's passage, the number of applications tripled. During the year following the law, the Pension Office received 101,481 applications, twice the total number of applications filed during the entire five-year period 1875 to 1879.[23] Incredibly, veterans filed 44,532 applications in June 1880 alone, the last month in which arrears applications could be filed.[24]

The surge of claims was not entirely unexpected. Years earlier, Secretary of War John Eaton had warned Congress that a law such as the Arrears Act would cause the pension rolls to surge upward as "men, at distant periods from the expiration of their service, become blind, and it is reported that, in consequence of being stationed at some particular place, injurious to vision the ill effect has been produced; they sink into consumptions, and it is traced to a cold caught while in service: in such case the recognized precedents go to establish the right of the party to being placed on the list of pensioners."[25]

Federal officials had warned that the bill's cost would be high, but little did they know at the time that they were writing into the statute books the single most expensive piece of legislation up to that point. The bill's Senate floor manager, Senator John Ingalls, had put the total at $18 to $20 million. Hayes administration officials estimated a much higher cost of between $50 and $150 million.[26] Both numbers proved to be underestimates. Two years after the law's passage, President Chester A. Arthur reported that arrears payments had already cost taxpayers $235 million.[27] It is likely that the law's ultimate cost was even higher. The law reversed the decade-long decline in pension outlays. Pension outlays had climbed from less than $27 million in 1878 to $56 million in 1880, to $60 million in 1884, and to $79 million in 1888. It is fair to conclude that the law added nearly $400 million to pension expenditures during the 1880s alone.[28]

Interest Group Lobbying

The role of lobbyists in the years preceding and subsequent to the Arrears Act provides an early example of the dynamic interplay between lobbying organizations and legislation that would become commonplace a century later. Claims agents led the advocates for arrears payments. These agents, certified by the Pension Office, assisted veterans and widows with the complex application process, represented claimants in appeals before the Pension Office, and received compensation for their services. With a large financial stake in pension legislation, particularly legislation that would increase the number of applicants, the claims' agents had emerged as a powerful lobbying force a decade earlier. As early as 1870, the chairman of the House Military Affairs Committee declared the claims agents to be "one of the most potent influence we have and one that we shall have to watch very carefully in the future, or millions and tens of millions will be taken out of the Treasury."[29]

The more successful claims agents used soldiers' newspapers and mass mailings to promote their cause. The legendary George Lemon established a widely circulated newspaper, the *National Tribune*, as its lobbying organ. Another famous claims agent, Captain R. A. Dimmick, established the "Pensions Committee" as its lobby. These agents generated mass petitions from veterans to Congress for arrears payments. In 1878, for example, the Senate received 200,000 such petitions, causing the arrears bill to be referred to as the "lobby bill."[30]

The Arrears Act was a financial bonanza for the claims agents, who received filing fees for each new claimant they represented. Enriched by these fees, the claims agent lobby became even more formidable. A story about a rather minor piece of legislation in 1884 provides ample evidence of its power. The legislation in question would raise the filing fee to $25 from $10, greatly benefiting George Lemon, who represented 120,000 claimants. While the bill was in conference and the outcome of the fee increase was in doubt, Lemon purchased 40,000 claims from Nathan W. Fitzgerald and Company for $10,000. The legislation passed with the filing fee included. When Fitzgerald learned the new legislation's contents, he proposed to repurchase the claims for $20,000. Lemon replied that he might have paid only $10,000 for the claims, but "it has cost me $50,000 to get the bill through Congress."[31]

The Arrears Act also spawned a second large national lobbying force: the Grand Army of the Republic (GAR). The GAR's evolution from a service organization to a special interest lobby is worthy of attention because the same path would be followed time and again by twentieth-century lobby groups, including American Association for Retired Persons (AARP), the American Federation of Labor and the Congress of Industrial Organization (AFL-CIO), the Chamber of Commerce, the American Public Welfare Association, and countless others.

Founded in 1866, the GAR's initial purposes were to assist veterans returning to civilian life and to support the widows and orphans of soldiers killed in battle. The organization sponsored social gatherings and charitable activities, including theatrical performances, campfires, lectures, and lotteries.[32] During its initial years, it confined its lobbying activities to promoting homes for disabled Civil War veterans at the state government level.[33]

The Arrears Act gave the GAR new life. When the flood of applications overwhelmed the Pension Office, the GAR created a Pension Committee to lobby the Pension Office to expedite claims processing. With an office in Washington, the committee soon began lobbying Congress for greater pension benefits and more Pension Office resources. The committee held meetings with Pension Office staff and members of Congress and their staffs. GAR officials also regularly testified at congressional hearings on pension matters. The GAR, the congressional veterans' pension committees, and the Pension Office formed what is perhaps the nineteenth century's most formidable iron triangle. One of its earliest successes was a doubling of the Pension Office budget in 1882. By the mid-1880s, the GAR had become the dominant interest group representing Civil War veterans. Members of Congress welcomed the organization as the "accredited representative of the soldier."[34]

Pensions and Electoral Politics

The mid-1880s marks the beginning of a widening national divide between the two major political parties on pension issues. Southern Democrats exerted a powerful influence on their party's national policy positions and, quite naturally, were unsupportive of pensions for Union soldiers. Their northern counterparts supported pension liberalizations. The divided Democrats could offer only vague promises on pension legislation. The Republican Party, dominated by northern interests, stood solidly behind more liberal pensions. The party differences on pensions were magnified by disagreements on tariff policy. By the mid-1880s in the aftermath of the Arrears Act, pensions had grown to one-quarter of federal spending. Excluding interest on the national debt, pensions had become the federal budget's largest single expenditure item, exceeding spending on both the army and navy combined. The budgetary importance of pension expenditures and the revenue importance of tariffs meant that decisions on pensions and tariffs became joined at the hip. Republicans had long supported high tariffs to protect their strong base in manufacturing states. Generous pensions became a politically efficient and politically beneficial way to distribute the tariffs' revenues. Democrats, reflecting their strong southern, western, and agricultural base, had long opposed high tariffs.

The sharpened national divide between the parties became apparent in the 1884 presidential election pitting Democrat Grover Cleveland against Republican James G. Blaine. By 1884, the number of Civil War pensioners had swelled to over 300,000, and pensions became a central campaign issue. The Democratic Party platform vaguely called for "sufficient revenue to pay all the expenses of the Federal Government . . . including pensions, interest, and the principal of the public debt." The Republican Party strongly supported pension liberalization with the specific pledge to repeal "the limitations contained in the Arrears Act."[35] The pension stakes were sufficiently high to cause the GAR to drop its thin veneer of nonpartisanship and throw its support behind the Republican candidates. The *National Tribune*, the GAR's official public organ, labeled James G. Blaine and his running mate, the former GAR head, John A. Logan, the "soldiers' ticket" and joined in to support the Republicans.[36]

The election campaign witnessed the use of the Pension Office as a political machine to gain partisan advantage. The agency had the sole authority to accept or reject pension claims and could expedite or delay decisions. One month before the presidential election, the Republican pension commissioner, William Dudley, moved more than one hundred pension examiners to the key swing state of Ohio where 40,000 claims awaited adjudication. Subsequent congressional investigations revealed that he expedited the approval of pension claims, in some cases in return for claimants' promises to vote Republican, and he ordered that no claims be rejected until after the election. After completing his election work in Ohio, Mr. Dudley moved to Indiana, where he performed the same activities. Commissioner Dudley's actions constitute an early demonstration of how an entitlement program can be used for partisan advantage.

Grover Cleveland overcame the GAR and Mr. Dudley's campaign efforts to become the first Democrat to hold the office of president in a quarter century. The new president entered office committed to restraining federal spending as a step toward his ultimate objective of reducing tariffs. The pension program's high cost and lax administration presented President Cleveland with a target for expenditure reduction. In 1879, a Pension Office investigation had concluded that about 25 percent of claims were fraudulent.[37] The flood of applications in the years since the Arrears Act's enactment had only worsened the problem. The fraudulent pensioners included those who suffered from disabilities that were unrelated to Civil War military service, those who were in fact quite healthy and capable of earning a living, relatives of long-deceased veterans to whom checks were still being delivered, and widows of Civil War soldiers who had remarried but had failed to inform the Pension Office.[38] In his first annual message to Congress, he declared that "it is fully as important that the rolls should be cleansed of all those who by fraud have secured a place therein, as that meritorious claims should be speedily examined and adjusted."[39]

Private pension relief bills provided President Cleveland with another inviting target. Veterans whose claims had been denied naturally turned to their congressmen or senators for help. Elected representatives regularly submitted claims to Congress on their constituents' behalf in the form of private relief bills. Using private relief bills for this purpose was an age-old practice, but following the Arrears Act, the practice grew to extraordinary dimensions. During the Forty-Ninth Congress, 1885–1887, 40 percent of all House bills and 55 percent of all Senate bills were private pension bills. On one day alone, April 26, 1888, the Senate approved four hundred special pension acts.[40]

Both the House and Senate used "pension time" for mass consideration of private relief bills. The House often reserved Friday afternoons, when only a handful of members were present, to take up private pension bills and pass them by general consent. Quick passage, after little or no time for serious consideration of individual bills, was followed by a "jubilant whoop" of satisfaction. The Senate followed a similar process.[41]

President Cleveland's effort to cleanse the rolls began on May 8, 1886, when he vetoed his first private pension relief bill. The occasion for his veto was a bill whose sole purpose was to benefit a private citizen, Andrew J. Hill. The bill, one of 240 private pension bills he received that day, would have retroactively doubled Mr. Hill's pension. Mr. Hill's claim in fact had been previously rejected by the Pension Office and President Cleveland used his veto to point out that the Pension Office, not the Congress, was the proper place for making eligibility determinations. The president argued that while the bureau could on occasion mistakenly reject worthy applications, Congress should not regularly override its decisions. If the Pension Office lacked the resources to do an adequate job, Congress should provide the office with additional funds. If the process for approving claims was inadequate, the process should be revised. If the Pension Office was not properly carrying out the congressional will, it should be reorganized.[42]

President Cleveland's veto message made clear that he was prepared to veto future private pension relief bills. By the end of August of his first year in office, he had vetoed more than 100 such bills. By the end of his first term as president, he had vetoed 228 bills, a record unmatched by any other president in history.[43]

President Cleveland's detailed veto messages highlighted the program's excesses. In one case, he explained that the potential beneficiary had not died as a result of wartime injuries, but "while engaged in recreation" during a prison stint after the war (he had fallen off a swing).[44] In another case, the president pointed out that the former soldier had died of "intemperate use of intoxicating liquors" while in jail for being drunk in public.[45] A third case involved a soldier, who, contrary to the claims of his widow, had not died in battle but rather had "choked to death on a piece of beef when gorging himself on a drunken spree."[46]

Despite these vetoes, the number of pensioners and pension expenditures continued to increase. By 1888, 452,557 individuals were collecting pensions. Pension expenditures accounted for one-third of the federal spending, excluding interest on the debt.

Tariffs and pensions remained the dominant issues in the 1888 presidential election. President Cleveland made tariff reductions the centerpiece of his reelection campaign. The Republican challenger, Benjamin

Harrison, campaigned on a platform of high tariffs to protect workers and to generate surplus revenues to support worthy veterans. The party's lighthearted jingle crystallized this message:

> Let Grover talk against the tariff, tariff, tariff
> And pensions too.
> We'll give the workingman his due
> And the pension boys who wore the blue.[47]

President Cleveland's record on pensions provided Republicans with considerable campaign fodder. Republicans and the GAR pounded President Cleveland's vetoes of private pension bills as "228 rounds of ammunition."[48] Senator Cushman K. Davis of Minnesota typified the attack by charging that the president's vetoes were "crueller than an assassin's knife stabbed through many a widow's heart, and old soldier's heart."[49]

Grover Cleveland won the popular vote by less than 1 percent, but Benjamin Harrison won the Electoral College vote. Numerous contemporaneous accounts attributed Harrison's victory to the "soldiers' vote."[50] The *Chicago Tribune* concluded that the Republican victory was not due to the "protected working men of the cities" but "the old soldiers and their sons."[51] Similarly, General Alvin Hovey, who won the Indiana race for governor, declared: "I am certain that in the Western States our comrades have gained the victory. . . . The tariff question cut no figure in the election, and our victory was obtained from the 'boys in blue.'"[52] Mr. Hovey estimated that twenty thousand veterans living in Indiana had voted for Benjamin Harrison.[53] From Abilene, Kansas, a newspaper reporter wrote to Grover Cleveland: "The Irish and the soldier vote primarily aided in the result. Out of six or seven hundred Grand Army men in this city (Abilene), a small percentage of them voted for you."[54] In Illinois, the Democratic candidate for governor, General John Palmer, blamed his defeat on the organized soldier vote, charging that the GAR had acted as a political machine during the campaign.[55] In two critical states, Indiana and Grover Cleveland's home state of New York, both of which had gone to Mr. Cleveland four years earlier, pensioners represented 7.0 and 3.4 percent of all votes that would be cast, respectively.[56] Benjamin Harrison won Indiana by a 1.2 percent margin and New York by a 3.4 percent margin. The two states provided President Harrison with his Electoral College margin of victory.

President Harrison entered office ready to fulfill the Republican Party promises to veterans with both political appointments and pension liberalizations. He appointed former Union soldier and long-time activist James Tanner as commissioner of pensions. Soon after the announcement of his appointment, Commissioner Tanner enthusiastically declared, "I will drive a six-mule team through the Treasury." In a widely publicized speech in Tennessee, after describing how he would use his position to increase veterans' pensions, Mr. Tanner exclaimed: "God help the surplus when I get my hands on it."[57]

With President Harrison's blessing, Commissioner Tanner mobilized the Pension Office to expand the number of pensioners and their benefits. It reevaluated the severity of disabilities for existing beneficiaries as a means of boosting pension benefits. During his first few months at the helm, the Pension Office reevaluated 7,000 to 8,000 beneficiaries per month.[58] These reviews were occasionally conducted without the pensioner's prior knowledge or consent.[59] In one instance, the agency rerated Senator Charles F. Manderson's disability without the senator's knowledge. Without any prior notification, the Treasury sent the senator a $4,300 check for retroactive benefits. The astounded senator promptly returned the check.[60]

Commissioner Tanner's aggressive actions were highly controversial, and before the end of his first year in office, the secretary of interior forced him to resign. His successor, General Green B. Raum, was also charged with serious improprieties. Claims agent George Lemon had requested a new internal Pension Office procedure that gave priority review to applications submitted by claims agents over those submitted by the veteran himself or by his widow. The new procedure was highly beneficial to Mr. Lemon, who handled twice the number of claims as any other agent. Over the objections of his staff, Mr. Raum implemented the new procedure. The very next day, Mr. Lemon gave Mr. Raum a much needed $12,000 loan to finance a private business venture that had fallen on hard times.[61] Commissioner Raum rode out the charges of accepting a payoff and served out his term.

The Dependent Pensions Bill

During the decades following the Civil War, federal budget surpluses piled up at a historic pace. In 1889, the federal budget recorded its twenty-fourth consecutive annual surplus. The surpluses persisted through repeal of the income tax in 1872, the panic of 1873, the abolition in 1883 of the excise tax on banking, and a 50 percent cut in the tobacco tax. In 1889, federal revenues exceeded expenditures by 37 percent.[62] The magnitude of these surpluses has only one parallel in U.S. history: the decade from 1825 to 1836, which produced the extravagant 1832 Universal Pension Law for Revolutionary War soldiers and the 1836 Jarvis bill for navy veterans and their widows.

The massive budget surpluses, the Revolutionary War pension program's precedents, a Republican president, and Republican majorities in both houses of Congress combined to make a large pension expansion inevitable. Under these circumstances, only divine intervention could have saved the surplus.

In his 1889 Annual Message to Congress, President Harrison proposed to entitle pensions to all Civil War veterans who suffered disabilities regardless of whether those disabilities were the result of wartime service. In the president's view, a "worthy and suffering class" of veterans who had nobly served their country had been denied benefits merely because the records that were necessary to support their claims had been lost. Echoing arguments that had been made fifty years before on behalf of service pensions for aging Revolutionary War veterans, the president contended that his proposal would prevent this special class of citizens from being thrown on the local relief rolls or placed in poorhouses.[63]

Congress, under additional public pressure from the GAR, responded with the Dependent Pension Act of 1890, a law that fundamentally changed the basis of Civil War pensions.[64] Under the law, a Civil War veteran's disability no longer needed to have resulted from injury or illness incurred during the war. Veterans and their survivors were now entitled to pensions regardless of whether the veterans' disability was war related. In addition, disabled veterans no longer needed to be indigent to qualify for benefits. They needed only to demonstrate that their disability impaired their ability to perform *manual* labor. Since the vast majority of Civil War veterans would reach their 50s and 60s during the coming two decades and would likely suffer disabilities normally associated with aging, the law, for all practical purposes, promised to expand the pension rolls to all aging Civil War veterans.[65]

Following the 1890 law's enactment, the pension rolls and its cost surged. Within three years, the number of Civil War pensioners rose to 935,084 from 455,858 in 1889, nearly 100,000 of them widows. In 1893, pension outlays swelled to $157 million from $89 million in 1889 and accounted for an extraordinary 40 percent of federal expenditures.[66] To fully appreciate the budgetary importance of pensions, consider for the moment that currently, the Social Security old-age and disability insurance programs and Medicare combine to account for 39 percent of the budget.[67]

As it had in the past, Congress vastly underestimated the cost of the pension expansion. The bill's chief sponsor, Congressman Justin Morrill, estimated the bill's first year cost at $40 million.[68] The bill's annual expense in fact proved to be $50 to $60 million, far eclipsing the cost of the previous record-setting Arrears Act.

Evidence of pension fraud accompanied the rising pension rolls, just as it had following the 1818 Revolutionary War service pension law. The extravagance of the 1890 Dependent Pension Act, pension fraud and allegations of Pension Office corruption that followed in its wake, and the high tariff engineered by Senator William McKinley became the central issues in the 1892 presidential election. The election line-up was a replay of the 1888 election, except that in 1892, President Harrison was the incumbent and Grover Cleveland was the challenger. The Democratic Party platform declared, "We denounce the present administration of that [Pension] office as incompetent, corrupt, disgraceful and dishonest."[69] The party's press ally, the *New York Herald*, declared "the entire burden of McKinleyism" would go "to pay bounties to a million men who are no longer doing anything in return for the burden they impose upon the people."[70] Candidate Cleveland renewed his previous campaign promise to "cleanse the pension rolls" and limit publicly provided benefits to "worthy" veterans.

President Harrison, in contrast, wooed the veterans' vote. He reminded veterans that he had delivered on his pension promises by signing into law the most liberal pension bill in history. But his ability to promise additional pension liberalizations was limited. The higher pension expenditures from the 1890 law had reduced the budget surplus to a mere $10 million in 1892, down from $88 million in 1889. With little money in the Treasury to finance additional benefit promises, the Republican Party platform, for the first time in two decades contained no separate plank for expanding pensions.[71]

Voter backlash against the tariffs and pension corruption contributed to President Cleveland's landslide victory.[72] The widespread charges that the Harrison administration was using the Pension Office to buy votes were, according to historian Mary Dearing, moderately successful in attracting voters to the Democratic Party's side.[73]

President Cleveland took immediate actions to curb the prior administration's pension excesses. Eligibility rules under the 1890 law were tightened and all those on the rolls were reevaluated. Pension Office commissioner William Lochren's efforts attracted considerable press attention, but his results didn't quite measure up to the hype. After two years, only 2,266 claimants, less than 1 percent of recipients under the 1890 law, had been removed from the rolls. Monthly benefits to another 3,343 pensioners were lowered.[74]

The GAR railed against this minor reform as if the pension rolls had been purged, decrying "false economy which shaves and pares to the quick at the expense of honor, justice, and principle."[75] The organization demanded the ouster of Commissioner Lochren. President Cleveland complied six months before the 1896 election by "promoting" Mr. Lochren to a federal judgeship. His successor, Dominic Murphy, promptly ended Commissioner Lochren's policy of reviewing the disability status of those on the pension rolls and announced that no more pensioners would be dropped.[76] So by the time President Cleveland left office in 1897, there were 12,500 more Civil War pensioners than when he had taken office.

The economic recession that began in 1893 was as deep, broad, and long as any recession in prior U.S. history. The recession ended twenty-eight consecutive years of budget surplus and produced large budget deficits for the remainder of the decade. The budget deficits caused all parties to the pension debate to moderate their demands. GAR commander in chief T. G. Lawler announced new objectives at the 1893 National Encampment by saying, "while we are not asking for any new pension legislation, we do ask and insist that when a law is passed . . . that its provisions . . . be carried out and not misapplied by any man . . . or any party."[77] The Democratic Party platform weakly called for a continuation of current pension policy. The Republican Party vaguely called for "such laws as are best calculated to secure the fulfillment of the pledges made to them [veterans] in the dark days of the country's peril."[78]

Republicans were able to use the free-silver debate, which dominated the 1896 presidential election, to their advantage when it came to the pensioners' vote. The party appealed directly to pensioners' financial interests by arguing that adoption of free silver meant a reduction in the purchasing power of veterans' pensions. Free silver would cause rising prices, while veterans' monthly pension payments were fixed in dollars. The *Chicago Tribune* claimed that under a free-silver administration, veterans' benefits would end up worth only half of their current value.[79] To this, President Cleveland had no effective response.

The deep recession, with an assist from the soldiers' vote, cost Grover Cleveland his job. William McKinley won the presidency in 1896, and Republicans retained the majorities in both houses of Congress that they had gained in the previous midterm election. The McKinley administration took major steps toward transforming the Civil War pension program into a service pension program. In 1899, the Pension Office ruled that under the Dependent Pension Act, disabled veterans and widows would henceforth be eligible "without any reference to the claimant's wealth or capacity to earn . . . support." The only requirement was that the applicant be unable to perform manual labor.[80] A year later, the Pension Office ruled that veterans age 75 or older would be presumed to be disabled by stipulating that "a claimant who has reached the age of 75 years is allowed the maximum rate for senility alone, even where there are no special pensionable disabilities."[81]

Following President McKinley's assassination in 1901, the Theodore Roosevelt administration transformed the Civil War pension program into a federal retirement program. President Roosevelt, facing election in 1904, sought to appease the demands of the veterans' lobby with

Pension Office Order Number 78, which declared that old age alone was a qualifying infirmity. For Civil War veterans age 62 and older, the order established a tiered payment system in which monthly benefits rose according to age. The order became effective in April 1904, seven months before the election.[82]

Two years later, when the Treasury returned to surplus, the GAR pressed for codification of the Roosevelt administration's policy. Congress responded just five months before the midterm elections in 1906 with a temporary law making 62 the age of eligibility for Civil War pensions.[83] A year later, Congress passed legislation making the age criterion permanent for Civil War and Mexican-American War veterans.[84]

The final step to making veterans' pensions a federal retirement program came in 1912, when the budget registered its first surplus in four years and a highly competitive presidential election was in full swing. All three candidates, President and Republican candidate William Howard Taft, former president and Bull Moose Party candidate Theodore Roosevelt, and Democratic candidate Woodrow Wilson—the last demonstrating that Democrats had learned their electoral lessons—joined together to support pension liberalization. These fiscal and political conditions created a highly favorable climate for expanding pension benefits. A 1912 law, enacted just before the national elections, granted Civil War pensions based solely on length of service and age, with higher benefits for longer terms of service and older veterans. Gone were requirements that veterans be disabled or be unable to perform manual labor.[85] During the congressional debate on the bill, Democratic congressman Martin Dies of Texas lamented the fact that "the naked truth is that the Democratic Party is just as cowardly in this pension question as ever the Republican Party dared to be."[86] Immediately on enactment, the Pension Bureau sent out 600,000 blank pension applications to members of Congress for distribution to their constituents. Congress returned the favor by increasing the appropriation for the Pension Bureau to hire temporary clerks to process the expected high volume of applications.

The Electoral Impact of the Pension Vote Revisited

The period from 1896 to 1912 marks the American electorate's great realignment behind the Republican Party. In prior decades, voters had been evenly divided between the two major political parties. From free-silver 1873 through 1894, control of the House of Representatives changed political parties five times and control of the Senate three times. Presidential election contests were most often decided by razor-thin margins. Starting with the 1894 midterm elections, a sizable majority of the electorate swung behind the Republican Party. Voters gave the Republicans continuous control of the White House from 1896 to 1912, the House of Representatives from 1892 to 1910, and the Senate from 1892 to 1912.

Scholarly studies have shown that the tariff issue, the silver question, urbanization, immigration, and the soldiers' vote played major roles in the electorate's realignment.[87] As this narrative suggests, the receipt of pension benefits also played a significant role in swinging the national electorate behind the Republican Party. The importance of pension benefits, separate and distinct from the "soldiers' vote," has been confirmed by more detailed statistical studies.[88] Strong evidence was found that the pension vote was large enough to swing the popular vote decisively in favor of Republicans Benjamin Harrison in 1888 and William McKinley in 1896 and 1900. The pension vote contributed importantly to Teddy Roosevelt's win in 1904 and William Howard Taft's in 1908, but not decisively in either election. In 1892, pensioners swung the popular vote by 5 percentage points, but this magnitude was not enough to prevent Grover Cleveland from retaking the White House. Similar evidence impact favoring Republicans was uncovered in House elections during presidential election years, when the two parties' differing positions on pension liberalizations were most visible to voters. There was little evidence, however, that the pension vote played an important role during midterm elections for the House of Representatives.[89] On balance, the evidence indicates that Civil War pensions were an early demonstration that a broad-based distribution of entitlement benefits among the voting population can provide elected officials with an electoral advantage.

Legislating Universal Coverage

Congress was far from finished enacting legislation on behalf of Civil War veterans. It continued to pass laws that liberalized pensions for another four and a half decades. In 1918, it enacted an across-the-board benefit increase that raised the average monthly benefit by 30 percent. Two years later, another even-numbered year, Congress raised the average monthly benefit by another 30 percent.[90] These increases were nearly sufficient to compensate pension beneficiaries for loss of the purchasing power of their pensions from inflation.[91] In 1930, Congress repealed the requirement that a soldier serve for at least ninety days during the Civil War to qualify for benefits, thereby making pensions nearly universally available to all Civil War veterans of the Union armed forces.[92]

Following the pattern set by Revolutionary War laws, Congress incrementally extended pensions to Civil War widows until they were provided to virtually all widows of Civil War soldiers regardless of their marriage date. As noted earlier, the 1890 Dependent Pension Act granted pensions to widows of Union soldiers who had married prior to 1890 and had not remarried. In 1901, Congress extended pensions to widows who had remarried but had become widows again and to divorced wives of Union soldiers. In 1920, Congress granted pensions to widows who had married Union soldiers after 1890 but before 1905. In 1944, Congress extended pensions to all widows of Union soldiers regardless of when the marriage occurred, but required the widow to have been married for at least ten years. In 1957, Congress dropped the ten-year requirement. Incredibly, a year later, Congress granted pensions to widows of Confederate soldiers.[93]

In addition to these general laws, Congress continued its practice of enacting private relief laws that granted pensions to individual veterans and their widows. The Sixty-Third Congress, which was in session from 1913 to 1915, passed 5,061 private relief laws for Civil War pensions, raising the total of such laws that had been enacted since the Civil War's beginning to 47,398.[94]

The Civil War pension program came under considerable criticism during the second decade of the twentieth century when the progressive movement for government reform was strong. The program's large cost and the highly visible nature of its excesses made the program an inviting target. Public sentiment still favored pensions to disabled veterans and widows of soldiers killed in action, but the many pensioners who could support themselves or had only marginal connections to the war, including some very young wives of some very old soldiers, led reformers to charge that graft, waste, and abuse permeated the program. A 1915 *Chicago Tribune* article reporting that total expenditures on Civil War pension had reached $5 billion carried the subtitle, "Grabbers Still Are Busy." Congressman Joseph Ransdell of Louisiana pointed to the "double-dipping" behavior of General John C. Black as an example of the program's excesses. General Black was pensioned in 1878 on the ground that he was "a physical wreck, maimed and diseased, incapable of any effort and much of the time confined to his bed."[95] The general, however, had then gone on to serve in the publicly visible positions of commissioner of pensions, a member of Congress, and chairman of the U.S. Civil Service Commission while continuing to collect his disability pension.

As age and time took their toll, the number of Civil War pensioners began to decline after the turn of the century—slowly at first, as liberalizations offset natural attrition, but then more quickly. The number of Civil War pensioners peaked in 1901 at slightly fewer than 1 million, declined to 863,000 in 1910, 534,000 in 1920, 217,000 in 1930, and 53,000 in 1940.[96] Owing mainly to the two large increases in monthly benefits that were enacted in 1918 and 1920, Civil War pension expenditures reached their peak at $247 million in 1921. But that year, pension expenditures accounted for only 8 percent of federal spending and only half a percent of the nation's output of goods and services. By 1930, Civil War pensions' share of the federal budget was down to 4 percent.[97]

For all practical purposes, the Civil War pension program was over by the time World War II started, but its expenses continued to dribble out of the U.S. Treasury for another seventy years. The last Civil War soldier who received a pension died in 1956. The last Civil War widow pensioner died nearly fifty years later, in 2003. As of this writing, there remains one person still receiving Civil War survivor benefits: Irene Triplett, the product of a May–December marriage. In 1924, her mother, Elida Hall, age 28, married Mose Triplett, a 78-year-old veteran of both the Union and the Confederate armies. Five years later, Irene was born.

In legislating Civil War pensions, Congress followed the same pattern it had established in expanding Revolutionary War pensions. In doing so, Congress reaffirmed and hardened the earlier legislative precedents but on a much grander scale. Along with this legislation came an important and powerful discovery by the Congress and the executive branch: broadly distributing cash benefits directly to a large segment of the voting population could produce significant electoral advantages. The important role that recipients of Civil War pensions played in the national electorate's realignment to the Republican Party was not lost on either Republicans or Democrats. This discovery ensured that future Congresses would address entitlement legislation with electoral benefits firmly in mind.

5 Repeating Past Mistakes

World War I Veterans' Benefits

> No political party or self-seeking politician should ever dare to attempt to resurrect the old, unjust [Civil War pension] system.
>
> *Professor W. F. Gebhart*[1]

I N SPRING 1917, AS CONGRESS BEGAN ITS DELIBERA-
tions over a World War I pension program, the high cost of Civil War pensions was firmly in the minds of many members. The United States was entering a new war, unprecedented in scale, and the Treasury was still spending an extraordinary sum on a war that had ended fifty years earlier. When the Treasury closed the budget books on 1916, the federal government's annual pension bill totaled $150 million—over one-fifth of that year's total federal spending. Congress was still confronting the exorbitant demands and continuous pressure brought by the politically powerful pension lobby, leading to a strong sentiment for alternative programs that would prevent a recurrence of the Civil War disability program experience.

In addition to providing disability pensions for World War I soldiers to compensate for the loss of life or limb during wartime service, Congress adopted a novel program designed to reduce the inevitable pressure to liberalize disability pensions as veterans aged. The new program provided soldiers with an option to voluntarily purchase government-provided disability insurance to compensate for any disabilities they might incur later in life, regardless of the cause of the disability. The insurance program was well intentioned, but it proved no match for the inevitable and overwhelming pressures to extend the World War I pension program to virtually all veterans with disabilities, regardless of their cause. In the end, Congress not only extended disability pensions, as had previous Congresses; it did so at a much faster pace. Once again, the existence of large budget surpluses provided the critically important fuel for the pension liberalizations, and the equally worthy claim provided the rationale.

Following the war, Congress established a second novel program that was designed to alleviate future pressures to liberalize benefits. The 1924 adjusted certificate program provided veterans with a certificate entitling them to a sizable lump-sum payment in 1945, when age-related disabilities would presumably become common. This attempt backfired, just as the attempt to build a navy fund had a century earlier. As appropriations to prefund future payments built up in a special fund, so did the pressures to spend those appropriations. As the Great Depression wore on and veterans' immediate needs increased, Congress bent to the inexorable "cash now" movement's pressure to permit veterans to collect their deferred payments earlier than the original law allowed.

The so-called bonus issue also ignited an extraordinary seventeen-year battle between Congress and the executive branch. The five presidents who served between the two world wars—Woodrow Wilson, Warren G. Harding, Calvin Coolidge, Herbert Hoover, and Franklin Roosevelt—opposed bonus bill legislation. All vetoed bonus bills except President Wilson, who was not presented a bill by Congress. President Coolidge vetoed two bonus bills. The House of Representatives overrode all five vetoes, and the Senate overrode two of them.

The bonus issued also spawned a remarkable phenomenon: mass marches by veterans throughout the country demanding a promised entitlement benefit. The most memorable of these was the 1932 Bonus Expeditionary Force march on Washington, D.C., which ended when troops under General Douglas McArthur's command drove the veterans from the city.

Voluntary Disability Insurance for
Veterans: A New Approach

Six weeks after the United States entered World War I on April 6, 1917, Congress instituted a national draft with the Selective Service Act. The conscription law was quickly followed by the enactment of the War Risk Insurance Act, which created three major programs: a conventional disability pension program, a rehabilitation program of vocational rehabilitation and medical care, and the voluntary disability insurance program.[2]

The insurance program was the law's novel feature. Veterans could make monthly contributions to purchase up to $10,000 of death and disability insurance from the Bureau of War Risk Insurance. Premium payments were deducted from the soldier's paycheck during military service.[3] The insurance benefit entitled a soldier who became disabled as a result of injuries or illness incurred after wartime service to a minimum of twenty years of monthly disability payments. In the event of the soldier's death, his dependents would be eligible for the remaining portion of his entitlement.

Premium payments and federal government general fund revenues constituted the program's primary means of financing. The latter were limited to covering the program's administrative cost and insurance payments that resulted from the additional death and disability risk incurred during wartime service.

The new insurance program was designed to obviate any future need for legislation to extend benefits to veterans whose disabilities were unrelated to wartime service. Congress wanted to avoid a repeat of the Civil War program's soaring costs, its political favoritism, and widespread abuse. The new approach promised to substitute insurance benefits that were determined by scientifically applied actuarial principles for pension benefits that were determined by political calculation. Congressman Sam Rayburn, a chief sponsor of the insurance program, spoke for the program's supporters by saying that unless the insurance bill passed "after this war is over, another saturnalia of pension frauds and pension claims will be put up to this Congress."[4] Academic and policy experts outside government supported the program as a way to apply scientific principles to social policy problems, a hallmark of the Progressive era. Many predicted that the new approach would render obsolete the ad hoc pension liberalizations that had plagued the Civil War program. Future Congresses, they argued, would consider it unfair to provide taxpayer-financed pensions to veterans who had rejected the opportunity to opt into the insurance program, while other veterans were making regular insurance contributions out of their own pay. W. F. Gebhart, a life insurance expert, promised that with the new program in place, "no political party or self-seeking politician should ever dare to attempt to resurrect the old, unjust system."[5]

The program was quite popular initially. But after the war, when federal authorities were no longer able to automatically deduct premium payments from paychecks of discharged soldiers, program participation dropped rapidly. Ultimately only 10 percent of soldiers who had made regular premium payments during the war continued to do so afterward.[6]

Disability Pension Liberalization

The novel program failed to dampen Congress's enthusiasm for expanding the conventional wartime disability program. Within a few years, the same legislative pressures that had produced soaring Revolutionary War and Civil War pension costs began operating on World War I pensions.

From 1921 to 1930, the federal budget experienced ten consecutive years of budget surplus. Over the decade, federal revenues averaged a full 25 percent more than expenditures. Congress first responded in 1921 by establishing a "presumption" that any veteran who suffered from tuberculosis or neuropsychiatric diseases within two years of discharge had incurred these diseases during wartime service and was therefore entitled to disability pensions. But the act of creating presumptions for one set of diseases generated pressures for additional presumptions later in the decade. Advocates for expanding qualifying disabilities asked what made veterans who suffered from tuberculosis more deserving of government aid than veterans who suffered from other equally debilitating diseases. So three years later, Congress added Parkinson's disease, sleeping sickness, and dysentery to the list.[7]

The additional presumptions only heightened the unfairness of granting pensions to veterans with certain diseases and denying pensions to veterans with other diseases. The perceived inequity grew as the passage of time made it more difficult for veterans with these other diseases to prove that their disabilities were related to wartime service. Large federal budget surpluses toward the end of the 1920s magnified the pressures for liberalization. In 1927, the surplus reached the $1 billion mark for the first time in U.S. history. The Treasury ledgers for fiscal year 1930 showed that revenues exceeded expenditures by 22 percent despite the stock market crash the previous October.[8] Few saw the monumental economic collapse just on the horizon.

By 1930, the pressures proved irresistible. That year, Congressman John E. Rankin of Mississippi proposed extending the presumption of service-connected disabilities to veterans suffering from a "chronic constitutional or analogous disease."[9] For all practical purposes, the proposed legislation granted pensions to all disabled veterans regardless of whether their disabilities were war related. The bill's coverage was broad enough to encompass virtually every chronic ailment, including obesity.

Opponents argued that in correcting one inequality, the bill was creating another. The War Risk Insurance Act of 1917 had given all veterans voluntary access to government-subsidized insurance in the event that they became disabled after wartime service. Premium contributions had been withheld from the paychecks of those who had opted into the program. Veterans who had chosen not to opt in had avoided making contributions. The bill would now grant these nonparticipating disabled veterans a monthly disability check provided entirely at taxpayer expense. Moreover, the 1917 law, by providing insurance for veterans with postwar disabilities, had been designed precisely to avoid extending pensions to veterans with nonservice-connected disabilities.

When Congress passed the general presumption bill, President Hoover promptly vetoed it. The president, however, objected to the means the bill employed, not to its ends. He argued that a blanket

presumption constituted "a wholly false and fictitious basis for legislation in veterans' aid."[10] His proposed alternative would extend pensions to all financially needy disabled veterans, regardless of the origin
of their disabilities. The need standard was set so high that virtually
all disabled veterans could qualify.[11] Thus, the practical outcome of his
plan was essentially the same as the Rankin bill. Congress passed the
president's proposal, providing pensions to veterans with nonservice-
connected disabilities.

With the bill's passage, the barrier that the architects of the 1917
veterans' insurance program had designed to prevent the expansion
of benefits to veterans with nonservice-connected disabilities lay in
shambles. A decade of large budget surpluses and the precedents set
by veterans' legislation of two earlier wars had proven to be too much.
The government-subsidized insurance program had not even slowed
the entitlement expansion. To the contrary, Congress took forty-nine
years to extend nonservice-connected pensions to Revolutionary War
soldiers, forty-eight years for Civil War veterans, and only twelve years
for World War I veterans.

As with previous liberalizations, the new law generated an unanticipated rush of claimants. The Veterans Administration reported that the
number of claims exceeded "the preliminary estimates based upon the
experience and records of (the agency)."[12] From July 1, 1930, to June 30,
1931, the bureau received 541,943 applications, far more than the record
363,799 in 1891 after passage of the Dependent Pension Act of 1890.
The total number of pensioners breached the one million mark for the
first time in 1931 and continued rising the following year. In 1932, there
were three veterans receiving pensions for every two in 1930. That year,
veterans on the pension rolls with nonservice-connected disabilities
rose to over 412,000, 20 percent more than the number of pensioners
with service-connected disabilities.[13]

Congress should have anticipated the rush of claimants. A seemingly minor amendment in 1926 law illustrates just how sensitive individuals are to disability entitlement incentives. The amendment raised
the monthly benefit to a flat $50 for any soldier diagnosed with tuber-
culosis. At the time, tuberculosis diagnosis was highly subjective: Any
scarring on the lungs was sufficient for a positive diagnosis. Before the

law, only 12,019 veterans with tuberculosis were receiving pensions. A year later, the number had increased to 31,040 and two years later to 38,701. The increase in pensioners, coupled with the increase in monthly benefits, produced a ninefold rise in annualized pension payments to soldiers with tuberculosis.[14]

The flood of claimants caused the 1930 law to be far more costly than Congress and the Hoover administration had anticipated. The 1930 law was estimated to cost about $500,000 per year, a rather modest increase over the approximately $200 million spent that year on World War I pensions. In 1932, the Veterans Administration reported that expenditures under the 1930 law had totaled $30 million in fiscal year 1931 and $75 million in fiscal year 1932.[15]

Adjusted Compensation

The cost of the 1930 law was dwarfed by a new type of World War I veterans' benefit enacted into law in 1924. Adjusted compensation, more commonly known as the bonus, was designed as a supplement to veterans' wartime pay.

The movement for bonus payments began with the massive demobilization after the November 11, 1918, armistice. When many discharged soldiers experienced severe difficulties readjusting to civilian life, Congress stepped in and voted each discharged veteran a one-time bonus of $60, about two months of pay. The one-time payment satisfied few people, and political support for additional payments, termed a bonuses, grew quickly. As one prominent veterans' leader put it, "Every political demagogue in the country was yelling 'Bonus' for his own selfish ends beginning about November 1918."[16]

Advocates for bonus payments did not offer any principled arguments. Their position, boiled down to its essential elements, was that economic circumstances during and immediately following the war had treated World War I veterans unfairly. First, wartime military pay had been unfairly low, below the amount "paid the lowest-paid common laborer."[17] The basic military pay rate of $1.25 per day for overseas service and $1 per day for domestic service remained fixed throughout the war. When the United States entered the war in 1917, the latter rate was only about half the average manufacturing wage. Second, the rapid rise in private sector wages and prices during the war caused military pay to lag even farther behind private sector wages. During the war's nineteen months, manufacturing wages rose 33 percent and consumer prices increased by 19 percent.[18] Thus, bonus payment advocates argued, men who stayed at home benefited from real-wage gains during the war, while men who went off to war not only fell behind private sector workers but suffered real-wage reductions.

The effort to enact a bonus payment became the primary legislative objective of a formidable new lobbying organization: the American Legion. Established in 1919, the American Legion's original mission, similar to the Grand Army of the Republic, was to help veterans adjust to civilian life. The American Legion initially declined to take a position on bonus legislation at its first meeting in November 1919. However, the organization quickly took on a lobbying role and, along with the Veterans of Foreign Wars and the Disabled American Veterans, formed a powerful lobbying triumvirate. The American Legion, which by 1920 had 843,000 members, was the largest and most influential of the three. It was commonly said in Washington that "opposing a Legion measure is like poking one's political head out of a train window."[19]

The Legion organized itself along the same lines as had the Grand Army of the Republic, with a permanent national legislative committee in Washington and 10,000 local affiliates. It relied on the same pressure tactic that the Grand Army of the Republic and the claims agents had pioneered in lobbying for Civil War pension liberalizations. When an issue of importance to veterans came up for consideration in Congress, the National Committee notified the Legion's posts, which would generate thousands of individual letters from veterans to their congressional representatives. This technique, which became known as "the barrage," continues to be widely used today, except that the medium through which the message is delivered is now the Internet and phone lines.

The bonus bill idea attracted considerable support in Congress, where over two hundred bonus bills had been introduced by early 1924.[20] None was successful. Congress passed a bonus bill in 1922, but President Harding vetoed it because it lacked a financing source. The main obstacle to enactment was congressional and presidential concern over the magnitude of the national debt, which had soared to an unprecedented $24 billion as a result of the war. Bonus payments could easily add another $2 billion to $3 billion to that number. The priorities of Presidents Harding and Coolidge were to reduce the national debt through spending restraint and lower income tax rates from their high wartime levels. Congress at first agreed with their priorities. But pressure from the veterans' lobby continued to mount as Congress made steady progress reducing the war debt. A string of five consecutive annual federal budget surpluses from 1920 to 1924 enabled the public debt to be reduced by $3 billion from its $25 billion peak in 1919.[21]

In 1924, the House and Senate passed the World War Adjusted Compensation Act that entitled World War I veterans to bonus payments based on length of service during the war payable in 1945. The bonus payment amounted to a dollar a day for time served within the United States and $1.25 per day for time served abroad, plus an additional 25 percent to each of those totals because the payment had been deferred. Veterans entitled to $50 or less would be paid in cash. Those who were entitled to more than $50 would receive an interest-bearing certificate in lieu of cash. The certificate, in effect a government bond, and the accumulated interest on it could be redeemed by each veteran in 1945. For the typical veteran, the future amount payable was just under $1,000. Importantly, as we shall see later in this chapter, the amount payable was shown on the certificate's face.[22]

The certificates' aggregate value at redemption was initially estimated at $2 billion, about half of the total of all federal program expenditures in 1924. To finance the certificates, the bill created a reserve fund that was modeled after the post–Civil War navy pension fund. The fund was credited with appropriations of both principal and interest from the general Treasury. Specifically, the bill authorized Congress to appropriate about $100 million to the fund each year for the next twenty years, which would amount to $2 billion by 1945. Interest receipts on "investments" of the fund balance in U.S. Treasuries would also be credited to the fund and would be available in the event that the cost of the certificates exceeded the estimated $2 billion. Thus, in 1945, when the adjusted certificates became payable, the federal government would supposedly have the money on hand to do so.[23]

The law satisfied two goals: It met the demands of the veterans' lobby for additional compensation for wartime veterans and it provided the additional assistance in a form designed to address the inevitable future demand Congress knew from experience would come as World War I veterans aged.

President Coolidge vetoed the bill, saying he recognized that while meeting the needs of veterans was "a sacred obligation," the additional benefits were unwarranted. He noted that $2 billion had already been spent on disabled veterans and their dependents; $500 million had already been spent on veterans' life insurance; and the federal government was spending $400 million per year on disability pensions, rehabilitation services, insurance payments, and hospital care. The federal government's priority, in President Coolidge's view, should instead be to reduce wartime taxes and the national debt.[24] Adherence to such priorities, he argued, was the country's path to economic prosperity.

The president also argued that the reserve fund did not in fact provide any advance funding to meet the bill's extraordinary expense. Instead, the appropriation was merely a bookkeeping entry.[25] In the ever-so-gentle language used in official presidential communications, President Coolidge wrote:

> If we are to have such a commitment it should be in some form which would be in harmony with recognized principles of Government finance. . . . Under it [the legislation] the Government will not have in the fund in 1945 two and a half billions of dollars. All it will have will be its own obligations, and it will owe two and a half billions of dollars of cash. It will then be necessary to sell to the public this two and a half billions of bonds—a major operation in finance which may be disastrous at that time and may jeopardize the value of Federal securities then outstanding.[26]

Congress overrode the president's veto and the Veterans Bureau went to work issuing adjusted compensation certificates. Within a year, 2.8 million veterans and their survivors had applied for certificates worth an estimated $3.1 billion. A few years later, when a more complete tally was made, the renamed Veterans Administration revised the value of the government's outstanding liability to $3.6 billion.[27] Again, Congress had substantially underestimated the cost of a major entitlement law.

The 1932 Bonus March

In 1931, the Great Depression brought the bonus issue back to the forefront. An amendment to the original adjusted compensation law in 1927 had allowed the government to offer loans to veterans against a portion of the value of their certificates. By July 1930, over 2 million veterans, about half of all World War I veterans, had borrowed against their certificates.[28]

The loan provision was just the beginning of veterans' demands on the U.S. Treasury. As unemployment rose and household income fell, the political clamor to allow immediate cash payment of the certificates grew. The cash-now effort was led by Congressman Wright Patman (D-TX), who argued that given the depressed economic conditions, veterans needed their promised bonus payments immediately, not in 1945. According to Mr. Patman, the federal government was not being asked to make a new commitment of federal funds, only to advance a future obligation the government had already made to veterans.

The facts, however, were not quite what the congressman claimed. Under the Patman bill, veterans would receive the face value of their certificates immediately rather than in 1945. The certificate's face value, the amount payable in 1945, was 50 percent more than the certificate's present value, so Congressman Patman's bill actually provided a large windfall over the amount promised by the 1924 law.

The congressman scheduled hearings in 1931 featuring Joseph Angelo, who had won the Distinguished Service Cross for saving George S. Patton's life on the battlefield. Angelo testified that he had walked the 140 miles from his home in Camden, New Jersey, to the nation's capital to testify: "I done it all by my feet—shoe leather. I was not picked up by any machine." When asked why he came to testify, Mr. Angelo replied, "I come to show you people that we need our bonus. . . . I have got a little home back there that I built with my own two hands after I came home from France. Now, I expect to lose that little place. Why? My taxes are not paid."[29]

With Angelo's testimony providing the necessary impetus, Congress passed a bill providing immediate cash payment of the certificates. President Hoover, who had signed the costly 1930 veterans' pension into law a year earlier, vetoed the measure. Congress promptly passed a compromise bill that allowed veterans to borrow up to 50 percent of the value of their certificates.

The compromise failed to deter Congressman Patman and his cash-now supporters, and he reintroduced his bill in 1932. The deepening depression boosted the bill's prospects. But President Hoover's new effort to combat the economic decline, the Reconstruction Finance Corporation (RFC), gave even more impetus to both the Patman bill and the Bonus March.

The RFC had begun operations in February 1932 by making loans to banks, railroads, and farms. By the end of March, it had issued loans to 974 banks, railroad companies, insurance firms, and a livestock credit corporation. By July, loans had been made to 5,000 private institutions. A steady stream of press reports accompanied these loans. The corporate loans, when contrasted with congressional inaction on advancing money already owed World War I veterans, seemed profoundly unfair. Were veterans not at least equally worthy of assistance? Father Charles E. Coughlin, whose weekly radio addresses already attracted tens of millions of listeners, put the question succinctly: "If the Government can pay two billion to the bankers and railroads, having had no obligation to them, why cannot it pay the two billion to the soldiers, already recognized as an obligation?"[30] The federal government's entry into the business of providing assistance to private enterprise had opened up a large new arena in which the equally worthy claim could be applied.

President Hoover had strongly objected to the bonus bill, saying that it would "undo every effort that is being made to reduce Government expenditures and balance the budget," but the RFC's $500 million expenditures in 1932 made this objection ring hollow.[31]

In early May, a few hundred veterans, calling themselves the Bonus Expeditionary Force (BEF), set out from Portland, Oregon, for Washington, D.C., to pressure Congress to enact the bonus bill. The BEF leader, Army Sergeant Walter Waters, explained their demand by saying that the veterans were not asking for anything new, merely an early release of a future payment: "These men [veterans] had fallen far down into the valley of despair. Some push was necessary to start them out and up over the hill. Jobs would have provided the best sort of impetus but there were no jobs. The Bonus, a lump sum of money, would act in the same fashion." To Waters, their demand seemed reasonable: "What man, having a promise to pay at a later date would not ask his debtor for it in advance if he believed that the debtor could afford the money and if his own need was not only great but critical? These men felt that the Government had the money."[32]

Along their cross-country march, the BEF was greeted sympathetically in small towns and large cities. Soon newspapers and radio stations around the country reported on their travels and their cause. As the news spread, veterans in other communities set out for Washington to join the BEF to demand "cash now."

Waters's contingent arrived in Washington on May 29 and set up camp just across the Anacostia River, and soon they were joined by other veterans and their families. By June, more than twenty thousand veterans and their wives and children were living in tents and shanties, washing themselves and their clothes in the Anacostia River and cooking on open fire pits.

In June, the $2.4 billion Patman cash-now bonus bill passed the House but failed in the Senate. With dashed hopes, some veterans gave up and began their journey home. But Waters and thousands of other veterans and their family members remained, intending, as Waters declared, "to stay here until 1945 if necessary to get our bonus."[33]

Rumors spread that Communists had infiltrated the camps and were planning violence—rumors that the Hoover administration accepted as fact. The charges were never substantiated. In fact, the vast majority of veterans were law-abiding citizens who were suffering from the depression's hardships. But their desire for assistance had become a demand on the government for other citizens' hard-earned money.

Hoover administration officials and the District of Columbia's administrators grew increasingly concerned about the possibility of violence as the summer stretched into July. Chief of police Pelham D.

Glassford, who had become well acquainted with and well respected by the marchers, warned the occupiers to vacate the buildings, to no avail.

On July 28, the District of Columbia police arrived to oust the veterans who had occupied an abandoned government building. Shots were fired. One veteran was killed, and three policemen were injured. The veterans' entitlement quest had claimed its first casualties.

Later that day, Army Chief of Staff General Douglas McArthur, acting on orders from the president, decided to end the occupation. In a scene never before witnessed in American peacetime history, General McArthur's tanks, two hundred mounted cavalry, and three hundred infantrymen with loaded rifles and fixed bayonets moved down Pennsylvania Avenue to confront former members of the U.S. military. Then, going beyond the president's instructions, General McArthur ordered his troops to storm the camp at Anacostia. Firing tear gas grenades and setting fire to the shanties, one generation of American soldiers drove another generation from their encampment. During the battle, one veteran was killed and about fifty veterans and District of Columbia police were injured.

Initial press reports had supported the administration's actions.[34] But a few days later, newsreels showed the reality: Against a background of fire and smoke, harmless men, women, and children had been driven from their camp by the U.S. military with bayonets and sabers. Public opinion quickly turned against the Hoover administration's actions. Although the impact of the "battle of Anacostia" on the 1932 presidential election is debatable, President Hoover lost his reelection bid three months later by 7 million votes.

The Bonus March incident was a cruel twist of fate for Herbert Hoover. In 1930, he had signed one of the most liberal veterans' pension bills in U.S. history that had added over 400,000 veterans to the pension rolls. He had presided over a 50 percent increase in the Veterans Administration's budget and upgraded its status within the executive branch. He had vetoed a bonus bill but reached a compromise that increased the amount veterans could borrow against their certificates, and over 2 million veterans had taken advantage of this opportunity. In many respects, President Hoover had done more to aid World War I veterans than any of his predecessors.

6 Retrenchment

Roosevelt and the Veterans

No person, because he wore a uniform, must thereafter be placed in a special class of beneficiaries over and above all other citizens. The fact of wearing a uniform does not mean that he can demand and receive from his Government a benefit which no other citizen receives.

President Franklin Roosevelt, veto message of March 27, 1934

FRANKLIN ROOSEVELT CAME TO OFFICE WITH well-formed views about the proper government role in providing assistance to veterans of war. He shared the founding fathers' belief that all citizens had an obligation to serve their country in wartime and therefore did not represent a special class of individuals entitled to government benefits merely because they had served during wartime. The federal government, in turn, had an obligation to support and care for veterans who suffered disabilities from injury or illness resulting from wartime service.

His views were decidedly at odds with Congress, which invariably concluded that all wartime veterans, especially when they reached old age, stood as a special class. Those who had come through their wartime service unscathed were as equally worthy of government assistance as those who had suffered disabling injuries or illness due to wartime service. The acts of 1818, 1832, 1837, 1890, and 1930 had established strong precedents.

The clash of view between the president and Congress over veterans' benefits for disabilities unrelated to wartime service produced a decade-long battle that began before the Roosevelt administration was even one week old and lasted until World War II. The conflict produced a half-dozen presidential vetoes of major veterans' bills. Congress overrode three of the vetoes.[1]

By early 1933, the Great Depression had become the worst economic crisis in American history. The unemployment rate stood at 25 percent, economic output was down by 43 percent since 1929, and 40 percent of all banks had shut their doors. The president recognized that a modern economy could not operate without the free flow of credit and made addressing the banking crisis his first priority. Congress moved swiftly by passing a bank bill on March 9, six days after the inauguration.

The federal government's finances were in shambles, so the president's second priority was to put the federal budget on a sound footing. The budget, facing a U.S peacetime record deficit, could not be balanced without reducing veterans' benefits. Spending on veterans' programs including pensions, rehabilitation, and health care, had risen to 25 percent of total spending.

During his campaign, the president had espoused the orthodox economic view that the federal budget should be balanced and had called for a 25 percent reduction in federal spending. But as is common in presidential campaigns, he offered few details. For that, the new president turned to his newly chosen budget director, Lewis Douglas. Mr. Douglas, who had served three terms in Congress and had served on the Appropriations Committee, was well known for his strong policy views and his courage to stand up for them. He had consistently supported restricting pensions to veterans with service-connected disabilities, and early in 1932, he had delivered a courageous speech proposing such a restriction on the floor of the House. In his speech, Mr. Douglas urged members to set aside politics: "This is no time to consider our own petty political careers."[2] When he ended his remarks, members rose and gave him a roaring ovation—and then promptly voted down his proposals. *New York Times* columnist Arthur Krock aptly summarized Douglas's speech and the subsequent House action by writing: "In rising and cheering Mr. Douglas, the House was paying tribute to honesty and courage. In voting against him it was recording its belief that these attributes in a politician do not pay."[3]

On his seventh day in office, the president delivered his budget message to Congress, asserting that the federal budget had "for three long years . . been on the road toward bankruptcy." He told Congress that the budget deficit "has accentuated the stagnation of the economic life of the people. It has added to the ranks of the unemployed." He stated emphatically his belief that the failure to address the budget deficit would lead to economic ruin. "Too often in recent history," he said, "liberal governments have been wrecked on rocks of loose fiscal policy."[4]

To put the government's finances on a sounder footing, the president proposed that Congress give him the extraordinary power to unilaterally reduce federal spending, including entitlements. Specifically, he proposed that Congress delegate to him the unilateral authority to cut spending on veterans' pensions, other veterans' programs, and the operational expenses of government agencies.

Despite the federal budget's dire circumstances, President Roosevelt's extraordinary popularity, and the deference Congress usually grants to a president's proposals at the beginning of a new administration, the proposal faced an uphill battle in Congress. No president since Grover Cleveland's ill-fated efforts nearly fifty years earlier had taken on veterans' pensions, the budget's most sacred cow. Moreover, the president was asking Congress to delegate to the executive branch enormous discretion to set policies that were normally determined by congressional legislation. The next day, in an unusual Saturday session, the House passed the president's proposals, but the bill's prospects in the Senate were bleak. A filibuster loomed.

Two actions by the president on Sunday and Monday proved decisive in causing the Senate's favorable vote. On Sunday night, the president gave the first of his legendary fireside chats, reassuring the public that the U.S. banking system was in sound shape. On Monday, he sent to Congress his third message: to modify the Volstead Act to permit the sale of beer and other low-alcohol beverages, an extremely popular proposal that passed the House on Tuesday, March 13. Now the Senate was in a bind. Under Senate rules, action on the Volstead Act modification could not take place until the Economy Act had been addressed. The Senate now could not duck a vote on the Economy Act by allowing a filibuster or recessing without also walking away from the president's proposal to allow the sale of beer. The president had devised this strategy on the preceding weekend and informed his senior staff of it by announcing that "it would be a good time for a beer."[5] Faced with this dilemma, the Senate passed the Economy Act on Wednesday and the Volstead Act modification on Thursday.

Ten days later, President Roosevelt signed the most consequential legislation in pension history, An Act to Maintain the Credit of the United States Government, commonly known as the Economy Act of 1933. The law repealed all entitlements to pensions that had been granted to veterans of World War I, the Spanish-American War, the Boxer Rebellion, and the Philippine Insurrection.[6] The entitlement repeal applied with equal force to pension entitlements for veterans who had suffered disabilities in wartime service and to those with disabilities unrelated to wartime service. It applied equally to entitlements for widows and orphans of veterans killed in battle. It also applied to entitlements for veterans currently on the rolls and new applicants. The new law gave the president discretionary authority to set new eligibility rules.[7] He could continue pensions for some or all of the affected veterans if he so chose, but he was under no legal obligation to provide pensions to all veterans who met statutorily prescribed eligibility rules. The Economy Act abolished all of them. Monthly benefits for veterans of all wars prior to the Spanish-American War were reduced across the board by 10 percent. The president could also set new monthly pension levels for all other veterans within the broad guidelines established by the law.[8] The Economy Act prohibited the executive branch's new rules and monthly benefit levels from being challenged in federal court and specified that the delegation of authority to the president would last two years.[9] Regulations then in effect could be changed only by an act of Congress.[10] For the first time in U.S. history, a large-scale entitlement had been repealed.

Moving quickly before veterans' pension advocates could mount a defense, the administration issued regulations on March 31 to overhaul the vast complex of veterans' pension rules and impose massive reductions in benefits. The number of pensioners would be cut in half, mainly by removing from the rolls veterans who had qualified for pensions under the presumptive disease provisions of the 1920s laws and denying pensions for disabilities unrelated to wartime service. Monthly pension benefits would be reduced for nearly all veterans.

The regulations ignited a year-long battle between President Roosevelt and Congress. The veterans' lobby, led by the American Legion and the Veterans of Foreign Wars, regained their footing and demanded that Congress undo the pension cuts. In an attempt to forestall congressional action, the Roosevelt administration issued revised regulations that restored some benefits.[11] But the effort failed. On June 16, Congress passed legislation that limited the size of benefit reductions to 25 percent for certain veterans, set a minimum benefit for all veterans of the Spanish-American War, the Boxer Rebellion, and the Philippine Insurrection who were age 55 and older, and authorized the creation of independent review boards to conduct the eligibility reviews. Importantly, the law left intact the repeal of the entitlement for World War I veterans whose disabilities were unrelated to their wartime service.[12]

Not satisfied, the veterans' lobby pressed for further relief. In January 1934, the administration again attempted to mollify Congress by issuing regulations that loosened eligibility rules. This attempt also failed. In March, Congress passed legislation that reestablished the pension entitlement and full pension benefits for World War I veterans with wartime disabilities, their widows, and survivors who were on the rolls prior to the Economy Act. The law also restored the pension entitlement and set a maximum cut of 25 percent in benefits for all disabled veterans of the Spanish-American War, the Boxer Rebellion, and the Philippine Insurrection who were on the pension rolls prior to the Economy Act, regardless of the source of their disability. Significantly, Congress again left intact the Economy Act's repeal of the pension entitlement for World War I veterans suffering from disabilities unrelated to their wartime service.[13]

President Roosevelt vetoed the bill, but Congress overrode his veto. Presidential advisor Harold Ickes lamented the override by writing that "man after man, like so many scared rabbits, ran to cover out of fear of the soldier vote."[14]

At the time, the veto override was regarded as a major setback for the president. Writing in the *New York Times*, Arthur Krock described the vote on the bill as "the President's first Manassas."[15] Although the override was a setback, the president still achieved 90 percent of what he desired. The reversals of the president's policy were on the margin and did not go to the heart of his policy objectives.

The president did not believe society owed an obligation to its citizens for their military service alone. His principal policy goal was to eliminate pensions for veterans with disabilities unrelated to their wartime service. He largely achieved this goal, at least for World War I veterans. On June 30, 1933, 412,482 veterans with nonservice-connected disabilities were on the pension rolls; a year later, there were only 29,903, all of whom were permanently and totally disabled. The pension entitlement for World War I veterans with disabilities unrelated to war had been all but terminated. These veterans were no longer a special class of people to whom the government was obliged to assist.

Overall, the Economy Act's reduction in the veterans' pensions program is the largest ever taken in any entitlement program in U.S. history. Although no official estimates of the law's impact on pension outlays were made, an estimate suggests that the law cut pension outlays nearly in half. In the year preceding the Economy Act, pension outlays were on the rise, as they had been since World War I ended. Yet during the law's first year in operation (1934), total pension outlays were 42 percent below the prior year's outlays—a $229 million reduction. One-third of these reductions came from terminating veterans with disabilities unrelated to their wartime service, the principal target group of the president's policy. The remaining reduction came from reducing monthly benefits paid to the lion's share of pensioners who remained on the rolls.[16] Pension expenditures in 1935, which accounted for the full-year impact of the 1934 veto override law, were still one-third below their 1933 level. The law's impact on the pension rolls was nearly as large. The Veterans Administration reported in 1935 that the

Economy Act and subsequent revisions resulted in eliminating 456,065 recipients from the rolls.[17] On June 30, 1934, after veterans and survivors had been restored to the rolls pursuant to the March 1934 law, there were 431,803 fewer people on the pension rolls than a year before, a one-third reduction in the pension rolls. Nine of every ten terminated veterans were World War I veterans with disabilities unrelated to their wartime service.[18]

Several factors account for President Roosevelt's remarkable success in reducing veterans' pensions. The economy and federal budget's dire situation presented the president with a national emergency, and in Washington, such emergencies are a strong predicate for action. The president moved quickly after his inauguration, proposing the Economy Act within a week of being sworn into office. For months following an inauguration, the president's influence typically is at its zenith, because Congress is usually willing to give his proposals considerable deference and interest groups tend to be in disarray.

President Roosevelt was also willing to use his veto power to sustain his policies. When Congress threatened to overturn major portions of the Economy Act in June 1933, he informed Congress that he would veto such a bill and warned that he would use a radio address to take his case directly to the American public, over the heads of Congress. His 1934 veto, although overridden, also served to induce Congress to produce a watered-down bill.

Finally, President Roosevelt employed his remarkable political skills to achieve his policy goal. In March 1933, he had used the sale of low-alcohol beer to circumvent the threat that the Senate's rules presented to his Economy Act. In May, when a second, much smaller Bonus Expeditionary Force returned to Washington, President Roosevelt, in sharp contrast to President Hoover, convinced the marchers to disperse without incident. He first issued an executive order setting aside twenty-five thousand jobs in his Citizens' Conservation Corps for veterans to work in the forests. The president then dispatched Eleanor Roosevelt, rather than the U.S. Army, to the veterans' encampment to sympathize with their plight. The protesting veterans left Washington satisfied that the president was doing what he could for them. President Roosevelt's actions served as a template nearly fifty years later for Ronald Reagan, the only other twentieth-century president to achieve significant entitlement restraint.

Over the next six years, under pressure from the American Legion and other veterans' lobbying groups, Congress repeatedly attempted to restore the president's cuts, resulting in many vetoes and little else. In 1934, President Roosevelt, in an effort to forestall legislation, issued regulations raising the basic benefit payable to veterans with 100 percent disabilities to its pre-1933 level of $100 per month. In 1935, Congress passed an American Legion–sponsored bill that restored monthly benefits paid to partially disabled veterans to their pre-1933 levels. The president vetoed this bill but was overridden. Most other efforts to expand benefits were rebuffed by presidential vetoes that were sustained by Congress.[19]

In 1940, as U.S. participation in World War II grew closer, the long battle between the president and Congress over veterans' pensions came to a close. President Roosevelt's success in reducing veterans' pensions is perhaps best measured by comparing pension outlays and the number of pensioners in 1940, right before U.S. entry into World War II, to 1933 when he took office. In 1940, benefits payable to World War I veterans and their survivors were still 22 percent below their 1933 level. The number of World War I veterans and survivors on the pension rolls was still 33 percent below the 1933 level.[20]

The Bonus Bill's Final Chapter

The final chapter of the bonus payment story was written in 1935 and 1936. Throughout 1934 and 1935, Wright Patman and the veterans' organizations continued to press for immediate payment of the adjusted compensation certificates. In 1934, as in 1932, the House passed the Patman bonus bill and the Senate did not. In 1935, Congress once again took up bonus legislation. This time the Senate followed the House's lead and passed the bill.

The arguments in favor of the bill were the same as in previous years, with one exception: A majority in Congress appeared to have cast aside the orthodox view that a balanced budget was essential to economic recovery in favor of a new theory advanced by British economist John

Maynard Keynes. Professor Keynes hypothesized that deficit spending was essential to economic recovery. Many in Congress, not surprisingly, eagerly embraced the theory. To them, the theory meant that Congress could vote to increase appropriations without imposing higher taxes. The resulting budget deficit, far from harming the economy, would actually increase the nation's wealth. The Keynesian theory was the politician's free lunch, and the members of Congress immediately understood it as such. The bonus bill that Congress passed included a preamble that unabashedly reflected this new theory: "Whereas since the Government of the United States is now definitely committed to the policy of spending additional sums of money for the purpose of hastening recovery from the present economic crisis, the immediate cash payment of the face value of the adjusted-service certificates . . . is a most effective means to that end."[21]

President Roosevelt, who had long before abandoned the orthodox economic view and had pursued deficit spending, vetoed the bill. In an extraordinary presidential act never seen before or since repeated in U.S. history, he appeared on Capitol Hill in person to deliver his veto message to a joint session of Congress. Standing before a Congress that was currently debating his signature New Deal bill to create a Social Security system, the president reminded its members of all that the federal government had done for World War I veterans: $7.8 billion had been spent on cash assistance, health care, and rehabilitation assistance; another $450 million was currently being spent each year on the same veterans' benefits. He believed the 1924 adjusted compensation law had been a fair settlement of the veterans' claims. Immediate payment of the certificates' 1945 face value amounted to a $1.6 billion gratuity to veterans. He was against any such payment because it was wrong to single out veterans as a special class on which to bestow benefits. In his words, "In this future of ours it is of first importance that we yield not to the sympathy which we would extend to a single group of class by special legislation for that group or class."[22]

The president used his veto message to state his views on this legislative application of the new Keynesian theory, challenging the application, if not the theory itself. In President Roosevelt's words, "Wealth is not created, nor is it more equitably distributed by this method (distributing cash or its equivalent directly to citizens). A Government, like an individual, must ultimately meet legitimate obligations out of the production of wealth by the labor of human beings applied to the resources of nature. Every country that has attempted the form of meeting its obligation which is here provided has suffered disastrous consequences." He stated flatly that the failure of an expenditure of this type to be accompanied by a corresponding tax increase "would in and by itself alone warrant disapproval." He justified the deficit spending that had occurred under his watch on an entirely different basis: government's responsibility to provide aid to suffering citizens in a time of crisis: "Every appropriation by the Seventy-Fourth Congress to date, for recovery purposes, has been predicated not on the mere spending of money to hasten recovery, but on the sounder principle of preventing the loss of homes and farms, of saving industry from bankruptcy, of safeguarding bank deposits, and more important of all—of giving relief and jobs through public work to individuals and families faced with starvation."[23]

The House overrode the president's veto, 322–98, but the Senate sustained it.

Less than four months later, in September 1935, a tragic natural disaster in the Florida Keys led to a final resolution of the bonus issue. Pursuant to President Roosevelt's 1933 promise, the Federal Emergency Relief Administration had established work camps for veterans. Workers were paid $30 per month and given food and shelter for their services. Three camps had been set up in the area between Miami and Key West to build Highway 1 along Florida's Atlantic Coast. The workers in these camps consisted primarily of World War I veterans who had been sent from Washington following the 1933 Bonus March. On September 2, 1935, as camp members took a Labor Day break, a hurricane of enormous strength hit the Keys. Stranded by bureaucratic bungling and miscommunications, 259 veterans in the federal government's charge died.[24]

When Congress returned in January 1936, sympathy for World War I veterans was at a fever pitch. Bills providing for immediate payment of the adjusted-service certificates were quickly introduced in both houses of Congress. The House and Senate passed bonus bills, the president issued a perfunctory veto, and Congress promptly overrode the president.

The bonus bill, in its final form, entitled veterans to immediate payment of the face value of their certificates. New certificates in $50 denominations were redeemable at once (starting June 15, 1936) or could be held until 1945, earning 3 percent interest. The Veterans Administration promptly issued $1.765 billion in cash and certificates. Total cash and redemptions in 1936, nineteen years after the United States signed the armistice ending World War I, totaled $1.43 billion, the largest disbursement of cash to veterans in any single year in U.S. history up to that time.

In the end, President Roosevelt's extraordinary efforts to rein in veterans' entitlement programs were only partially successful. Through the use of the veto, he was able to prevent Congress from reinstituting nonservice-connected pensions for a large portion of veterans whom his administration removed from the rolls in 1933. He was able to forestall the early payout of the bonus, but only for three years. President Roosevelt's efforts to create a New Deal for Americans, in part by extending federal entitlement benefits to the general population, were far more successful, as we will see in the next chapter.

7 The Birth of the Modern Entitlement State

We can never insure one-hundred percent of the population against one-hundred percent of the hazards and vicissitudes of life, but we have tried to frame a law which will give some measure of protection to the average citizen and to his family against the loss of a job and against poverty-ridden old age.

Franklin Roosevelt, statement on signing the Social Security Act[1]

THE NEW DEAL PRODUCED A FUNDAMENTAL PIVOT in the evolution of the U.S. government. The gradual expansion of the federal government's reach that had taken place during the twentieth century's first three decades gave way to a sharp acceleration. The New Deal also permanently altered the balance in the federalist system that the founding fathers had carefully constructed by profoundly changing the relationship between the federal government and the individual, the allocation of authority between federal and state governments, and the role of the federal courts in making public policy.

Before the Great Depression, the federal government bore no significant responsibility for poverty relief. Individuals were expected to provide for their own economic well-being. Local and state governments and private charities furnished assistance to those who were unable to provide for themselves, especially the elderly, disabled people, and children of financially needy widowed, divorced, and deserted mothers. Similarly, unemployment assistance lay outside the federal sphere.

Although the U.S. economy had periodically experienced economic contractions, the federal government had refrained from involving itself in labor market issues. Unemployment was addressed by local public works projects, state and local aid programs, and private charitable relief. Direct cash assistance to families with a temporarily unemployed breadwinner, in the rare instances when it was provided, was given out only with great care so as to not encourage idleness and sloth.

The New Deal policies were premised on the view that unemployment and poverty, especially elderly and child poverty, were beyond individuals' control, a by-product of larger social and economic forces that operated in a modern industrial economy. New Deal advocates believed that state and local governments were ill equipped to deal with these overwhelming national forces. The federal government, with its extraordinary taxing and borrowing capacities, was considered better positioned to address them. In the New Deal view, the federal government not only had the fiscal capability but also the moral obligation and constitutional authority to do so.

The New Deal extended the application of federal entitlements far beyond existing limits. Until the New Deal, federal entitlements were restricted to those who had performed specific government service— veterans and former government employees. The New Deal expanded entitlements to those who had not previously performed any federal government service, to state governments, and to private businesses.

The New Deal used the federal government's fiscal powers to induce or coerce state governments to create new or expand existing state government entitlements. It used a federal payroll tax to forcefully induce the states into creating unemployment insurance programs. It used threats to withhold federal matching funds for state-run welfare programs to induce states to expand eligibility for their welfare programs.

The New Deal entitlements ushered in a new era for the federal courts. First, the Supreme Court allowed the New Deal entitlements to pass constitutional muster under the "general welfare" clause. This ruling's ramifications went beyond the realm of entitlements by removing any practical limitation on federal spending power. The ruling also caused the Court to lessen its role as the guardian of the boundary line between federal and state powers, just as James Madison had warned,

120 years earlier, that such a constitutional interpretation would do so.[2] Second, once federal entitlement rights had been granted, the nature and extent of these legal rights had to be adjudicated. The courts were the institution established to perform this role. In the 1960s and 1970s, the federal courts used their adjudicatory role to expand the legal rights of entitlement claimants in welfare, health care, and nutrition. Ultimately federal court decisions created welfare entitlement rights where none had been legislated.

The New Deal extended the reach of federal government entitlements, but it did not repeal the precedents that Congress had already set, including its susceptibility to the allure of "equally worthy" claims and the temptation to use entitlements for electoral advantage. The operation of these forces in the new era would produce a proliferation of entitlements that would ultimately distribute government aid to more than half of all U.S. households.

The degree to which New Deal entitlements represented a sharp break from the past can be fully appreciated only by first understanding the federal government's role in assisting the poor and elderly before the 1930s.

Nineteenth-Century Welfare Policy

Since colonial times, aid to those unable to care for themselves had been recognized as a local community responsibility, carried out by private charities and local governments. Local government aid was limited to long-time residents. The primary role of state governments was to help finance local aid to the so-called unsettled poor, that is, homeless people who migrated from town to town. State aid was necessary because local governments feared that local aid attracted poor transients and would drain the community's scarce resources.[3]

Throughout colonial times and well into the late nineteenth century, welfare administrators and social reformers distinguished between two groups. The first consisted of poor people who through no fault of their own were unable to provide for themselves and were viewed as worthy of help: the frail elderly, the disabled, and children of single mothers unable to care for them. The second group consisted of able-bodied adults who could work but were nevertheless destitute. Welfare administrators and social reformers believed that poverty among the latter group resulted from human frailties: idleness, intemperance, and immorality. Great care, therefore, was taken in providing government aid for fear that it would encourage greater dependency. As one social reformer put it, "Next to alcohol, and perhaps alongside it, the most pernicious fluid is indiscriminate soup."[4]

The provision of public assistance to "worthy" individuals and the denial of such assistance to "unworthy" individuals created a public policy dilemma with large moral overtones. Drawing eligibility rules too narrowly would leave destitute some individuals who were in need through no fault of their own. But drawing eligibility rules that were too loose would, in effect, compel working individuals to support individuals who were perfectly capable of providing for themselves. Moreover, regardless of where eligibility rules were drawn, the provision of assistance would create incentives for potential recipients to modify their behavior to qualify for aid, often in ways detrimental to their own long-run interests. We will return to this dilemma when we consider twentieth-century welfare entitlements.

State and local governments of the early nineteenth century quickly found that it was difficult to distinguish between the two groups. Over time, welfare rolls increased and the financial burden of caring for the poor grew heavier. Blame was placed squarely on the method of providing welfare assistance. In most towns, aid was provided directly to families in need, foster families, and families that took on poor people as apprentices or indentured servants. Experience had shown that this policy of "outdoor relief" encouraged greater dependency by allowing too many able-bodied people to receive community-financed aid.

In response, state and local governments began to emphasize the alternative of institutional care: almshouses for the elderly poor and disabled, orphanages for children, mental asylums for the insane, and workhouses for the able-bodied poor. Care that could be provided in an institutional setting was thought to be more suited to the needs of the nonable-bodied poor. Institutional care, reformers believed, could also help control costs because it served as a deterrent to the able-bodied poor seeking aid.[5] The growth in institutional care was accompanied by a gradual centralization of public welfare as states and counties assumed a larger share of the financial burden.

As local governments reduced outdoor relief efforts, charities, churches, and mutual aid societies increasingly took up responsibility for providing short-term aid to the able-bodied poor. Because poverty among the able-bodied was believed to be a consequence of human weaknesses, charitable assistance was provided on a case-by-case basis and was usually accompanied by a heavy dose of counseling. As one counselor stated, "It is not bread the poor need, it is soul; it is not soup; it is spirit."[6] Temperance and morality were believed to be the keys to rehabilitation and self-reliance.

From time to time, there were attempts to secure direct federal aid to certain classes of poor people, but these efforts ran counter to strongly held beliefs that welfare should not, and could not, be a federal responsibility under the U.S. Constitution. There are two notable examples of this general sentiment. The first was Dorothea Dix's twenty-year quest to obtain federal aid for state institutions for the insane. She reached the edge of success in 1854 when Congress enacted legislation that would have granted 10 million acres of federal land to states for mental asylums. President Franklin Pierce then vetoed the bill. Reflecting the conflict between human compassion and constitutional principles that prevailed at the time, President Pierce wrote to Congress, "I readily, and I trust feelingly, acknowledge the duty incumbent on us all, as men and citizens, and as among the highest and holiest of our duties, to provide for those who, in the mysterious order of Providence, are subject to want and to disease of body or mind, but I cannot find any authority in the Constitution for making the Federal Government the great almoner of public charity throughout the United States."[7] Congress sustained the veto, and Dorothy Dix's effort came to an end.

The second example occurred during Reconstruction. Most of the 4 million emancipated slaves were ill prepared for their freedom. Lacking education, adequate clothing, shelter, and money, the freed slaves had been, in the words of Frederick Douglass, "turned loose, naked, hungry and destitute to the open sky."[8] After the war, most freed slaves continued to live in the South, where large segments of the white population remained overtly hostile to them. Racial animosity toward African

Americans and the poor condition of the former Confederate states' economies combined to limit assistance.

Congress responded by creating the Freedmen's Bureau, the federal government's first large-scale welfare agency. During its brief existence from 1865 to 1872, the bureau administered programs throughout the South that provided health care, education, welfare assistance, and legal aid, mainly to former slaves. Its schools taught over 240,000 students, its health care facilities treated over 500,000 people, and its welfare administration provided food rations to 20 million refugees.[9] The bureau's activities made the agency the nineteenth-century equivalent of three modern federal government cabinet departments: Health and Human Services, Education, and Labor.

Despite the large scale of its operations and its importance in alleviating hardship, the Freedmen's Bureau appears to have had no significant long-term impact on the evolution of U.S. welfare policy. Its chief proponents in Washington regarded it as a temporary agency established to meet an immediate postwar need. Once it had completed its duties, Congress terminated its operations. Until the New Deal, the federal government's only role in providing welfare aid was to sufferers of natural disasters.

Attitudes among officials and reformers about providing care for poor people in institutional settings began to change after the Civil War, prompted by the deplorable conditions found in many institutions. State examinations, such as those in New York State and South Carolina, described state-financed institutions as filthy and generally unhealthy, poorly constructed, and with insufficient heating and ventilation. The conditions were more characteristic of an abandoned warehouse than a house of care. Institutionalized people living in these overcrowded and often wretched conditions received little supervision, little attention to their personal needs, and poor-quality health care. They were often treated as societal castoffs rather than individuals who would benefit from care and rehabilitation.

By the 1890s, the failure of institutional care to live up to its promises was readily apparent. The pendulum of social reform began to swing back toward noninstitutional care, first in the care and treatment of impoverished children and then more consequentially for modern entitlements in the provision of elderly assistance.

Children became the primary focus of attention mainly because poverty was entirely beyond a child's control, and the long-term consequences of child poverty were believed to be severe. As Robert Hunter wrote in his classic 1904 work on poverty, "Poverty degrades all men who struggle under its yoke, but the poverty which oppresses childhood is a monstrous and unnatural thing, for it denies the child growth, development, strength; it robs the child of the present and curses the man of the future."[10]

Late nineteenth-century social reformers were aghast at the conditions of institutions within which poor, motherless children were often housed. Initially they pressed for removing children from institutions that also housed the mentally insane, the disabled, and the elderly, placing children in separate orphanages. Then, as the new century dawned, the reformers began to emphasize that the family unit was critical to children's physical, emotional, and intellectual development. Home life was to be maintained whenever possible. If the mother was incapable of properly raising her child, the next best alternative was to place the child in a home that had a proper environment. The early twentieth-century reformers regarded orphanages as a last resort.

The new views about the importance of home life gained widespread attention in 1909 when President Theodore Roosevelt convened the first White House Conference on the Care of Dependent Children. The conference brought together two hundred leading social reformers of the day, including Homer Folks, Lillian Wald, Jane Addams, and Florence Kelley. The conferees' white paper proclaimed that "home life is the highest and finest product of civilization. It is the great molding force of mind and character."[11] The objective of governmental aid, according to the reformers, should be to prevent children from being separated from a mother left destitute by the absence of the child's father. The conference report stated flatly that no child "should be deprived of his family by reason of poverty alone."[12]

The reformers recognized that not all mothers were capable of providing a proper home environment. Financial aid, they believed, should be limited to households that were suitable for child rearing. As the report stated, "Children of worthy parents or deserving mothers should, as a rule, be kept with their parents at home."[13] In the reformers' view, government had a responsibility to ensure that any home receiving aid had a proper environment. But the desire to provide financial assistance to single mothers had to be balanced against the reality that any such public aid relieved fathers of their financial responsibility and would thereby weaken the family life they were trying to strengthen. The reformer recommended local administration in the delivery of assistance and that local authorities have considerable discretion in determining eligibility and the amount of financial assistance.

The conference launched a new era in child welfare policy. Two years later, Missouri and Illinois enacted laws that provided cash assistance to mothers who had been left destitute by their husband's death. By 1913, sixteen additional states had mothers' aid programs on their books. By 1933, forty-six states had established programs (only Georgia and South Carolina lacked them). Financing mothers' pensions was primarily a local responsibility. In 1934, only seventeen state governments contributed to financing.[14]

Enactment of publicly funded mothers' aid programs was highly controversial. Opposition was especially strong among private charities that were the primary source of aid to mothers and children without husbands. The charities argued that the "mechanical nature" by which government bureaucracies worked would result in financial aid becoming a permanent entitlement-based dole that would trap women and children in a lifetime of poverty and dependency.[15] Moreover, dependency would be transmitted from one generation of recipients to the next, according to social reformer Homer Folks, because children would "grow up accustomed to the idea that they are depending upon it. It takes the life of independence out of them."[16] Government agencies, they warned, could not exercise sufficient discretion in choosing which families would actually benefit from assistance. Neither could government agencies provide the individualized counseling and services necessary for single mothers to become self-reliant. In their view, the lessons of the early nineteenth-century outdoor relief programs had demonstrated the validity of these concerns.

These concerns were large when applied to widows, but they were overwhelming when applied to families in which the child was born out of wedlock or was fatherless because of divorce or desertion. Homer

Folks in 1914 argued that "to pension desertion or illegitimacy would, undoubtedly, have the effect of a premium upon these crimes against society. . . . It is a great deal more difficult to determine the worthiness of such mothers than of the widow, and a great deal more dangerous for the State to attempt relief on any large scale."[17]

Proponents of expanding aid countered that to deny aid to a child of a financially needy unwed, widowed, divorced, or deserted mother punished the child for the sins of the parent. In the proponents' view, all needy children, regardless of circumstances, were equally worthy of assistance.

Concerns that aid might encourage divorce and illegitimacy held sway, causing states to be initially reluctant to extend aid beyond the children of widows. Thus, the initial dependent children programs, commonly called "widows' pensions," were limited to assistance to mothers with deceased husbands.

During the decades leading up to the Social Security Act, many state programs expanded eligibility to include children of mothers who were divorced or whose husbands were disabled or had deserted the family. Nevertheless, in the early 1930s, 82 percent of families receiving assistance were headed by a widowed mother. By 1934, only three states specifically granted eligibility to children of unmarried mothers, and fewer than half the states granted eligibility to children of divorced parents.[18]

By the early 1930s, regulations that conditioned welfare aid on a demonstration that the child's home was a satisfactory place for child rearing were firmly embedded in state welfare policies. Such "suitable home" laws often contained specific behavioral prohibitions or requirements on adult caretakers. Michigan and Massachusetts, for example, specified that no male boarder other than the mother's father or brother could live in the home. Delaware required children who attended school to maintain satisfactory performance. Minnesota specified that mothers could be required to learn English.[19]

Aid to the Elderly

Strong demographic, economic, and political forces led to a change in attitudes regarding aid to elderly people during the early twentieth century. The number of elderly had been steadily rising for decades. In 1890, the number of people age 65 and over, although only 3.9 percent of the population, was nearly 50 percent greater than in 1860. By 1920, the elderly population had grown another 50 percent, to 5.7 percent of the population. Changes in the U.S. economy's structure from agrarian to industrial over the same period loosened family ties as sons and daughters of rural farmers moved to cities for industrial jobs. As the ties loosened, familial support for elderly people declined.

By the turn of the century, Civil War veterans' pensions served as an effective support program for a large but increasingly exclusive segment of the elderly population: white males. The vast majority of women, African American men, and Southerners who fought for the Confederacy were not part of the Civil War pension system. After 1915, pension coverage began to decline as the march of time took its inevitable toll on Civil War veterans.

By the 1920s, two main groups advocated for government aid to the elderly. One school, led by social reformers Jane Addams and Paul Kellogg of the National Conference of Charities and Corrections, believed that aid should be limited to elderly people who had no other means of support, including support from their children. Aid should be granted on a voluntary basis at the discretion of those providing assistance. This "relief and charity" school of thought emphasized private charitable assistance and state-provided aid but did not oppose federal assistance.

A second school of thought, led by I. M. Rubinow and Abraham Epstein under the banner of the American Association for Old-Age Assistance, favored a social insurance approach. This approach, which had been embraced by many European countries, granted a right to assistance to all elderly people regardless of income and was financed by federal taxation. Writing in 1912, Mr. Rubinow, a leading progressive intellectual, argued that a federal program of assistance to the elderly did not represent a radical departure from existing policy. In his view, the Civil War pension program had evolved into little more than a thinly disguised general retirement program. Federal aid to the elderly was a natural extension. He wrote that it was "idle to speak of a popular system of old-age pensions as a radical departure from American traditions, when our pension roll numbers several hundred thousand more names than that of Great Britain."[20]

The volunteer or charity approach advocated by Ms. Addams and Mr. Kellogg met with considerable success after World War I. Pennsylvania, Montana, and Nevada enacted legislation providing aid to the elderly poor in 1923, with eligibility for aid restricted to those age 70 or older who had resided in the state for at least fifteen years. Participation by counties was optional. Five other states followed suit. In 1929, California became the first state to enact an old-age program that was mandatory in all political jurisdictions. The program was administered by counties, and financing was shared equally by the county and state governments.[21]

There was little public support for a federal program to assist the elderly during the 1920s. Philosophical opposition ran deep. Presidents Harding, Coolidge, and Hoover all believed that federal aid to the elderly, unemployed workers, and single mothers with children should remain the sole province of the states. Neither Republican nor Democratic Party platforms of the 1920s expressed support for federal welfare programs. The furthest either party went was the Democratic Party in 1932, when its platform pledged to "advocate unemployment and old-age insurance under state laws."[22] Also reflecting this lack of support was the absence of any organized large-scale national lobby that pressed for a federal program. The groups advocating for federal aid were small and unorganized. Abraham Epstein's American Association for Old-Age Assistance, founded in 1927, was largely a one-man think tank. Jane Addams and Paul Kellogg's National Conference of Charities and Corrections was larger and more organized, but it focused mainly on state governments. Organized labor, which eventually became a potent lobbying force, had opposed federal old-age assistance until the mid-1920s.

As the Depression deepened, support for federal involvement gained a stronger foothold. In 1933, Francis Townsend, a physician in Long Beach, California, introduced his radical plan to provide federal assistance. The Townsend Plan promised $200 per month to every person age 60 or older who agreed to retire from active employment. The payment, equivalent to an annual $45,000 in today's dollars, was a bounty to all elderly people, including those who were able-bodied and in no need of help. The plan was to be financed by a tax on the earnings of younger workers. The payments would increase annual federal outlays tenfold and double the national debt in the plan's first year. Remarkably, public opinion polls in 1935 showed that 56 percent of the population favored the plan: a petition calling on Congress to enact it into law was signed by 10 million people.[23]

Congress felt the pressure for action but gave serious consideration only to more measured proposals. Although Congress was reluctant to venture into the welfare arena, it was sympathetic to the fiscal plight of state and local governments, which were overwhelmed by the need for relief assistance. When nine states closed their old-age assistance programs in 1934, support coalesced around a proposal to provide federal matching grants to these programs. President Roosevelt supported the proposal but preferred to go much further. In June 1934, as the curtain closed on the Seventy-Third Congress's first session, he announced his intention to submit a more comprehensive Social Security program to Congress.

The Social Security Act

The Social Security Act was arguably the twentieth century's most consequential legislative act. The law's flagship program, which provided federal benefits to people 65 and older, represented the sharpest break from the past. The program not only brought the federal government squarely into the social welfare arena; it did so with a social insurance program in which benefits were not conditioned on need. It also introduced a new form of federal taxation, a payroll tax, to finance its benefits. The Social Security program has grown into the dominant social program of the latter half of the twentieth century and into the twenty-first century. The largest nondefense program in U.S. history, it will continue to be so until early in the next decade, when it will be surpassed by its sister program, Medicare.

The act also created three major new programs that entitled states to federal matching payments for state-operated programs: Old-Age Assistance, Aid to Dependent Children (ADC), and Aid to the Blind.[24] Decades later, ADC evolved into the nation's principal and most controversial post–World War II welfare program. The matching programs for poor elderly people and the blind were expanded to include poor disabled people in 1950. The three programs were federalized in 1972 into what is known today as the Supplemental Security Income program.

Finally, the act created the federal-state unemployment insurance program. Although it did not create a new federal unemployment insurance entitlement, it led directly to state entitlement programs that served as the infrastructure on which a large federal entitlement would be built in the 1970s.

The president's June 8, 1934, message to Congress marked the beginning of the pivot of government toward the modern entitlement state. He declared that the time when families and communities could be relied on to provide economic security to the elderly and poor had passed. The federal government had a duty to step in and provide that security for its citizens. He explained the need for government actions:

> Security was attained in the earlier days through the interdependence of members of families upon each other and of the families within a small community upon each other. The complexities of great communities and of organized industry make less real these simple means of security. Therefore, we are compelled to employ the active interest of the Nation as a whole through government in order to encourage a greater security for each individual who composes it.[25]

President Roosevelt, despite doubts raised by constitutional scholars, believed the federal government had the constitutional authority under the general welfare clause. He declared that "if, as our Constitution tells us, our Federal Government was established among other things 'to promote the general welfare,' it is our plain duty to provide for that security upon which welfare depends."[26]

President Roosevelt's sweeping Social Security plan was enacted by Congress and signed into law on August 14, 1935. The Social Security

Act was the most path-breaking and far-reaching of all the New Deal programs. For the first time in its history, the United States adopted a compulsory social insurance program of providing monthly cash assistance to participating people age 65 and older regardless of financial need or ability to work. Monthly retirement benefits were based on earnings over recipients' working years, with program benefits financed by an entirely new form of federal taxation: a payroll tax that was levied equally on workers and employers.[27]

The elapsed time between President Roosevelt's transmittal to Congress on January 17, 1935, to Social Security's enactment in August was short. Most of the plan's critical features were decided without controversy. The principal exception was whether it would be compulsory, an issue that opened up a long-standing partisan divide on Social Security.

Republicans desired an optional program. Led by Senator Bennett Clark of Missouri, Senate Republicans proposed that employees and employers who were participating in private pension plans be exempt. The Roosevelt administration and Senate supporters of a compulsory program countered that if the exemption were permitted, high-wage workers would opt out, leaving only low-wage workers as program participants, and the program would be unable to pay low-wage workers adequate benefits. The debate over the Clark amendment revealed the considerable amount of income redistribution that was buried in complex benefit formulas but did little to alter the legislative outcome. The amendment was defeated in the Senate Finance Committee.

Two interrelated features of the Social Security program proved to be crucial to its enactment, its long-run endurance and, ultimately, its enormously high cost. The first feature was a linkage between taxes paid in and benefits received. The use of payroll taxes to finance benefits served as the linchpin of this linkage. Paying payroll taxes gave program participants a sense that by contributing to the program during their working years, they were establishing an earned right to benefits when they retired. Welfare provides benefits to needy people as an act of public charity. As such, its recipients, while they might be grateful for the public's generosity, possess no compelling claim on benefits. Social Security's earned-right underpinning, in contrast, gave its recipients a powerful claim on benefits. This distinguished Social Security from welfare, as Senate Finance Committee chairman Walter George noted: "Social Security is not a handout; it is not charity; it is not relief. It is an earned right based upon the contributions and earnings of the individual."[28]

President Roosevelt understood far better than his advisers the importance of an "earned right." When he was challenged about financing Social Security with a regressive payroll tax rather than general fund revenues from the progressive income tax, he replied: "We put those pay roll contributions there so as to give the contributors a legal, moral, and political right to collect their pensions and their unemployment benefits. With those taxes in there, no damn politician can ever scrap my social security program. Those taxes aren't a matter of economics, they're straight politics."[29]

Historians have puzzled over the fact that the Civil War pension program was not immediately followed by a broader federal retirement for the general population because the elements seemed to be in place. Congress had transformed Civil War pensions into a retirement program and thus accepted the idea of a federal program. In the century's second decade, Civil War pension expenditures had begun to decline, freeing up resources that could be used to finance a new retirement program. Finally, by the 1920s, the new federal income tax was demonstrating its extraordinary ability to produce large sums of revenue that could also be used. Yet Congress had not enacted a federal retirement program. The concept of an earned right helps explain why.

Public support for Civil War pensions hinged on the view that soldiers, through their sacrifice to "save the Union," had earned a right to pensions in their old age. So strong was this view that the pension program, despite its numerous frauds, its widely publicized scandals, its large excesses, and its long history of political manipulation, had not only endured; it had remained popular. Elderly people had performed no government service and therefore had established no such earned right.

President Roosevelt understood well the power of the concept of the earned right. He believed that the earned right a person established by paying a working lifetime of payroll taxes would carry a political weight equivalent to the earned right established by wartime military service.

History has proven the president correct. Social Security's earned right, though certainly less morally compelling than that of wartime military service, nevertheless proved to be crucial to sustaining the program.

The extent of Social Security's earned right depended on the degree of linkage between workers' benefits and their payroll tax contributions: the stronger the link, the firmer the program's earned-right foundation. To achieve a strong link, the 1935 law based a worker's retirement benefits on his or her lifetime earnings: the higher the worker's lifetime earnings, the higher were that person's monthly benefits.

Although the law's linkage was strong, it was not perfect. Congress built in a degree of progressivity. Lower-wage workers would receive monthly benefits that were higher as a proportion of their lifetime earnings than would higher-wage workers. In addition, virtually all retirees during the program's first few decades would receive benefits far in excess of their tax contributions.

The use of payroll taxes rather than general revenues to finance the program allowed Social Security to be self-financed; that is, benefits were to be entirely funded by payroll taxes and, in later years, by interest earned on investments of the surplus payroll tax revenues. The self-financing policy had broad-based support. Both the president and key members of Congress viewed it as necessary to avoid imposing a large unfunded liability on future generations. The president, in transmitting his Social Security proposal to Congress, had stated emphatically that self-financing was a condition for an acceptable plan. An old-age insurance program, he said, "should be self-sustaining in the sense that funds for the payment of insurance benefits should not come from the proceeds of general taxation."[30]

President Roosevelt was surprised in January 1935 when his cabinet committee responsible for drafting the Social Security plan presented him a plan that contained a large unfunded liability. Previously he had roundly criticized the Townsend Plan for imposing a large unfunded liability on future generations and refused to endorse his committee's plan. He told Secretary of Labor Frances Perkins, chair of the committee, "This is the same old dole under another name. It is almost dishonest to build up an accumulated deficit for the Congress of the United States to meet in the 1980s. We can't do that. We can't sell the United

States short in 1980 any more than in 1935."[31] Lacking sufficient time to alter the plan before the previously announced date for its transmission to Congress, the president allowed the plan to go forward, but only as one of eight alternatives. His public advocacy for a self-supporting program left no doubt about where he stood.

In its final form, the Social Security law established an initial payroll tax of 2 percentage points on the first $3,000 of a worker's earnings. The tax was shared equally between workers and their employers and would begin in 1937. The law scheduled the payroll tax to increase by equal increments every three years until it reached 6 percent in 1949. The tax applied mainly to manufacturing and trade workers and covered only about half of the labor force. Farmworkers, professionals, and domestic workers were excluded from coverage.[32]

The choices of the initial tax rate and the $3,000 ceiling on taxable wages were somewhat arbitrary. At the time, neither the Roosevelt administration's Social Security architects nor Congress had much information on the proportion of wages the $3,000 ceiling would cover or how many workers earned below this threshold. Ultimately the choice was made, according to one of the program's architects, by applying "aesthetic logic," a euphemism for pulling a number out of thin air.[33] After the program was up and running, it would turn out that over 95 percent of all covered workers earned less than the $3,000 ceiling on taxable wages and, hence, were taxed on their entire earnings.[34]

The Social Security payroll tax also turned out to be the first permanent, large-scale direct tax on the incomes of middle-class households in U.S. history. Before 1937, the temporary Civil War income tax and the modern income tax that had begun in 1916 were primarily imposed on wealthy individuals. In 1937, only 1.8 million households with incomes below the $3,000 ceiling on Social Security taxable earnings paid any federal income taxes, accounting for only 3 percent of total federal income tax collections. In contrast, Social Security compelled 25.8 million workers to pay payroll taxes. Even allowing for two covered earners in each household, the Social Security tax generated a sixfold increase in the number of households paying federal taxes. The 1 percent payroll tax that Social Security imposed on the earnings of middle-income employees, though it may seem small by current standards, was by no means small in 1937. For the typical family with only one wage earner, the payroll tax more than tripled the household's federal tax burden.[35]

Under the Social Security Act, benefit payments would not begin until 1942, five years after payroll tax collections began. A typical new retiree in that year could expect to receive about $210 per year.[36] The choice of benefit levels was somewhat arbitrary. Neither the president nor Social Security's supporters in Congress specified the policy objective that was to be achieved by the chosen benefit levels. Instead, they relied on vague references, such as preventing impoverishment or ensuring financial security. The Senate Finance Committee report on the Social Security bill, for example, described the benefit as one "which will provide something more than merely reasonable subsistence."[37] But what constituted "reasonable" the committee was unwilling to specify. Later, program advocates would claim that existing benefits were "unrealistically low" or "inadequate." But how "low" or "inadequate" compared to what standard, program advocates rarely specified.

The law's specific tax and benefit provisions made Social Security, when viewed as a retirement program, quite generous. Seventy percent of workers in covered jobs in the late 1930s could expect to receive a rate of return on their contributions that was in excess of what they could expect to earn on savings invested in financially safe securities. The program was exceedingly generous for workers who were nearing retirement age at the time of the law's enactment. For example, the typical covered worker who was age 60 in 1937 could expect to pay about $144 in payroll taxes (including the employer share) before reaching Social Security's age of eligibility in 1942. Upon retiring, this worker could expect to receive $17.50 per month in benefits for the remainder of his or her expected life (about twelve years at the time). The benefits stream represented a staggering 54.3 percent rate of return on the worker's contributions. So large was the return that within nine months of retiring, the typical retiree in 1942 could expect to receive benefits that equaled all of his or her own and employer's contributions plus interest at 3 percent per year.

The 1935 program was also quite generous for middle-age workers. A 40-year-old worker in 1937 could expect to receive in benefits an amount equal to his or her own and employer's contributions, plus interest at 3 percent per year, in less than five years of this person's remaining expected thirteen-year life span. This amounted to a 6 percent inflation-adjusted annual rate of return, twice the return that could be expected from investments that provided a similar degree of financial safety.[38]

A second feature of the new law, though its existence was short-lived, was the creation of a large reserve fund to finance the program's future high cost. The "large reserve" policy set payroll tax levels during the program's early years high enough relative to benefits to generate annual revenue surpluses, which were appropriated to a reserve fund and invested in U.S. Treasury bills. In later years, when annual expenditures exceeded annual payroll tax collections, the interest receipts and the reserve fund's principal balance could be drawn on to finance benefit payments instead of relying on revenue from higher taxes.

The Roosevelt administration and a majority in Congress favored the large reserve policy over its main alternative, a pay-as-you-go financing approach. Under the latter policy, payroll taxes would be set so that revenues in each year would roughly match that year's Social Security expenditures. The preference for the large reserve fund was based on the proposition that it would smooth out the program's cost between current and future generations. In 1935, demographers projected that the number of people age 65 and older would double by 1960 and triple by 1990.[39] As a result, Social Security expenditures were projected to rise substantially to 10 percent of taxable payrolls by 1980. Under a pay-as-you-go policy, the Social Security tax rate would be required to rise to this level. While a 10 percent payroll tax may not seem overly burdensome today, a tax of this magnitude on middle-class workers in the 1930s was unthinkable. At the time, the average personal income tax rate faced by taxpayers with incomes below Social Security's taxable $3,000 annual earnings ceiling was just half of 1 percent.[40]

The manner in which the reserve policy was intended to work will be important for understanding the issues that we discuss in later chapters. Under the large reserve plan, surplus payroll tax revenues raised during the program's early years would be used to reduce the publicly held debt. Years later, when Social Security outlays were anticipated to be in excess of payroll tax revenues, tax revenues that would have been required to finance principal and interest payments on the publicly held debt would be available to finance Social Security benefit payments. In this manner, the reserve policy was a means of smoothing out the tax burden across generations. As Treasury Secretary Henry Morgenthau explained, surplus payroll taxes "would be used progressively to replace the outstanding public debt. . . . To the extent that the receipts from the old-age annuity taxes are used to buy out present and future holders of Government obligations, that part of the tax revenues that is now paid out to private bond holders will be available for old-age annuity benefits; thereby minimizing the net additional burdens upon the future."[41]

The reserve fund served as an accounting device to officially record these transactions. During the early years of Social Security, the fund would be credited, dollar for dollar, with the amount of this debt reduction plus the interest payments the government was no longer required to pay holders of public debt. During the program's later years, the fund would be debited, dollar for dollar, with program expenditures that were in excess of its revenues. The excess would be financed by issuing debt to the public up to the level the outstanding debt would have reached without Social Security. According to projections at the time, projections that could not have anticipated either World War II or the federal government's emerging tendency to incur peacetime deficits, surplus Social Security revenues would enable the publicly held debt to be reduced by 50 percent by 1950 and would enable the debt to be eliminated entirely a decade later. Neither Congress nor the Roosevelt administration addressed how the surpluses would be used after 1960.

The supporters of the large reserve policy, led by President Roosevelt, contended that a large reserve was the only way to ensure that Social Security would not impose a large unfunded liability on the next generation of taxpayers. In their view, the issue was more fundamental than one of financing; it was whether one generation of Americans should impose a large financial burden on subsequent generations.

The large reserve policy looked sound on paper, but in practice, its financial soundness depended critically on Congress's ability to use the surplus funds to reduce the publicly held debt. That would require a degree of discipline and long-term focus that previous Congresses had not demonstrated. In fact, the lesson of nineteenth-century history was that the reserve fund policy would cause Congress to liberalize Social Security, just as federal budget surpluses had invariably caused Congress to liberalize veterans' pensions. The navy pension fund debacles of the 1830s had also shown the folly of attempting to preserve even dedicated revenue in a separate fund. The fund's large balances had merely served to concentrate the pressure to liberalize the program.

The warnings of history were not enough. The White House and Congress were also turning a blind eye to their own actions regarding bonus payments for World War I veterans. The prefunding plan for bonuses in 1924 had created a pot of appropriated funds that had already been used to finance loans to veterans well in advance of the original date that bonus payments were payable. Now Congress was considering the large Social Security reserve fund at the same time it was also considering, and would shortly pass, a bill that would allow veterans to immediately claim the full value of their 1945 certificates on the ground that Congress had already set aside most of the necessary funds.

The inability to set aside funds for the future was not unique to Congress. During House Ways and Means Committee hearings, Princeton economics professor Douglas Brown informed Congress that state and local governments had found pressures to spend pension surpluses irresistible. According to the professor, "It has happened in almost every policeman's and almost every fireman's pension plan in the country. You permit large reserves and the popular demand is for increased benefits."[42]

Some members of Congress understood that Social Security surpluses would generate irresistible pressures to expand benefits. Senator Daniel Hastings (R-DE) asked rhetorically during the floor debate on the Social Security bill: "Does anybody believe that such a huge sum of money, accumulated for any purpose, could be preserved intact? Does anybody doubt that it would be subjected to all kinds of demands?"[43]

Other members expressed the view that even if Congress could manage to resist pressures to expand Social Security benefits, it would eventually use the surplus funds to finance additional government activities. Congressman Allen Treadway (R-MA), for example, asked, "Would it [the large reserve] not be an invitation for all sorts of pork-barrel schemes and wild spending sprees?"[44]

The use of surplus Social Security funds to finance non–Social Security programs was a pernicious one because under Social Security's accounting rules, the reserve fund would be credited with surpluses regardless of how the surplus funds were used. Even if Social Security surpluses were spent on the federal government's general operations, the government accounting system would nevertheless credit the reserve fund with surplus funds as if they had actually been used to reduce the publicly held debt. Thus, the reserve fund's balance would continue to grow, giving the public the false impression that surplus funds were being set aside and invested for future recipients when, in fact, the money was being spent. When it came time to draw on the reserve fund, the public would find an empty bucket. The publicly held debt and its annual interest burden would be just as high as it would have been had the Social Security surpluses never existed. In the end, the members of Congress who understood the dangers of large surpluses were too few in number. Despite the lessons of history and their warnings, Congress voted to adopt the large reserve policy.

The Social Security Act settled the issue in 1935, but the settlement was only temporary. Two years later, the large reserve policy would generate a firestorm of criticism from both liberals and conservatives and collapse under the weight of attacks from both the Left and the Right. The fund's existing reserves would be spent primarily by expanding benefits. Out of this debate would come yet another account device to "protect" the revenues that were dedicated to paying benefits: a Social Security trust fund.

Social Security's Federal Matching Programs

The Social Security Act's three entitlement-based matching programs were designed to bolster state welfare programs for the elderly, the blind, and children of poor mothers who were widowed or left destitute by desertion or disability. At the time, thirty-nine states had established welfare programs for the elderly poor, thirty-three states had adopted programs for the blind, and forty-six states were running welfare programs to assist needy children. These programs operated on a statewide basis in most states. Local governments provided the main source of financing and were responsible for program administration.[45] By 1935, the toll the Great Depression had taken on state government finances had severely weakened state and local governments' ability to maintain their public assistance programs.

The Old-Age Assistance program supplemented state assistance to poor people age 65 and older. The congressional committees responsible for writing the law regarded the Old-Age Assistance program, not Social Security, as the federal government's main new vehicle for alleviating old-age poverty.[46] The Roosevelt administration and the New Deal supporters in Congress, however, regarded the program as a stop-gap measure to provide immediate relief to states until Social Security benefits began in 1942. The New Dealers expected the Old-Age Assistance program to gradually phase down over time as the Social Security program matured. The Aid to the Blind program, the furthest Congress was willing to venture into the realm of assisting disabled adults, provided similar matching payments to state aid to the blind programs. The Aid to Dependent Children program was designed to assist state efforts to help poor children in households headed by widowed and divorced mothers, and mothers whose husbands were disabled or had deserted the family. But as we will see in later chapters, children of never-married women would come to dominate the recipient rolls. Their inclusion in the ranks of eligible people would engulf the program in national controversy that would last four decades.

The Social Security Act established a clear entitlement to states for federal matching payments by requiring the federal government to match state benefit payments in any state that met the law's minimal statutory requirements. No discretion was allowed.[47] State Old-Age Assistance and Aid to the Blind payments were matched on a fifty-fifty basis up to a limit; that is, the federal government would match each dollar of state spending with a dollar of its own up to a maximum monthly benefit amount. State Aid to Dependent Children payments were matched at a lower rate. For every two dollars of state monthly benefits to needy children, the federal government would provide one dollar of aid up to a maximum monthly benefit amount.

The law imposed only minimal requirements on states to qualify for federal matching payments. It required that public assistance programs be operational in all jurisdictions within the state, that the state provide at least some level of financial assistance, that applicants who were denied benefits by local welfare agencies be given the right of appeal to a state agency, and that the length of state residency requirements for the Old-Age Assistance and Aid to the Blind benefits be no longer than five years and no longer than one year for the Aid to Dependent Children benefits.[48]

Significantly, the Social Security Act did not grant individuals a legal right to welfare assistance. It wasn't until an extraordinary series of federal court decisions during the late 1960s and early 1970s that welfare recipients were given legal rights to welfare benefits.

The Social Security Act's federal matching programs enjoyed widespread bipartisan support in Congress. The only significant point of contention was the extent of authority over state programs that would be given to the federal government. The focal point of this debate was state eligibility rules that required individuals to reside in the state for a minimum number of years. At the time of the debate, virtually all states had such residency requirements for their public assistance programs. For example, two-thirds of the states required recipients of old-age assistance to have lived in the state for fifteen years or more. Arizona, with its attractive climate, required thirty-five years of residency for eligibility. Most states required two or more years of residence to qualify for mothers' aid program benefits.[49]

New Dealers within Congress and the Roosevelt administration favored a federal welfare system with nationally uniform benefits and had opposed these state requirements. They sought to use the Social Security Act's matching payments to induce states to voluntarily eliminate residency requirements. But a large congressional majority, with strong support from state governors and legislators, viewed residency requirements as essential. They argued that such requirements were necessary if states were to provide adequate benefits without becoming havens for nonresidents seeking assistance. Absent residency requirements, a state with high benefit levels relative to its neighbors would likely face an influx of nonresidents that would overwhelm its resources and jeopardize benefits to poor people with established residency. The debate produced a legislative compromise that established maximum time limits on state residency requirements. More than three decades later, the Supreme Court struck down these limits as an unconstitutional restriction on the right to travel.

The Social Security Act established the New Deal welfare policy, a hands-off policy that effectively limited the federal role to providing financial assistance to states. States retained control over eligibility rules, benefits levels, and administrative arrangements between it and local governments. The matching payment's entitlement feature, besides providing states with certainty over the amount of federal funding, also gave state governments a degree of protection from federal policy interventions.

The hands-off policy did not last long. The protections Congress sought to give to states were hardly worth the paper on which they were written. During the 1950s and 1960s, federal welfare officials chipped away at the policy by using the federal government's financial leverage to induce states to modify eligibility rules and approval processes. Then, in the late 1960s and early 1970s, Congress and the federal courts effectively ended the New Deal policy by imposing mandates on state welfare programs.

The federal entitlement to states was accompanied by a corresponding loss of federal budgetary control. In any given year, the amount the federal government would spend on matching payments depended entirely on how much the states individually chose to spend on their federal-state public assistance programs. Thus, federal spending was determined more by the priorities of state governments than on the availability of federal resources.[50] At the time, the matching payments constituted less than 1 percent of total federal spending, so the loss of control didn't seem important.

However, the Social Security Act's federal matching payments would prove to be a recipe for rapidly growing welfare expenditures. Under the matching provisions, state governments need to raise only a portion of the money required to provide a dollar's worth of additional assistance benefits to constituents. This created a distorted incentive for state legislators to expand federally supported welfare programs over programs that were state financed exclusively or programs that were partially funded by fixed-dollar discretionary federal grants. The matching payments created a similar distortion of incentives at the federal level. Federally mandated eligibility and benefit expansions on state welfare programs required Congress to allocate only part of the cost of each dollar of mandated benefits.

Unemployment Insurance

The movement for unemployment insurance began in the Progressive era. The dominant school of thought on it, led by University of Chicago professor John Commons and his organization, the American Association for Labor Legislation, favored mandates on employers. They would require employers to establish and finance their own unemployment benefit plans or contribute to a state-sponsored unemployment insurance program. A later variant of this approach, advocated by another University of Chicago professor and a future senator, Paul Douglas (D-IL), would instead require firms to make payroll contributions to a state-run unemployment insurance program.

The initial movement met with little success at federal or state levels. A 1916 bill to establish a commission to recommend a national unemployment insurance program was introduced in the House but never emerged from committee. American Federation of Labor President Samuel Gompers testified against it, saying that compulsory unemployment insurance would "be a germ that shall devitalize the American Citizenship and take away from them the vital principles of freedom of action in the exercise of their normal activities and their higher and best concept of human welfare, combined with freedom."[51] A 1928 proposal for a national unemployment insurance program met a similar fate. At the state level, unemployment insurance bills had been introduced in more than a half-dozen states by 1931. Only Wisconsin enacted a program, but it would not begin to pay benefits until 1934.

The onset of the Great Depression generated more interest in Congress for a federal unemployment insurance program. Liberals pressed for a federal program on the ground that states could not be expected to enact their own programs because the taxes required to finance such a program would put business in the state at a competitive disadvantage with respect to its neighbors. New York senator Robert Wagner, the chief advocate for a federal program, made this case by arguing that state programs would never "impose such a burden upon its industries for fear of handicapping them in the competition with other States."[52] But a majority of members opposed a federal program, some on philosophical grounds and others on the more practical grounds of cost. A 1931 Senate committee report succinctly summarized the opposing argument by concluding, "It will readily be seen that the imposition of such a function upon the Federal Government will bring into being a bureaucracy extending its activities all over this country such as we have never known. No one has yet hazarded a guess as to the extent to which we must go both in the way of supervision and expense if the Federal Government shall launch into such an experiment."[53]

As the Depression deepened during the early 1930s, support for an unemployment insurance program grew. In early 1934, Senator Wagner joined forces with Congressman David J. Lewis (D-MD) to introduce a compromise federal-state program that would use the federal taxing power to induce states to adopt their own unemployment insurance programs. Under the Wagner-Lewis plan, businesses in states that did not adopt a federally approved program would be subject to a new federal payroll tax. Businesses in states that adopted such a program would receive a relief from the tax in the form of a credit. The Roosevelt administration endorsed the plan in 1934, but the Ways and Means Committee rejected the bill.

The following year, after President Roosevelt called for a federal-state unemployment insurance plan, the Wagner-Lewis bill's major provisions were incorporated into the Social Security Act. Under the new law, the federal government imposed a 3 percent federal tax on the payrolls of U.S. business firms. These firms were then given a credit equal to 90 percent of the new tax if the state in which they operated enacted a federally approved unemployment compensation program. The remaining 10 percent was returned to the states in the form of federal grants to finance the administrative cost of state unemployment programs.[54]

The unemployment insurance program was a novel use of the federal taxing power. The tax and credit provisions effectively compelled states to enact unemployment compensation programs. The law also required the states to transfer the proceeds of their own unemployment insurance taxes to the U.S. Treasury, which then acted as banker. States could make withdrawals from their bank accounts to pay benefits by requesting release of their funds. In the meantime, Treasury would invest state funds in U.S. Treasury securities and credit state accounts with interest earned on these securities. In practice, this meant that the federal government had the use of state funds during the period between deposit and withdrawal. Finally, the grants to states for administrative expenses meant that while states were free to set unemployment insurance eligibility rules and benefit levels, the federal government would decide the minimum amount they must spend to administer their programs.

The Supreme Court Approves

The constitutionality of the Social Security and unemployment insurance programs was immediately challenged in federal court. The Supreme Court's decisions in these cases would have far-reaching ramifications not only for these two programs, but for the establishment of subsequent entitlements and, more generally, the welfare state's future.

The issue in the Social Security case was whether the Constitution's spending power was sufficiently broad to permit the federal government to spend its funds to support senior citizens. In 1935, the scope of the federal spending power was unclear. Surprising as it may seem, the Supreme Court had not ruled on its limits in nearly a century and a half since the Constitution's ratification. The issue in the unemployment insurance case was whether the federal government could use its taxing power to induce states to enact unemployment compensation programs.

Since the federal government's earliest days, the scope of its spending power had been a matter of dispute. James Madison, the father of the Constitution and author of many of the *Federalist Papers*, believed that the spending power was limited to expenditures required to carry out the specific powers enumerated in the Constitution's Article 1, section 8. The taxing power, in Madison's view, was never meant to provide a means to expand the spending power beyond the enumerated powers.[55]

Alexander Hamilton, the originator of the *Federalist Papers* and the nation's first Treasury secretary, believed that the power to spend was broader than the government's other legislative and regulatory powers. In his view, Congress could spend federal funds to promote the general welfare. The only restriction on the spending power, according to Hamilton, was that the expenditure be for a national, not local, purpose.[56]

In the intellectual world, the battle between adherents of these two views took place largely out of the public view—mainly in law journals, books on the Constitution, and law school classrooms. The Hamilton view was bolstered by the publication of Supreme Court Justice Joseph Story's highly influential *Commentaries on the Constitution* in 1833. Justice Story argued that the opening phrase of Article 1, section 8, which authorizes Congress to "lay and collect Taxes, Duties, Imposts and Excises, to pay the Debts and provide for the common Defence and general Welfare of the United States," should be properly read to mean that Congress was authorized to impose taxes *in order to* promote the general welfare. Since the purpose of collecting taxes was to finance expenditures, Congress also had the power to spend to promote the general welfare. Story rejected Madison's view because it amounted to an assertion that the Constitution's words, "to provide for the common Defence and general Welfare of the United States," had no meaning. They were, according to Judge Story, *vox et preterea nihil*—an empty sound and vain phraseology.[57]

But the Hamilton-Story view created constitutional anomalies. The view implied that the founders had, in effect, designed two constitutions to operate side by side.[58] One constitution conferred on Congress a broad power to spend federal funds to promote whatever activities it deemed to be in the general welfare. The other constitution applied to all other legislative matters and regulatory actions and limited the federal powers to those the Constitution enumerates. Under this anomaly, Congress could appropriate funds for projects that could be controlled only by state and local governments, but it could not control or regulate these very same projects.

A related anomaly is that the Hamilton-Story view implies that Congress can appropriate federal funds raised by the issuance of debt only to carry out the enumerated powers' activities, whereas federal funds raised by taxation can be used more broadly to promote the general welfare. The phrase "to promote . . . the general welfare" appears only in the taxing power clause and is therefore applicable only to federal funds raised by taxation. The phrase does not appear in the clause that gives the federal government the power to issue debt. Thus, under the Hamilton-Story logic, debt-financed expenditures must be limited to enumerated powers' activities. To argue otherwise is to give substantive meaning to words the founders chose to exclude from the debt clause.[59]

The first federal spending power cases had come before the Supreme Court in 1923. *Frothingham v. Mellon* and *Massachusetts v. Mellon* involved a congressional appropriation to assist state maternal and child health programs. Mrs. Frothingham, a taxpayer, and the state of Massachusetts both argued the Constitution did not permit the federal government to spend money on health services as they were properly the responsibility of the states. The Court threw out both cases, ruling that Mrs. Frothingham suffered no harm from the law because the expenditure was such a small part of the government's total expenditures that her tax burden was unaffected by the program's existence. The Court also ruled that the state of Massachusetts suffered no harm. The statute contained nothing to coerce the state into operating a federally approved health care program. In effect, in both cases, the Court ruled "no harm, no foul."

For the Social Security Act, the rulings meant that the federal matching programs for old-age assistance and dependent children could not be successfully challenged in federal court. In a larger context, the rulings effectively precluded citizens and states from constitutionally challenging the vast majority of federal expenditure programs on the grounds that their purpose lies beyond the enumerated powers.[60]

However, the position that the Supreme Court might take on the constitutionality of the Social Security and unemployment programs, both financed by specific taxes, was far from clear. Would the Court view the retirement benefits and the payroll tax as separate and distinct and, following the Frothingham precedent, deny all challenges?

Or would it see the expenditure and the tax as parts of the same policy and hear the case? If it chose to hear the case, would it adopt Madison's interpretation and strike down the program, or would it adopt the Hamilton-Monroe-Story interpretation and uphold the program? Would the Court view the unemployment insurance program's tax and credit scheme as a constitutionally proper use of the tax power to induce state action or an improper use of the tax power to coerce state action?

As these legal challenges were winding their way through the courts, so were cases challenging other elements of President Roosevelt's New Deal. The most important of these cases was *United States v. Butler*, decided by the Supreme Court in January 1936, just five months after the Social Security Act was signed into law.[61] The *Butler* decision involved the 1933 Agricultural Adjustment Act, one of the first New Deal measures, which authorized the U.S. Department of Agriculture to make monetary payments to farmers who agreed to withhold acreage from cultivation. The payments were financed by a tax on food processors.

The Court struck down the act as an invasion of the constitutional rights reserved to the states. According to the Court, the act's basic purpose was to regulate farming activities. The tax on food processors, in its view, was merely incidental to achieving the law's regulatory objectives.[62] Regulating farm production was, in the Court's opinion, outside the federal government's constitutional power.

In the logic of the Court's decision, the power to tax to promote the general welfare was not relevant to its decision. Once the Court reached its conclusion that the Agriculture Adjustment Act was a regulatory action, issues of taxing and spending and hence, the general welfare clause, were irrelevant to its decision on the act's constitutionality.[63]

Nevertheless, the Court chose to opine on the age-old dispute over the interpretation of the general welfare clause. In its opinion, the Hamilton interpretation was correct, and Madison was wrong. Congress, according to the Court, had the power to spend federal funds to promote the "general welfare." The scope of the spending power was indeed broader than the other legislative and regulatory powers, which the Constitution restricted to those enumerated in Article 1, section 8. [64]

Perhaps because the Court's opinion that the Hamilton view prevailed was immaterial to its decision in *United States v. Butler*, the Court offered no studies or analyses in support of its general welfare clause interpretation beyond citing Judge Story's and Alexander Hamilton's writings. In expressing a view that would have potentially profound and far-reaching consequences, the Court merely alluded to an unidentified body of literature and asserted that a "study of all these [writings] leads us to conclude that the reading advocated by Mr. Justice Story is the correct one."[65] The Court also offered no criteria for distinguishing expenditures that were national in character from those that were local.

Under Supreme Court jurisprudence, the Court's opinion on the general welfare clause in *Butler* would not normally serve as a precedent for subsequent Court decisions. Under judicial procedural rules, opinions that venture beyond those required to form the legal basis of a decision are regarded as dicta—little more than editorial comments. Yet fourteen months after the *Butler* decision, the Supreme Court used the view on the general welfare clause it expressed in *Butler* as precedent for its decision that both the Social Security and unemployment insurance programs were constitutional.

In the Social Security retirement program case, *Helvering v. Davis* (1937), the Court ruled that Congress had the constitutional power to spend to promote the general welfare. Therefore, the Social Security program was constitutional. Justice Cardozo elevated the Court's dicta in the *Butler* case to the status of precedent by declaring for the Court's majority, "It is now settled by decision. *United States v Butler, supra*. The conception of the spending power advocated by Hamilton and strongly reinforced by Story has prevailed over that of Madison."[66]

In the Court's view, Congress, not the Supreme Court, is vested with the discretion to determine whether a particular expenditure promotes the general welfare. The Court chose not to offer any criteria by which expenditures that were national in character could be distinguished from those that were local. The only guidance the Court offered on how it would apply the general welfare clause to judge the constitutionality of future spending laws was that the expenditure could not be "clearly wrong," not be "a display of arbitrary power," and must be the result of "an exercise of judgment."[67]

The unemployment insurance case, *Steward Machine v. Davis* (1937), involved the relationship between the states and the federal government. At issue in the unemployment case was its tax and credit scheme. The law's opponents claimed that the taxing power was being used not for the purpose of raising federal revenues, but instead to coerce states into establishing unemployment programs that, under the Constitution, were areas reserved for states. The opponents argued that the law's "dominant end and aim is to drive the state legislature under the whip of economic pressure into the enactment of unemployment compensation laws at the bidding of the central government."[68] In their view, the Court's decision in Butler served as ample precedent for striking down the federal unemployment insurance law. Employment and unemployment policy, like agricultural policy, was an area the Constitution reserved to the states. The federal government countered that unemployment was a national problem. Under the Constitution's general welfare clause, the federal government had the authority to enlist the states in a "cooperative endeavor to avert a common evil."[69]

The Court upheld the unemployment insurance law's constitutionality, agreeing with the executive branch that unemployment was a national problem that demanded an urgent solution. Each state, according to the Court's majority, had failed to "contribute its fair share to the solution . . . [because each] . . . was paralyzed by fear."[70] Because of this failure, "a disproportionate burden, and a mountainous one, was laid upon the resources of the Government of the nation."[71] Thus, the unemployment law was not invading "upon fields foreign to its function." It was merely taking steps to "safeguard its own treasury."[72]

Moreover, according to the Court, the law's tax did not represent coercion, merely an inducement for states to act. What factors separated inducement from coercion, the Court did not say. It was no more willing to draw a boundary line between inducement and coercion than it was between government expenditures that were national and local in character. In the Court majority's words, "We do not fix the outmost line. [It is] enough for present purposes that, wherever the line may be, this statute is within it. Definition more precise must abide the wisdom of the future."[73]

The Supreme Court's Social Security Act decisions put the nation on a path from which there would be no return. These decisions, by expanding the spending power's breadth, fundamentally changed the relationship between individuals and the federal government. The Congress could now use its taxing and spending power to extract income from one set of citizens and give income to another with no other purpose than to redistribute income from a group that it deemed to be less preferred to another that it deemed to be more preferred. The result has been a vast escalation of federal government entitlement spending.

By weakening the wall that separates state and federal responsibilities, these decisions fundamentally altered the relationship between the federal and state governments. Since the 1930s, the federal government has moved inexorably to encroach on activities that had previously been the sole province of the states. In the late 1940s, the federal government entered the housing market, in the 1950s it moved into education and disability insurance, in the 1960s it assumed a large role in health care and nutrition, and in the 1970s it entered the mass transit and environmental cleanup arenas. Today, it is hard to think of a single traditional state government activity that has not also been undertaken by the federal government. Most all of the federal encroachments have been justified under the general welfare clause.

In addition, the federal government has repeatedly used taxing and spending power to induce states and municipal governments to carry out federal policies and administer federal programs. Not content to spend federal funds to promote its vision of the general welfare, Congress has established a practice of attaching conditions to its spending that are designed to induce lower levels of government to also promote its vision.[74]

The decisions also profoundly altered the Supreme Court's role in protecting the federalist system that the Constitution had created. The Constitution established the Supreme Court as the arbiter of the boundary line between federal and state responsibilities. Its rulings meant that it would remove itself from its arbiter role as it would be unwilling to substitute its judgment for that of Congress and the president.[75] It would be unwilling to declare that any appropriation that had been debated within Congress and had been signed into law by the president had been "an arbitrary exercise of power" or was not "an exercise of judgment." Indeed, since 1937, the Supreme Court has not declared a single appropriation of federal funds to be unconstitutional on the ground that the expenditure was on an activity that lay outside the Constitution's enumerated powers.

8   The Consequences of Social
       Security Surpluses

*We use the proceeds of a gross income tax on labor, raised in the pious
name of social security, to cushion the General Treasury.*
        Senator Arthur Vandenberg, 1937[1]

THE INK WAS BARELY DRY ON THE 1935 SOCIAL
Security Act law when Congress enacted a major overhaul
and expansion of the program. The 1939 Social Security Amendments
greatly increased benefits, especially for workers who were nearing
retirement age. The amendments also added new benefits for spouses,
children, widows, and survivors. The law's large-scale benefit expansion was fueled by Social Security surpluses. The amendments abandoned several key principles on which the original Social Security
program had been built and undermined others. In doing so, Congress
profoundly altered the program's character and began a transformation
of Social Security to a tax-and-transfer program.

During the years leading up to World War II, there was little congressional action on unemployment insurance and the New Deal's
welfare programs. Congress was content to let states develop their programs in response to the New Deal's measures and incentives. Thereafter, the all-encompassing world war consumed the country's energy
and resources.

Following the attack on Pearl Harbor, Congress turned its attention almost exclusively to war-related issues. One notable development was the wartime debate over the use of surplus payroll taxes. The Roosevelt administration precipitated the debate by pressing Congress to allow previously scheduled payroll tax increases to take place. In making its case, the administration, peculiar though it seems, argued that the same surplus payroll tax dollars could be used simultaneously to finance both Social Security benefit expansions and the cost of wartime operations. Surplus Social Security revenues were, in the administration's view, a financial "twofer." Although the argument failed, it would be used repeatedly with some success throughout the postwar years.

The Collapse of the "Large Reserve" Policy

A student of history, especially one knowledgeable about veterans' pensions, would have known that any attempt to maintain a large reserve fund was likely doomed from the start. The pressure from within and outside Congress to spend surplus funds would grow once the surpluses emerged, inevitably leading to a liberalization that would soak up the excess revenues. From this perspective, the 1939 Social Security liberalization is not surprising. What is surprising is the manner in which the liberalization occurred.

The story of the 1939 amendments unfolded like a Greek tragedy. Within months following the Social Security law's enactment, the large reserve policy came under heavy criticism. Objections that a large fund would eventually lead to either excessive Social Security expansions or a large increase in government spending were first raised in professional journals, then in newsstand magazines, and eventually on the Senate floor. The rise in the publicly held debt in 1937 and 1938 seemed to confirm public allegations that Social Security funds were being used not to reduce the debt, as the White House had promised, but to finance current government operations. The charges, which came primarily from the large reserve policy's critics, played a key role in the enactment of the 1939 amendments. Thus, what began as an attempt to prevent a large reserve fund from leading to a major increase in government spending had, ironically, contributed to that precise outcome.

The cause of the uproar over the reserve fund was its reported size. The reserve fund was projected to grow to $47 billion by 1980, an amount that was greater than national debt. Many members of Congress and the public believed that the large reserve would inevitably be used either to liberalize the Social Security program or increase spending on other government programs. The idea that Congress could raise $111 billion in payroll taxes over a forty-year period and withhold $47 billion of that sum was, in the words of one commentator and critic, nothing short of a "hoax."[2]

Both liberals and conservatives raised concerns about the large reserve. A highly influential Social Security supporter, Arthur M. Linton, vice president of the American Society of Actuaries, kicked off the criticism with a paper written in a professional journal for actuaries in late 1935. Linton argued that the reserve policy, while appropriate for private insurance companies, was unsound when applied to a government enterprise. The federal government, in his view, would inevitably spend the reserve funds because the "politician had but scant appreciation of the significance of the reserve fund and of the necessity of foregoing the expenditure of current revenue in favor of investing it to benefit voters of the more or less distant future."[3] Linton pointed out that maintaining a large reserve was contrary to experience abroad. Both Germany and Great Britain, two countries with national old-age insurance plans, had abandoned their initial attempts to build surpluses and now operated their programs on a pay-as-you-go basis. In a second article, this one written for the *Atlantic Monthly*, he warned that the reserve plan's inherent problem was not that a large reserve fund would actually materialize, but that it would "lead either to a dangerous liberalization of the benefits or to a program of unsound governmental spending."[4]

The debate turned partisan during the 1936 presidential elections when the Republican Party announced its opposition to the large reserve. The controversy spilled onto the Senate floor in January 1937 when Senator Arthur Vandenberg (R-MI) introduced a resolution directing the Social Security board to abandon the plans for a large reserve. The resolution called the reserve "a fiscal and economic menace" and called on Congress to either raise benefits or lower taxes.[5]

Three weeks later, on the occasion of Senate consideration of the first appropriation of funds to the reserve account, Senator Vandenberg took the floor again to denounce the reserve as "the most fantastic and the most indefensible objective imaginable."[6] Furthermore, the senator charged, the Roosevelt administration was currently using surplus payroll taxes to finance the federal government's operating expenses. As he put it, "We use the proceeds of a gross income tax on labor, raised in the pious name of social security, to cushion the General Treasury."[7]

Federal budget data released in 1937 and 1938 added fuel to the fire. The data appeared to show that current surplus payroll taxes were being used not to reduce the publicly held debt, but instead, as critics had warned, to finance the government's current operations. In both years, payroll tax collections exceeded the program's expenses by $700 million. Yet the publicly held debt failed to decline by this amount; rather, it rose by over $2 billion.

From 1937 to 1939, the critics grew increasingly vitriolic. Both friends and foes of Social Security attacked the reserve as a "swindle," a "solemn and cruel farce," a financial "hocus pocus," and a scheme of "hollowness and humbuggery." Inside Congress and in public forums, critics charged that payroll tax proceeds were currently "misappropriated" or "embezzled" to fund government programs and projects other than Social Security.[8]

Abraham Epstein, a leading supporter of Social Security and author of the highly influential 1932 book, *Social Insecurity*, added his voice to the mounting criticism. The liberal Mr. Epstein joined conservative critics by arguing that the reserve would create inexorable "political pressure for benefits larger than socially necessary and beyond the country's capacity to sustain."[9] Furthermore, Mr. Epstein declared, even if Congress could practice the self-denial required to use surplus payroll taxes to reduce the public debt, such a policy would be unfairly regressive. He said, "even if it were wise and possible to reduce the National Debt no more antisocial means of accomplishing this could be imagined than through a tax on workers directly or indirectly—a tax hard to bear and repressive of employment."[10]

As opposition to the large reserve fund grew, so did the attractiveness of proposals to dissipate the reserve's funds by liberalizing

Social Security benefits. New Dealers feared that Social Security was in danger of becoming a secondary vehicle for delivering assistance to elderly people. As noted in the previous chapter, state governments had responded to the 1935 act's matching programs by liberalizing eligibility rules and raising benefit levels. Social Security wouldn't begin to pay benefits until 1942, and it was likely that its monthly benefits would be well below those provided by state-operated old-age assistance programs. The Social Security surpluses provided an opportunity to raise benefits and expand eligibility to ensure that Social Security would be the primary vehicle for assisting the elderly.

Others in Congress were willing to support a limited expansion rather than continually confront charges that Congress was misappropriating Social Security funds. Ironically, to many members, the large reserve policy—a policy to set aside funds for the future—had become a political liability. It would remain so until the federal government produced budgets that would reduce the publicly held debt, a prospect that was not viewed as likely in the late 1930s.

By the time the Seventy-Ninth Congress convened in January 1939, there was little question that the large reserve would be abandoned and a large-scale Social Security liberalization would be the means by which this would occur.[11] At that time, the reserve fund had an enormous accounting balance of over $1 billion—enough to finance benefits for more than a decade.[12] Early in 1939, the Social Security Advisory Council, a group of outside Social Security experts the president had appointed two years earlier, recommended spending the reserve fund by initiating benefit payments earlier than 1942, sharply increasing monthly benefits, and expanding eligibility to widows and survivors of covered workers.[13] President Roosevelt endorsed these proposals. The fact that the federal budget showed a deficit for a peacetime-record ninth consecutive year hardly mattered. The Social Security program, like the navy pension fund one hundred years before, had its own dedicated source of revenue. Congress would consider Social Security legislation in the context of its own finances, not the overall federal budget's condition.

Congress passed the landmark 1939 Social Security Amendments by overwhelming majorities in both houses. The massive law's main benefit provisions included moving forward the date at which monthly benefits would begin to 1940 from 1942; adding new monthly benefits for spouses and children, and widows and survivors of deceased covered workers; and sharply increasing monthly benefits.[14] The spousal benefit raised the monthly benefits for all retired workers with a spouse age 65 or older by 50 percent. The child benefit did the same for retired workers with children under age 18. The widows' and survivors' benefits added a life insurance component to the retirement program.[15] The new benefit schedule provided far more generous benefits for current retirees and those nearing retirement. For example, the typical worker who was nearing retirement (age 62 in 1939) would receive a benefit that was 50 percent higher than under the 1935 law. Such a worker with a spouse the same age would receive a monthly benefit that was more than twice as high. The new law, setting a precedent for future Social Security legislation, also made the benefit schedule more progressive by increasing monthly benefits payable to lower-wage workers as a proportion of their wage earnings and reducing the monthly benefits payable to high-wage workers. These changes significantly weakened the relationship between an individual worker's payroll tax contributions and that worker's monthly benefits and thereby greatly eroded the program's earned-right principle. The law's main revenue provision was to delay the previously scheduled payroll tax increase, originally due in 1940, for two years.

The 1939 law abandoned the large reserve policy the president had so steadfastly demanded just four years earlier. Under the new policy, according to Treasury Secretary Morgenthau, the reserve would be no larger "than is necessary to protect the system against unforeseen declines in revenues or increases in the volume of benefit payments."[16] The "contingency reserve" policy looked only five years into the future. The new policy was, for all practical purposes, the pay-as-you-go financing policy that the president had emphatically rejected four years earlier.

In addition, the 1939 law took a step away away from Social Security's self-financing policy. Without a large reserve, maintaining the self-financing policy required raising future payroll taxes above the 1935 law's ultimate 6 percent tax rate. But neither the Roosevelt administration nor Congress was willing to do that. Dealing with future deficits would be left to future Congresses, and the law allowed general revenues to be used to support benefit payments.[17] The new policy would have no near-term need for general revenues, as revenues from the existing payroll tax schedule were sufficient to finance benefit payments for several decades.[18]

Finally, to create the perception that surplus Social Security funds would thereafter be protected from misappropriation, the 1939 law relabeled the reserve fund a "trust fund," a term that was synonymous with safety. The trust fund's creation had no effect on the manner in which the Treasury Department handled Social Security's cash transactions. The Treasury would continue to collect payroll taxes along with corporate and personal income taxes and issue Social Security checks drawn on the United States Treasury. Surplus payroll taxes would not be set aside in a trust fund any more than they were set aside in a reserve fund.

Similarly, the trust fund's creation had no effect on government's accounting system treatment of Social Security's transactions. The trust fund, like the reserve fund, was merely a bookkeeping device in which a ledger entry would be made to credit Social Security with the payroll tax receipts and interest payments and debit Social Security for its expenditures. Surplus payroll taxes would continue to be credited to the trust fund regardless of how the cash proceeds were actually used, just as surplus payroll taxes had been credited to the reserve fund. Interest payments continued to be credited to the trust fund as they had been to the reserve fund.[19]

The only consequence of the trust fund's creation was that payroll tax proceeds would now be automatically appropriated to the trust fund without any congressional action instead of being annually appropriated. This new process would enable Congress to avoid annually confronting difficult questions about how the cash proceeds of surplus payroll taxes were being used.

The War Years

Throughout the war years, President Roosevelt and New Deal activists within his administration continued to work to expand the New Deal's entitlements. In his January 1942 budget message for the upcoming fiscal year, delivered to Congress just one month after the attack on Pearl Harbor, the president proposed to expand Social Security coverage to workers who had not been included in the original 1935 law and create new social insurance programs to provide disability benefits and health care assistance. A year later, the National Resources Planning Board (NPRB), an interdepartmental working group within the Roosevelt administration, issued a massive 600-plus-page report containing a comprehensive blueprint for expanding the New Deal.

The report called for universal Social Security coverage, new social insurance programs for disability and health care, and a new federal social insurance program to provide supplemental unemployment benefits. To address the unmet need of those who were not covered by these social insurance programs, the report proposed a menu of welfare programs to provide health care, food stamps, school lunches, college grants, and social services to the indigent. The report also proposed that the Aid to Dependent Children program be expanded to provide single mothers, as well as their young children, with benefits. To finance these welfare programs, the report recommended that funds should be redistributed from high-income states to low-income states.

The report, reflecting the Roosevelt administration's views, favored social insurance over welfare as the means for providing assistance. Under the social insurance approach, applicants would not have to undergo the degrading experience of proving impoverishment. There would be no "welfare stigma," no loss of dignity, attached to the receipt of benefits. Whether the country could afford the social insurance and welfare programs envisioned by the New Dealers was another matter.

The next year, President Roosevelt followed the NPRB report with his broader vision of the economic rights to which individuals should be entitled. In his 1944 State of the Union address, the president called for an "economic bill of rights": "the right to a useful and remunerative job"; "the right to earn enough to provide adequate food and clothing and recreation"; "the right to a good education"; "the right to adequate medical care"; and the "right to adequate protection from the economic fears of old age, sickness, accident, and unemployment."[20]

But Congress was in no mood to consider New Deal expansions. Winning the war was the government's central and overriding objective, consuming all of Congress's energy and the vast majority of the nation's financial resources. In addition, Republicans and southern Democrats had forged an "unholy alliance," in the words of Democratic senator Paul Douglas, to block New Deal expansions. The alliance served notice on the president by abolishing the NPRB just three months after it released its blueprint. Under these conditions, there would be no significant entitlement liberalizations during the war years, except the GI Bill, discussed in the next chapter.

War Finance and the Social Security Payroll Tax Freeze

The only entitlement-consequential issue during the war was the debate over Social Security financing, which featured the Roosevelt administration's novel claim that each dollar of additional payroll taxes could finance both wartime military expenditures and postwar Social Security benefits. In other words, payroll tax revenues were a financial "twofer." Similar fallacious arguments would be made in the post–World War II years to justify payroll and other taxes used to finance trust funds. Hence, the claim merits further discussion.

The war imposed a staggering economic cost on the nation. By 1943, annual war expenditures alone were more than half of the nation's entire prewar output of goods and services and five times the federal government's entire budget in 1940. War expenditures would climb another 25 percent before the war was over.[21]

The administration called for a combination of higher taxes and the issuance of debt to finance the war effort. Its 1941 plan proposed that one-sixth be financed by higher taxes; the 1944 plan proposed 50 percent.[22] To meet its goals, the administration pressed Congress to raise personal and corporate income taxes and establish personal income tax withholding. It also called for higher payroll taxes by allowing the previously scheduled payroll tax rate increase to take effect and extending coverage to additional industries and occupations.

Congress repeatedly rejected the proposed payroll tax increases, voting them down seven times from 1941 to 1947.[23] Each time, Congress voted against extending Social Security coverage and in favor of freezing the payroll tax rate at its 1940 level. Thus, the combined employee-employer payroll tax remained at 2 percent throughout the decade rather than rising to 6 percent as called for in the 1935 law.

The prevailing congressional view was that a payroll tax increase was unnecessary as a Social Security financing measure. World War II was a boon for Social Security's finances. The war produced higher domestic employment and delays in retirement in 1940, a combination that quickly increased the Social Security trust fund accounting balance far above the level needed to meet the contingency reserve requirement. At the end of 1942, the trust fund balance was twice the amount needed to meet the contingency reserve requirement; two years later, the balance was ten times the required amount.[24] Just a few years before, Congress and the administration had agreed to finance Social Security on a pay-as-you-go basis. Revenues from the existing payroll tax rate were more than enough to carry out this policy.[25]

The Roosevelt administration articulated the "twofer" claim in its first wartime budget. The budget, submitted to Congress one month after Japan attacked Pearl Harbor, proposed to raise Social Security taxes by $2 billion as part of its $9 billion war financing program. One billion dollars would come from allowing the previously scheduled payroll tax rate increase to take effect on January 1, 1943. The other $1 billion per year would come from expanding Social Security coverage to employees in industries and occupations that previously were not covered.[26]

President Roosevelt spelled out how these additional revenues could be simultaneously available to finance postwar Social Security benefits and the immediate war effort in his budget message to Congress in 1942: the "increased [payroll tax] contributions would result in reserves of several billion dollars for postwar contingencies. . . . Investment of the additional reserves in bonds of the United States Government would assist in financing the war."[27] Moreover, the president made clear that he would withdraw his Social Security tax increase unless the legislation raised postwar Social Security benefits; stating flatly that he "oppose[d] the use of pay-roll taxes as a measure of war finance unless the worker is given his full money's worth in increased social security."[28]

The president's message was reinforced by Treasury Secretary Morgenthau. In testimony before Congress on the administration's war financing plan, Mr. Morgenthau explained, "We shall have to tax in accordance with the magnitude of that program and in accordance with the seriousness of the position in which we stand. The President's Budget message in January called for the raising of $7,000,000,000 in new revenue from taxes, together with an additional $2,000,000,000 to be obtained from the social-security program."[29] In contrast, Social Security board officials justified the payroll tax rate increase as necessary to meet Social Security's long-run financing needs. In testifying before the Ways and Means Committee, the same committee that heard Morgenthau's testimony, Arthur Altmeyer explained that without the tax increase, Social Security revenues "are probably inadequate to meet the [future] benefit payments provided in the existing law."[30]

The administration's argument was made possible by government trust fund accounting rules that credit surplus payroll tax revenues to the Social Security trust fund regardless of how those revenues are actually spent. The administration hardly believed that it could spend the same dollar simultaneously on two different activities. Its argument was an attempt to appeal simultaneously to two audiences: one consisting of people concerned about war finance, the other of people who were concerned about Social Security financing matters.

Although the administration's novel argument was unsuccessful with wartime Congresses, it would be repeated throughout the post–World War II era to justify a raft of higher taxes, including payroll taxes for Social Security, Medicare, and disability benefits; gasoline taxes for roads, bridges, and mass transit systems; airline ticket taxes for airport construction projects; and taxes on coal for black lung benefits.

9 A New Kind of Entitlement

The GI Bill

We may be a war-weary people by the time we have shattered the Axis. . . .
There will be an urge to let down after the fast pace we maintained to win
this war, to dump men willy-nilly back into civilian life, to let them find a
job as best they can and where they can. . . . But the Army will not take that
easy way.

Robert P. Patterson, assistant secretary of war, 1943[1]

THE SERVICEMEN'S READJUSTMENT ACT OF 1944
was the only major new entitlement created during World
War II. Popularly known as the GI Bill, the law granted educational
assistance, cash readjustment assistance, and government-backed
home, farm, and business loan guarantees to all veterans regardless
of their disability status. The educational program provided aid for
tuition, books, supplies, and living expenses while the veteran was in
school. The GI Bill is important for three reasons.

First, the law permanently established as national policy the view
that society owed a debt to all wartime veterans, not just to those who
had suffered from disabling wartime injury or illness. Moreover, the
law's underlying premise was that all wartime veterans should, to the
extent possible, be assisted in returning to the status in civilian life that
they had achieved when they had departed for war. The policy and the

premise were sharp departures from prior wartime veterans' programs that had initially restricted benefits to veterans who suffered wartime injuries.

Second, the GI Bill's noncash, or in-kind (as they are now called), benefits were a new type of entitlement benefit. Entitlements to in-kind benefits bestow a right to reimbursement on people and institutions that provide the benefits prescribed by the law. Under the GI Bill, educational institutions, college professors, training instructors, and school administrators were entitled, directly or indirectly, to compensation for the educational services they provided to veterans. Bankers and financial institutions that provided guaranteed home loans were entitled to receive repayments from the government on defaulted loans. These service providers had a vested financial interest in the program. Along with veterans' organizations, their lobbies were powerful advocates for maintaining and expanding benefits.

Thus, the GI Bill serves as the forerunner of the raft of in-kind benefit entitlements enacted in the 1960s and 1970s to provide health care, nutrition, and social services for the elderly, the poor, and the disabled. These entitlements spawned a vast expanse of service-provider lobbying organizations that exerted a profound influence on entitlement expansions.

Third, veterans receiving the GI bill were free to choose almost any school and any education or training he or she wished. Hence, the program operated as the federal government's first large-scale voucher program.

The GI Bill is unique among entitlements in that it operated on a grand scale for a relatively short period of time. By 1955, after the program had nearly run its course, 80 percent of World War II veterans—12 million people—had received benefits from one or more of the GI Bill programs. More than half of all returning GIs—7.8 million veterans—had participated in far-reaching educational tuition and subsistence aid from the Veterans Administration. At its enrollment peak in 1947, over half of all men enrolled in U.S. colleges and universities were receiving aid from the GI Bill. The home loan program was only slightly less important. By 1955, 3.8 million veterans had received a home loan guaranteed by the Veterans Administration.[2]

Although the GI Bill's programs provided a large segment of the veteran population with benefits, it did so at a relatively modest cost to the Treasury. At its peak in 1947, GI Bill outlays accounted for 16 percent of federal noninterest spending, less than half the Civil War pension program's largest share in the 1890s.

Origins of the GI Bill

From its inception, the primary rationale for the GI Bill was different from that of prior wartime veterans' legislation, when veterans' benefits served as both a recruitment tool and a means to meet a societal obligation to injured wartime veterans or the families of those who died in the conflict. In 1944, a high level of patriotism and the 1940 Selective Service Act made recruitment a nonissue.

The GI Bill was motivated primarily by concern about the economic and social consequences of the massive demobilization that would occur at the war's end. There was fear that the simultaneous discharge of up to 15 million soldiers into a 60-million-person labor force and the reconversion of the U.S. economy from wartime to a peacetime footing would result in massive unemployment. A program that eased the transition for soldiers was desired to prevent severe unemployment and unrest among returning war veterans.

The Roosevelt administration had begun to focus on educational assistance as a means to aid the readjustment of returning war veterans as early as 1942. That year, Congress lowered the Selective Service Act's draft age from 21 to 18, interrupting the education of large numbers of college students.[3] Ensuring that young men who wished to return to school when the war ended received assistance was a natural extension of the principle established in the 1940 Selective Service Act. That act, the nation's first peacetime military draft law, had granted draftees a legal right to their former jobs on their return from military service.

President Roosevelt kicked off the legislative campaign to enact the GI Bill in July 1943, following the successful outcome of the military campaign in North Africa and Mussolini's fall from power. In his July 28, 1943, fireside chat, entitled a "First Crack in the Axis," he informed the nation of the war's progress and then called for legislation providing for mustering-out pay, government educational assistance, and temporary unemployment benefits for all veterans, along with improved health care services for disabled veterans. In reversing his long-held views on the nation's obligations to its citizen soldiers, the president acknowledged that "the members of the armed forces have been compelled to make greater economic sacrifice and every other kind of sacrifice than the rest of us, and they are entitled to definite action to help take care of their special problems."[4]

After five months of little legislative progress, the American Legion stepped into the breach in January 1944 with an omnibus "GI Bill of Rights" that included all of the benefits President Roosevelt had proposed. Subsequently renamed the "GI Bill," it proposed to extend benefits to all veterans—both the able-bodied and the disabled. The legion declared that veterans "should be aided in reaching that place, position, or status which they had normally expected to achieve and probably would have achieved, had their war service not interrupted their careers."[5] Society, the organization said, had an obligation to minimize any economic harm a veteran suffered as a consequence of wartime service. GI Bill benefits, according to the American Legion, were "earned certain rights to which they are entitled. Gratuities do not enter the picture."[6]

Teaming up with Hearst Newspapers, the lobby group regularly blasted Congress for its procrastination on veterans' legislation, just as the Grand Army of the Republic had teamed up with the *Herald Tribune* seventy years earlier. William Randolph Hearst waited until Christmas Eve 1944 to pen a letter to his own newspaper imploring readers to "let us continue to urge our great political leaders to think less about their own personal 'place in history' and think more about the men whose heroism and self-sacrifice made that place possible."[7]

The Legion bill's centerpieces were new education and home loan programs. The education program would provide a monthly subsistence allowance and tuition assistance for up to four years to veterans whose education or job training had been interrupted by military service. The home loan program authorized the Veterans Administration to grant loans to veterans to help finance a home or farm. The bill also included mustering-out pay and fifty-two weeks of unemployment benefits for all honorably discharged veterans.

The bill, sponsored by eighty-one of ninety-six senators, passed the Senate by a unanimous vote.[8] The fact that J. Bennett Clark, the chairman of the Senate committee with jurisdiction over the bill, had been one of the American Legion's founders ensured the bill's quick passage.

In the House, the bill's route to enactment was somewhat slower. There was widespread agreement that the federal government was obligated to help veterans whose civilian lives had been interrupted by the war. However, there was also a general concern that the Roosevelt administration would use the legislation as a vehicle to advance its New Deal programs. The worry was that New Dealers would transform a program designed for veterans into a general education program that would be available to all citizens. The bill, it was feared, was a Trojan horse to further its New Deal programs. As Congressman Bernard Gearhart (R-CA) put it, "The thing we have to fight down is the crafty effort of so many different groups to use the war for the reorganization of the world."[9]

These concerns were not without considerable justification. An administration-supported bill to subsidize public education for the general population had passed the Senate the year before but had failed in the House. The Congress had also recently fought a bitter battle over another administration-supported bill to extend rehabilitation services to all disabled civilians, veteran or not.[10] Congress had little stomach for another fight.

A more specific concern, one that generated most of the debate in both chambers, centered on the new education program. The bill's overriding objective was to guarantee returning GIs the greatest freedom in choosing their educational institution and their field of study. As Congressman Leonard Allen (D-LA), a member of the House Committee on World War I Veterans' Legislation, explained, "We tried to guarantee to the veteran the greatest liberty of choice to the individual in letting him select his own school anywhere, with no restrictions. . . . The federal government would not set standards for approved educational institutions, nor standards for acceptable courses of study. These regulatory decisions would be left to the states. Congressman Allen explained, "The bill specifically provides on page 55, paragraph 6, against any Federal interference."[11]

But allowing the states to determine all the rules and regulations regarding their education programs while the federal government paid the bills was an open invitation to abuse and extravagance. During House debate, Congressman William Poage (D-TX) expressed his concern about the arrangement of responsibilities:

> Mr. Chairman, it is always surprising to me to see how Members of this House can be so intelligent as individuals and yet act as a mass with such utter disregard of the facts of ordinary human relationships. There is not a man or woman on this floor who does not know that if we establish a program whereby six or seven million young people . . . receive training at the Government's expense . . . that there is going to be a racket established all over this country of so-called institutions of learning that are simply going to spring up here, there, and yonder to get the kids' money. . . . You and I could make money by quitting Congress and going into the school business.[12]

Allowing the federal government to set rules and regulations on educational course work and educational institutions would open up the field of education to federal control. Some members of Congress feared that once federal funds began to flow from the Treasury, the pressure to ensure, through regulations and federal standards, that taxpayer funds were properly spent would inevitably lead to an unacceptable level of federal intrusion into education. Southern representatives were particularly concerned that federal authority would be used to force desegregation.

The dilemma, which Congress would confront many times in the future, was well stated by John Rankin, chairman of the House Committee on World War II Veterans Legislation (D-MI) during the House debate on the bill:

> As far as the States' rights are concerned, there is not a man in this House who has fought harder to maintain the rights of the States than I have, but we are representing now the Federal Government, and . . . since this is Federal money that is being spent, some Federal agency must have the power to say whether or not that money is being wisely spent or is being wasted. . . . Some men talk as if we ought to send the

Federal Treasury off down here and have some professors handle it. We are not going to do that. This is Federal money.[13]

Eventually the issue was decisively settled against allowing any federal involvement in regulating education. The final legislation emphatically prohibited any federal influence over educational institutions or curriculum. The bill stipulated that "no department, agency, or officer of the United States in carrying out the provisions of this part shall exercise any supervision or control whatsoever over any State educational agency or State apprenticeship agency or any educational or training institution."[14] The House passed the bill overwhelmingly.[15]

The only moment of real drama in the process of enacting the GI Bill came during the final stage of the legislative process. The story, which undoubtedly contains certain embellishments, is now a Washington legend and worth retelling.[16] The House and Senate bills went to a conference committee to iron out their differences. After three weeks of deadlock, the committee agreed on June 9 that if the logjam couldn't be broken by a vote scheduled for 10:00 a.m. the next day, the bills would be sent back to their respective chambers. If this happened, in the words of committee member, Pat Kearney (NY), "the bill will be lost."[17] The tie-breaking vote in the bill's favor was held by Congressman John Gibson, a Democrat from rural Georgia. Unfortunately for the bill's supporters, the congressman had recently left Washington to return home. He had given his proxy, but the chairman of the house conferees, in a violation of standard protocol, had rejected it. Gibson had to return to Washington to cast his vote in person.

In the early evening of June 9, a scant sixteen hours before the 10:00 a.m. vote, word went out from the bill's supporters in Congress to the American Legion officials in Washington: "Find Gibson!"

But Gibson was nowhere to be found. Legion officials who phoned his home were informed by the long-distance operator that all calls to Georgia involved a five- to six-hour wartime delay. They contacted Georgia radio stations, which agreed to run the following news alert at regular intervals: "Anyone knowing the whereabouts of Congressman John S. Gibson ask him to call Operator 2 in Washington."

Working through the editor of the *Atlanta Constitution*, a newspaper that had priority wartime phone access in case of an emergency, Legion officials finally reached the local operator in Gibson's home town of Douglas, Georgia. The operator, when informed of the Legion's reason for trying to contact Gibson, responded: "My husband just landed in Normandy. I'm with you," and promptly phoned Gibson's friends. She discovered that he was en route from Valdosta to Douglas, a distance of 70 miles. Phone calls went out to the Georgia State Police to "Find Gibson!"

Finally, around 11:00 p.m., the police located the congressman who, according to one account, was playing poker at a highway truck stop and unaware of the desperate attempts to reach him. Gibson immediately agreed to return to Washington. But to the dismay of those seated at the poker table, he looked to the kitty for his return flight fare to Washington.[18]

Finding John Gibson was difficult enough, but getting him to Washington in time for the scheduled vote proved more challenging. Initial efforts to secure a military plane from the base in nearby Waycross failed because the only available plane was grounded due to mechanical difficulties. Then Legion officials discovered that a commercial Eastern Airlines flight from Jacksonville to Washington National Airport was scheduled for takeoff at 2:00 a.m. But there was not enough time. Jacksonville was 150 miles away.

With the help of the editor of the Hearst Newspapers, a late-night call was placed to the airline's traffic manager to request that the flight be delayed until Gibson could arrive. The official hardly needed persuading. His immediate supervisor was Eddie Rickenbacker, an active legionnaire and America's World War I flying ace. Gibson, escorted by Georgia and then Florida state police through a driving thunderstorm, arrived in Jacksonville to board the delayed flight. The plane landed at Washington National Airport on June 10 at 6:37 a.m. Gibson arrived at the Senate conference promptly at 10:00 a.m. to register his vote. Before doing so, he announced, "Americans are dying today in Normandy in the greatest invasion in all history. I'm going to hold a press conference after this meeting and castigate anyone who dares to vote against this bill." The conferees who had objected to the bill quickly folded their tents, the House-Senate differences were ironed out, and the conference bill sailed through both chambers. The president signed the GI Bill into law on June 22, 1944.

The Law and Its Impact

Under the GI Bill, all World War II veterans who had served at least ninety days and were age 25 or younger were presumed to have had their education interrupted and entitled to educational assistance. Veterans over age 25 were required to demonstrate that their education or training had been interrupted. Veterans were granted entitlements for up to four years of federal assistance for education or training at any educational institution certified by state governments or by the Veterans Administration.[19] They could receive up to $500 per year for tuition, books, materials, tools, and supplies. Additional subsistence allowances during their time in school or training were set at $50 per month for single veterans and $75 per month for veterans with dependents ($500 and $750 per month in today's dollars). Veterans were allowed two years from the date of their discharge or the end of the war to initiate their education or training.

The education and training program operated as a voucher program. The veteran was responsible for applying for financial assistance. The federal government, through the Veterans Administration, had responsibility for certifying veterans' eligibility. The states were responsible for determining eligibility of schools and on-the-job training programs.

The GI loan program guaranteed loans to veterans for the purchase of a home or farm or for expenses in starting a business, with the amount of the guarantee equal to 50 percent of the loan up to $2,000. The maximum interest rate that lenders could charge on the loan was set at 4 percent, and the federal government paid the interest during the loan's first year. In addition, the bill provided readjustment pay in the form of 52 weeks of unemployment benefits at a rate of $20 per week.

During deliberations on the law, Congress gave scant consideration to the cost of the new entitlement. Neither the Senate nor House reports on the bill provided estimates of its cost. The estimates that were provided during congressional debate underestimated the entitlement's cost. The House bill's floor manager, Chairman John Rankin, citing a Veterans Administration report, put an upper bound of the law's total cost at $6.5 billion. Within this total, the education and training portion was estimated to be $3 billion, well short of the law's eventual cost of $18.5 billion for the entire bill and $14 billion for the education and training portion.[20] Similarly, initial estimates of the number of GIs who were expected to enroll in education and training programs were invariably too low. The Veterans Administration's administrator, General Edward Hines, testified that at most 2 million veterans would enroll. Eventually nearly 8 million veterans took advantage of the bill's education and training benefits.[21]

The veterans' lobby played an instrumental role from start to finish in structuring the GI Bill and marshaling it through Congress. An indication of the extent of their influence is provided by a rare public exchange among Veterans Committee members Edith Nourse Rogers (R-MA) and chairman John Rankin (D-MS), and Congressman Thomas Jenkins (R-OH). The exchange begins with Mrs. Rogers answering a question about support for the bill:

> Mrs. Rogers: There was no opposition to any of the provisions that are in the bill. They are very few. The veterans' organizations, the schools, and everybody else agree to what is in the bill. . . . It was unanimous.
>
> Mr. Jenkins: I understand that the Veterans of Foreign Wars has some complaint against the GI bill. Has there been an effort to relieve that situation?
>
> Mr. Rankin, Yes.
>
> Mr. Jenkins: May I compliment the leadership and the gentleman from Mississippi. . . . We have now come to the place where we can all agree to pass this bill.[22]

The Impact of the GI Bill

Military demobilization occurred far more rapidly than U.S. military leaders had initially planned, though perhaps not fast enough for many GIs. By June 1945, 2.5 million soldiers and naval personnel had been mustered out. During the next year, another 10.5 million were discharged. By July 1947, demobilization was virtually complete: 14.4 million had been discharged.[23]

At first, the take-up rate was slow. Of the 2.5 million GIs who had been discharged by July 1945, only 83,016 had applied for education or training assistance and only 15,455 had applied for guaranteed loans. The fears within the administration and in Congress that the U.S. economy would not be able to absorb such a large number of returning veterans proved unfounded. Only 180,798 had filed for unemployment insurance, and about 70 percent were able to find work within a year of their discharge.

The slow take-up of the GI Bill's education and loan guarantee benefits led the Congress to liberalize the program in December 1945.[24] The law now extended the presumption that military service had interrupted an individual's education to all World War II veterans regardless of age, not just those under age 25. The law also increased the time allowed for application to four years for education and training assistance and to ten years for a loan guarantee. Finally, the law increased subsistence allowances and the maximum loan guarantee amount.

Thereafter the program's participation soared. By July 1946, 2 million returning GIs were receiving education or training subsidies. *Time* magazine reported that due to the surge in enrollment by veterans, there was "standing room only" at universities and junior colleges. Half of all college students were on the GI Bill. A year later, enrollment in the GI Bill education and training programs reached its peak of 2.5 million. Over 500,000 veterans were enrolled in on-the-job training programs.[25] Housing loans had been guaranteed for over 700,000 veterans.[26]

The GI Bill had become the federal government's largest program. Its 2.5 million recipients dwarfed the Social Security program's 1 million.[27] Its $3.2 billion expenditure was 50 percent higher than the next largest program, veterans' compensation payments.[28]

The law's fiscal impact was large but brief. By June 30, 1955, only 70,000 World War II veterans were receiving GI Bill education and training assistance. Its outlays on World War II veterans had declined to $141 million.[29]

By the time the education and training program had nearly run its course in 1955, two-thirds of all World War II veterans had received

GI Bill benefits.[30] Six million of all World War II veterans had availed themselves of education and training assistance. Over 4 million had received VA-backed loans, mainly for the purchase of a home, and the number of new loan guarantees was still running at more than 500,000 per year.[31] A total of $18.5 billion had been spent: $3.9 billion on tuition, $10 billion on subsistence payments, and the remaining $4.6 billion on loans and loan guarantees.

The GI Bill's impact on the country is hard to overestimate. Its unemployment benefits eased the transition to civilian life for 6 million of the 15 million returning GIs. For most recipients of tuition and subsistence assistance, the skills they earned were profoundly beneficial not only to them but to the larger society. Because of GI Bill aid, many veterans went on to build successful careers as part of America's burgeoning middle class. The aid also helped some GIs reach the pinnacle of their chosen profession. It supported the education of Supreme Court Chief Justice William Rehnquist, U.S. senator Robert Dole, and Congressman Charlie Rangel, who represented Harlem for nearly four decades.

Despite the GI Bill's extraordinary successes, the law was not without its scandals. With a staggering 40,800 educational institutions and 500,000 business firms approved to receive education and training subsidies by 1950, a certain amount of fraud and abuse was hardly unexpected.[32] Congressman Poage's prediction of inevitable excesses and abuses in an open-ended entitlement with no federal oversight of educational suppliers proved accurate. Although with time these scandals have faded from the public's memory, they were important to the GI Bill during its operations and in shaping subsequent veterans' legislation.

The largest of the GI Bill's scandals, involving vocational education schools, generated considerable press attention and were the subject of congressional hearings, a special investigation by a select House committee, and several Veterans Administration reports. By 1949, 8,800 vocational schools had been approved by the Veterans Administration; 5,600 of these schools had come into existence since the GI Bill's enactment. Some schools were operating as many as three shifts a day churning out graduates but providing few marketable skills. Newspapers and magazines regularly reported the frivolous nature of many of their course offerings. In Mississippi, students were studying to become baseball players. In New York and New Jersey, students were taking courses in "bartending mixology." So-called charm schools were springing up throughout the nation. A seven-month course in "chicken sexing" was highlighted in *Collier's* magazine. After reviewing the excesses in the GI Bill program for vocational schools, Senator Paul Douglas concluded, "We wasted millions and millions of dollars on the thing. They [the Veterans Administration] certified a lot of fake schools and some of the schools milked the system."[33]

Flight schools were particularly popular. The high demand for flying lessons induced by the GI Bill's generous subsidies brought forth a large supply of schools. Most, however, gave recreational, as opposed to commercial, lessons. Between 1944 and 1949, the number of flight schools approved by the VA registered a tenfold increase, from 351 to 3,134.[34] The law had virtually created an industry.

Vocational schools engaged in a variety of practices to fraudulently increase the tuition charged to the government. Dummy corporations, reminiscent of the railroad financing scandals in the 1870s, were set up by school operators to sell tools and supplies to their schools at inflated prices. One school, for example, used inflated prices for supplies to justify charging students $2,626.50 for a fifty-one-week course in luggage fabrication. Another school did the same to charge $1,467.52 for a fifty-week course in laying linoleum.[35]

The abuses, although concentrated among vocational education schools, were also present among colleges and universities, albeit in less spectacular terms. Under the original terms of the GI Bill, public universities and colleges were permitted to charge the government nonresident tuition rates for veterans who lived out-of-state, even if the tuition charge exceeded $500 per year. After examining this practice, VA administrator Omar Bradley found that some public educational institutions abused it. He delicately told Congress that "it was found that certain universities and colleges had increased the nonresident fee to an amount which, in some cases, appeared in excess of the cost of teaching personnel and supplies for instruction."[36]

The GI Bill's successes and its abuses had a direct impact on the next major veterans' legislation: Korean War veterans' benefits legislation.

The GI Bill policy—that society owes an obligation to all veterans, not just to those disabled by wartime injuries—was affirmed once again in the Veterans Readjustment Act of 1952. Although the Korean War veterans' benefits were decidedly less generous than those of the GI Bill, the underlying philosophy policy was the same.[37]

The GI Bill's impact on the acceptance of entitlements among the broad population beyond veterans is hard to gauge. The tuition and subsistence aid was extraordinarily popular among veterans and profoundly valuable to many veterans' future earning capacity. The home loans enabled millions of veterans to buy their first homes as they were starting their families. By 1960, some 30 million people were in families that had benefited directly from the bill.[38] They saw firsthand the difference that a government entitlement program could make in individuals' lives. This recognition would make many veterans more accepting of a philosophy that favored similar government interventions on behalf of a broader segment of the population beyond veterans.

The GI Bill, however, had been justified, defended, and ultimately enacted only on the ground that veterans were a special class of Americans. By their wartime service in defense of the nation, they were entitled to benefits to which those who had not served in the military during wartime were not. But the obligation that society owed to wartime veterans did not necessarily extend to those who had not served. Indeed, the efforts by the Roosevelt administration to use World War II veterans' benefits as a means to extend its social welfare programs had been decisively rejected by the Congress.

10 Setting the Postwar Entitlement Agenda, 1946–1950

Under the Social Security Act, national policy contemplated that old-age and survivors insurance would be the primary Government measure affording economic protection to the needy aged and dependent children. . . . Public assistance was designed as a backstop, a second line of defense, eventually to be replaced in large measure by social insurance benefits.

President Harry S. Truman, budget message to Congress, 1949

AT THE END OF WORLD WAR II, THE AMERICAN entitlement state stood at a crucial policy juncture. The New Deal had set the building blocks of the modern American entitlement state firmly in place, but its future remained highly uncertain.

The world war and congressional opposition by the unholy alliance of conservative Democrats and Republicans had combined to check the advancement of the New Deal during the first half of the 1940s. The legislative hiatus meant that the size and reach of New Deal entitlements remained almost as they had been before the war. Social Security was still far from universal. In 1946, only one in every six people age 65 and over received monthly benefits. More than a third of all workers were still exempt from paying Social Security payroll taxes.[1] State government unemployment insurance programs provided benefits to only one in every three unemployed workers. The Old-Age Assistance, Aid to the

Blind, and Aid to Dependent Children programs assisted fewer than 3 million of the nation's 140 million residents. Only one welfare program, Old-Age Assistance, had grown significantly. State-run Old-Age programs provided aid to over 2 million poor elderly people, making it, not Social Security, the principal program for assisting the elderly. Only 385,000 children received benefits from the much smaller Aid to Dependent Children program, and a mere 71,000 people received Aid to the Blind benefits.[2]

The direction Congress would take with entitlements after the war was not clear. Would it follow the same pattern of extending assistance to those in the general population that it had in extending wartime veterans' pensions? Would the existence of surplus revenues produce the same pressures to extend eligibility? If so, where would the extensions end? Where would Congress draw the line between those worthy of assistance and those who were not worthy? How important would electoral considerations be in influencing entitlement legislation?

The biggest question at the time was whether social insurance, led by Social Security, or welfare would become the primary vehicle for delivering assistance to individuals. The answer would have important ramifications for the relationship between the federal government and recipients of assistance, the federal government's role in providing assistance, and the eventual size and reach of entitlements.

First, social insurance's earned-right basis for assistance gave individuals a legal claim to assistance and imposed a corresponding legal obligation on government administrative agencies to meet this claim. In this manner, social insurance put individuals on more or less equal legal footing with administrative agencies. Federal-state welfare programs, on the other hand, gave claimants few legal rights to benefits and, correspondingly, gave state and local government agencies broad discretion to determine which claimants were worthy of its charitable assistance. The welfare programs therefore put individuals in the role of supplicants who had to prove impoverishment.

Second, social insurance put the federal government in the primary role of determining who would receive assistance, how much each person would receive, and the terms and conditions of such aid. The New Deal's federal-state welfare programs had left these decisions primarily in the hands of state and local governments, where it had resided for two centuries.

Third, social insurance would extend the reach of entitlements farther and impose a greater financial burden on society than welfare would. Since social insurance provided assistance independent of an individual's financial need, it extended entitlement assistance to middle- and upper-income individuals, as well as to poor people. Welfare, in contrast, limited government assistance to impoverished individuals who were unable to provide for themselves.

President Truman emerged from the war years committed to completing the New Deal's unfinished social insurance agenda. His goal was to make social security the main vehicle for providing cash assistance to the elderly and establish a new federal disability insurance program and a new national health insurance program. The four-year battle over these initiatives culminated in the massive 1950 Social Security Amendments. While Congress rejected the call for disability and health care entitlements, the amendments represented a major advance toward ensuring that Social Security, not Old-Age Assistance, would be the principal governmental program providing assistance to the elderly. The law reaffirmed the New Deal paternalistic view that individuals could not be counted on to be solely responsible for meeting their needs in retirement. Government must step in to meet not only these needs but also to mitigate life's hazards encountered along the way to retirement.

President Harry Truman's Postwar Agenda

President Harry S. Truman wasted no time in kicking off an ambitious effort to expand the New Deal entitlement programs. In a series of speeches and messages to Congress beginning in September 1945 and ending with the State of the Union the following January, the president outlined his postwar domestic policy plans with increasing specificity. New and expanded rights to federal entitlements were at the top of his domestic agenda. On September 6, just five days after announcing to the world that Japan had surrendered, he called on Congress to enact President Roosevelt's economic bill of rights into law. "Let us make the attainment of those rights," he urged, "the essence of postwar American economic life."[3] A month later, on November 19, he proposed a national health insurance plan.[4] In his 1946 State of the Union, he proposed to make Social Security universal by expanding its coverage to nearly all private sector workers, establish a national disability insurance program, and create a federal unemployment benefits program to supplement state benefits. In addition, he called on Congress to enact a host of nonentitlement programs, including a national school lunch program and a sweeping housing assistance program for low-income households. The president made clear that his Fair Deal program, as the collection of proposals would later be called, would not only vigorously complete the New Deal's unfinished business, it would enlarge it.

President Truman's proposals made clear his support for the New Deal idea that social insurance should be the nation's first line of defense against poverty in old age and the loss of income due to unemployment, ill health, and disability. He expressed his support in the context of the Social Security program, but it applied with equal force to his other social insurance proposals:

> Under the Social Security Act, national policy contemplated that old-age and survivors insurance would be the primary Government measure affording economic protection to the needy aged and dependent children, and that unemployment compensation would provide temporary assistance to the unemployed. . . . Public assistance was designed as a backstop, a second line of defense, eventually to be replaced in large measure by social insurance benefits.[5]

The basis for this view is that all members of a given class are worthy of receiving federal assistance because of their circumstances and regardless of their income. The worthiness of the class is guaranteed by a grant of an entitlement to assistance among all members of the class. The entitlement right is secured by the payment of a compulsory payroll tax. A universal Social Security program would give all elderly people a legal right to federal assistance simply because they had reached a particular age. A national health insurance program would give all citizens a legal right to federal assistance to meet medical expenses. National disability and unemployment insurance programs would entitle workers who suffered from ill health or job loss through no fault of their own to government aid.

Initially the president's Fair Deal agenda was stymied by other postwar policy imperatives. Demobilization, debt reduction, and tax relief dominated Congress's legislative calendar. Millions of returning veterans were seeking jobs. The outstanding public debt had risen to over 100 percent of GDP. Taxes had climbed to 20 percent of GDP, three times their prewar level.

In Congress, the large divide between the political parties and, to a lesser extent, between northern and southern Democrats, that had emerged during President Roosevelt's second term remained a fact of life. This divide reflected, in part, strong philosophical differences on the proper federal government role in providing direct assistance to individuals. Northern Democrats who represented the party's liberal wing strongly favored social insurance over welfare. Social insurance put the federal government, not the states, in charge of policy. The federal government, they believed, was more financially equipped than the states to obtain the resources necessary to assist individuals and could provide uniform benefits across all states. Social insurance bestowed federally uniform legal rights to assistance and thereby avoided the stigma and demeaning application process associated with welfare. Liberal Democrats believed that as social insurance programs expanded, the federal role in existing federal-state welfare programs would gradually decline. In their view, a universal social security program, a federal disability insurance program, and a national health insurance would so reduce welfare costs that only a residual responsibility for states would remain.[6]

Republicans and southern Democrats distrusted a large federal role and favored an alternative policy of federal financial support for state-run, means-tested welfare programs. In their view, state and local governments were better positioned to care for individuals than the federal government. In providing aid, distinctions had to be drawn between the deserving poor, who were unable to provide for themselves, such as children, disabled, and elderly people, and the undeserving poor, consisting mainly of able-bodied individuals who had the ability but not the inclination to be self-supporting. Making these distinctions required knowledge of individual and family circumstances. Local governments were much closer to the poor in their communities and thus more likely to possess this knowledge. Most Republicans and southern Democrats accepted a universal Social Security program but resisted extensions of social insurance beyond retirement benefits. Conservative Republicans also feared that if Social Security benefits grew too large, they would become a substitute for private savings, undermining individual self-reliance and reducing the available supply of funds for private investment, thereby impairing economic growth.

In 1945 and 1946, the unholy alliance between southern congressional Democrats and Republicans, mainly an alliance of convenience for southern Democrats when it suited their interest, blocked President Truman's proposed New Deal social insurance liberalizations. When Republicans took control over Congress in 1947 for the first time in sixteen years, they did the same, but without the assistance of southern Democrats. The "Do Nothing Congress," as Truman labeled the Republican Congress of 1947–1948, didn't get its name for nothing.[7]

President Truman's surprise victory over Thomas Dewey and the return of Democrat majorities in both chambers of Congress in the 1948 elections gave new life to liberals' domestic agenda, setting the stage for the first large-scale postwar entitlement expansion. The vehicle for this expansion was the massive 1950 Social Security Amendments. But before Congress passed this law, it dealt liberals a severe blow by rejecting the president's national health insurance and disability insurance plans.

The Failed Quest for National Health Insurance

Within months of his election, President Truman called on Congress to enact legislation "providing for a nationwide system of health insurance."[8] In the president's view, the American health care system suffered from the twin problems of high cost and a lack of access to medical care. The president declared that the high cost of medical services acted as a barrier to accessing health care: "As treatment has become more expensive, families have found it more and more difficult to meet the extraordinary costs of accidents, serious illness or major surgery. . . . It is no longer just the poor who are unable to pay for all the medical care they need—such care is now beyond the means of all but the upper income groups."[9]

President Truman's national health insurance plan was modeled on the New Deal cash assistance programs. The primary vehicle for providing health care to all individuals would be a new social insurance program that would operate like Social Security. Working individuals and their families would earn an entitlement right to government-sponsored health insurance by contributing payroll taxes that would support the program. "Health insurance," the president said, "will mean that proper medical care will be economically accessible . . . as a right and not as a medical dole."[10] Insurance for poor people with little or no labor force attachment would be provided by state governments and would be financed by federal public assistance matching grants to states.

President Truman's national health insurance proposal, the first concrete plan of this type, represented a milestone. Social reformers had begun advocating for government provided health insurance during the Progressive era. These efforts, led by the American Alliance for Labor Legislation (AALL), were premised on the view that private health care markets and charity care could never meet the nation's health care needs. In fact, in their view, charities and churches were obstacles on the path to achieving AALL's vision of a higher collective good. I. M. Rubinow, AALL's chief architect of health insurance reform, represented this view well by writing, "A new movement for social policy must meet its strongest opponent in the fetishism of self-help."[11] Only a government-imposed mandatory system, AALL believed, could ensure adequate health care for all citizens.

The AALL proposal, like President Truman's, compelled employers and workers to contribute to a government pool of funds that would be used to finance health insurance and compensation for lost wages due to ill health or injury. Government contributions, funded by another layer of taxes, would be added to the pool. Thus, universal health care would be a "shared responsibility" among workers, employers, and other taxpayers. Government agencies would specify the plan's minimum benefits.

The plan's opponents charged that compulsory insurance infringed on personal freedom and other natural rights of citizens. The essayist T. L. Thompson expressed this objection: "If any citizen can by law be compelled to carry health insurance and pay therefor a part of his earnings, he can be compelled under the same principle of legislation to do anything else and pay the cost out of his hard earnings, if somebody thinks it will be beneficial to him. Such a doctrine is absolutely destructive of a man's rights to do or not to do whatever his judgment may dictate as to matters that solely affect him personally. It is the exercise of absolute and arbitrary governmental power over the individual."[12]

AALL's proposals encountered stiff opposition in each state in which it was proposed, and by 1919, the effort to enact compulsory health insurance was dead, having been rejected by every state legislature that had considered it. Its defeat was so thorough that fifteen years later, President Roosevelt rejected proposals to include it in his Social Security plan fearing that a national health insurance proposal might jeopardize his plan. President Roosevelt did, however, keep the idea percolating on Congress's back burner throughout the remainder of the 1930s.[13]

Emboldened by the 1948 election, liberals in Congress pressed for action in early 1949. The leading congressional plan, introduced by Senator Robert Wagner (D-NY), Senator James Murray (D-MT), and Congressman John Dingell (D-MI), was of similar design to President Truman's. By any standard, the scale of the plan was enormous. The plan provided hospitalization, physician services, laboratory services, dental care, and care in nursing homes.[14] It would require a 4 percent payroll tax on the first $3,600 of earnings, double the Social Security payroll tax at that time. Similarly, the proposal's outlays would more than double those of Social Security.

Republicans, knowing that in legislative matters "you can't beat something with nothing," offered an alternative plan to provide federal grants to states for health care services to the poor. The 1949 Republican plan is important because it marks the point in history in which both major political parties embraced a federal role in financing health care services to a significant segment of the U.S. population other than veterans. Democrats favored a federal entitlement-based social insurance approach; Republicans, a grants-to-states program for only the poor. These party differences have remained fundamentally unchanged over time as Congress has periodically considered and debated national health care proposals.

President Truman's proposal produced a short-lived but titanic battle among the nation's large interest groups. National health insurance supporters included the American Federation of Labor and the Congress of Industrial Organizations. Opponents, led by the American Medical Association, included virtually all major health care providers: the American Dental Association, the American Hospital Association, the American Catholic and Protestant hospital associations, Blue Cross–Blue Shield Commissions, and numerous physician specialty groups. Opponents also included the Chamber of Commerce, the American Bar Association, and the American Farm Bureau.

The terms of the debate presaged those of the 1970s and 1990s and are the same as those we hear today. National health insurance advocates began with the premise that health care is a fundamental right to which all citizens are entitled regardless of income. Opponents emphasized that the plan was a threat to individual liberty. Senator John McClellan (D-AR), for example, forcefully declared that "a 'compulsory' health program requires not only submission of the person, but demands surrender of the individual's will to the master authority. It denies freedom of choice in the exercise of the inherent right of a human being to act independently and of his own free will in the all-important matter and duty of preservation of the health and life of himself and that of his family." The issue, according to the senator, is a "test that will determine whether the moral stamina, self-reliance and character of the American people have so deteriorated that they can now be seduced into approving and accepting the socialization of medical science in the vain expectation that it will prove to be a health Utopia."[15]

National health insurance proponents argued that private health insurance markets left too many individuals without adequate health insurance coverage. President Truman made the case by declaring,

Voluntary plans have proved inadequate to meet the need. Most voluntary plans give only very limited protection. While some fifty million people now have some form of health insurance (38 percent of the population), this insurance usually provides only limited protection so far as hospitalization is concerned and in most cases makes no provision at all for other medical services. Only three and one-half million of our people have insurance which provides anything approaching adequate health protection.[16]

Echoing President Truman, Oscar Ewing, the administrator of the Federal Security Administration, declared "that the voluntary insurance plans can never do the job that the national interest requires to be done."[17] After studying the issue, he concluded that "this examination of the facts makes it clear that, at a maximum only about half of the families in the United States can afford even a moderately comprehensive health insurance plan."[18]

National health insurance opponents countered by arguing that individuals' freedom to choose their physician and competition in private health care markets were the keys that had enabled the U.S. medical system to provide the highest-quality medical care in the world. As John Hayes, the president of the American Hospital Association, told Congress, adoption of national health insurance would result in the loss of the "spirit and initiative for progress that have brought American medicine and health services to the forefront of the world today."[19]

Proponents asserted that national health insurance would provide universal health care at a lower cost to society. President Truman declared that his program would provide health insurance coverage to an estimated 85 million individuals and "will save a great deal more than it costs. We are already paying about four per cent of our national income for health care. More and better care can be obtained for this same amount of money under the program I am recommending."[20] The cost reduction would be achieved, according to the proponents, without altering the doctor-patient relationship. Oscar Ewing proclaimed that "the only change . . . is that, instead of the patient paying as the money is available, he would receive a service for which the doctor would be paid by the insurance system at a rate and by a method to which he has agreed."[21]

The AMA's lobbying campaign was unprecedented in its sophistication, scope, and intensity by the standards of the late 1940s. During its nine-month nationwide campaign in 1949, the organization spent $1.2 million financed by a first-time-ever $25 fee assessed on its 140,000 members. Its public relations firm, Whitaker and Baxter, reported that its flyers, radio commercials, and advertisements in national newspapers and magazines had reached over 100 million readers. One commercial asked, "[Do you want to face] . . . a nameless, unknown man on the desk end of a long pill line?" Another warned that the president's plan "would bring a third party—a politician—between you and your Doctor." The AMA's campaign was tailored to particular audiences. Advertisements designed for restaurants and soda fountains read, "There's no Such Thing as a Free Lunch." Those designed for retail drug outlets read, "From pills to penicillin . . . This progress is more than statistics—it's people. And the people we know don't want it tampered with!"[22]

The AMA's campaign turned public opinion against the president's plan. By October 1949, the plan was dead, buried under the avalanche of AMA-financed campaign materials. President Truman continued the fight for his liberal dream throughout his remaining years in office, but his efforts proved futile. Public aversion to government control over health care and strong opposition from large interest groups gave national health insurance no chance.[23]

A year later, Congress enacted a scaled-down version of the congressional Republican plan, a small consolation prize for the president. In the Social Security Amendments of 1950, Congress authorized state governments to use a portion of their federal grants under the Old-Age Assistance and Aid to Dependent Children programs to reimburse health care providers for medical services delivered to recipients of these programs. The compromise legislation was important because it established the first permanent federal entitlement program to finance direct health care services to individuals.

A New Start for Social Security

With the defeat of national health insurance, the outcome of President Truman's proposed expansions of Social Security took on great importance. The Social Security program was still in its infancy in the late 1940s. How the program would evolve in the give-and-take world of congressional and executive branch policymaking remained to be determined. Congress had limited prior experience with large-scale entitlements, and this experience had largely been confined to veterans' programs. The Civil War veterans' pension experience had not been positive, and the experience of World War I veterans' programs had been only marginally better. Elected officials found the temptation to use these programs to improve their political fortunes irresistible and readily acceded to demands by the veterans' lobby for lavish benefits and lax eligibility standards. The demands and temptations caused these well-meaning programs to grow unnecessarily expensive and become rife with fraud and abuse. In contrast, the popular GI Bill, although not entirely free from fraud, nevertheless was regarded as a successful government program. Which experience would apply to Social Security remained to be played out.

As the flagship social insurance program, the success or failure of Social Security would crucially affect the future of liberals' social insurance agenda. State-run old-age assistance programs had grown far more rapidly than Social Security. Between 1937 and 1947, the number of recipients of these programs had increased by 50 percent, and expenditures had registered a fivefold increase.[24] To the consternation of liberals, Old-Age Assistance, not Social Security, had become the dominant vehicle for delivering aid to the elderly. By 1946, it not only assisted twice as many elderly people, the program paid monthly benefits that were twice as high as Social Security's.[25] Unless Social Security was significantly liberalized, it would likely wither away and take social insurance along with it.

In 1948, with his electoral mandate firmly in hand, President Truman proposed that Congress raise Social Security's monthly benefits significantly, relax eligibility standards so that new retirees could qualify immediately for benefits, and expand its coverage to virtually all workers in previously uncovered industries and occupations.[26]

Inflation provided a rationale for a general increase in monthly benefits. The original Social Security law had not included automatic updates in benefits to compensate recipients for increases in the cost of living. In 1935, Congress had not been concerned about inflation, since the U.S. economy had exhibited none, except for a brief four-year period following World War I.[27] But the post–World War II inflation experience had been different. The price level had risen by 70 percent from 1940 to 1949, severely reducing the purchasing power of benefits.

By 1949, there was widespread agreement that wartime and postwar inflation had rendered Social Security benefits "inadequate."[28] Although Congress had never established a standard for measuring the adequacy of benefits, the 1949 benefit levels seemed to be quite low. That year, the typical Social Security retired worker received $26 per month, or $312 per year. Although the federal government had yet to establish an official poverty measure, these Social Security benefits were certainly well below what could reasonably be considered a poverty level. To see this, we can construct a 1949 poverty line by extrapolating the official poverty line back in time and compare the level of Social Security benefits to that poverty threshold. The constructed 1949 poverty line for a single person was $1,153. Thus, the average Social Security benefit provided a typical retired worker with only 27 percent of the money needed to move out of poverty.[29]

Abundant current and projected Social Security revenue surpluses in 1949 provided ample revenues to finance a sizable benefit expansion. Annual surpluses that had emerged during the war continued after the war. By 1950, the Social Security trust fund's accounting balance reached $11.3 billion, an amount that by itself was sufficient to finance nearly a decade of benefits.[30] Social Security trustees projected that the surplus for 1951, the first full year in which any Social Security expansion would be in effect, was more than enough to finance a threefold expansion in Social Security outlays. Moreover, with wage and salary disbursements growing at an annual compound rate of 8 percent and with more than forty workers contributing payroll taxes for each Social Security recipient, the outlook beyond 1951 was even brighter. [31] The trustees projected that the trust fund balance would reach $22 billion by the end of fiscal year 1954, an amount equal to eighteen times that year's projected outgo.[32]

The large Social Security surpluses had generated the usual political pressures for a general benefit increase despite the poor overall condition of the federal budget. The high priority that Congress had assigned to reducing wartime debt had produced disappointing results. In October 1949, the debt had been reduced by only 8 percent from its 1946 peak, and was 84 percent of GDP. The Korean War, which was less than a year away, virtually guaranteed budget deficits for the foreseeable future.

In a rational budget system, Social Security would have been considered one of many federal programs with a competing claim on federal resources. Congress would have weighed the merits of higher expenditures on Social Security benefits against the merits of higher expenditures on other federal programs. It would have weighed the economic costs of higher payroll taxes against the costs of other forms of taxation. It would have considered payroll tax revenue as a potential resource to finance government activities, including the nascent Korean War.

But the state of the overall federal budget mattered little to the Eighty-First Congress, as it had not mattered a century before when Congress considered navy pension legislation. Neither the existing budget deficit, nor the national imperative of reducing the World War II debt, nor the financial needs of the pending Korean War were an issue during congressional debates. In 1950, Congress considered President Truman's proposals as if Social Security were completely separate from the rest of the federal budget.

The House and Senate overwhelmingly approved a modified version of President Truman's Social Security proposals in June 1950. The Social Security Amendments provided a mammoth across-the-board increase in monthly benefits. The law's sliding scale of benefits that averaged 77 percent per recipient provided larger increases to retirees with lower wages and vice versa.[33] The 1950 Act also rewrote Social Security's eligibility rules to enable hundreds of thousands of workers with little history of contributing payroll taxes to begin collecting benefits.

The 77 percent benefit bonanza was the single largest monthly entitlement benefit increase in the twentieth century, and it was timed for maximum electoral advantage. The legislation called for the higher benefits to be included in the October 1950 Social Security checks that were sent to 1.3 million recipients.

The 1950 law's eligibility liberalization allowed previously uncovered workers age 65 and older with as few as eighteen months of employment to start collecting benefits.[34] For as little as $135 in lifetime payroll tax contributions, these new retirees could start collecting $600 per year in Social Security benefits. An estimated 550,000 retired people qualified for the benefit bonanza on July 1, 1951, a 30 percent increase in the number of Social Security recipients.

The 1950 Social Security Amendments extended the payroll tax to an additional 8 million self-employed workers, domestic servants, and regularly employed agriculture workers. Another 2 million state and local government employees and workers in nonprofit firms could voluntarily opt in to Social Security. For every four covered workers in 1950, there were five in 1951. The list of witnesses appearing before Congress in hearings on the amendments demonstrated just how far the reach of the proposed coverage extensions would go. Those testifying included Underwear-Negligee Associates Inc., the New York Candy Club, and the national Handbag and Accessories Association.[35]

Newly covered workers would begin paying payroll taxes on January 1, 1951, and thereby partially finance the higher benefits paid to existing retirees. At the same time, the newly covered workers would be earning entitlement credits toward their own retirement benefits. Taxing newly covered workers and, in return, promising them future benefits based on their contributions, while simultaneously raising current retiree benefits, added to the program's Ponzi-like feature.

Congressional supporters of the coverage expansion argued that uncovered workers were no less deserving of Social Security's umbrella of security than covered workers. President Truman put the argument well by saying, "The protection afforded by old-age and survivors benefits under our existing social insurance program is unfairly and unnecessarily restricted. More than 20 million persons at work in an average week are in jobs where they cannot earn any rights toward these benefits. People in these jobs are in at least as great need of insurance protection as those in [covered] jobs."[36] Using the equally worthy claim to justify a tax mainly on low-wage workers might seem at first blush to be a political nonstarter. But the policy was quite popular. The extraordinary generosity of Social Security at the time explains the apparent anomaly. In 1950, recently retired workers who had worked continuously since 1937 could recover in Social Security benefits all of their and their employer's payroll tax contributions plus a 3 percent annual interest rate earned on those contributions within less than a year of retirement. Moreover, the 1950 amendments promised newly covered 50-year-old workers that they could expect to recover all of their and their employer's payroll tax contributions plus interest within twenty-seven months of retiring.

The 1950 Amendments greatly weakened the already tenuous link between a worker's payroll tax contributions and the monthly retirement benefit. After reviewing the law, Senator Paul Douglas, a staunch New Dealer and one of the 1935 Social Security Act's chief congressional advocates, lamented that the law "virtually abolishes any connection between the total amounts contributed by the insured persons and the total benefits paid to those insured persons."[37]

Despite the weakened link, Congress continued to extol what they saw as the program's virtues of self-reliance and independence. The House Ways and Means Committee's majority bill report to the full House of Representatives illustrates this phenomenon:

> A contributory system, in which both contributions and benefits are directly related to the individual's own productive efforts, prevents insecurity while preserving independence. . . . Because benefits are related to average earnings and hence reflect the standard of living which an individual has achieved, ambition and effort are rewarded. . . . Because benefits under the insurance system are paid as a matter of right . . . , the worker's dignity and independence are preserved.[38]

In reality, the legislation was another significant step to transforming Social Security from a retirement program to one that was financed like other federal programs. After the 1950 law, it is safe to conclude, just as Senator Douglas had concluded, that Social Security was a conventional income transfer program that was dressed up to look like a retirement program. For the remainder of the twentieth century, the myth continued on as one of Social Security's enduring features.

The 1950 Social Security Amendments dramatically increased the program's short- and long-term expenditures. The law increased outlays during the first full year of its impact, 1951, and in 1952 by 130 percent. The $1.2 billion annual increase equaled the entire amount spent by the federal government to assist states with their welfare programs.[39] The higher immediate costs could be financed out of existing and projected surpluses. No significant tax rate increase was required and none was imposed. Although the 1950 law raised the ceiling on taxable wages starting in January 1951, it delayed the previously scheduled tax rate increase that was to take effect on that same date.

Over the long term, the law was projected to roughly double Social Security annual expenditures for the foreseeable future. To finance these costs, the 1950 Amendments specified that the payroll tax rate would increase to 4 percent in 1955, 5 percent in 1959, 6 percent in 1965, and an ultimate rate of 6.5 percent in 1970.[40]

The higher future payroll tax generated a debate in the House about Social Security's intergenerational fairness. Was it fair for Congress to impose high taxes on future generations that it was unwilling to impose on the current generation? During the debate, Congressman John Byrnes (R-WI), who would spend the next two decades in Congress warning of Social Security's future cost, asked his fellow members to consider the fairness of the bill they were about to enact into law:

> Would we vote for this bill today if it carried with it a 6.5 percent payroll tax, which is necessary to pay actually for the benefits going to be granted by it? If we are not willing to do that, if we are not willing to impose that tax, which is necessary to pay for these benefits, on ourselves and the present generation, how can we vote to place it on the next generations? . . . As I said in the beginning, it would be the easiest thing in the world to vote for this bill, because you are giving the beneficiaries who are now on the rolls and who will go on the rolls within the next 20 or 25 years something for nothing; but you are not giving something for nothing to future generations. Those future generations will pay for what you are giving away today for nothing. I just do not

believe it is honest or sound to burden my children or your children on that basis. Remember we give them no voice whatever in what we are committing them to.[41]

Byrnes's plea to consider the interests of future generations fell on deaf ears. No member rose to answer his questions. No member rose to either compliment him or challenge his remarks. There was no round of applause, no round of cheering, as there had been in 1932 when Congressman Lewis Douglas had taken the House floor to deliver his impassioned warning about the future cost of veterans' pensions. Instead, immediately after Congressman Byrnes took his seat, Congressman Robert Hale (R-ME) rose to ask the bill's floor manager for a technically precise definition of a lumber industry employee for the purpose of Social Security coverage. The House of Representatives had quickly moved on to matters they perceived to be of more immediate consequence.

According to official actuarial projections at the time, the schedule of tax rate increases provided payroll tax revenues that would be sufficient to finance Social Security outlays each year until the mid-1980s, thirty-five years into the future. How the deficits would be financed after this point was left unaddressed. Those deficits were too far in the future and subject to too much uncertainty to be of any significant concern to legislators.[42]

The 1950 Amendments reaffirmed Social Security's self-financing policy.[43] Payroll tax revenues would be used exclusively to finance benefits for the foreseeable future. The original Social Security law had established the principle, but actions taken since then had called the policy into question.[44]

The 1950 Social Security Amendments set several important precedents for subsequent Social Security legislation. First, to maximize political gain, benefit increases were enacted or scheduled to take effect during election years. Second, to redistribute income, benefit increases were scaled to provide larger increases for retirees who were receiving lower benefits than for retirees receiving higher benefits. Third, to increase the inflation-adjusted value of benefits for new retirees, benefit increases were larger than the amount necessary to compensate recipients for inflation.

Reaffirming the New Deal Welfare Policy

The federal role in providing welfare assistance had changed little during the war years. Congress continued the New Deal policy in which state and local governments retained responsibility for designing and administering welfare programs and the federal government provided financial assistance.

The Truman administration had conflicting views on federal welfare policy. On one hand, it held that the current welfare system provided inadequate benefits, left too many needy people without assistance, and allowed states too much discretion to treat poor people in similar situations differently. On the other hand administration officials worried that any significant welfare expansion would undercut social insurance's role as the first line of defense against poverty. The conflict caused the Truman administration to propose, and Congress to enact, only modest welfare expansions.

The main thrust of President Truman's welfare proposals was to extend federal matching payments to states for assisting impoverished people who were not covered by existing programs. The additional payments would cover poor disabled people, people in state general assistance programs, and children in financially needy two-parent families. The Truman administration also proposed to broaden the federal Aid to Dependent Children (ADC) program matching payments to include the mother or other caretaker of eligible children. The proposal would raise family benefits by nearly 20 percent for families in which there were four children to nearly 100 percent in one-child families. The objective of the expansion, consistent with the tenor of the times, was to allow single mothers to remain at home to care for their children.

With two notable exceptions, President Truman proposed to continue the New Deal welfare policy of not interfering with state welfare programs. He proposed that state residency requirements be banned and welfare offices be required to provide a fair hearing to all welfare applicants on a timely basis.

Immediately following the war, welfare rolls had increased sharply in the first of three great surges in the welfare rolls that would occur during the twentieth century. From 1945 to 1949, the number of public assistance recipients increased by more than 50 percent. Large caseload increases occurred in all three federal-state welfare programs. But the biggest increase was registered by the ADC program: the number of children on the welfare rolls more than doubled.[45]

The surge accelerated longer-term changes that had been taking place in the ADC program's demographic makeup. In 1934, four out of every five recipients of state mothers' aid programs were the children of widows. By 1948, only one in four were. That year, nearly half of all recipients (45 percent) were children in families in which the father was absent because of divorce or desertion or because the child had been conceived out of wedlock.[46] The program was becoming one that primarily supported children in divorced families and children born out of wedlock.[47]

Large societal changes in the postwar structure of families, compounded by state government welfare program liberalizations, drove the surge. Hasty wartime marriages, lengthy wartime periods of separation between spouses, and high migration rates produced a sharp rise in postwar divorce rates and out-of-wedlock births. By 1948, the U.S. divorce rate was 35 percent higher than its prewar level in 1940; the out-of-wedlock birth rate was 44 percent higher.[48]

These demographic changes came on the heels of program liberalizations that were stimulated in part by higher federal matching rates. The 1939 Social Security Amendments had increased the match rate from 33 to 50 percent. States responded by raising monthly benefits and relaxing eligibility rules.[49]

Accompanying this demographic change was a phenomenon that had disturbing long-term ramifications: the ADC program itself was apparently contributing to the rising number of broken homes and out-of-wedlock births. Welfare's incentives made it too easy for fathers to avoid their parental responsibility and for poor mothers to rely on government aid rather than their own resources to meet their living expenses. Within a decade, the phenomenon would make the ADC program the most controversial welfare program in U.S. history.

The 1950 Social Security Amendments enacted more limited welfare changes than President Truman had sought. Congress rejected extending federal aid to state general assistance programs, providing ADC payments to two-parent families, and banning welfare residency requirements. Congress did allow states to use federal funds to support mothers and other caretakers of eligible children. It also approved a new public assistance program that provided federal matching payments for state programs for impoverished permanently and totally disabled people, a consolation prize for the president who desired a sweeping social insurance–based disability program. Congress also broke new ground by permitting states to use existing federal matching funds to pay medical care services delivered to recipients of public assistance. These provisions mark the federal government's permanent entry in the field of disability and health for people in the general population who were not veterans or government employees.

The law also contained two federal mandates on state governments. To address the growing problems of desertion and illegitimacy, the law required public welfare agencies to notify law enforcement officials whenever an abandoned or deserted child became eligible for ADC. The law also required states to provide a "fair hearing" to any individual whose application was denied or not acted on with "reasonable promptness." Although the Social Security Act was only fifteen years old, the cracks in the New Deal policy of allowing states to run their programs as they saw fit were beginning to show.

Conclusion

The congressional debate over and enactment of the 1950 Social Security Amendments made clear that the forces that had produced the previous liberalizations of veterans' entitlements were operating with equal potency on Social Security. The timing of the across-the-board monthly benefit increase demonstrated that Congress had learned how to use entitlement legislation for political advantage.

Although the forces behind entitlement expansions remained potent, it was still not clear just how far they would drive the size and scope of entitlements. It was also unclear whether federal social insurance or state-run welfare programs would become the primary vehicle for providing direct assistance to individuals other than retirement benefits. Congress had rejected President Truman's proposals for national health insurance and for a Social Security disability insurance program. But in the process, Congress had established a federal role in partially financing state-run health care and disability programs. Although in 1950 Congress had reaffirmed the New Deal's hands-off policy for state welfare and unemployment insurance programs, it was unclear how long this policy would last. The temptation to use federal financing as a lever for exerting federal control over was strong. With the federal government now firmly in the business of partially financing cash welfare, health care, disability, and unemployment benefits, its potential to exert policy control in each of these areas was large.

For the next fifteen years, from 1951 to the beginning of Lyndon Johnson's Great Society, social insurance and welfare programs grew at demonstrably different rates, and their growth involved very different issues. The next two chapters review the development of the two types of assistance programs, beginning with social insurance.

11 Establishing Social Insurance Dominance, 1951–1964

This is an election year and, naturally, in an election year we must, if we can, sweeten up the voters a little bit. So we did increase the benefits a little bit to sweeten up the voters.

Congressman Noah Mason, 1958[1]

THE ENACTMENT OF THE 1950 SOCIAL SECURITY Amendments was a major step toward making Social Security the main government vehicle for providing assistance to the elderly. But the defeat of national health insurance and federal disability insurance and the reaffirmation of the New Deal no-strings-attached federal welfare policy raised a serious question about whether the federal government's entitlement reach would be further extended.

From 1950 to the beginning of Lyndon Johnson's Great Society, Congress answered this question by steadily expanding Social Security so that by the mid-1950s, the program's coverage was nearly universal. By the mid-1960s Social Security had replaced old-age assistance as the first line of defense against old-age poverty.

The liberalizations followed a familiar pattern. Benefits were incrementally expanded, as had nineteenth-century and World War I veterans' entitlements, except at a far faster pace. The increases in benefits were the result of pressures generated by the large Social Security surpluses and without regard to the overall federal budget's often poor condition. In enacting these benefit increases, Congress raised the use of entitlements to gain electoral advantage to a fine art. Five of the six Social Security retirement and disability insurance laws from 1951 to 1964 were enacted during election years, and all but one was enacted with overwhelming bipartisan support. Five of the six laws provided benefits that began one month before a congressional election.

The major new entitlement of the 1950s was the Social Security Disability Insurance program. The new entitlement passed by the thinnest of margins and only as a result of crafty maneuvering by the Senate's majority leader, Lyndon Johnson. Once it was enacted, Congress immediately began expanding the program, and each expansion established a new base on which subsequent liberalizations would be built.

Incremental Expansion

The decade began with two laws that demonstrated that the 1950 amendments had been just a starting point for raising Social Security benefits. In 1952 and 1954, Congress provided current and future retirees with double-digit benefit increases.

Large Social Security surpluses and Congress's focus on the short term played key roles in both benefit hikes, just as they had in prior liberalizations. During the first half of the 1950s, on average, forty-five workers were paying payroll taxes for each retiree. Economy-wide aggregate wages were growing at an extraordinary annual rate of 8 percent. These demographic and economic factors produced exceptionally strong payroll tax revenue growth. Legislated coverage extensions in 1950 and 1954 pushed revenue growth even higher. Although the taxes collected from these newly covered workers would eventually be needed to finance the benefits to which they would be entitled, Congress paid little mind to the future. Under its pay-as-you-go policy, Congress regarded all payroll tax revenues as available to finance immediate benefit increases.

In early 1952, the Social Security trustees projected that revenues for 1952 and 1953 would run at twice each year's expenditures. Official projections made two years later also showed large surpluses. Revenues for 1954 and 1955 would exceed expenditures by at least 50 percent. As had so often happened in the past, the surpluses created political pressure to raise benefits.

Although Congress's public rationale for benefit increases was to compensate recipients for the loss of purchasing power due to rising consumer goods prices, both benefit increases, 12.5 percent and 13 percent, respectively, raised benefits for future retirees by more than necessary to compensate for inflation. This is because Social Security benefits for future retirees are linked to their earnings, which typically increase over time with inflation, in addition to worker productivity.

The timing of both increases followed the vote-buying precedent set in 1950. The 1952 and 1954 benefit hikes were scheduled to take effect in October, one month before the national elections.

Congressional consideration of Social Security legislation in 1958 occurred in an environment that was quite different from earlier times. In early 1958, the Social Security trustees reported that current year outlays were running 5 percent in excess of revenues. The deficit, the first in the program's nearly twenty-year history, were projected to reach $428 million by year's end and $1.1 billion shortfall the following year. The shortfalls, a consequence of the 1957–1958 economic recession, the cumulative impact of liberalizations in the early 1950s, and an unanticipated rush of women claiming early retirement benefits that had been granted in 1956 were projected to continue well into the next decade.[2]

At the same time, Congress was under intense pressure to liberalize the program even more. Precedents had firmly ingrained a need to enact an election year increase in Congress's collective DNA. Over five hundred bills had been introduced in the Eighty-Fifth Congress (1957–1958) to liberalize the program in one way or another. Four years had elapsed since the last benefit increase, and consumer prices had increased by nearly 8 percent during this time. Congressman Noah Mason (R-IL), a critic of an election year increase, stated sarcastically during debate on the benefit hike, "This is an election year, naturally and, in an election year we must, if we can, sweeten up the voters a little bit. So we did increase the benefits a little bit to sweeten up the voters."[3]

The Social Security committees in both houses were adamantly unwilling to allow the deficits to continue. The Senate Finance Committee declared, "A situation where outgo exceeds income for 7 or 8 years is one that should not be permitted to continue. Doing so would only impair public confidence in the system."[4] The House Ways and Means Committee message was nearly identical. The committees declared that deficits would have to be eliminated before a benefit increase would be considered and any benefit increase would be matched by a corresponding increase in payroll taxes. Social Security's pay-as-you-go-policy would be maintained even if it required a tax increase during an economic recession.

But in the end, the legislation the committees sent to the floor did not match their strong words. The election year pressures overwhelmed their fiscally conservative intentions. Congress easily passed the committees' bill to raise benefits by an average 7.5 percent, just enough to compensate current recipients for the loss of purchasing power due to inflation.[5] In contrast to previous increases which were scheduled to occur just before national elections, the effective date was January 1959.

The law also raised both the ceiling on taxable wages and the schedule of payroll tax rates. But these tax hikes were not sufficient to eliminate the program's deficits. A year later, when the books were closed on 1959, the program recorded a $1.7 billion deficit, an amount 50 percent greater than the projected 1959 deficit the year before and before the legislation.[6]

The debate on the House bill produced one notable proposal. Congressman John Byrnes suggested an automatic cost-of-living adjustment (COLA) for Social Security benefits. The adjustment would allow Congress to "avoid the problem which has presented itself during the last 3 election years . . . that no Congress can adjourn before an election without at least making some changes in the Social Security Act."[7] The need to compensate for inflation had made election year Social Security bills "must-pass" legislation, so members felt free to attach other Social Security liberalizations to these bills knowing that few members would dare vote against a bill containing a COLA. The 1958 Social Security Amendments, for example, contained eighteen program liberalizations in addition to the general benefit increase.

A majority of representatives was unwilling to deny itself the ability to vote on election year benefit increases, and Byrnes's proposal died on the House floor. The opportunity to use Social Security benefits to

gain electoral advantage was too great and the cost of the accompanying liberalizations had not become large enough. It would take another
fourteen years, a series of massive election year Social Security benefit
increases, and an astonishing bidding war between leading congressional Democrats and President Nixon before Congress voted to enact an
automatic annual COLA for Social Security.

Social Security's relatively poor financial showing proved to be even
more of a constraining force on Social Security expansions from 1959
to 1964. The coverage expansions that Congress had put in place in
the early 1950s were producing large numbers of retirees who claimed
generous benefits. Outlays for benefits were rising as fast as revenues
from rising wages and growing labor force participation. Each year,
the Social Security trustees reported the program's financial woes to
Congress and that the deficits would most likely continue into the near
future without any changes in taxes. If any future surpluses appeared,
they were likely to be small. Lacking surplus revenues, Congress's major
actions were limited mainly to modestly raising Social Security's initial
benefits in 1960 and, in 1961, allowing men to collect early retirement
benefits at age 62.

The Social Security liberalizations in the 1950s, especially the ad
hoc benefit increases in 1952, 1954, and 1958, further weakened the
link between the benefits an individual received and the taxes the individual paid. These liberalizations were financed by a combination of
existing Social Security surpluses and legislated increases in payroll
taxes. The 1952 benefit increase, for example, was financed entirely
from existing surplus revenue. The 1954 benefit increase was financed
partially by existing surpluses and partially by an increase in the ceiling on taxable wages. The 1958 increase was financed by higher payroll
taxes because no surplus existed. In the two latter instances, the payroll taxes paid by current workers were used to finance higher benefits
for current retirees. In addition, the 1952 and 1958 laws raised benefits
most for recipients at the lower end of the benefit spectrum. Both laws
made the program more of an income redistribution program and less
of an insurance program.

The 1956 law allowing women to claim early retirement benefits at
age 62, though at a reduced monthly rate, provides another example

of the tendency of Congress and executive branch officials to under-state individual responses to the incentives provided by entitlement program liberalizations. Social Security actuaries, who admittedly had little prior data on which to make projections, estimated that within five years, about 700,000 women would elect to take early retirement benefits. Five years later, four times that number—2.8 million women—had availed themselves of the option.[8] Because early retirees received a reduced level of benefits, the long-run cost underestimate may not have been significant. In the short run, however, the large number of early retirees contributed to the trust fund's financial woes during the late 1950s and early 1960s.

Throughout the 1950s, not surprisingly, Social Security enjoyed widespread popularity. In a nationwide 1952 Roper poll that asked whether Social Security was a "good thing" or a "mistake," 90 percent of those surveyed responded that it was a "good thing," only 3 percent thought it was a "mistake," and 7 percent had no opinion.[9]

The program's popularity should not have been surprising given the large monetary returns recipients received relative to their payroll tax contributions. The average male worker retiring in 1952 recovered all of his and his employer's tax contribution plus interest in twelve months, earning him an inflation-adjusted annual rate of return of 19.4 per-cent.[10] Perversely, but quite understandably, the fiscally reckless 1950 benefit bonanza that gave retirees benefits that they had not paid for had served to make Social Security more popular.

Social Security's popularity led to a widespread belief in the nation's capital that it was a program that worked: that the social insurance approach could achieve important socially desirable goals and be polit-ically popular at the same time. This belief was reinforced by support from the capital's leading newspaper, the *Washington Post*. In its edito-rials, the *Post* regularly supported extending Social Security coverage, raising the general level of monthly benefits, and increasing benefits for retirees who continued to work. It opposed any delay in previously scheduled payroll tax increases and lauded the president and Congress when they expanded the program. Only once from 1951 to 1964 did the *Post* editorialize against a Social Security expansion. That was in 1956 when it argued against establishing the early retirement benefit for women on the ground that it was "discrimination in favor of the distaff side."[11]

Social Security's popularity contributed to a change in the position of congressional Republicans from resisting program expansions to supporting them and even proposing limited program extensions. The change had been gradual. The party platforms of 1944 and 1948 had supported the concept of universal Social Security but offered no details as to the program's structure. After World War II, congressional Republicans resisted President Truman's proposed expansions.[12] However, lacking any viable alternative to the president's plan and the votes to block his plan, they ultimately joined with Democrats to support the 1950 Social Security Amendments. Two years later, Republicans offered no resistance to the 1952 benefit increase which Democrats had proposed. The turning point came with the election of Dwight Eisenhower and Republican congressional majorities in 1952. Within a week after taking control of Congress, Republicans signaled that there would be no rollback in Social Security when House Social Security Subcommittee chairman Carl Curtis announced that he had reluctantly concluded that Social Security is "here to stay." Early the following year, President Dwight Eisenhower proposed raising Social Security benefits and making the program virtually universal on the basis of the old "equally worthy" argument, by saying benefits should be extended to "those justly entitled to it but who are now excluded."[13]

A little more than a year later, Congress, with the overwhelming support of Republican majorities that controlled both chambers, passed the 1954 Amendments into law.

Congressional Republican support for the program, however, only went so far. In the coming years, Republicans continued to object to program expansions, such as lowering the age of eligibility for benefits below age 65, and to favor benefit increases that were invariably less than those proposed by Democrats. Thus, they remained on the political defensive as liberal congressional Democrats continued to propose Social Security liberalizations.

Disability Insurance

The 1954 elections returned Democrats to majority control in both houses, a position they would hold for the next twenty-six years. With Social Security now on its way to becoming the nation's principal vehicle for delivering assistance to elderly people, liberals turned to the second prong of their social insurance agenda: creating a disability insurance program. The Social Security Disability Insurance program law was enacted in 1956, but only by the use of special rules in the House of Representatives and by the thinnest of vote margins in the Senate.

Since the turn of the century, progressives and New Deal liberals had sought a disability program that would replace lost earnings. Early efforts in the form of state-run workman's compensation laws, led by the American Alliance for Labor Legislation, were moderately successful. President Roosevelt had considered a national disability program but ultimately did not recommend one to Congress.[14] Following the war, President Truman proposed a disability insurance program modeled on Social Security as part of his effort to complete President Roosevelt's New Deal agenda. The House of Representatives had passed a payroll tax–financed program along the lines of the president's proposal in 1949. But the Senate had refused to go along in the face of strong American Medical Association (AMA) opposition and because of concerns about program costs. The 1950 compromise that provided federal matching grants to state-run welfare programs for the disabled poor disappointed social insurance advocates.

Following passage of the 1950 law, disability insurance advocates within and outside the Federal Security Agency developed a scaled-down strategy for a federal insurance program. The strategy exploited a perceived unfairness in Social Security's existing treatment of the disabled and, along with the 1950 disability program, proved to be important in leading to passage of the federal Social Security Disability Insurance program in 1956.[15]

Under the Social Security retirement program, workers' eligibility for benefits depended on the amount of time they were employed in a covered job. Similarly, the level of their monthly benefits depended on their average monthly earnings. Thus, workers with disabling injuries that kept them out of the workforce for a number of years could, at worst, fail to qualify for retirement benefits or, more often, receive a sharply reduced benefit. Disability advocates argued persuasively that such a penalty was patently unfair. A disabling injury that was no fault of the worker did not make that worker less deserving of Social Security retirement benefits.

Program advocates proposed to correct the unfairness by preserving, or "freezing," the retirement rights of the disabled, in much the same way that private insurance companies often waive a person's premium contributions in times of economic distress.[16] The correction simply excluded the period of time that a worker was disabled from the calculation of Social Security eligibility and benefit levels.

The disability freeze provision had been included in the House version of the 1952 Social Security Amendments, but the Senate had rejected it, setting the stage for a bizarre House-Senate compromise. The compromise authorized a temporary disability freeze that would expire on June 30, 1953, but then stipulated that no applications by disabled people could be accepted until the day after the law expired. What the compromise gave with one hand, it took away with the other.

The 1952 disability freeze compromise contained another provision that proved important for the Social Security Disability Insurance program's enactment four years later. The compromise placed authority for determining a worker's disability status with state disability agencies rather than with the federal government in the event that the disability freeze provisions were ever to become operative.

This part of the compromise was designed to mollify the AMA.[17] The powerful 140,000-member AMA had played an important role in 1950 in blocking President Truman's plan. The organization regarded a federally administered disability program as a vehicle for socialized medicine, or in the colorful words of Social Security scholars Edward Berkowitz and Kim McQuaid, "the Trojan Horse that could let national health insurance within the gates."[18] The AMA believed that since disability determinations necessarily involved medical examinations performed by physicians, a federal program would eventually make physicians employees of the federal government or put physicians under contract to perform medical exams under rules and procedures promulgated by the federal government.[19] The AMA had fewer concerns about its involvement in state-run disability programs. In 1952, its members were already working with state officials to make disability determinations.

The compromise was a foot in the door that could be opened later by merely extending the life of the disability freeze. Two years later, Congress did so with the Eisenhower administration's support by passing the 1954 Social Security Amendments.

By 1955, when the new Democratic-controlled Congress was seated, all of the elements for a politically acceptable, administratively feasible, federal disability program were in place. State agencies had been making disability determinations under their welfare programs for four years and had already begun making determinations under the aegis of the Social Security administration, which was now using these determinations to adjust Social Security benefits for retirees. As long as a new federal disability program relied on state agencies to conduct disability reviews, the AMA's opposition would be minimized.

The House easily passed its disability insurance program as part of a larger Social Security bill in 1955. The House plan was a tax-financed, federally administered program that was structured along the same lines as Social Security. The program was to be financed by raising the Social Security payroll tax 1 percentage point, with proceeds credited to a newly created Social Security Disability Insurance Trust Fund. Benefits would be paid from the fund, and the fund would operate in all respects like the Social Security trust fund.

The argument in favor of its social insurance approach was compelling. Under the existing welfare approach, disabled workers and their families were required to prove that they were economically destitute in order to receive assistance. The social insurance approach gave workers an entitlement to assistance that was based on their individual payroll tax contributions. This right, according to social insurance advocates, preserved the worker's dignity and self-respect. In addition, the fiscal burden of the existing welfare program fell on state governments and local communities. The social insurance approach, by relying on payroll tax contributions to finance benefits, relieved these jurisdictions of these burdens.[20]

In 1956, the Senate Finance Committee failed again to include a disability program in its version of the larger Social Security bill. The committee's arguments against granting entitlement rights to disability recipients were equally compelling: "Lack of objectivity indetermination of disability makes it both easier for the claimant to maintain, and harder for the administration to deny, the presence of qualifying disability. In many instances, physical disability does not necessarily produce economic disability, although this would in many cases be the tendency if monthly benefits were available."[21] According to the committee, the entitlement would also serve as a deterrent to a disabled person's rehabilitation and achieving self-sufficiency. Once on the benefit rolls, a disabled individual would have a diminished incentive to undertake the difficult and demanding rehabilitation necessary to be able to return to work. Furthermore, an entitlement-based disability program would be subject to widespread abuse. In many instances, whether a disabled person is unable to be gainfully employed is a judgment call. Few objective medical standards can be applied to all, or even most, disability cases. There is no bright line that separates disabled people who can be gainfully employed from those who cannot. Under such circumstances, workers with a marginal attachment to the labor force could be expected to magnify the extent of their disabilities to qualify for benefits. Sympathetic physicians would give these applicants the benefit of the doubt in making medical assessments. Sympathetic government employees responsible for making disability determinations would find it difficult to deny benefits in cases of economic hardship.[22] As a result, costs would spiral out of control and ultimately jeopardize the Social Security program.[23] Considering the experience with Civil War disability pensions, the committee's arguments had merit.

For a while, it appeared that the proposed program would suffer the same fate as its predecessors. But when the Social Security bill came to the Senate floor, the venerable Senator Walter George (D-GA), a former Finance Committee chairman, offered an amendment to add the disability insurance program. Senator George's program was drawn along the same lines as the House plan, but with tight eligibility rules that attempted to overcome the Senate Finance Committee's objections. The amendment granted an entitlement of monthly cash only to workers who had sufficient work experience in Social Security–covered employment, who were age 50 and above, and who were *totally* and *permanently* disabled. Workers with temporary disabilities were not eligible for benefits, nor were dependents of disabled workers. The definition of *disabled* was strict. It required workers to prove that they were unable to perform any job in the American economy by reason of a medically determinable physical or mental impairment. As a further guard against abuse, disability recipients were required to wait six months from the disability's onset before receiving benefits.

Senate Finance Committee chairman Harry Byrd (D-WV) warned that Congress would fall prey to the "equally worthy" claim and gradually relax each of the restrictions. He asserted that "cash payments to the totally disabled of 50 years of age and over is merely the entering wedge" and predicted, "As the years go by, . . . it is certain that any disability provision will be greatly liberalized in the future, either by changing the age limit or increasing benefits to dependents, or adopting a program for partial disability."[24] Senator Everett Dirksen (R-IL) echoed Senator Byrd's concerns by saying: "It is not logical to give the benefits to a man 50 years old, without dependents, and deny them to a man 30 or 35 years of age, with dependent children, which a man of 50 would not ordinarily have." The fact that the disability program was projected to run surpluses made it even more likely that the restrictions would not last. Senator Dirksen predicted that when the program's revenues exceeded its expenditures, "then of course it will be very easy to strike 'permanent' [from the disability requirement] and make it 'temporary' and to strike 'total' [from the disability requirement] and make it 'partial.'"[25]

Senator Lyndon Johnson of Texas countered by arguing that private sector workers were no less deserving of disability insurance coverage than members of Congress and federal employees, all of whom already had that coverage.[26] Senator William Knowland (R-CA) responded that to the contrary, these programs showed the difficulty of controlling disability program costs: "The retirements because of physical disability under the railroad retirement system in 1954 represent 36 percent of the retirements due to age" and "for civil service the same number is 40%."[27] Data that were unavailable to Senator Knowland at the time showed that civil service disability claims had more than doubled since 1950 and the Railroad Retirement disability claims had grown by 44 percent.[28]

Under Senator George's amendment, program administration, including especially the job of making disability determinations, was to be performed by state disability agencies, not the Social Security Administration (SSA). The SSA could overrule state approvals of disability claims but not state agency rejections of claimants. According to Senator George, the state disability determination process instituted by the disability freeze legislation was working: "We know that disability determinations are being made successfully every day, not only in connection with the 'disability freeze' provision . . . but also in numerous public programs." To others in Congress, the idea that state agencies would make eligibility determinations for a federally funded entitlement was an invitation to excessive cost. Senator Knowland recognized that states "would have no financial interest in the result" and asserted that "it is not unreasonable to anticipate widespread abuses. . . . If a State is in a position to be relieved of a relief load of possibly an entire family by making a determination of physical disability of the head of that family, is that not an incentive for them to make such a finding if they can do it?"[29]

After a prolonged debate, the Senate passed the George amendment by the narrowest of margins: 47–45. Following the crucial vote, disability program opponents joined supporters and voted to pass the 1956 Social Security Amendments by a unanimous "hoorah!" vote of 90–0.[30]

Senate passage was, in large measure, the handiwork of the Senate majority leader, Lyndon Johnson. When the Senate roll call on the George amendment was taken, two votes recorded in favor raised eyebrows throughout the Senate chamber. One was that of Senator George "Molly" Malone (R-NV). A staunch conservative, Malone was one of the last senators anyone would expect to vote for a national disability insurance program. The other was Senator Earle Clements (D-KY), who, in the midst of a tough reelection fight, had publicly gone on record against the program. The votes of these two men provided the disability insurance program with its razor-thin vote margin.

As Lyndon Johnson's biographer Robert Caro tells the story, the majority leader separately convinced the two senators to switch their crucial votes. Earlier, Senator Malone had been seeking support for legislation that would guarantee that the federal government would purchase $69 million worth of tungsten from Nevada mines. The Eisenhower administration and most Senate Republicans opposed the earmark, but Majority Leader Johnson offered to provide the necessary votes if Senator Malone would agree to support the Social Security Disability Insurance program when it came to the floor.[31] The agreement was a private affair between the two men. Later that month, when Senator Malone received a surprising twenty-eight Democratic votes in support of his tungsten purchase guarantee and the measure passed, Senate observers wondered where the votes had come from. Why had Democrats voted for the earmark? The answer was straightforward: Lyndon Johnson asked them to.

In July, with the disability insurance program standing two votes shy of passing the Senate, the majority leader called on Senator Malone to make good on his side of the bargain. According to columnists Roland Evans and Robert Novak, who were covering the Senate at the time, Senator Malone was desperately trying to avoid pressure from the Republican leadership. He "stayed in the cloakroom, appearing only momentarily to call the 'aye' vote for the disability amendment, then fairly ran out of the Chamber—disappearing . . . before Knowland [the Senate Republican minority leader] could get a crack at him."[32]

Needing one more vote to pass the disability insurance program, majority leader Johnson turned to Senator Earle Clements, who was facing a strong Republican challenger in the fall elections. Senator Clements had publicly announced that he would vote against disability insurance. A reversal of this position would put his reelection in serious jeopardy. Senator offered Senator Clements a simple deal: The majority leader would provide him with large sums of cash to support his reelection campaign if Mr. Clements would promise to vote for the disability insurance program. Senator Clements could initially vote against the George amendment, but if his vote was ultimately needed to pass the amendment, he must agree to change his vote. The senator accepted the deal.

On the day of the vote, the story, as related by Senate aide Bobby Baker to Robert Caro, is as follows: "As the roll call proceeded on the

Senate floor, Johnson ordered Clements to stay close at hand. The bald old pro 'was seated right next to Johnson and heat was coming off his head,' Bobby Baker recalled. 'He was down there, just hoping and praying' that his vote would not be needed. But it was. Johnson told him to change it and he changed it, and, as Baker said, 'We won by Clements' vote.'"[33]

Senator Clements's vote ensured Senate passage of the disability insurance program, but it ended his career. Despite Lyndon Johnson's financial help, which, according to Johnson campaign aide Booth Mooney, included a "suitcase just stuffed with currency," Earle Clements lost his Senate seat.[34] The vote that may have cost Mr. Clements his Senate career had given the nation a new disability insurance entitlement.

Because of the tight restrictions, the Social Security administration's actuaries projected that the program's outlays would be well below its projected revenues for the foreseeable future, and that proved accurate initially. The Social Security Disability Insurance trust fund immediately experienced large annual surpluses. In June 1958, the trust fund reached $1 billion against annual outlays under $200 million. That year, the Social Security trustees reported that absent any legislative change in taxes or benefits, large annual surpluses would continue for the foreseeable future.

But the warnings by Senators Byrd, Dirksen, and others also proved prescient. Congress responded to the surpluses in 1958 by expanding benefits to dependents of disabled workers and by making disability benefits retroactive to one year from the onset of a disability.[35] These provisions became effective in October 1958, one month before the midterm congressional elections.

Congress repeated this behavior two years later. In early 1960, the Social Security trustees reported that the disability insurance trust fund balance had reached $2 billion, nearly four times the upcoming year's projected outlays. Over the next four years, annual disability payroll tax revenues would exceed annual expenditures by 80 percent. In response, Congress passed the 1960 amendments that removed the requirement that a disabled worker be at least 50 years of age. The liberalization granted an entitlement to all but very young adult workers.

These liberalizations helped disability expenditures to grow at an astounding 25 percent annual rate from the program's first full year in operation in 1958 to 1965. In 1965, disability expenditures were three times larger than the projection the Social Security trustees made when the law was enacted in 1956.

The 1958 and 1960 disability program liberalizations stand in sharp contrast to the restrained increases in retirement program benefits and eligibility rules that were enacted in the same legislative bills. The contrast highlights the importance of the availability of surplus funds.

12 The Beginning of the Great Turn in Welfare Policy, 1951–1964

Public welfare, in short, must be more than a salvage operation, picking up the debris from the wreckage of human lives. Its emphasis must be directed increasingly toward prevention and rehabilitation.[1]
President John F. Kennedy, February 1962

A N UNEASY POLITICAL EQUILIBRIUM ON FEDERAL welfare policy existed throughout the 1950s. Both Presidents Truman and Eisenhower resisted major welfare expansions, the former because they undermined efforts to make social insurance the primary means of providing assistance to individuals and the latter because they would "weaken the sense of state and local responsibility."[2] In Congress northern liberal Democrats continued to favor expanding the federal welfare role. While the alliance between southern Democrats and Republicans supported greater federal funding, it opposed federally prescribed benefit levels and eligibility rules. The result was a relatively quiet decade for federal welfare legislation.

Legislation during the 1950s was limited primarily to increasing the federal financing role. From 1951 to 1959, Congress passed five legislative acts, each of which modestly increased federal matching rates for existing welfare programs.[3] Not one of these acts contained a welfare system contraction of any consequence.

The liberal forces for a larger federal welfare presence gained momentum in the early 1960s. Congress enacted the Kerr-Mills program in 1960 to provide medical care to poor elderly people; it curbed state Aid to Families with Dependent Children (AFDC) restrictive eligibility policies in 1962; it created the food stamp program in 1964; and it launched the federal War on Poverty the same year.

The years 1951 to 1964 witnessed the appearance of major fissures in the New Deal's two-bedrock welfare policy principles: state autonomy and cash assistance. State and local governments responded to rapidly rising welfare rolls, particularly among children of never-married women and divorced mothers by curtailing welfare eligibility. These actions, particularly those taken by southern state governments with a history of discriminatory treatment of African Americans, led federal welfare officials to take preventive measures. Using federal matching funds as a lever, welfare officials threatened states that continued to employ so-called moral codes as a condition of welfare eligibility. As tensions between the two levels of government mounted, Congress stepped in with legislation to strengthen federal authority. By the mid-1960s, the bedrock principle of state autonomy had been greatly eroded.

At the same time, federal and state welfare officials began to question the wisdom of further cash assistance to the poor. Concerned that this assistance encouraged recipients to act in ways that were detrimental to their own long-term interests, federal policymakers turned to providing in-kind benefits in lieu of cash. Under a new paternalistic approach, Congress authorized new welfare entitlement programs that provided nutrition assistance, medical care for the elderly, rehabilitation services, and other social welfare services. The Economic Opportunity Act, enacted at the very end of this period, created a host of additional nonentitlement services programs. These laws marked the beginning of a major turn away from the New Deal's cash assistance principle and toward providing in-kind benefits.

Rising Tensions between Federal and State Governments

While the New Deal welfare policy held in Congress during the 1950s, tensions over the policy steadily mounted between state governments and federal welfare officials. The focal point was the extent of legal rights that states granted to AFDC program recipients.

At issue were policies that referred to a "suitable home" and "substitute parent." The objective of these policies was to protect the child's well-being and the taxpayers' interests. The implementing laws focused primarily on the mother's moral character. Most commonly, these laws prohibited a single mother from living in a nonmarital union or cohabiting with another adult. The laws denied eligibility if the unmarried mother was found to have a male adult living in the home or if a man frequently visited the home for the purpose of having sexual relations with her. An Oregon law, for example, used the catchy phrase "Roger the Lodger" to define an unmarried adult living in a household who was expected to contribute to the child's financial support.[4] Other state laws stated simply that the home environment should promote "good character."[5]

These policies had been central features of state pension programs for mothers since the first mother's aid program was enacted by Illinois in 1911. At the time of Social Security's enactment, most aid programs contained "suitable home" or "substitute parent" policies.[6] The widespread acceptance of these policies is reflected by the 1935 American Public Welfare Association's guidelines for model state mother's aid laws, which recommended that state laws include the following language: "Assistance shall be given under this Act to any dependent child . . . who is living in a suitable family home meeting the standards of care and health, fixed by the laws of this state. . . . The maintenance of a proper home environment for dependent children is vital to the success of any child welfare program."[7]

The consistency of the policies with the Social Security Act's objectives was assured by the Federal Security Agency in 1940. In a letter to states, the agency wrote: "Many state plans for aid to dependent children require that the state agency shall determine that conditions in the home . . . will protect the interest and promote the welfare of the dependent child. Such a provision is in keeping with the purposes of the federal act."[8]

Following World War II, as the welfare rolls became increasingly dominated by desertion and illegitimacy claims, states began to more rigorously enforce their existing suitable home and substitute parent laws, and states lacking such laws began enacting them. During the 1950s, nine additional states enacted such laws. Nineteen states attempted to adopt specific policies to deny or restrict aid to families in which the mother had an additional illegitimate child while she was receiving welfare.[9] A New Jersey grand jury investigating the AFDC program during the 1950s explained the rationale for its policies in this way: "There is no . . . logic, justice, or morality . . . in granting State Welfare funds to a mother who has had two, three, four or even five illegitimate children fathered by two or three different [men]. Immorality, promiscuity, and unwed motherhood seem to be rewarded and encouraged by the easy allowance made upon a simple application of need."[10]

These state actions caused federal welfare officials to change their views. Federal officials came to believe that suitable home provisions did not serve a child's best interest. Nonmarital unions may not provide an ideal environment for a child, they argued, but when all factors are considered, the environment might be entirely suitable for ensuring the child's health and welfare.[11] This view went even further. Since the conditions that might make a home unsuitable were often caused by a lack of financial resources, denying welfare aid would only cause the home to become less suitable for a child's proper upbringing. Moreover, in federal officials' self-described "modern" view, a child's eligibility should not depend on the parent's behavior. A policy that did so effectively punished the child for the sins of the parent.

Federal officials also opposed suitable home and substitute parent policies because the policies lacked objectivity and uniformity. Caseworkers could make rulings based on their judgments about the physical condition of the child's home or their assessments of the parent's character gleaned from periodic, and often unannounced, home visits. This broad latitude gave rise to a degree of arbitrariness in eligibility determinations that federal officials deemed unacceptable. Federal officials were particularly concerned about the application of these policies in the South. The relatively high prevalence of poverty, nonmarital unions, and out-of-wedlock births among African Americans made them particularly subject to the arbitrary application of these policies. In southern states, which did not allow black children to attend the same schools as white children and did not allow blacks to eat at the same lunch counters or drink at the same water fountains as whites, federal officials rightfully feared that these regulations were a powerful instrument of discrimination and control. Their concern was widely shared, especially after the publication of Gunnar Myrdal's *The American Dilemma: The Negro Problem and Modern Democracy*, a monumental 1944 study of race relations in the United States. Addressing southern welfare practices, Myrdal wrote that suitable home regulations "may easily lend themselves to rather arbitrary interpretations whereby . . . many Negro families can be cut off from any chance of receiving this kind of assistance."[12]

The Federal Security Agency's (FSA) solution to arbitrary state welfare eligibility rules, regardless of whether the rules were racially motivated, was to provide welfare as a matter of right rather than as a gratuity. In 1946, FSA formally advised all state governors that state laws could "be further strengthened by a provision to the effect that assistance is to be provided as a matter of right to eligible persons."[13] Although the Social Security Act clearly prohibited federal officials from imposing their policy preferences on the states, federal officials nevertheless frequently attempted to do so. Efforts to dissuade states from adopting policies that denied aid to families in which mothers gave birth to an illegitimate child while already on the welfare rolls were largely successful. But efforts to prevent states from adopting "substitute parent" policies proved less effective.[14]

The disagreements between federal and state authorities over "suitable homes" and "substitute parent" laws for the most part took place out of the public eye. All this changed in 1960 when actions taken by Louisiana and later Newburgh, New York, precipitated a federal-state welfare crisis and led to a Supreme Court decision striking down state suitable home provisions nearly a decade later in *King v. Smith* (1968).

In spring 1960, Louisiana enacted a suitable home law that denied AFDC benefits to an entire family if its unmarried mother gave birth to an illegitimate child while the family was receiving AFDC benefits. Under the Louisiana law, the second illegitimate child was evidence that the home was not suitable. Families could appeal their terminations and benefits would be reinstated if the mother could demonstrate that she was not engaged in a continuing illicit relationship and that the home was suitable.[15] Louisiana moved aggressively to implement its law and applied the law retroactively. Welfare officials sent letters to 5,991 families, containing 22,501 children, notifying them that their benefits would be terminated in August. Ninety-five percent of these families were African Americans.

The Social Security Administration declared that the state's actions were not in conformity with the Social Security Act. Federal officials demanded that Louisiana officials appear in Washington, D.C. to explain their actions and threatened to cut off federal matching funds. The state countered that the agency "has never issued a bulletin, has never issued a regulation, has never published a rule, has never ordered us or any of the states by a directive to the effect that a suitable home provision was not valid."[16] In its response, the Social Security Administration reluctantly admitted that there was little it could legally do to prevent Louisiana from implementing its suitable home policy.

But the battle was far from over. Six months later, three days before John F. Kennedy's inauguration, President Eisenhower's outgoing secretary of health, education, and welfare, Arthur Flemming, ordered the Social Security Administration to take action. The agency then issued a regulation stipulating that states could remove families from the rolls only if the state made other arrangements for the affected children's care. If Louisiana did not comply with the new regulation, the federal government would withhold its share of AFDC matching funds, resulting in the removal of an estimated sixty-five thousand children from the welfare rolls.[17]

The Louisiana incident threatened to ignite a nationwide crisis. At the time, twenty-three states had suitable home policies in effect, and many of them had no provision for supporting alternative living arrangements for children who were removed from the AFDC rolls.[18] A previously enacted Mississippi law raised the stakes considerably. Wary of federal sanctions for its suitable home policy, the state had enacted a law that rescinded the state AFDC appropriation if federal funds were withheld from the state.[19] The rescission would immediately terminate benefit payments to all of the state's AFDC children.

Louisiana's harsh action, occurring at a time when the country was awakening to the extent of discrimination against black Americans, especially in the South, was roundly criticized in the national press. In the court of public opinion, the action was indefensible. However, in the court of law, the Flemming rule was illegal. The Social Security Act unambiguously obligated the federal government to make federal matching payments. Moreover, since the Eisenhower administration was due to leave office three days later, Secretary Flemming was in no position to enforce his regulation. The issue was left for President Kennedy and the Seventy-Eighth Congress to address.

In May 1961, Congress passed and President Kennedy signed into law a provision that postponed implementation of the Flemming rule for fourteen months, an amount of time sufficient for all states to bring their laws into compliance with the regulation. The next year, Congress wrote the Flemming rule into the federal statute books. The 1962 Public Welfare Amendments stipulated that states could discontinue AFDC benefits under a suitable home provision only "if a state provides other adequate care and assistance with respect to the child."[20]

A year later, a similar incident occurred when the city of Newburgh, New York, attempted to address its rising welfare problem. Coming on the heels of the Louisiana incident, the Newburgh controversy made welfare a national issue.

Newburgh, located on the banks of the Hudson River just beyond the New York City suburbs, had a population of thirty-one thousand in 1960. During the war years, the city had thrived as its naval shipyards and textile mills employed tens of thousands of workers. But after the war, as shipbuilding slumped and textile mills moved south, Newburgh suffered through a prolonged period of industrial and economic decline. Throughout the 1950s, its population and per capita income fell steadily. By 1960, its median income was well below the state median.[21]

During the 1950s, Newburgh's fruit and berry farms had attracted large numbers of migrant workers, most of them southern blacks. Initially the workers arrived during harvest season and then returned to the South once the crop had been picked. By the late 1950s, however, large numbers of migrant families had begun to stay in Newburgh. The dearth of year-round employment opportunities and a federally mandated state law that outlawed local welfare residency requirements put Newburgh at the mercy of the large economic and migration trends that were taking place throughout the nation. The city's welfare budget soared. By the early 1960s, Newburgh was spending more on welfare than it was on police and nearly as much as it was on fire protection.

When Orange County, within which Newburgh was located, refused to provide financial support, the financially distressed Newburgh took action. In June 1960, the Newburgh city council approved a thirteen-point plan designed to curb perceived excesses in its public welfare programs. Key elements included providing vouchers for food, clothing, and rent in lieu of cash assistance; requiring that recipient families maintain suitable homes and, if not, placing the families' children in foster homes; limiting AFDC benefits to three months within any twelve-month period; and requiring recent migrants to have a concrete job offer before receiving temporary assistance. The welfare reform applied to all public assistance recipients, but the town council's concern was mainly with the AFDC population. A stark warning accompanied the plan: "All mothers of illegitimate children are to be advised that should they have any more children out of wedlock they shall be denied relief."[22]

Many, if not most, northern and western cities were experiencing similarly rising welfare burdens, so news of Newburgh's welfare plan spread quickly. During July and August, newspaper coverage was extensive. Television documentaries appeared on NBC and CBS, and editorials were written in the conservative *National Review* magazine and liberal *Nation* magazine.[23] Senator Barry Goldwater (R-AZ), who became the Republican presidential nominee in 1964, publicly supported the Newburgh plan as a model for all cities.[24]

A Gallup poll found that a large majority of Americans supported the Newburgh plan, as did five of New York City's seven newspapers.[25]

Most Americans recognized that local governments bore a responsibility to assist people who were unable to help themselves, but they were troubled by rising welfare rolls, especially because the rolls were increasingly dominated by families with able-bodied adults, those that had been deserted by the father, and those with children born out of wedlock.

Social welfare professionals, state and federal government officials, and leading liberals, however, decried the plan as callous and unnecessarily harsh. The *New York Times* lambasted Newburgh as "a city where mercy took a beating." The newspaper lamented the prevailing public opinion in favor of the Newburgh plan by writing, "The voice of man's inhumanity to man is loud in the land applauding Newburgh."[26]

The New York State Welfare Agency declared parts of the plan to be in violation of federal and state laws and took the city to court. When in December 1960, the New York State Supreme Court enjoined the city from putting the plan's main elements into effect, the issue, as far as Newburgh was concerned, was over. Commenting on the court's position, the *Wall Street Journal* moaned, "It's a fine commentary on public morality in this country when a local community's effort to correct flagrant welfare abuses is declared illegal."[27]

The Louisiana and Newburgh stories were the most visible parts of a growing cloud of concern and controversy enveloping public assistance programs. Nationally, welfare costs were 60 percent higher in 1960 than in 1950. Aid to the Blind had increased 77 percent, and AFDC had risen 91 percent over the same period of time. Aid to the Permanently and Totally Disabled, which had not been enacted until late in 1950, had grown 84 percent in the previous five years. Old-Age Assistance had increased 29 percent. Caseload increases were equally concerning. In the prior five years, AFDC was up 37 percent, Aid to the Disabled was up 53 percent, and Aid to the Blind was up 10 percent. Only Old-Age Assistance registered a caseload decline of a modest 9 percent. Rising wages and employment seemed to have had little impact on welfare costs and caseloads. If economic growth couldn't slow the growth in the welfare rolls, what could?

The changing composition of the AFDC caseload was perhaps even more cause for concern. By 1961, only 8 percent of AFDC families were on the rolls because the mother was widowed, down from 25 percent in 1948. In contrast, one-third of all recipient families were on the rolls because the father was absent due to divorce, separation, or desertion. Another one-in-five recipient families were on the rolls because a child was born out of wedlock. Also, more mothers who were already on welfare were having additional children out of wedlock. Over half of all recipient families had three or more children, and 18 percent had five or more.[28] The program, which was originally designed to support widows and their children, had continued to evolve into a program that supported illegitimacy and desertion. The AFDC program also appeared to be becoming a permanent way of life instead of a temporary helping hand. In 1961, 40 percent of all recipient families had been on the rolls for three or more years, and nearly half (48 percent) for four years or more.[29]

The welfare system was front-page news in most big city newspapers. The press regularly reported on the large caseloads and costs.[30] The stories often singled out the AFDC program and, to a lesser extent, the Aid to the Permanently and Totally Disabled program, as the principal source of the system's rising costs. A *Los Angeles Times* story highlighted the "all-time local champion" of welfare. The woman had been the recipient of $50,000 in public aid over thirty-four years on welfare (over $400,000 in today's dollars). She had given birth to twenty-two children fathered by seven different men, none of whom had ever been married to her.[31]

Although welfare fraud and abuse attracted considerable press attention, the rising welfare caseloads were, in large measure, a consequence of major demographic trends. National divorce rates and out-of-wedlock births had continued to rise throughout the 1950s, producing a continuing rise in the number of AFDC-eligible families. In addition, the epic migration of African Americans from the rural South to northern cities had gathered momentum in the 1950s. This great movement of people, one of the largest migrations in U.S. history, provided industrial jobs for many migrants. But others who were unable to find work found themselves living in large poverty-ridden ghettos in the urban industrial centers of the North. For many of them, welfare became a necessary means of support.

Regardless of the causes of the welfare system's growth, the New Dealers' predictions that the welfare rolls would wither away as social insurance programs matured had proven dead wrong. In 1939, Social Security had added benefits for widows and survivors to alleviate, in part, the burden they imposed on state-run mothers' aid programs. Yet the number of families receiving AFDC had quadrupled since then. Social Security Disability Insurance benefits had been added in 1956. Yet four years later, 200,000 more people were receiving public assistance disability benefits than in 1956. By 1960, the number of elderly people receiving Social Security benefits had grown to more than 10 million. Yet nearly 600,000 more elderly people were receiving old-age welfare benefits in 1960 than at the depths of the 1937–1938 economic recession. Reflecting on the public assistance program growth, Alabama senator Lister Hill, who had been in the House of Representatives when the Social Security law was enacted, remarked in 1962, "I remember when we passed the act in 1935 the thinking was that the public assistance grants were being only for more or less of a temporary period, that soon everybody would be under OASI [Old-Age and Survivors Insurance] and you would not have any need for public assistance grants."[32]

By the early 1960s, it was clear to all that the federal-state welfare system was malfunctioning. The widespread publicity given to its shortcomings had imprinted the system's failures on American public conscious. At the same time, books by Michael Harrington and others had made intellectuals and policymakers aware of the desperate conditions of those in poverty.[33] The status quo, it seemed, could no longer be maintained. A new approach was needed.

The Kennedy Years: A New Services Approach

President John F. Kennedy promised a fresh approach. His new policy, delivered in the first presidential message to Congress ever exclusively devoted to welfare, placed a priority on preventing welfare dependency by helping welfare recipients become self-sufficient. In the president's words, "Public welfare, in short, must be more than a salvage operation, picking up the debris from the wreckage of human lives. Its emphasis must be directed increasingly toward prevention and rehabilitation."[34]

The new approach proposed federal matching funds for state and local government welfare services. The new services approach was designed to prevent potential welfare recipients from becoming dependent on welfare and to rehabilitate existing recipients to a self-sufficient life. The proposed new services included family planning and financial counseling, remedial education, vocational education, job training, work experience, and day care assistance. These services would be provided by professional social workers who would be educated and trained, also with the assistance of federal funds.

The Kennedy administration's "hand up, not a handout" policy was warmly embraced by congressional Democrats and Republicans. The policy was incorporated on a bipartisan basis into the Public Welfare Amendments of 1962.[35] The law's central feature was to provide state governments with an entitlement to receive federal reimbursement for 75 percent of the costs of providing a broad array of ill-defined social welfare and psychosocial services. The law's open-ended language provided federal reimbursement for "services to maintain and strengthen family life for children, and to help . . . [adults] . . . with whom children . . . are living to attain or retain capability for self-support or self-care."[36] In committee reports on the bill, Congress anticipated that the services would "usually be provided by trained social workers, or by workers employed under the direction of social workers."[37] To ensure a sufficient number of professional social welfare workers, the law also authorized additional federal funding for their training.

Thus, the law's big winner was the social welfare profession. Three-fourths of the salaries and expenses associated with their work would now be federally financed. This higher match rate stood out in contrast to the 50–60 federal match rate paid on cash benefit payments to poor welfare families.

The law signaled a significant change in welfare policy away from providing cash assistance. A related provision in the 1962 law, one that would have important ramifications four years later, allowed state welfare agencies to provide welfare benefits in the form of vouchers that could be used to purchase clothing or make monthly rental and utility payments.[38]

The 1962 law also took action to address the problems of desertion and illegitimacy that plagued the AFDC program. President Kennedy had long recognized that AFDC, by limiting aid to single mothers, created a financial incentive for men to desert their children and for mothers to remain unmarried. His proposed solution, now a customary one for entitlement programs, was to expand federal welfare assistance, this time to two-parent households. Congress concurred by establishing a three-year program of federal matching funds for state welfare programs for two-parent families if one parent was unemployed.

Kennedy administration officials expressed complete confidence that the new services approach would prove highly successful. The assurance that Health, Education, and Welfare Secretary Abraham Ribicoff gave to the House Ways and Means Committee typified the conviction of administration officials: "These efforts, we know from experience will pay."[39] This confidence was echoed by public welfare officials and social welfare experts inside and outside government who asserted that only a lack of trained welfare personnel stood in the way of the success of the new approach. Administration officials argued that although prevention and rehabilitation services would be costly in the short run, the new approach would have a long-run payoff by increasing self-sufficiency among welfare recipients and therefore lowering welfare costs. The New York Times wrote, "The initial cost will actually be higher than the mere continuation of handouts. The dividends will come in the restoration of individual dignity and in the long-term reduction of the need for government help."[40]

The administration's confident predictions and the support it received from social welfare experts created a high expectation that the new approach would work. As would often occur in the 1960s, the reliance placed on the perceived wisdom of experts, the conclusions of so-called scientific studies, and outcomes of government-funded demonstration projects were misplaced. There was, in fact, precious little evidence to support the contention that social welfare services would prevent welfare dependency or help existing recipients achieve self-sufficiency. The 12 percent rise in the AFDC program's caseload over the next two years should have been enough to dispel the idea that a comprehensive service approach would not work. But as subsequent events show, it wasn't.

The First Phase of the War on Poverty

In the wake of President Kennedy's assassination, Lyndon Johnson enlarged Kennedy's incremental approach to an all-out war to combat poverty. Standing before Congress just six weeks after the assassination, President Johnson launched his antipoverty program by declaring: "This administration today, here and now, declares unconditional war on poverty in America."[41] Johnson's War on Poverty would be a Texas-style war: bigger, bolder, and more comprehensive than anything the federal government had previously contemplated.

The war would be fought on two fronts to attack the root causes of poverty. One front would consist of a host of new federal programs and services in addition to those established under the Kennedy administration to help the poor become self-sufficient. New programs included higher-quality preschool and adult education, a new work-study program for college students, an additional array of community services, enhanced youth employment and job training services, and a domestic Peace Corps to train young volunteers to support local community antipoverty efforts. A novel feature of the president's approach was that the poor themselves would be actively involved in designing many of the new local programs.

The second front would consist of creating new federal programs and expanding existing ones to address malnutrition, poor housing, and ill health among the poor. A food stamp program, only a pilot program at the time, would be given legislative authority. Decades-old housing programs would be given new life. A new Medicaid program would provide health care. The creation of these new programs reflected President Johnson's view—and the views of the Economic Opportunity Act's congressional supporters at the time—that cash welfare assistance was not an answer to the nation's poverty problem. These and other new in-kind welfare programs would grow to eventually provide safety-net assistance on a scale that New Deal and Fair Deal architects could only have imagined. It also would create an elephantine network of service provider lobbying groups that no one could have imagined.

The First Front: The Economic Opportunity Act

In July 1964, Congress passed the centerpiece of President Johnson's War on Poverty: the Economic Opportunity Act (EOA). The statute faithfully incorporated the president's vision by stating in its preamble the goal of eliminating "the paradox of poverty in the midst of plenty" by "opening to everyone the opportunity for education and training, the opportunity to work, and the opportunity to live in decency and dignity."[42] To achieve these ends, the EOA authorized new youth employment programs, loans and grants for small family farms, employment and housing assistance for migrant workers, small business loans for low-income people, community work and training programs for welfare recipients, grants for preschool education and adult education, and grants for volunteers to help provide services to the poor in underserved communities.

Notably, the EOA did not authorize any new entitlement programs or expand existing New Deal welfare entitlements. Instead, it created several new programs that were annually funded with discretionary appropriations. The landmark law's centerpiece, and ultimately a major source of its undoing, was Title II, which authorized federal grants for community action programs "to provide stimulation and incentive for urban and rural communities to mobilize their resources to combat poverty."[43] The law did not spell out precisely how community action funds were to be used, but it did require grant recipients to include poor people in the community as active participants in developing and implementing solutions to poverty. The law's "maximum feasible participation" requirement was designed "to see to it that the poor do have a say in the planning and operation of welfare programs."[44]

The EOA, like the Public Welfare Amendments of 1962, was enacted with confident promises that the new approach would bring about an end to the seemingly endless growth in the welfare rolls. Upon signing the EOA into law, President Johnson famously declared, "We are not content to accept the endless growth of relief rolls or welfare rolls. We want to offer the forgotten fifth of our people opportunity and not doles. . . . The days of the dole in our country are numbered."[45]

Title II's premise that poverty was best combated by local community efforts was an entirely reasonable one. The federal government was too remote from the problems of poor communities to be able to provide effective solutions. But Title II's assertion that local government bureaucracies were obstacles to effective poverty solutions was dubious. The proposition that community-based organizations, often consisting of impoverished individuals, could solve America's poverty problem proved to be an unattainable utopian dream.

Two years following the EOA's enactment, the AFDC rolls and its costs were soaring faster than at any other time in U.S. history; community organizers were using federal funds to organize welfare mothers to march on welfare offices across the country demanding higher benefits; and legal service lawyers were using federal funds to bring lawsuits against all levels of government, including the federal government, challenging welfare regulations. Ironically, the EOA, which contained no welfare entitlement expansions, fueled an extraordinary surge in welfare rolls.

The rapidly rising welfare rolls brought American welfare policy to the beginning of an important turning point in the early 1960s. The New Deal consensus that had prevailed over the federal and state government roles in welfare policy and financing was breaking down. The era of state autonomy in setting welfare policies was coming to an end, and an era of active federal intervention in welfare polices was just starting. At the same time, both state and federal welfare officials had begun to develop serious doubts about the wisdom of providing additional cash assistance to welfare recipients, another hallmark of the New Deal welfare policy. The national provision of nutrition assistance and health care services were not far behind.

The Opening of the Second Front: Food Stamps
in Lieu of Additional Cash Assistance

Throughout the 1950s, liberal Democrats had repeatedly pressed for a food stamp program. Such a program had operated for a few years during the late 1930s and early 1940s but was disbanded during World War II.[46] The Democratic Party platforms of 1956 and 1960 called for the establishment of a federal food stamp program, and congressional liberals had regularly introduced food stamp bills in Congress. Opposition by the Eisenhower administration, southern Democrats, and

Republicans in Congress had caused food stamp bills to be rejected in 1957 and 1958. In 1961, President Kennedy went around Congress by establishing a pilot food stamp program by executive order.

In August 1964, one month after passing the EOA, Congress gave legislative authority to the food stamp program. The Food Stamp Act of 1964 overcame the opposition of southern Democrats and a few rural Republicans in what has become a classic case of legislative logrolling.

The logroll tied food stamp and farm price supports together in a single legislative package. Urban members of the House Agriculture Committee, led by Representative Leonor Sullivan (D-MO), refused to vote for extending wheat and cotton price supports until the rural farm members voted for food stamps. After considerable delays, committee members reached an arrangement in which rural members voted to authorize the food stamp program and, in return, urban members voted for price support payments.[47]

The food stamp program's enactment reflected a growing unease within the executive and legislative branches about the wisdom of additional cash welfare assistance. Both the Kennedy and Johnson administrations favored food stamps over cash assistance on the paternalistic ground that recipients couldn't be trusted to spend cash assistance wisely. The paternalistic sentiment behind the food stamp program was expressed by Secretary of Agriculture Orville Freeman, the Kennedy administration's leading food stamp advocate. Speaking about senior citizens, Secretary Freeman declared, "When they give them the money, they do not use it for food. They go out and play bingo with it."[48] With only a slight modification, the secretary's comment could have just as well applied to other welfare recipients.

Under the 1964 law, eligible individuals were allowed to purchase a monthly allotment of food stamps. The amount a family was required to pay rose with the family's income. The difference between the amount the family was required to pay, the "purchase requirement," and the value of the monthly allotment, termed the "bonus value," was a subsidy to the family. The stamps could be used only to buy food items at grocery stores. Purchases of alcohol and tobacco products with food stamps were prohibited. Grocery stores could redeem the stamps for cash. The theory behind this arrangement was that the purchase requirement would obligate a recipient family to its normal expenditure on food. The goal of the subsidy was to enable the family to consume a nutritionally adequate diet.

The 1964 food stamp program gave considerable deference to the states' role in welfare. As a result, the program operated only at a state's request and only in areas where the state government gave permission. But states could not operate both a food stamp program and a commodity distribution program in the same area. They had to choose between the two. States set eligibility standards that in general were similar to those used for their public assistance programs. Some states also extended eligibility to other low-income individuals and families. The federal government, however, set the monthly allotment of food stamps that participating individuals would receive and the amount of the purchase requirement. It also financed the entire cost of benefits, but states financed 70 percent of the program's administrative costs. The curious federal-state arrangement of responsibilities, the same arrangement used for the Social Security Disability Insurance program, would later prove to be a recipe in both programs for excessive payments, fraud, and abuse.

The program also had multiple personalities. Members of both houses of Congress from farm states viewed the program as one that would benefit farmers by increasing the demand for foodstuffs. Some urban members saw the program as a nutrition assistance program that would raise nutrition levels among the poor, while others saw it as an income maintenance program that helped offset the unequal public assistance benefits across the states.

13 The First Great Society

They give you freedom with one hand and take it away with the other. They give you a little money and they treat you as if you were in jail.
  Brenda Foster, welfare mother, 1966[1]

THE LAUNCH OF LYNDON JOHNSON'S GREAT Society program in 1965 marks the beginning of a remarkable ten-year period of entitlement legislation that is unprecedented in all of U.S. history. This chapter covers the first phase of this period, from Lyndon Johnson's election as president to the end of his term in office. Chapter 15 discusses the second phase during Richard Nixon's presidency.

The first phase saw the creation of new and explosive health care entitlement programs, Medicare and Medicaid; an expansion of Social Security disability insurance to temporarily disabled workers; two large general increases in Social Security retirement and disability benefits; and the largest expansion in the Aid to Families with Dependent Children (AFDC) program in its thirty-year history.

Revenues from a rapidly expanding economy and an even more rapidly growing labor force provided the fuel for this legislative blitzkrieg. The revenue surge, as with previous surges, made irresistible the desire to expand entitlement benefits. Congress applied the additional revenues to financing the new Medicare program and expanding the existing Social Security programs. The AFDC expansion was the unanticipated outcome of an attempt to curtail exploding program costs.

The period also witnessed a new phenomenon: welfare mothers, urged on by government-funded activists, were organizing and marching on federal, state, and local governments to demand higher welfare benefits and fewer restrictions on eligibility.

The 1964 Elections and Lyndon Johnson's Program

In 1964, American voters overwhelmingly reelected President Johnson. "Landslide" Lyndon's long coattails carried Democrats to post–World War II record majorities in both the House and Senate. When the Eighty-Ninth Congress convened in January 1965, Democrats held more than two-thirds of the seats in both legislative chambers. Claiming an electoral mandate and having the votes to carry it into effect, Democrats set out to complete the major unfinished business of Franklin Roosevelt's New Deal, Harry Truman's Fair Deal, and John F. Kennedy's New Frontier. Elections matter, and the 1964 elections mattered a lot.

The election sweep came during a propitious decade for liberals. Following a recession that ended in 1961, the economy began a twelve-year period of extraordinary growth. National income, adjusted for inflation, grew at 4 percent annually, a rate unmatched by any twelve-year period following World War II. By 1973, the nation's real income was 70 percent higher than it was in 1961. This growth provided a revenue bonanza that could be used for higher Social Security retirement and disability benefits, a Medicare program, and new entitlements to assist lower-income households.

President Johnson put new federal health care programs for the elderly and the poor at the top of his first-year agenda. The president proposed a Medicare program for people 65 and older who were receiving Social Security benefits and a new federal-state Medicaid program for recipients of public assistance to the elderly, the disabled, and families with dependent children. Both plans stemmed from well-intentioned desires to help the elderly and the poor meet their medical expenses.

As a policy matter, liberals believed that these programs would have two collateral benefits. First, passage of Medicare and Medicaid would set the stage for enactment of a health insurance program covering everyone, an elusive liberal goal since the turn of the century. Pressure would mount to lower Medicare's eligibility age, just as it had for disability insurance, and to expand Medicaid beyond recipients of public assistance. Second, passage of the president's health care proposals would break the legislative logjam that had prevented Social Security benefits from being increased. Throughout the first half of the 1960s, legislative proposals containing increases had been considered by Congress, but each time, they had been tethered to Medicare proposals. When Medicare plans died in Congress, the Social Security benefit increases died with them. As a result, Social Security monthly benefits had not been raised since 1958.

Combating poverty remained high on the president's domestic agenda. The annually funded, discretionary antipoverty programs established by the Economic Opportunity Act the preceding autumn were now fully operative. The president believed that these programs would be far more effective if Congress doubled their funding. Expanding cash entitlement assistance to the poor was low on his initial priority list.

Medicare and Medicaid

Democrats in Congress eagerly awaited Johnson's proposals, especially his Medicare plan. The defeat of Harry Truman's national health insurance proposal in the late 1940s had been a severe setback. Following its defeat, liberal Democrats adopted a scaled-down approach to health care reform similar to that taken on disability insurance. The approach proposed to extend payroll tax–financed insurance coverage of hospital and nursing home expenses to Social Security retirement beneficiaries, a more sympathetic target. To temper objections from the American Medical Association (AMA), the scaled-down approach did not cover physician services. The plan shifted the health care debate away from national health insurance to a more limited program of health care assistance to the elderly. But these proposals, opposed by

President Eisenhower and the alliance between conservative congressional Democrats and Republicans, went nowhere. The opposition favored an alternative program that was modeled on existing public assistance programs: a state-run program for poor elderly people partially financed by federal matching payments.

Congress passed such a program in 1960. The Medical Assistance for the Aged program, with federal match rates ranging from 50 to 80 percent and state autonomy, was a continuation of the New Deal welfare policy.[2]

President Kennedy's election had done little to change Medicare's political prospects. He offered a scaled down proposal: a health insurance plan for Social Security retirees financed by a small increase in the payroll tax. For the next four years, the health insurance debate was a replay of the debate over President Truman's plan, and so was the outcome. The AMA, which led the opposition, labeled the proposal "fedicare" and condemned it as "a costly concoction of bureaucracy, bad medicine, and an unbalanced budget."[3] Proponents countered that high health care costs among the elderly and the inability of private markets and states to provide coverage demanded a federal solution.

There was one notable development during these debates: the emergence of two organized lobbying groups for senior citizens. Since the Townsend movement had fizzled out in the early 1950s, no large-scale lobby group for the elderly had emerged to take its place. In 1961, the American Federation of Labor provided funds, personnel, equipment, and offices for a new lobby: the National Council of Senior Citizens (NCSC), which quickly grew to 250,000 to 300,000 members and became a potent force behind the push for Medicare. The second lobby group was the American Association for Retired Persons (AARP). Founded in 1947 as an association of retired teachers, the organization reincorporated itself into a lobby group for all senior citizens in 1958. Although the AARP would later become a potent lobby for Medicare, in the early 1960s the organization favored a private sector program over the proposed compulsory social insurance approach.[4]

Washington's major newspapers, the *Washington Post* and the *New York Times*, added to the pressure for a federal program to provide health care to elderly people. The *Post* repeatedly pressed the case.

When Congress failed to pass Medicare and other social legislation in 1963, the *Post* offered the opinion that "Congress now is the real problem child of our Federal System."[5] A year later, the *Post* awarded Senator Russell Long (D-LA) a special prize for employing "the most devious legislative tactic of the session for his efforts to prevent Medicare's enactment." Second place went to Senator George A. Smathers (D-FL) "for the best performance as a supporting obstructionist."[6] After the 1964 elections, the newspaper applauded the defeat of three Republican House Ways and Means Committee members who had opposed Medicare by opining that they "suffered a fate in the elections that befits men of Neanderthal-like fiscal mentality."[7] In early 1964, the *New York Times* told its readers that there was no reason Congress had to choose between higher Social Security benefits and Medicare for seniors by writing that "both the Medicare and the pension-increase proposals have substantial merit, and there is no reason why they should be dangled before the elderly on an either-or basis."[8] The *Times* singled out the House Ways and Means chairman, Wilbur Mills, as the chief obstacle to Medicare by labeling him a "One-Man Veto on Medicare."[9]

From 1961 to 1964, the efforts of the Kennedy administration, the NCSC, and the press could not overcome congressional opposition. A Medicare bill never emerged from committee in either congressional chamber, and until 1964, attempts to add a Medicare program on the Senate floor were defeated.[10] Finally in 1964, a breakthrough occurred in the Senate when a Medicare amendment to that year's Social Security bill mustered enough votes to pass. Four liberal Republicans, who had formerly opposed Medicare, changed their votes to provide the necessary margin. The amendment, however, was rejected in the conference committee.

Following President Johnson's sweeping electoral win, three alternative health plans for the elderly emerged as contenders. The first was the social insurance approach that covered hospital and nursing home care for elderly Social Security recipients. The second, a Republican alternative, allowed elderly people to voluntarily choose among a set of private health care plans that covered a full range of benefits, including physician services. Participating seniors would pay monthly premiums to finance a portion of the program's cost.[11] General fund tax revenues would cover the remainder. The third alternative, the AMA's Eldercare plan, which also covered a broad range of services to the elderly, would be administered by the states with the assistance of federal financing.

Wilbur Mills, the powerful chairman of the Ways and Means Committee, who for fifteen years stood in staunch opposition to federal government–provided health care, reversed his position. Moreover, instead of choosing one of the competing alternatives, Mills combined all three plans into a single one, dubbed the "three-layered cake."[12] For good measure, Mills added his own significant expansion. The first layer contained the social insurance approach advocated by Presidents Johnson and Kennedy. This layer (now Medicare Part A) granted Social Security recipients an entitlement to hospital benefits, financed by an add-on to the existing Social Security payroll tax. The second layer (now Medicare Part B), taken from the Republican alternative, gave Social Security recipients the option of enrolling in a federal government–subsidized fee-for-service plan that covered physician, outpatient, and laboratory services. Half of the cost of this layer, Supplementary Medical Insurance, was financed by flat premiums charged to enrollees and half by general fund tax revenues. The third layer (now Medicaid) provided states with federal matching payments for medical care services delivered to recipients of federal-state public assistance programs and, at state option, to lower-income "medically needy" who were not receiving welfare assistance.

When Chairman Mills brought the Medicare bill to the House floor for debate, House Democrats knew they were on the verge of passing the most important social insurance program since the passage of Social Security thirty years earlier. When the chairman rose to introduce his bill, Democrats gave him a standing ovation.

After some modifications, the "three-layered cake" passed overwhelmingly in both congressional chambers. On August 30, 1965, President Johnson flew to Independence, Missouri, the home of Harry Truman, to sign the bill in the company of the former president. The Medicare program entitled all people age 65 and older who qualified for Social Security to government assistance to defray the cost of their medical care. Medicare Part A covered hospital expenses, outpatient care, and a limited amount of home health and skilled nursing care.

Like Social Security, Part A was financed by an increase in the Social Security payroll tax, shared equally between employees and employers. Medicare Part B covered physician services and the costs of related services, including lab tests and X-rays. Half of Part B expenditures were financed by monthly premiums paid by Medicare beneficiaries and half by general fund revenues. Medicare deductibles and coinsurance payments were set at low levels to ensure that all covered people paid little out of their own pocket for covered services.

Medicare created as much of an entitlement to health care providers as it did to elderly people. Hospitals and other Part A providers were entitled to receive federal reimbursements for the reasonable costs of services provided to Medicare beneficiaries. Physicians were entitled to receive reimbursements for all service charges that were "reasonable" or "customary" for the physician and were within the "prevailing" range of charges among physicians in the community.

In deference to long-standing concerns about federal government potential interference with the doctor-patient relationship, Medicare set no limit on the amount of physician care an individual received and the frequency of this care. Limits on hospital care and home health services were set so generously that they were irrelevant for most providers and patients. Initially, because of concerns about the deleterious impact of government price controls on the quality of medical care, reimbursement rates for physician services were determined by private health insurance companies under contract to administer the program. Medicare bills were paid by the insurance companies, called financial intermediaries and carriers, which in turn would be reimbursed by the federal government.

These reimbursement arrangements were a recipe for an immediate sharp rise in health care inflation and a long-term increase in government spending. Medicare's reasonable hospital cost reimbursement system provided hospitals with no incentive to restrain costs and a large incentive to add costly services to patient care. Medicare's fee-for-service arrangement allowed doctors and eligible patients virtually complete freedom to decide between themselves on a medical regime. Since the federal government paid most of the costs and the patient paid little, neither doctor nor patient retained any incentive to limit the amount of care and every incentive to provide additional care, regardless of its effectiveness. Cost reimbursement for administrative services by Medicare carriers and financial intermediaries gave them little incentive to exercise control over the program's costs. At the same time, the law gave the federal government little, if any, ability to control Medicare reimbursement rates or the quantity of services provided. Its job was simply to write the check.

As had so often happened in the past, the new entitlement's costs quickly exceeded the official projections. Medicare hospital care expenditures during the program's first six months in operation exceeded the Social Security trustees' official estimates by 21 percent. During the next twelve months, they exceeded estimates by 50 percent. Expenditures for physician services also rose sharply, but at the time of the Medicare law's enactment, the Social Security actuaries had not even attempted to forecast their growth.

The new Medicaid program was created to defray the costs of medical care provided to those who were impoverished through no fault of their own. The program followed the New Deal welfare model. States set the policies and administered their programs within broad federal guidelines. The federal government helped finance these programs with matching payments. The law required that states cover public assistance recipients: members of single-parent households, disabled people, and elderly people. States could cover medically needy people who were not living in poverty and would otherwise qualify for public assistance. Medically needy people were expected to finance their health care expenses out of their own resources until additional payments would pull their income down to a level that would qualify them for public assistance.

Medicaid's federal-state cost-sharing arrangement was a prescription for rapidly rising expenditures. Neither state legislatures nor Congress faced the full cost of program liberalizations. Low-income states, for example, were required to pay only twenty cents of each dollar of Medicaid expenses and, hence, could finance five dollars of medical care for only one additional dollar of state revenue. High-income states were required to pay fifty cents of each dollar and thus could provide two dollars of medical care for each additional dollar of state revenue.

Similarly, the federal government could finance more than one dollar of Medicaid benefits for each dollar of federal revenue it devoted to the program. Such a financial arrangement gave the federal government an incentive to impose additional coverage mandates and service requirements on states and gave states a corresponding financial incentive to expand their Medicaid programs (and less incentive to oppose federal coverage mandates and service requirements).

Cost sharing also distorted budget allocations, particularly at the state government level. Each additional dollar of state revenue could finance two or more dollars of Medicaid benefits. But an additional dollar of revenue could only finance one dollar of state infrastructure or education expenditures.

Medicaid's expenditures quickly skyrocketed. Federal budget officials had projected in early 1966 that Medicaid would cost under $400 million during the federal government's 1967 fiscal year. Its actual cost exceeded $1.1 billion. One source of the excess costs was several high-income states that responded to Medicaid's incentives by establishing generous income standards for those deemed medically needy. New York, for instance, set the income threshold for its medically needy program at about twice the poverty line, a level generous enough to allow nearly half the state's residents to qualify. Congress moved quickly to rein in state medically needy programs before too many states followed New York's lead. It capped the medically needy income standard at 133 percent of the poverty line in 1967.

The large increase in demand for health care services caused by Medicare and Medicaid created an immediate sharp rise in health care costs that spread throughout the entire U.S. health care system. The cost of a day in a U.S. hospital, which had been rising at a 6.4 percent annual rate from 1961 to 1965, rose by 16.6 percent in 1967, 15.4 percent in 1968, and 14.5 percent in 1969.[13] Recent research has estimated that Medicare alone produced a 37 percent increase in hospital costs between 1965 and 1970.[14] The cost of physician care, which had been rising at an annual rate of 3.2 percent during the five years leading up to Medicare's enactment (1961–1965), rose by 7.5 percent in 1967, 6.1 percent in 1968, and 6.7 percent in 1969. The rise in hospital and physician costs during these years was more rapid than at any other time in prior U.S. history.

Social Security

The inability to enact a Medicare bill from 1961 to 1964, along with budget shortfalls in the Social Security retirement program, stymied efforts to pass Social Security benefit increases. In 1965, however, Medicare turned from being an obstacle to a vehicle, and the retirement program's annual deficits turned to surpluses. The Social Security trust fund's return to a surplus position began in 1964, and in spring 1965, the trustees projected that the program would run billion-dollar surpluses the following year. The projected surpluses, a result of steadily growing taxable payrolls and a previously scheduled payroll tax rate hike that would take effect on January 1, 1966, would be the program's first near-term billion-dollar surplus.

Congress responded by including a benefit increase that averaged 7 percent for Social Security recipients in the law that created the Medicare program. The amount was just enough to compensate recipients for inflation since the last general benefit increase in 1958, but it came with a twist: the benefit increase, first payable in September 1965, was made retroactive to January. The retroactive portion, amounting to 56 percent of a typical recipient's monthly benefit, was included as a lump-sum add-on in the September monthly benefit.

Along with the benefit increase, Congress raised the maximum earnings subject to the payroll tax to $6,600, setting a pattern that it would follow for the next eight years. Congress's principal motivation for the increase, besides a desire to raise more revenue, was that the payroll tax had become more regressive over the previous five years. The strong economic growth had reduced the proportion of workers with earnings below the Social Security maximum taxable earnings. The proportion, which had hovered around 70 percent during the 1950s, had dropped to 65 percent by 1964, and it would drop even further in the absence of additional legislation. The previously scheduled tax rate hikes set for 1966 and 1968 would fall more heavily on low-wage workers whose entire earnings would be subject to the higher tax rates. Legislation enacted from 1966 to 1973 would raise the maximum taxable earnings four more times. By 1974, the taxable wage threshold would reach $13,200, nearly three times its 1964 level.

The 1965 Social Security benefit increase was followed by a larger one in 1967. Again, surplus Social Security revenues provided the fuel for a benefit hike, and, again, the president and Congress ignored the federal budget's overall financial condition in considering the increase. That year, after two more years of strong economic growth, the trustees reported that the Social Security trust fund had run a $2.3 billion surplus in 1966 and was well on its way to a $3.4 billion surplus in 1967. The rest of the budget, the so-called administrative budget, with expenditures exceeding revenues by 8 percent, was in the process of incurring a reported $10 billion deficit, its largest budget deficit of the decade.

With surplus Social Security funds available, President Johnson made poverty reduction an explicit goal of his Social Security policy. In a special message to Congress in early 1967, he told Congress that despite the progress of Social Security, "5.3 million older Americans [one-fourth of the total] have yearly incomes below the poverty line."[15] The level of benefits, according to the president, was "grossly inadequate." To achieve his poverty reduction goal, the president proposed to combine a 59 percent increase in monthly benefits for people who received the lowest benefits with at least a 15 percent increase for all other Social Security recipients.

Congress responded with a scaled-down benefit increase along the lines of the president's plan. The 1967 Social Security Amendments increased benefits by 25 percent for retirees with low earnings and 11 percent for those with high earnings. The average benefit increased by 13 percent, more than twice the growth in consumer prices that had occurred since the last increase in 1965.

The poverty reduction goal was laudable but costly to achieve through a program that was not means tested. The law's $3 billion of additional benefits, most of which went to people living above the poverty line, exceeded the combined total of all federal spending on cash welfare entitlement programs.

Diverting Funds from Social Security
Retirement to Disability Insurance

The disability program, in contrast to the retirement program, was mired in financial trouble. The program incurred deficits in 1963 and 1964 and was experiencing another deficit in 1965. The trustees projected that continuing deficits would cause the disability trust fund to be exhausted by 1970. The deficits were largely a consequence of the 1960 law that allowed workers under age 50 to qualify for benefits. The surge of beneficiaries had caused disability program expenditures to triple from 1959 to 1964.

The program's unsustainable financial situation should have forced Congress and President Johnson to confront an unpleasant choice: Tighten eligibility rules or raise payroll taxes. But the retirement program's surpluses provided another way out, and Congress took it. The 1965 Social Security law shifted .2 percentage points of the payroll tax from the Social Security retirement program to the disability program, the practical effect of which was to divert revenue from the retirement program to the disability insurance program. With the additional disability insurance revenue, Congress not only left disability benefits and eligibility intact, it expanded eligibility to include temporarily disabled workers.

In 1956, the votes required to secure the disability program's passage had been obtained only after members were given assurances that Social Security retirement funds would not be diverted to the new program. The assurances had lasted less than a decade. As we will see, the diversions would continue in increasing amounts for the next five decades.[16]

The War on Poverty

By 1967, it was becoming clear that the War on Poverty was not working out in the way that its architects had predicted. Welfare rolls, instead of declining as President Johnson's "best and the brightest" promised, had soared to record levels, and the welfare system was careening toward a crisis. That year, the number of AFDC recipients reached 5 million, 1.3 million more than in 1962 when John Kennedy introduced his new welfare services approach. The 1967 caseload was also 1 million people higher than it was when Lyndon Johnson had launched the War on Poverty three years earlier. The days of the dole, far from being numbered as President Johnson had promised, were just beginning.

Broken homes and out-of-wedlock births had become even more important reasons why families were receiving AFDC benefits. In 1967, three-quarters of all AFDC families were on the rolls due to divorce, separation, illegitimacy, or desertion by one of the child's parents, up from one-half in 1961.[17] Welfare was also becoming a way of life for an increasing number of AFDC households. In 1967, one-third of all AFDC households had been on the rolls for four or more years. AFDC and race had been intertwined since the program's inception. But in 1967, when African Americans constituted 47 percent of all AFDC recipients, the program came to be viewed as primarily one for African Americans.

The bold and confident promises of the War on Poverty's architects were turning out to be empty. By 1967, federal spending on AFDC welfare services had ballooned to $392 million from a negligible amount in 1962. The main beneficiaries were the service providers, mainly middle-class professional social workers in and outside government welfare agencies, educators in schools of social work, legal services lawyers, and academicians. The federal government was spending more on professional social workers than on school lunches for poor children. Daniel Patrick Moynihan would subsequently describe the services approach as "a policy of feeding the sparrows by feeding the horses."[18]

The Department of HEW reported that welfare services, such as counseling in family life, health, financial activities, and family planning, were being delivered to 80 percent of all AFDC families, but there was little to show for it. While these services may have helped recipient families with their daily lives, they appeared to have been of little assistance in helping welfare recipients become self-sufficient.[19]

The rapidly rising welfare rolls and the increasing prevalence of families from broken homes and children from out-of-wedlock births was evidence that the 1962 AFDC program for families with an unemployed parent (AFDC-UP) was failing to achieve its stated objective of reducing welfare due to desertion and illegitimacy. The program had been adopted in twenty-one states and appeared to have no other effect than to add another 160,000 families to the rolls.

The War on Poverty's Community Action Program (CAP) had become mired in controversy. The program architects distrusted local governments and private charities as being unresponsive and neglectful of the needs of the poor. Too often, they contended, local governments erected obstacles to the advancement of the poor. So by design, CAP funds most often bypassed local governments and were distributed instead to local community action agencies, or antipoverty councils. These agencies quickly became vehicles for professional agitators to organize the poor into pressure groups for more housing, education, health care, and welfare assistance. Tensions between the community action organizations and local governments mounted when elected officials pushed back. Complaints were filed against local agencies, charging them with mismanagement and embezzlement and with encouraging demonstrations, sit-ins, and protests. Syracuse's mayor, William Walsh, charged that the poor in his city were "being urged to storm City Hall" by federally funded, professional antipoverty agitators. Los Angeles's mayor, Sam Yorty, went further, writing that the community action agency in his city was "a reckless effort to incite the poor for political reasons" and claimed that the agency's actions were a factor in precipitating the Watts riot in August 1965.[20] Other mayors charged that CAP program funds were being used for political purposes. Mayor Richard Daley of Chicago contended that the list of people funded by the city's antipoverty agency read "like a fund-raising committee for the Democratic Party." These complaints were echoed in Congress. Congressman Adam Clayton Powell (D-NY) charged that the Office of Economic Opportunity was creating "giant fiestas of political patronage." In somewhat less colorful terms, House Education and Labor Committee Republicans contended that "the community action program has been turned into a political pork barrel by big city machines whose only interest in the poor is to exploit them."[21]

In addition, the OEO's programs helped spawn two extraordinary phenomena that were just becoming apparent in 1967. One took place on the streets of inner cities, the other in courtrooms around the country. In the streets, welfare mothers, aided by federal War on Poverty funds and federally funded volunteers and community organizers, mobilized and marched on city halls and local welfare offices demanding higher welfare benefits and relaxed eligibility rules. In courtrooms, legal services lawyers, also aided by War on Poverty funds, brought lawsuits in federal courts challenging long-standing federal, state, and local government rules. Both phenomena had a profound impact on welfare entitlements, so each is worthy of an in-depth discussion. We turn first to the actions of welfare mothers. Our consideration of the legal services lawyers is deferred to the next chapter.

Welfare Rights Movement

The welfare mothers' rights movement began in 1963 when welfare mothers in various cities independently formed groups to pressure state and local governments for higher benefits and better treatment by welfare officials. The first of these groups, ANC Mothers Anonymous (named after California's Aid to Needy Children program), was established in 1963 in the Watts area of Los Angeles by Johnnie Tillmon, an unmarried welfare mother with five children. [22] The movement accelerated dramatically in 1965 when the Office of Economic Opportunity's CAP began distributing federal funds to community action agencies. By early 1967, 188 separate welfare rights organizations existed throughout the country.[23] Virtually every major industrial city had at least one such group. New York City, which had the largest concentration of welfare mothers, had ten so-called welfare leagues.

The first national organization of the poor formed in the United States, the National Welfare Rights Organization (NWRO), was established in 1967. It grew quickly from an organization that coordinated the activities of local organizations and served as a clearinghouse of welfare information to a national welfare lobby. By summer 1969, the NWRO represented twenty-two thousand dues-paying families from 523 local welfare rights groups.[24] The organization used its resources in Washington to fight the welfare work requirements in the 1967 Social Security Amendments and President Nixon's welfare reform initiative.

Acting on the belief that they were entitled to government benefits, groups of welfare mothers began marching on welfare offices in cities across the nation in the mid-1960s. On June 30, 1966, welfare mothers staged their first coordinated marches on welfare offices in twenty-five cities.[25] The demonstrations in such cities as New York, Boston, Chicago, Los Angeles, Columbus, Ohio, and Washington, D.C., drew in six thousand welfare recipients from one hundred different welfare rights organizations and were widely covered by the news media.[26] A large demonstration occurred a few months later in New York City when welfare mothers demonstrated to demand winter school clothing at the start of the school year.[27] On the first anniversary of the June 30, 1966, marches, welfare mothers were demonstrating, picketing, and petitioning welfare offices in forty cities across the United States.[28] That same year, they marched for special Christmas grants in New York.

Welfare mothers primarily sought higher welfare benefits, not social welfare services. As welfare rights activists in Boston put it, "What you really need is money, not social workers."[29] Most welfare rights marches were organized around demands for grants that were provided on top of regular welfare payments to finance purchases of specific goods. The grants were usually provided at the welfare caseworker's discretion after an assessment of the family's needs. If, for example, the family did not have a kitchen table, the caseworker would authorize a special grant to enable the family to purchase one. The special grants were an outgrowth of concern in the early 1960s that welfare recipients were misusing their cash welfare benefits.[30] Operationally, local welfare offices developed detailed lists of items that could be purchased with special grants. Items included hats, "dressy" dresses, stockings, refrigerators, washing machines, kitchen tables, dish cabinets, beds, playpens, strollers, sofas, lamps, alarm clocks, eggbeaters, and towels.[31]

The special grants became a principal tool for recruiting welfare mothers to march and demonstrate. Welfare activists in Massachusetts distributed a flier that read, "Do each of your children have their own bed? Did you know that you are entitled to a separate bed for each? Come to the first meeting of the Pilgrim City Welfare Rights Organization . . . In no time at all, you'll have the furniture."[32] New York activists distributed a flyer targeting the large number of Puerto Rican single mothers that proclaimed in large bold letters: *Welfare Le Debe* (welfare owes you). Under the heading, the flyer informed welfare recipients that they were entitled to *ropa para verano* (summer clothes), *telephonos*, *lavarropas* (clothes washers), and *nuebles becentes* (decent furniture). The flier closed with a call to attend a demonstration at the local welfare center *para demander sus derechos legales* (to demand your legal rights).[33] Boston activists held "benefit of the month club(s)."[34]

These efforts helped convince welfare mothers, who typically had little education and no knowledge of the law, that they were entitled to the specific benefits. One New York welfare mother, upon seeing the list of minimum standards items, said she "couldn't believe the things that were in [them]. . . . There was a law in the books that said you are entitled to these things."[35] Another welfare mother remarked that she was "shocked [because] this was a legal fact sheet with all the items you were entitled to . . . and you were just to check off if you needed these things, so we did."[36]

Welfare mothers also marched against the demeaning treatment they received at the hands of welfare caseworkers. They particularly objected to man-in-the-house regulations, residence requirements, income tests, and the intrusive methods welfare agencies used to enforce these AFDC regulations. They protested that midnight raids, unannounced visits by welfare caseworkers, and financial status checks were degrading and demanded the right to an appeal before an impartial referee before benefits were terminated or an application was denied.

Welfare mothers saw these eligibility requirements and the way in which they were enforced as a loss of personal freedom. One Washington, D.C., welfare mother and demonstrator charged, "They give you freedom with one hand and take it away with the other. They give you a little money and they treat you as if you were in jail."[37] Johnnie Tillmon described the sacrifice of freedom in a *Ms.* magazine article: "If the kids are going to eat, and the man can't get a job, then he's got to go. . . . You trade in a man for *the man*. But you can't divorce him if he treats you bad. He can divorce you, of course, cut you off anytime he wants. But in that case, he keeps the kids, not you. The man runs everything."[38]

The welfare rights movement peaked in the late 1960s. Thereafter, beset by internal disagreements on direction and methods, financial difficulties, and a strongly negative public reaction, the movement began to decline. By 1972, for all practical purposes the movement was over. That year saw only a handful of marches organized by local welfare rights groups. At the national level, the NWRO reported that it was in severe financial distress.

Another New Approach to Welfare

Faced with soaring welfare rolls, more broken homes, large federal budget deficits swelled by the costs of the Vietnam War and the War on Poverty, and the street demonstrations of welfare mothers, President Johnson and Congress were prepared to take yet another new approach. This one, recommended by a new set of experts, emphasized the importance of work incentives over welfare services.

The new emphasis on work incentives stemmed in part from recognition that most state AFDC programs exacted a heavy price for working by reducing a welfare mother's AFDC benefit by a dollar for each dollar of wages she earned. This feature, an effective 100 percent tax on her earnings, meant that an AFDC mother could not improve her economic circumstances by working unless she could earn so much that she worked her way completely off AFDC.

The addition of Medicaid benefits for AFDC recipients severely exacerbated this work disincentive. In most states, a welfare mother who worked her way off AFDC also faced the loss of Medicaid benefits for herself and her children. For a mother and two children, the loss of Medicaid in monetary terms equaled two months of full-time work at the minimum wage.[39] Partly as a result of these severe work disincentives, only 20 percent of women on AFDC worked.

The new emphasis on work and work incentives was also recognition of larger societal changes that were taking place in the labor force behavior of women with children. Throughout the 1950s and 1960s, women with young children in the home had entered the labor force with steadily increasing frequency. By the mid-1960s, 58 percent of all widowed, divorced, or separated women who had children in the home were in the labor force. Among these heads of household who had children under age 6, nearly half were in the labor force. The increasing prevalence of working women with young children at home altered beliefs about the ability of welfare mothers to work without harming their children's development. If a majority of women with children in the home could both work and raise their children, shouldn't women on welfare do the same?

The new approach was incorporated into the 1967 Public Assistance Amendments in two important ways. First, states were required to disregard the first $30 of earnings per month (about $200 in today's dollars) and one-third of a person's earnings in computing AFDC benefits and eligibility.[40] The "thirty and a third" earnings disregard was designed to reduce the welfare system's financial penalty for working. The monthly benefit for a mother earning more than $30 per month was now reduced by only two dollars for every three she earned. By allowing her to keep one out of every three dollars she earned, the earnings disregard reduced the AFDC work disincentive.

Second, states were mandated to implement a work requirement for AFDC recipients. The newly authorized Work Incentive (WIN) program required states to register welfare mothers for work, job counseling, or job training. The family of a welfare mother who refused the offer of work or training would be declared ineligible for continued AFDC payments.

The "thirty and a third" earnings disregard enjoyed bipartisan support, but the work requirement appeared harsh and was highly controversial. The Johnson administration opposed it. Senator Robert Kennedy (D-NY) criticized the requirement as based on "medieval poor law philosophy."[41] During the House Ways and Means Committee hearings on work requirements, welfare mothers representing the NWRO held a sit-in for three hours before they were forcibly removed from the hearing room. Southern Democrats and Republicans supported the policy as a necessary measure to stem the soaring welfare rolls and to ensure that women who were able to work did not continue on the welfare rolls.

As a result of the controversy, the requirement, delayed until July 1969, would be largely ineffective. The law granted exemptions for mothers with preschool-age children, mothers who cared for a disabled family member, and mothers who were in school. The law also granted a blanket exemption if the state government had not made adequate provision for day care. The last of these exemptions proved crucial in undermining the WIN program. With state welfare budgets already burdened with heavy costs, states were unwilling to spend any significant amount of funds to set up day care centers.[42]

The economists, like the social welfare experts before them, expressed great confidence that the new incentives would reduce welfare rolls. Lower caseloads would mean a reduction in welfare costs for federal, state, and local governments and reduced dependency among the poor. Their confidence led Ways and Means Committee chairman Wilbur Mills to predict that the 1967 law's work-related provisions would reduce the welfare rolls by 400,000 people by 1972.[43]

Once again, the confidence of the experts was misplaced. The welfare rolls not only continued their inexorable rise but grew at an even faster rate. The earnings disregard, instead of being a solution, caused an even larger problem. Although the disregard reduced the work disincentives of welfare, it also significantly raised the income threshold below which a family could qualify for AFDC. In most states, the threshold increased by over 50 percent.[44] Under the previous AFDC program, single mothers who had earnings that were sufficiently high to disqualify them from AFDC could now qualify for assistance with the disregard in place. Thus, the earnings disregard dramatically increased the pool of eligible recipients. Those who opted to receive AFDC now faced work disincentives that were far higher than they had previously faced. During the first full year that the new earnings disregard was in place, AFDC rolls rose an astonishing 25 percent.

Moreover, for those on the AFDC rolls, the earnings disregard improved work incentives, but only up to a point. The 1967 amendments did nothing to alter the fact that welfare mothers who worked their way off AFDC typically lost their Medicaid eligibility.

Reflecting congressional frustrations with the growing number of AFDC children who were born out of wedlock and the absence of any compassionate and effective ideas for reducing the growth, the 1967 law capped each state's future federal matching payments for assistance to such children. But this highly controversial policy, the first of its kind for any major entitlement program, was repealed two years later before it became effective.

The 1967 amendments marked the death knell of the New Deal's hands-off welfare policy. Congress viewed the explosion in the AFDC rolls as the fault of the states for failing to avail themselves of options the federal government had given them. By mandating the earnings disregard, Congress took a major step of asserting policy control over state welfare programs. In doing so, Congress refused to acknowledge the federal government's own role in the welfare crisis by limiting state eligibility restrictions and providing federal funds to social welfare professionals and community organizers who encouraged increased welfare participation. This initial step would quickly be followed by others, and within a decade, the federal government would dominate welfare policymaking, with the state government role receding primarily to administering federal policy in return for federal funds.

Rising federal welfare expenditures, a surge of spending on the new Medicaid and Medicare programs, and sharply escalating Vietnam War costs combined in 1967 to produce the largest federal budget deficit since World War II. Federal outlays for the AFDC program, up 60 percent from 1964, broke through the $1 billion threshold. The new Medicaid and Medicare programs had grown far more rapidly than the Johnson administration's experts had predicted. Medicaid's cost had doubled the initial projection and also breached the $1 billion mark in 1967. Medicare's cost, at $2.7 billion in its first year of operation, was more than double the federal expense of both AFDC and Medicaid. Both the Social Security retirement and disability programs had registered sizable two-year increases: retirement benefits were up 24 percent and disability benefits 33 percent.

The 1967 budget deficit was the federal government's seventh consecutive budget deficit. This fact was particularly disconcerting to members of Congress and the Johnson administration since the record string of peacetime deficits had occurred despite exceptionally strong economic growth. From 1961 to 1967, the growing economy had increased the annual flow of revenue to the U.S. Treasury by a whopping 50 percent. President Johnson had chosen to fight two wars simultaneously. He was losing both and in the process was adding large sums to the national debt.

The Great Society was the culmination of two decades of liberal efforts following World War II. Republicans had initially opposed these efforts, but then had acquiesced when it became clear that they did not have the votes to prevent them. The 1968 election of Richard Nixon, a presumed conservative Republican, created what was thought to be a genuine opportunity not only to block further liberalizations but also possibly roll back recently enacted ones. Contrary to these expectations, as we will see, President Nixon not only did not change course; he embarked on an entitlement path even more expansionary than his predecessor.

But before turning to the Nixon era, we need to address the creation of legal entitlement rights by the Supreme Court.

14 A Legal Right to Welfare

It may be realistic today to regard welfare entitlements as more like "property" than a "gratuity."

Justice William Brennan, 1970[1]

T HE 1930s SUPREME COURT SOCIAL SECURITY RUL-
ings upheld the constitutionality of entitlement programs for members of the general population. However, these decisions did not address the extent of legal rights of claimants. In fact, before the 1960s, federal courts repeatedly resisted the temptation to define legal rights to entitlement benefits. The few exceptions mainly involved wartime veterans' pension benefits. In these cases, the Court declared that although an entitlement statute compelled the executive branch to provide benefits to all who met the law's requirements, there was no vested right to benefits. Congress could change benefits and eligibility requirements. In 1960, when the Supreme Court heard its first Social Security entitlement case, the Court applied the same reasoning to conclude that recipients had no vested right to Social Security benefits.

This legal view, when applied to welfare benefits, underwent a significant change in the mid-1960s and early 1970s that began when legal aid attorneys brought suits in federal court challenging federal and state eligibility laws and regulations. The suits culminated in three major Supreme Court decisions, issued in rapid-fire succession from 1969 to 1971, that radically expanded the legal rights of welfare recipients and claimants. The Court (1) declared that long-standing state "suitable home" regulations violated federal law, (2) struck down state residence requirements for welfare as a violation of an individual's constitutional right to travel, and (3) ruled that welfare benefits were akin to property and were therefore protected by the Constitution's due process requirements. This last case established a legal entitlement right to welfare benefits that was stronger than the legal rights that had been granted to disabled veterans of prior wars and to the legal rights that were granted to disabled Vietnam War veterans who were returning at the time of the Supreme Court's decisions.

The Nature of Entitlement Rights Prior to the 1960s

All veterans' pension laws from the Revolutionary War to the Vietnam War required the executive branch to provide pensions to qualifying veterans.[2] The laws were silent on whether the qualifying veteran had a vested right to the pension as if it were a contractual benefit or a gratuity. Could Congress modify, reduce, or terminate pensions of existing beneficiaries? What legal rights did claimants who had been denied benefits possess? In particular, did such veterans have the right to appeal adverse decisions to the federal courts?

Supreme Court rulings during the nineteenth century and first half of the twentieth century answered these questions emphatically and unambiguously: The Court consistently ruled that veterans' pensions were not a contractual obligation of the federal government. In 1883, the Court reaffirmed this view in *United States v. Teller*, declaring, "No pensioner has a vested legal right to his pension. Pensions are the bounty of the government, which Congress has the right to withhold, distribute, or recall at its discretion." Subsequent rulings followed suit.[3]

During the same period, the Supreme Court consistently ruled that veterans had no legal right to appeal adverse pension decisions to the federal courts. The Court also made clear that veterans' pension laws had not given the judiciary the authority to resolve disputed pension claims, and they actively resisted any such role.

Congress initially attempted to assign the federal courts the role of adjudicating Revolutionary War pension claims. But the circuit and district courts rebelled against these mandates on the ground that Congress could not constitutionally impose a nonjudicial function on the judiciary, a coequal branch of government. When neither the executive branch nor Congress directly challenged the judiciary, the responsibility for determining the validity of Revolutionary War pension claims was assumed entirely by the executive branch.

The federal judiciary's continuing reluctance to adjudicate veterans' pensions is exemplified by its decision in an 1840 case, *Decatur v. Paulding*. Susan Decatur, widow of the famous navy captain Stephen Decatur, had been granted two pensions by two separate laws Congress enacted on March 3, 1837. A general pension law granted her a half-pay pension for five years, and a private relief law gave her another half-pay pension for five years plus a half-pay pension retroactive to the date of the captain's untimely death seventeen years earlier. The Pension Office granted her the general law pension but rejected her claim for the private relief law pension. Mrs. Decatur sued. The Supreme Court ruled that the Pension Office had acted within its discretion in granting the widow only one pension. After reaching its decision, the Court warned that involving the federal courts in adjudicating veterans' pension claims was unwise and unlawful. Chief Justice Roger B. Taney wrote for the Court: "The interference of the court with the performance of the ordinary duties of the executive departments of the government, would be productive of nothing but mischief, and [furthermore] this power was never given to them."[4] The Court reaffirmed its denial of judicial review of veterans' pensions eighty-seven years later in *Silberschein v. United States*.[5]

In 1934, the Supreme Court declared that not all entitlement benefits were gratuities proffered by the government; entitlement statutes could establish contractual obligations.[6] *Lynch v. United States* addressed the 1917 War Risk Insurance Act's voluntary disability insurance program discussed in Chapter 5. That program permitted soldiers to voluntarily purchase government disability insurance by contributing regular premium payments. The 1934 cases before the Court were brought by two widows of soldiers who became disabled while their insurance policies were in force. Contrary to the law's requirements, the Veterans Administration had failed to make premium payments to its insurance fund to finance the policy's continuation. When the soldiers died, the administration denied their widows' death benefit claims.

Writing for the majority, Justice Louis Brandeis declared that the disability insurance policies were "contracts of the United States" and therefore "legal obligations of the same dignity as other contracts of the United States."[7] The veterans' voluntary insurance premium payments secured a contractual right to disability and widows' payments.

Justice Brandeis distinguished conventional veterans' pensions from the War Risk Insurance Act disability insurance program by writing, "Pensions, compensation allowances, and privileges are gratuities. They involve no agreement of parties, and the grant of them creates no vested right. The benefits conferred by gratuities may be redistributed or withdrawn at any time in the discretion of Congress."[8]

With these cases serving as precedent, the Supreme Court decided its first post–New Deal Social Security case, *Flemming v. Nestor*, in 1960. The case involved Ephram Nestor, an immigrant who arrived in the United States in 1913. He worked in a Social Security–covered job, and both he and his employer had regularly contributed payroll taxes since 1937. As a consequence of his earnings and his age, Nestor became eligible for Social Security benefits in 1955. But the 1954 Social Security Amendments had stipulated that a noncitizen who was deported was not eligible for benefits. Nestor had been a member of the Communist Party from 1933 to 1939 and, because of this association, was deported in 1955. When the Social Security Administration promptly terminated his benefits, he appealed, and his appeal went to the Supreme Court. At issue was whether Social Security pensions were a contractual obligation, like War Risk Insurance disability insurance benefits, or a gratuity like veterans' pensions.

The Supreme Court's landmark ruling, following more than a century of precedents, declared that Social Security benefits were a government gratuity, not a contractual benefit. Thus, Congress could change benefits and eligibility rules at its discretion. In the words of the Court, Congress had the "right to alter, amend, or repeal any provision of the Act." The Court warned that treating Social Security as a contractual benefit would "graft upon the Social Security system a concept of 'accrued property rights' that would deprive it of the flexibility and boldness in adjusting to ever-changing conditions."[9] Crucial to the Court's decision was that a worker's monthly Social Security benefit was not directly tied to the worker's payroll tax contributions but to the worker's earnings.[10] Thus, President Roosevelt's earned-right concept, the cornerstone of his Social Security program, although perhaps a moral right, was not a legal or contractual right.

In a larger context, the Court's ruling in *Flemming v. Nestor*, coupled with its decision in *Lynch v. United States*, meant that the nature and extent of an individual's entitlement rights were critically dependent on the particular statutory language that authorized the entitlement. Not all entitlement laws created the same rights.

The Rise of Federally Funded Poverty Lawyers

Long before the 1960s, attorneys operating through legal aid societies had provided legal services to poor people, much of it on a pro bono basis or financed by charities and private foundations. The Economic Opportunity Act's Legal Service Program brought a marked change. The initial legal services' $42 million budget in 1965 was nearly ten times the total amount spent by all civil legal aid offices in the United States in 1959.[11] Within a year, the OEO program had funded 300 legal services organizations that were operating in 210 communities across the United States. By 1971, the program's $60 million budget was funding 265 organizations that employed 2,500 lawyers to represent poor people. Working out of 850 storefront offices in poor neighborhoods, these lawyers handled over 1 million cases annually.[12]

The Legal Service Program funds were a boon to activist legal services lawyers who stood ready to use federal funds to obtain greater legal rights for welfare recipients. The goal of the lawyers was to establish a welfare system that guaranteed poor people a legal right—an entitlement—to a decent standard of living. In the words of one prominent poverty lawyer, the goal was "a right to live." The right would be attained by transforming welfare into a system in which benefits depended exclusively on financial need. Toward this end, poverty lawyers sought to use the courts to strike down all eligibility conditions except financial need. Eligibility requirements—including living arrangements and living conditions, marital status, length of residence, status of citizenship, and ability to be gainfully employed—would be declared unlawful. Benefits levels would be uniform across all political jurisdictions and adequate to provide recipients with a decent standard of living. The entitlement right would be ensured by imposing constitutional due process requirements on the eligibility determinations and using constitutional equal protection requirements to ensure that minimum benefits were adequate.

Armed with federal funds, poverty lawyers brought lawsuits in federal courts on behalf of welfare recipients. They filed suits on behalf of individual claimants and entire classes of claimants against all levels of government: municipal, county, state, and federal. For the first time in history, federal funds were being used on a grand scale to sue not only lower levels of government but the federal government itself. The suits charged governmental units with both constitutional and statutory violations of welfare recipients' rights. The poverty lawyers challenged virtually every welfare eligibility rule, including residence requirements, suitable home provisions, and willingness-to-work requirements. They challenged state and local government processes for determining eligibility and their methods for ensuring compliance with program rules and regulations, the adequacy of benefits and intrastate variations in benefits based on cost-of-living differences, the definition of household income used to calculate benefits, and even the adequacy of federal outreach efforts to enroll individuals in welfare programs.

The main target of these challenges was the AFDC program. With 5 million people on the rolls in 1967, AFDC was the federal and state governments' main welfare program. But their efforts extended beyond AFDC to the entire welfare system, which by the early 1970s also included food stamps and Medicaid.

Federal judges at all levels, from the smallest district courts to the Supreme Court, were more than willing to hear welfare cases and grant welfare recipients constitutional and statutory entitlement rights. The federal courts of the 1960s had come a long way from those courts of the 1790s. Welfare cases occupied only a negligible portion of federal court activity before the 1960s and accounted for only 7 percent of all court decisions from 1968 to 1974. The Supreme Court had not heard a welfare case before 1968. But from 1968 to 1974, it accepted at least forty-six public assistance cases and issued decisions on eighteen of them.[13] Each Court agreement to accept a welfare case was preceded by numerous lower court decisions, and each of its decisions on case merits was succeeded by an even larger number of lower court decisions implementing the Court's ruling.

By 1970, the poverty lawyers had succeeded in fundamentally transforming welfare from an act of legislative charity—a government-granted gratuity—into an entitlement that ensured all eligible people a legal right to benefits. This radical change, occurring without any accompanying legislation, overturned nearly two hundred years of established welfare policy.

Three landmark Supreme Court decisions were pivotal in creating an individual entitlement right to public assistance benefits, and all three cases involved the AFDC program. *King v. Smith*, decided in 1968, struck down the man-in-the-house rule and, along with it, a host of other state eligibility regulations as violations of the Social Security Act. *Thompson v. Shapiro*, decided the following year, struck down state welfare residency requirements as a violation of the Constitution's implied right to travel. *Goldberg v. Kelly*, decided in 1970, ruled that welfare was akin to property and therefore was protected by the Constitution's due process provisions.

King v. Smith, the first welfare case to reach the Supreme Court, involved Mrs. Sylvester Smith, a widowed black mother of four children. Alabama state welfare officials declared Smith and her family ineligible for AFDC benefits on the ground that by cohabitating with a Mr. Williams, she was in violation of the state's man-in-the-house regulation. Under Alabama law, any man who lived in the home of the mother or visited frequently for the purpose of "cohabitation" was defined as a "substitute parent." Mrs. Smith and her children were dropped from the rolls.

A three-judge lower court panel ruled that the Alabama law violated the Constitution's Fourteenth Amendment. The goal of discouraging immorality, the lower court argued, "is wholly unrelated to any purpose of the AFDC statute."[14]

Alabama appealed and the case reached the Supreme Court in 1968. The state defended its regulation on two grounds: (1) discouraging illicit sexual relationships and illegitimate births was in the best interest of the unmarried mother's children and (2) the state had a legitimate interest in protecting the state's fiscal interest, and its regulation was designed to ensure that a substitute father, a parent under its AFDC program, supported Mrs. Smith as would any parent in a traditional marital union.

The Supreme Court's unanimous 9–0 decision avoided the constitutional issue raised by the lower court and struck down the Alabama regulation on the ground that it violated the Social Security Act. Chief Justice Earl Warren, writing for the Court, rejected both of Alabama's justifications. Discouraging illicit sexual relations and illegitimacy, he wrote, "would have been quite relevant" in the 1930s. But "Federal public welfare policy now rests on a basis considerably more sophisticated and enlightened than the 'worthy person' concept of earlier times." Furthermore, according to the Court, Congress, by codifying the Flemming rule and providing matching payments for state social welfare services in the 1962 Public Welfare Amendments, "has determined that immorality and illegitimacy should be dealt with through rehabilitative measures rather than measures that punish dependent children and that protection of such children is the paramount goal of AFDC." In the Court's view, poor children were no less worthy of assistance because of their parent's behavior.

The Warren Court's decision rewrote the Social Security Act's meaning. The 1962 Public Welfare Amendments did not preclude states from using "suitable home" provisions to determine eligibility for AFDC. The law expressly permitted states to terminate a family's welfare benefits if the state provided "other adequate care and assistance" for the family's children, such as foster care, for a dependent child. The 1962 law's social services provisions merely provided states with additional federal funds to rehabilitate AFDC mothers. The law was silent on issues of immorality and illegitimacy.

The Court also ruled that Alabama did not have the statutory authority to require a "substitute father" to support the mother's children. It argued that in 1935, Congress "must have meant by the term 'parent' an individual who owed to the child a state-imposed legal duty."[15] Thus, according to the Court, states could not consider the income or resources of an unrelated adult in determining AFDC eligibility unless the adult had a legal duty to support the family.[16]

Yet the 1935 Social Security Act contained no restrictions on the states' ability to define a "substitute parent." To the contrary, the act's intent was to leave such decisions entirely to the states. The Senate Finance Committee's bill report explains the intent: "This program does not represent an attempt to dictate to the States how they shall care for families of this character, but is recognition of the fact that many States need aid to carry out the policy which they have already adopted."[17]

The Court's decision had far-reaching immediate consequences. At the time, eighteen states had various forms of man-in-the-house laws. In Alabama alone, the regulation had resulted in the removal of an estimated twenty thousand individuals, mostly children, from the AFDC rolls. Nationwide, similar man-in-the-house rules had removed an estimated half-million individuals from the welfare rolls.[18]

The long-term ramifications were even larger. The Warren Court had concluded that the original 1935 Social Security Act "intended to provide programs for the economic security and protection of all children."[19] The law therefore could not have intended to leave "one class of destitute children without meaningful protection."[20] With these words, it reinterpreted the original Social Security Act to mean that every destitute child was equally worthy of receiving benefits under the law. State laws that imposed eligibility conditions other than financial need were legally suspect.

Armed with the *King v. Smith* decision, poverty lawyers brought a flurry of court challenges to state eligibility regulations. Lower courts, adopting a broad reading of *King*, embraced the Court's claim that all impoverished children were equally worthy to receive welfare benefits. In lower court cases from California to New York, courts struck down requirements that the mother identify the child's paternity and statutes that counted the income of a stepparent in determining the family's AFDC benefit, and that implemented work requirements. Finally, although the 1935 Social Security Act and subsequent amendments were silent on the issue of AFDC coverage of pregnant women, the federal government had allowed states the option of covering pregnant women and their unborn children. During the 1970s, ten out of fourteen district court decisions and five out of six circuit court decisions on pregnancy coverage determined Congress's legislative intent to mean that states must cover pregnant women and their (unborn) dependent children.[21]

In 1969, the Supreme Court struck down state welfare residence requirements. The lead case, *Shapiro v. Thompson*, involved Vivian Thompson, a 19-year-old unmarried mother who had moved from Dorchester, Massachusetts, to Hartford, Connecticut. She applied for AFDC benefits but had been rejected because she had not lived in Connecticut for the required one year.

Massachusetts and Connecticut argued that residence requirements were necessary to prevent states that provided high welfare benefit levels from becoming havens for nonresidents seeking assistance. An influx of nonresidents, they argued, would overwhelm the government's fiscal capacity and thereby jeopardize benefits to all poor people.

In a 7–2 decision, the Supreme Court ruled that state welfare residence requirements violated the U.S. Constitution. The majority opinion, written by Justice William Brennan, asserted that the Constitution guaranteed individuals a "right to travel." He wrote, "The nature of our Federal Union . . . require[s] that all citizens be free to travel throughout the length and breadth of our land uninhibited by statutes, rules, or regulations."[22] The right to travel, according to the Court, included the right to move from one state to another to obtain more generous welfare benefits. Justice Brennan brushed aside objections that the right to travel to collect state welfare benefits appears nowhere in the Constitution by arguing that "a right so elementary was conceived from the beginning to be a necessary concomitant of the stronger Union the Constitution created."[23] Justice Brennan then concluded that this "elementary" right applied only to welfare, not to other activities. The decision was highly consequential, adding an estimated 100,000 to 200,000 families to the welfare rolls.[24]

In dissent, Chief Justice Warren asked why the majority's concept of the right to travel did not make illegal state residence requirements for voting in federal elections, state-supported college tuitions, and state occupational licenses. The Court's majority had no answer. Two years later, the Court still had no answer when it upheld state college tuition differentials based on residence without a mention of its *Shapiro v. Thompson* decision.[25]

The radical nature of the Court's ruling can be best appreciated by briefly reviewing the history of welfare residence requirements. During congressional consideration of the Social Security Act, limits on existing state residence requirements were extensively debated, but no member appears in the record questioning their constitutionality. In 1950, Congress rejected the Truman administration legislative proposal to prohibit residence requirements in public assistance programs.[26] In 1960, Congress prohibited state residency requirements in its new Kerr-Mills health care program but allowed the requirements to continue in other public assistance programs. Two years later, Congress rejected President Kennedy's legislative proposal to reduce the allowable time limits on state welfare residency requirements.[27] From these actions, it is fair to conclude that presidents and most members of Congress spanning the first thirty years of federal involvement in welfare policy regarded state welfare residency requirements as constitutional.

In 1969, Justice Brennan and a Supreme Court majority concluded that Presidents Roosevelt, Truman, and Kennedy and the numerous Congresses that served with them had incorrectly interpreted the Constitution. The Court also concluded that although federal involvement in public welfare had never entered the founding fathers' writings, the founders had meant to prohibit state welfare residence requirements.

The third case, *Goldberg v. Kelly* (1971), did more than any other single court case to establish an individual entitlement to welfare. The narrow issue before the Court was whether welfare agencies must grant recipients an evidentiary hearing before terminating benefits. The broader issue was the extent of the individual's right to welfare benefits.

Since the late 1930s, states had been required under the Social Security Act to provide a fair hearing to everyone who was denied aid under federal-state public assistance programs. The federal law sought to ensure that welfare applications were acted on in a timely manner but allowed the states considerable flexibility in designing their hearings' procedures. In most states, benefits were terminated immediately when a caseworker declared a welfare recipient no longer eligible.[28]

New York State maintained that it had the authority to grant benefits when it found an applicant to be eligible and it had a corresponding authority to terminate benefits when it found a recipient to be no longer eligible. Furthermore, the state argued, its administrative procedures, which provided welfare recipients with advance notification that benefits would be terminated and appeal rights, struck a reasonable balance between the recipient's interests and governments' fiscal interests.

In its 5–3 decision, the Supreme Court ruled that states were constitutionally required to provide an evidentiary hearing. In a sweeping decision written by Justice Brennan, the Court's majority rejected the idea that welfare is "merely charity" but was in fact protected by the due process clause. An evidentiary hearing before welfare benefits could be terminated was essential to ensuring these protections. Justice Brennan, citing the lower court's finding that welfare recipients faced "brutal need," ruled that an individual welfare recipient's interests outweighed the government's interest in limiting fiscal burdens on the general public.

Justice Brennan articulated the new liberal view of welfare that had emerged in the 1960s. "We have come to recognize that forces not within the control of the poor contributed to their poverty. . . . Welfare, by meeting the basic demands of subsistence, can help bring within the reach of the poor the same opportunities that are available to others to participate meaningfully in the community." Welfare, by "fostering dignity" and preventing "social malaise," was also a "means to 'promote the general Welfare.'"[29] This liberal perspective was a far cry from the liberal perspective that had prevailed when Franklin Roosevelt had ushered in the federal welfare role with the warning that welfare was a "subtle destroyer of the spirit."

The Court's opinion provoked a withering dissent from Justice Black, who found that the decision "as a matter of constitutional law finds no precedent in our legal system."[30] He chastised the majority for using its judicial power "to wander out of their field of vested powers and transgress into the area constitutionally assigned to the Congress and the people." Taking on Brennan's view that welfare should be regarded as property, Black wrote, "It somewhat strains credulity to say that the government's promise of charity to an individual is property belonging to that individual when the government denies that the individual is honestly entitled to receive such a payment."[31]

Federal district and circuit courts were even more aggressive than the Supreme Court in expanding welfare rights. Some federal judges overrode specific statutory language with their own interpretations of a law's overarching goals. Others interpreted the absence of any statutory language that would prevent states from implementing eligibility rules as meaning that the states had no authority to implement these rules. Still other judges invoked constitutional rights to strike down long-standing federal and state laws that restricted eligibility.

An example from legal scholar Shep Melnick illustrates how far certain lower court judges were willing to go granting welfare rights. In *Rothstein v. Wyman* (1969), district court judge Walter Mansfield struck down a New York State policy that provided higher benefits to AFDC recipients living in New York City than to those living in outlying areas on the ground that it violated the U.S. Constitution's equal protection clause.[32] In the judge's words:

> Among our constitution's express purposes was the desire to ensure domestic tranquility and to promote the general welfare. Implicit in those phrases are certain basic concepts of humanity and decency. One of these voiced as a goal in recent years by most responsible leaders both federal and state is the desire to ensure that indigent and unemployable citizens will have the bare minimums required for existence without which are expressed fundamental constitutional rights and liberties frequently cannot be exercised and therefore become meaningless.

After the Supreme Court decision in *Goldberg v. Kelly*, lower courts moved to the next step of establishing a constitutionally protected minimum welfare benefit level. The key case involved a Maryland law that, like many other state laws, set a maximum family AFDC benefit. Once a family reached the limit, it would receive no additional benefits for additional children. A federal district court ruled that Maryland's policy violated the Social Security Act and the equal protection clause of the Constitution's Fourteenth Amendment. The court held that the

Constitution required the state to treat younger and older siblings in large families as equally worthy individuals and therefore equally entitled to benefits. The family benefit limit, by denying benefits to younger children in large families, violated the Constitution.

The Supreme Court was unwilling to go that far. In *Dandridge v. Williams* (1970), it rejected all claims that either the Constitution or the Social Security Act required states to pay minimum levels of benefits. The Court noted that neither the executive branch nor Congress had ever disapproved of any of the twenty state maximum grant policies that were in effect at the time. The Court recognized Maryland's policy dilemma: "Given Maryland's finite resources, its choice is either to support some families adequately and others less adequately or not to give sufficient support to any family."[33] The Court held that maximum grants were a constitutionally and statutorily permissible policy for striking this balance.[34]

By the mid-1970s, the Supreme Court's period of welfare activism was coming to an end. In *Matthews v. Eldridge* (1976), the Court pulled back from its *Goldberg v. Kelly* ruling and held that Social Security disability benefits could be terminated without a hearing. It argued that the circumstances of the former case differed from those of *Goldberg*: "Still, the disabled worker's need is likely to be less than that of a welfare recipient. In addition to the possibility of access to private resources, other forms of government assistance will become available where the termination of disability benefits places a worker or his family below the subsistence level."[35]

Nevertheless, the entitlement rights the court established during its period of welfare activism, along with increasingly generous benefits, caused the number of welfare recipients to soar. The length of time welfare recipients remained on the rolls grew as additional court-ordered procedural rules greatly increased the difficulty of terminating recipients' benefits. The impact was felt by the federal judiciary as entitlement cases came to dominate the court's workload.

15 The Second Great Society

> In this past third of a century, government has passed more laws, spent
> more money, initiated more programs than in all our previous history. . . .
> We shall plan now for the day when our wealth can be transferred from the
> destruction of war abroad to the urgent needs of our people at home.
>
> *Richard Nixon, Inaugural Address, January 20, 1969*

RICHARD NIXON TOOK OFFICE AT A TIME OF SOAR-
ing entitlement expenditures. In the two years since passage
of the 1967 Public Assistance Amendments, federal Aid for Dependent
Children (AFDC) expenditures had risen by an astonishing 53 percent, and Aid to the Permanently and Totally Disabled expenditures
increased by 26 percent. Expenditures on the Medicaid and food stamp
programs, both operating in only parts of the country, had doubled.
Since 1967, spending on the three-year-old Medicare program had
risen by 33 percent, far outstripping experts' projections. Outlays for
Social Security retirement benefits, which dwarfed all other entitlement
programs, had grown by 26 percent.

Rapidly growing entitlement spending and the high cost of the Vietnam War had produced seven consecutive annual budget deficits, a
post–World War II record. The fiscal year 1969 budget that the new
president inherited showed a nominal surplus of revenues over expenditures.[1] But that surplus was due entirely to a temporary retroactive
10 percent surcharge on all individual and corporate income taxes that

had been enacted in June 1968. After 1969, another twenty-eight years would elapse before the federal budget would be balanced again.

Under these grim fiscal circumstances, President Nixon proposed a federal entitlement agenda that was even more ambitious than President Johnson's. In May 1969, he proposed to "end hunger in America itself for all time" by making the five-year-old food stamp program a national entitlement program free of charge for the poor. In July, the president proposed to provide thirteen weeks of federally financed unemployment benefits during economic downturns on top of the existing twenty-six weeks provided by most states. Also in July, he foreshadowed a later proposal for national health insurance by declaring that "We face a massive crisis . . . in our medical system." In August, he announced a welfare reform plan that would provide "a basic income to those American families who cannot care for themselves" and federal income supplements to workers higher up the income ladder. That same month, he proposed to replace an array of existing discretionary categorical grant programs with a new revenue-sharing program that would permanently entitle states and municipalities to a portion of federal revenues. The president capped off this list of first-year initiatives by calling for a 10 percent across-the-board increase in Social Security benefits and indexing benefits to the rate of inflation. Remarkably, in the midst of these proposals, President Nixon called for a "reversal of the trend toward ever more centralization of government in Washington, D.C."[2]

The proposals would add $15 billion in new entitlement spending on top of the existing $54 billion base of entitlement spending that was already growing by 10 percent per year. In theory, the array of new entitlements would be financed by a "peace dividend" that would be available by ending the Vietnam War. Yet early assessments indicated that any defense funds that might be freed up would likely be required to finance existing entitlements. As presidential advisor Daniel Patrick Moynihan put it, "The Vietnam dividend is as evanescent as the clouds over San Clemente."[3]

Two of President Nixon's most significant proposals, his family assistance plan and his national health insurance proposal, did not pass Congress. They ultimately proved to be a bridge too far for a large number of Republicans and southern Democrats. But the new programs spawned by these failed proposals, along with the proposals that were enacted, produced a series of entitlement liberalizations that proved to be every bit as expansive as those of the Great Society.

The Social Security Bidding Wars: 1969–1973

The years 1969 to 1973 witnessed several high-stakes bidding wars between the Republican president and the Democratic-controlled Congress over larger monthly Social Security benefits. In each case, the Democrats outbid the president and achieved success by attaching the benefit increase to important bills on other topics. Congress attached an across-the-board 15 percent Social Security benefit increase to a major tax measure in 1969. In 1971, 1972, and 1973, Congress appended across-the-board benefit increases of 10 percent, 20 percent, and 11 percent, respectively, to bills raising the national debt. President Nixon reluctantly signed the first three of these benefit hikes. Weakened and distracted by the Watergate and abuse-of-power scandals that rocked his administration, the president offered no objections to the 1973 increase.

The benefit increases were ostensibly designed to compensate beneficiaries for loss of purchasing power, but as had happened in prior legislation, the increases generally exceeded inflation. Taken together, the four benefit increases raised benefits for a person on the rolls since 1968 by 69 percent—or 50 percent more than the growth in consumer prices.[4]

In the late 1960s, most Social Security beneficiaries were still receiving benefits far in excess of their contributions. Retirees in 1968, for example, earned on average an inflation-adjusted rate of return on their Social Security contributions of about 10 percent. It took typical new retirees only three and a half years to receive in Social Security benefits all of their payroll tax contributions plus a 3 percent annual return on them. The next seven and a half years of the retiree's expected life span were lived on someone else's contributions.[5] With such windfall benefits, Social Security's popularity remained high. The temptation for elected officials to use the program for their electoral ends was too much to resist.

The story of the 1972 Social Security benefit increase illustrates the extent to which Social Security had become a powerful instrument for both Democrats and the president to secure electoral advantage.

In late 1971, the legislative machinery for a benefit increase began to move forward in more or less usual fashion. The House of Representatives included a 5 percent across-the-board increase in Social Security monthly benefits, to become effective in June 1972. Two months later, the Senate passed a 10 percent increase. Then presidential politics intervened.

The four major Democratic Party presidential candidates began bidding for votes with higher Social Security benefits as the chits. Speaking to senior citizens in February 1972, Senator George McGovern (D-SD) initiated the bidding war by calling for a 20 percent Social Security benefit increase. Ten days later, Wilbur Mills (D-Ark) announced his candidacy and also proposed a 20 percent benefit increase. Not to be outdone, Senator Edwin Muskie (D-Me), speaking to senior citizens in March, raised his previous bid from 15 to 20 percent. Later in March, Senator Hubert Humphrey (D-MN) upped the ante to 25 percent.[6] In early June, Russell Long (D-LA), the Senate Finance Committee chairman, saw the handwriting on the wall and announced his support for a double-digit benefit increase, declaring, "If there is going to be a parade, I think I'd rather be at the front of the parade rather than on the tail end."[7]

Looking for a vehicle to which the benefit increase could be attached, Senate Democrats found one in that year's debt ceiling bill. The debt ceiling imposed a limit on the total amount of debt the federal government could have outstanding at any point in time. The previous debt ceiling law was set to expire on July 1. Unless a new bill was enacted, the federal government would be forced to either default on its maturing debt or be required to sharply reduce government spending on all projects, programs, and services.[8] Because of such consequences, Congress had never failed to pass a necessary debt ceiling bill.

On June 28, less than thirty-six hours before the debt ceiling was scheduled to expire, Senator Frank Church (D-ID) proposed to append a permanent 20 percent Social Security benefit increase to the House-passed debt ceiling bill. He justified his proposal on the ground that it would remove "from poverty in one stroke almost 1.5 million older people."[9] To maximize the amendment's political benefit, Church's amendment called for the benefit increase to first appear in the October 1972 Social Security checks, one month before the upcoming federal elections.

The benefit increase would cost the Treasury a staggering $7.4 billion in its first year.[10] The amount was more than all annual federal spending on World War II, the Korean War, and Vietnam War veterans combined, twice the amount annually spent by all federal food and nutrition programs, and equal to the entire annual Medicare budget. Hardly a less efficient means of reducing poverty could be found. Less than 20 percent of the benefit increase would go to those living in poverty. The remainder would benefit mainly middle-income senior citizens.[11]

The Church amendment did not include any revenue provisions to finance the expensive benefit increase. Yet Senator Church claimed the higher benefits would not adversely affect Social Security's finances, explaining that "this welcome and seemingly astonishing result can be realized because my proposal is based upon new actuarial assumptions."[12]

Those assumptions were a new methodology that the Social Security trustees had endorsed three weeks earlier. The new method assumed that rising labor productivity would cause wages to increase far faster than prices of consumer goods, with the result that projected surplus revenues sufficient to finance the 20 percent benefit increase were suddenly and magically available.[13] The new methodology had been roundly criticized, particularly by Robert J. Myers, the long-time and highly respected former chief actuary of Social Security. Mr. Myers, who had been evaluating the financial impact of Social Security legislation for Congress since 1949, called the new methodology an "unsound actuarial procedure." Its adoption, he charged, was tantamount to "borrowing from the next generation to pay the current generations' benefits, in the hope that inflation of wages would make this possible."[14] His argument fell on deaf ears.

On June 30, with the clock ticking down, the Senate voted 82–4 to attach the 20 percent Social Security benefit increase to the debt ceiling bill and send it back to the House. During the ensuing eleventh-hour House debate, Ways and Means Committee member John Byrnes (R-WI) warned members:

> At no point has there been a study by the Ways and Means Committee of the new method of financing that has produced the "windfall" that now is going to be used for the 20-percent benefit increase. Not one word of testimony in public or executive session has been received on this subject. This fundamental change in the criteria by which the soundness of the social security trust funds has been measured for one-third of a century is being adopted willy-nilly by the Congress without even a cursory review.[15]

Congressman Byrnes predicted that enactment of the Church amendment "may well mark a turning point in Social Security's financial soundness."[16] Just before midnight, the House, having no practical alternative, passed the Senate bill 302–35, and sent the take-it-or-leave-it proposition to the president.[17] President Nixon criticized the bill as failing "the test of fiscal responsibility" and reluctantly signed it. In fact, he had only himself to blame: he had appointed the Social Security trustees who, by endorsing the new methodology, had given it legitimacy.

In October, just five weeks before the 1972 presidential elections, the first Social Security checks containing the increase were mailed to recipients. The envelopes containing the checks included a message from the Social Security Administration that made clear to all 28 million Social Security beneficiaries just who was responsible for the benefit increase: It had been "enacted by the Congress and signed into law by President Richard Nixon."[18]

The Church amendment also included a provision automatically indexing Social Security benefits to the cost of living and the maximum taxable wage to the economy-wide growth in covered wages. If consumer prices rose by 3 percent, monthly benefits would automatically rise by the same amount. If covered wages rose 5 percent, the maximum amount of each worker's wages on which payroll taxes would be levied would automatically rise by 5 percent. In each case, no congressional action was required. Both indexing provisions would become effective on January 1, 1975.

The automatic indexing of Social Security benefits enjoyed widespread bipartisan support in Congress. Most members agreed that the guarantee of inflation protection was desirable. Conservative members also supported indexing because they recognized that Social Security bills had become vehicles to which other measures that could not pass as free-standing bills were opportunistically attached. They objected to these "Christmas tree" bills but were reluctant to vote against any bill containing a Social Security increase. Among these members, there was a certain "stop me before I kill again" rationale. Republicans, who had rarely been willing to increase benefits as high as Democrats, had long supported indexing. They believed that their position during election year debates over Social Security benefit hikes had worked to their electoral disadvantage.

The double-digit benefit increases from 1969 to 1973 were fueled by large surpluses that provided the ammunition for the bidding wars. In each year, the Social Security surpluses were more than large enough to finance the benefit increases. But as before, the financial condition of the rest of the budget was immaterial in Congress's consideration of benefit increases. In each of these years, the rest of the federal budget was in deficit.

In spring 1974, the Social Security trustees ominously warned that both the retirement and disability trust funds had experienced a sudden reversal of fortune. Instead of running long-run surpluses, the trust funds were projected to be in long-run deficit. An immediate and permanent increase in payroll taxes of about 25 percent would be necessary to restore both programs to long-run solvency. A year later, the trustees reported that the financial status of both funds had deteriorated significantly: within a decade, neither program would be able to pay its promised benefits.[19]

The extraordinary reversal of the programs' short-run finances was in part due to the severe economic recession into which the country had fallen. Economic activity, which had begun to decline in late 1973, plummeted by summer 1974. Declining real wages and employment meant less payroll tax revenue, and high inflation that persisted during the recession meant greater Social Security outlays.

But the economic downturn could not explain the programs' projected long-term deficits. The longer-term problem was in part due to the fact that the United States was in the midst of a massive demographic shift. Newly available Census data at the time showed that the birth rate decline that had begun in the late 1950s had continued during the 1960s. The demographic shift meant that in the future, there would be far fewer workers to support a growing number of Social Security beneficiaries.

The 1975 trustees' report hinted that another factor was more seriously, and more fundamentally, behind Social Security's deteriorating finances. In vague terms, the trustees explained that the programs' insolvency was "due to unintended results of the automatic benefit adjustment provisions enacted in 1972."[20] In fact, Congress had written a flawed indexing formula for monthly benefits into the Social Security law: It overly indexed initial benefits for all new recipients starting in 1975.

How could such an error happen to the nation's largest and most important domestic program with millions of senior citizens and disabled workers relying on its benefits? For all of its forty-year history, the Social Security program had benefited from expert financial advice, counsel, and oversight. Professional actuaries inside and outside government carefully evaluated the financial impact of congressional legislation and made annual assessments of the program's finances. Decades of high-quality work had earned them considerable respect within their profession and on Capitol Hill. These policy experts from academia, congressional staffs, and the Social Security Administration had provided careful advice on how to design legislative changes to achieve major goals. The various Social Security advisory councils had provided the same services in a more formal role. And the House Ways and Means and Senate Finance committees, which had jurisdiction over Social Security, had always been attentive to detail and careful to avoid legislative errors.

Yet somehow a fundamentally flawed formula that put the program on a certain path to financial insolvency had been enacted into law without anyone raising a public notice or comment that anything was wrong. Now, three years after passage of the midnight law that wrote the flawed formula into the statute books, the Social Security trustees were vaguely hinting that there was an error in the indexing formula.

Congress had an opportunity to fix the problem in 1975 and 1976 but chose to do nothing. It would take a presidential election before Congress would address the problem and then four additional years before a change in the benefit formula could be put into effect.

The Family Assistance Plan

President Nixon's Family Assistance Plan was the first attempt by any president to comprehensively reform the federal-state welfare system since it was established in 1935.[21] The proposal produced an epic three-year battle that engaged all of Washington's major institutions. Although in the end Congress rejected the president's plan, the effort spawned two new federal entitlement programs: Supplemental Security Income and the Earned Income Tax Credit.

The president launched his Family Assistance Plan (FAP) on August 8, 1969, in a televised address to the nation. He declared the welfare system "a colossal failure" and explained this judgment by saying, "What began on a small scale in the Depression [in the] thirties has become a huge monster in the prosperous sixties. And the tragedy is not only that it is bringing states and cities to the brink of financial disaster, but also that it is failing to meet the elementary human, social, and financial needs of the poor."[22] His indictment of the AFDC program was blunt: "It breaks up homes. It often penalizes work. It robs recipients of dignity. And it grows." For these reasons, the president proposed that Congress "abolish the present welfare system and that we adopt in its place a new family assistance system."[23]

A negative income tax (NIT) was the centerpiece of the president's proposal. It would provide a federally guaranteed annual income floor to families with children in which the adult family head was unable to work. In the president's words, "The federal government [would] build a foundation under the income of every American family with dependent children that cannot care for itself."[24] The nationally uniform income guarantee would be set at about 40 percent of the poverty line, about $1,600 for a family of four (about $10,000 today). The plan would allow recipients to retain a portion of their assistance as their earnings rose by reducing benefits by 50 cents for each dollar of earnings. Assistance would phase out when the family's income nearly reached the poverty line. The phase-down in benefits stood in sharp contrast to the AFDC program, which eliminated almost all of the financial rewards from work by reducing benefits by a dollar for each dollar earned. The improved work incentives were the plan's major selling point.

The NIT had an illustrious intellectual lineage. The idea was developed during World War II by Nobel laureate Milton Friedman as a replacement for existing welfare programs. His NIT, which had been well known to economists since the early 1950s, attracted considerable public attention when Professor Friedman included the idea in his widely read 1962 book, *Capitalism and Freedom.*

The NIT had several features that attracted conservatives. Foremost among these was its ability to provide income support for the poor without severely discouraging work. But the program would maintain work incentives only if it replaced all existing welfare programs, a point that Professor Friedman repeatedly stressed. Conservatives were also attracted by the fact that all households would be eligible for assistance. They believed that providing assistance independent of family structure was less likely to encourage mothers to have children out of wedlock and fathers to desert their families. Finally, since the program depended solely on a household's income, the NIT program could be administered by the Internal Revenue Service, allowing the large welfare bureaucracy to be eliminated.

The NIT gained liberal adherents during the mid-1960s as the realization set in that the Kennedy-Johnson services approach was failing to produce its promised results. For liberals, NIT's main attraction was its guaranteed income. Liberals had long regarded an entitlement to a basic income level, an "income by right," as welfare policy's holy grail. The NIT's entitlement was a means of achieving this long-sought goal. Ralph Helstein, the liberal activist and president of the Packinghouse Workers of America, expressed this viewpoint well. When he learned of Professor Friedman's NIT, he exclaimed: "That's it, this conservative has provided us with a way to get a guaranteed income."[25] Liberals also preferred use of an impersonal Internal Revenue Service code rather than an often arbitrary and capricious welfare bureaucracy to determine benefits. Finally, liberals regarded income support as only part of the answer to poverty. Nutrition, housing, and health care assistance were equally necessary. Thus, an NIT program should supplement, not replace, existing in-kind benefit programs.

At its core, the NIT represented a radical extension of the class of worthy welfare claimants. It legally entitled government aid to any family or any individual whose income fell below a certain threshold regardless of the reasons. It drew no distinctions: all low-income families and individuals were worthy of receiving government assistance.

The FAP was a large step toward this end. President Nixon declared, "For the first time, the government would recognize that it has no less an obligation to the working poor than to the nonworking poor; and for the first time, benefits would be scaled in such a way that it would always pay to work."[26] The Nixon plan would establish a legal entitlement to federal cash welfare benefits. (The Supreme Court's *Goldberg v. Kelly* ruling was a year away.) The entitlement would apply to families with children, the poor elderly, the disabled, and the blind. The plan required all able-bodied adults, except those with preschool children in the home, to accept work or training as a condition of receiving assistance.

The FAP also represented a sharp and costly departure from the New Deal welfare policy. The Nixon plan also went far beyond Harry Truman's Fair Deal, John F. Kennedy's New Frontier, and Lyndon Johnson's Great Society to exert greater federal control over the provision of welfare assistance. The federal government would set virtually all welfare eligibility rules, benefit levels, and operational details. States would be relegated to administering the federal program. In its first year, the reform plan would double the amount of money the federal government was spending on the public assistance programs it was replacing and would add 12 million individuals to the 12 million already on the welfare rolls.[27]

The initial press reaction to the proposal was overwhelmingly positive. The *New York Times* described the president's plan as "by far, the most original and constructive initiative of his Administration."[28] (And this was after the president had proposed to "end hunger in America.") Similarly, the *Los Angeles Times* called the plan "a bold new blueprint" and an "imaginative, innovative-and a refreshing change from the past."[29] In reporting this news coverage to President Nixon, Daniel Patrick Moynihan advised him, "Enjoy it while you can, Mr. President. The criticism will soon start."[30] Subsequent events would prove him prescient.

A bidding war over the plan's guaranteed level of income began immediately. The AFL-CIO supported a national uniform income floor "at no less than the poverty level" and decried the Nixon administration's proposal as "grossly inadequate." The NWRO's welfare mothers pressed for a higher floor under the banner "$5,500 or Fight," a level 40 percent above the poverty line for a family of four. Not to be outdone, the National Federation of Social Service Employees called for a guaranteed income of "at least $6,000" plus indexing benefits to the future cost of living. Senator George McGovern, the Democratic Party's eventual presidential candidate in 1972, raised the stakes further by introducing an even more generous NWRO bill in Congress that would establish a $6,500 annual income floor, an amount equal to 150 percent of the poverty line. His Democratic presidential primary opponent, Hubert Humphrey, charged that the plan would cost $72 billion per year (increasing federal spending by about one-third) and would put half of the U.S. population on the welfare rolls.[31]

The NWRO led the liberal attack on the president's proposal, dubbing the FAP the "Family Annihilation Plan." For three years, the welfare mothers' confrontational style and fiery rhetoric had worked well in agitating for higher benefits in large northern cities. In 1969, they brought these same tactics to the nation's capital. In November, the organization's vice chairman, Beulah Sanders, in testimony before the Ways and Means Committee, threatened to disrupt the nation's capital, telling the committee, "Either you include us in decisionmaking that is going to govern our lives, or I am going to tell you right now, we are going to disrupt this State, this country, this capital and everything that goes on."[32] In January 1970, the NWRO carried through on its threat by disrupting a Department of Health, Education and Welfare (HEW) hearing. In May, the organization staged an eight-hour sit-in at the office of the secretary of HEW before being arrested.[33]

During the 1960s, the phrase "There's money in poverty" had circulated widely through the nation's capital. The money had spawned an array of new welfare services' lobbying groups, including the National Federation of Social Services Employees, the National Conference of State Welfare Administrators, and the Day Care and Child Development Council of America, along with the National Assembly for Social Policy and Development, which represented an alliance of twenty-two state and local social welfare organizations. When added to the old guard organizations with a stake in welfare policy, including the AFL-CIO, the National Association of Social Workers, and the American Public Welfare Association, the combination represented a formidable lobby.

These lobby groups exerted a powerful influence on the welfare debate. The main thrust of their argument was that the assistance plan would work only if there were a further infusion of federal funds for day care centers, vocational rehabilitation, job training, and legal services for the poor. The AFL-CIO called for "comprehensive manpower and training programs" that the organization had a large hand in administering. The Day Care and Child Development Council noted the "lack of physical facilities" and "lack of a trained manpower pool" needed to meet current day care requirements. The American Public Welfare Association asked "for greater Federal financial support for child welfare services" by making welfare services an entitlement with no limit on the amount that could be appropriated.[34] Self-interest, of course, was not limited to those who argued for expanded benefits. The president of the American Federation of State, County and Municipal Employees Union, whose thirty thousand social service workers were jeopardized by the president's plan, bluntly warned Congress that "this legislation threatens to eliminate the jobs of our people."[35]

The president's plan passed the House of Representatives in April 1970 with bipartisan support but immediately encountered a serious roadblock in the Senate. The issue of work incentives caused the trouble and ultimately played a critical role in FAP's defeat.

The president's plan did not replace existing in-kind welfare benefit programs, such as food stamps, Medicaid, and federal housing assistance.[36] Each of these programs contained its own work disincentive. The food stamp program reduced the "bonus" value of stamps between 20 cents and 30 cents for each dollar of additional family income. Both

Medicaid and housing programs had "sudden death" provisions that terminated lump-sum benefits entirely when a family's income reached a certain threshold. A working mother earning the minimum wage who lost eligibility for Medicaid, for example, would have to work an additional four months just to make up for the market value of the lost health care benefits.[37]

When the work disincentives of these programs were added to those of the FAP, little, if any work incentive remained. In the jargon of economists, the marginal tax rate, the rate at which total welfare benefits decline as family earnings rise, was at least 70 percent for FAP families that also received food stamps. The rate could exceed 100 percent for FAP recipients who also received Medicaid. The high marginal tax rates due to the failure of FAP to replace existing in-kind benefit programs led Professor Friedman to oppose the president's FAP, declaring that it was "a striking example of how to spoil a good idea."[38]

The large work disincentives in the president's plan were brought out dramatically in Senate Finance Committee hearings in May 1970. Senate Finance Committee chairman Russell Long (D-LA) and ranking Republican senator John Williams (R-DE) demonstrated that a family could actually end up worse off by working under the FAP program than by earning nothing at all. Chairman Long delivered a mortal blow to the proposal by asking, "What is the point of requiring the man to go to work if he's going to end up with less money? . . . Why do that?"[39]

Arguments that workfare would mitigate these work disincentives were met with great skepticism and damning data. The early results of the 1967 Work Incentive (WIN) program were dismal. According to one widely cited study, ninety-two thousand adult welfare recipients had been referred to work or training. Of this total, only thirteen thousand had jobs at the end of the first year. Worse, only two hundred welfare recipients nationwide had been removed from the rolls for refusing to take an appropriate job or training.[40] For all practical purposes, the WIN program was being ignored by state officials. In New York City, only 2 percent of the 2.8 million eligible recipients had been employed, and only 4 percent were enrolled in an approved training program.[41]

For the next two years, the White House attempted to fix FAP's fatal flaw. The effort forced the administration to confront the unpleasant but inescapable trade-offs between work incentives, the adequacy of benefits, and the number of families that received government aid. The work incentives could be improved by more slowly phasing down FAP assistance as a family's earnings rose, but that would necessarily increase the number of families receiving government assistance and the total cost of assistance to taxpayers. To offset these costs and case-load increases, the guaranteed benefit floor could be reduced or benefits provided by other programs could be cut, but that would make benefits less adequate. Liberals vehemently objected to program cuts. Conservatives, for their part, were unalterably opposed to welfare caseload increases. None of these efforts succeeded, and the president's FAP finally died in the Senate Finance Committee in spring 1972.[42]

After rejecting the plan, Congress sifted through the wreckage to see whether any elements could be salvaged. Although replacing the AFDC program with an NIT had been the centerpiece of the president's reforms, his proposal to establish a federally financed minimum benefit standard for the three other federal-state welfare programs was attractive. The proposal had been greeted warmly by the nation's governors and mayors, who would be relieved of a $1 billion annual burden. It was also supported by liberal welfare groups as an incremental step toward a nationally uniform federal floor for all welfare programs.

Congress went farther than the president had proposed when it abolished the three federal-state welfare programs and replaced them with a new federal entitlement program in the Social Security Amendments of 1972. The new federal program, Supplemental Security Income (SSI), replaced the Old-Age Assistance, Aid to the Blind, and Aid to the Permanently and Totally Disabled programs with a new program that established uniform federal benefits and eligibility rules for poor people age 65 and older, poor blind people, and poor disabled people.

The new $2 billion-plus entitlement represented another sharp break from the nearly forty-year-old New Deal consensus welfare policy. States would no longer determine eligibility and benefits for the poor elderly, blind, and disabled. The federal government would do so. States could supplement federal benefits but were otherwise relegated to administering the program under heavy federal oversight. Two decades later, the poorly drafted statute would lead to court decisions that allowed benefits for millions of children with dubious disabilities and newly arrived legal immigrants.

The new SSI program was part of only one of several significant entitlement liberalizations contained in the 1972 Social Security law. The Senate Finance Committee did not understate the magnitude of the law when the committee called it "the most massive revision of the social security laws that Congress has ever undertaken."[43] Besides creating the new SSI program, the law increased Social Security benefits for certain groups of recipients on top of the 20 percent across-the-board increase that had been enacted three months earlier; extended Medicare benefits to Social Security Disability Insurance recipients; adopted a policy of gradually reducing monthly Medicare premiums from financing 50 percent of program costs to 25 percent, thereby shifting more of the cost onto general taxpayers; extended Medicare coverage to people suffering from renal disease regardless of age; and expanded Medicaid coverage to mentally ill children in state mental institutions. Indeed, the 1972 law ranks as one of the most expensive statutes in the post–World War II era, just behind the 1965 law creating the Medicare and Medicaid programs and nearly on a par with the 1950 Social Security Amendments. The Senate Finance Committee estimated that the law, when combined with the previously enacted 20 percent Social Security benefit increase, would increase federal nondefense spending the following year by an astonishing 16 percent. Ironically, the AFDC program, which was most responsible for the welfare crisis and was the impetus for the reform effort, remained largely unchanged.

The final legislative fallout from the welfare reform's failure came two years later, when Congress enacted the earned income tax credit, which provided wage supplements to working poor and near-poor families with children. The debate over welfare reform demonstrated that work incentives had become increasingly important to Congress, reflecting the high rate at which mothers of young children in the general population continued to enter the labor force.

Food and Nutrition Assistance

President Nixon took office amid a remarkably sophisticated public campaign to convince Congress that America faced a widespread
hunger crisis.[44] The campaign, conducted by liberal food and nutrition activists, physicians, social welfare experts, members of Congress
and their staffs, and national media outlets —aptly named the "hunger
lobby"—sought to create a legal entitlement right to federal food assistance. Operationally, they did this by pressuring Congress to transform
the food stamp program and the various child nutrition programs into
federal entitlements. They succeeded on both counts.

In 1969, the federal government operated two major nutrition programs: food stamps and child nutrition. When President Nixon took
office, the food stamp program was still in its infancy. It operated at the
discretion of state governments in roughly half of the nation's cities and
counties. Food stamps, for example, were not available in New York
City until 1970.[45] Where it did operate, only 22 percent of the poor were
receiving benefits. The school lunch program, which partially reimbursed school districts and nonprofit child care centers for the costs
of meals served, operated largely at the discretion of school districts.[46]
A school breakfast program was added in 1966. Federally subsidized
summer meals to schools, day care, and recreation centers located in
poor neighborhoods were authorized in 1968.[47]

When President Nixon entered office, the food stamp and the child
nutrition programs were not entitlements. Congress funded the programs with fixed annual appropriations that were apportioned to the
states by a statutory formula. The programs also adhered to the New
Deal hands-off welfare policy. The federal government provided partial
financial support, and the states set eligibility rules and administered
the programs.

Senators Robert Kennedy (D-MA) and Joseph Clark (D-NY)
kicked off the campaign with a widely publicized trip to the Mississippi delta in 1967 to explore the extent of hunger and malnutrition.
The trip was followed by congressional hearings and two reports sponsored by special commissions affiliated with the United Auto Workers
that confirmed and extended the senators' findings to other parts of

the country. The second of these reports, "Hunger U.S.A," contained a scathing indictment of America and its food policy. The report's authors, the Citizens Board, wrote, "If you will go look, you will find America a shocking place. . . . To make four-fifths of a nation more affluent than any people in history, we have degraded one-fifth mercilessly."[48] Its central finding was "a prevalence of chronic hunger and malnutrition hitherto unimagined." The report identified the existence of chronic and severe hunger in 250 counties in 20 states. The devastating consequences of widespread hunger, according to the report, were "infant deaths, organic brain damage, retarded growth and learning rates, increased vulnerability to disease, withdrawal, apathy, alienation, frustration and violence."[49]

In May 1968 the CBS television network sensationalized the Citizens Board findings in a documentary, *Hunger in America*. The CBS program was narrated by Charles Kuralt, who was well known for his "On the Road" segment on the *CBS Evening News with Walter Cronkite* show, and was produced by Don Hewitt who would later produce *60 Minutes*. *Hunger in America* opened with the bold, unqualified assertion that "ten million Americans don't know where their next meal is coming from. Sometimes it doesn't come at all." This opening was followed by a scene of a hospitalized child who was near death. Kuralt informed the audience that the child was "dying of starvation. He was an American. He is now dead."[50]

Both the Citizens Board and CBS embraced the view that the hunger problem stemmed from a lack of income, which led them to recommend free food stamps for all recipients, higher monthly benefits, looser eligibility requirements, and an entitlement to school lunches for all elementary and secondary school children. CBS declared that food, "the most human need, must become a human right," and recommended eliminating the food stamp purchase requirement and replacing commodity distribution with cash.

There was some truth about hunger in the Citizens Board report and in the *CBS News* show. But the real problem in America was not hunger but malnutrition, which stemmed only partly from a lack of income. Other factors, such as ignorance, a lack of education, poor dietary choices, and the rise of convenient fast-food outlets, were at least as consequential. The possible health care consequences of hunger—high neonatal morbidity rates, growth and learning retardation, and vulnerability to disease—were caused by a complex of cultural and environmental factors. Malnutrition was a problem only in certain areas of the United States, mainly in rural areas and in pockets of central cities. The proper remedies of hunger and malnutrition are quite different from one another. Yet the Citizens Board report made no recommendations for improving public health services other than to call for more middle-class subsidies in the form of greater federal funding for health care professionals. CBS made no recommendations for improved nutrition education, sanitation, or public health services to address the problem.

Nevertheless, major newspapers accepted the hunger lobby's findings at face value. The *Washington Post* lauded the Citizens Board for "its eloquent and dismaying picture of the effects of dietary deficiencies in this country."[51] The *Post* called on Congress to transform the food stamp program into an open-ended entitlement, declaring that there should be "no limit on how much may be appropriated to fill the need." The *New York Times* opined, "It is a disgrace that, in this richest nation in the world, babies are dying of hunger and children are growing up sick and stunted."[52]

Later analysis showed that the Citizens Board report contained little factual evidence to support its conclusions. The report presented no data on food consumption by families in any income group. Its main evidence of widespread "chronic hunger" came from earlier food consumption surveys that found that one-third of all low-income families had "poor diets." The USDA had previously advised readers that a poor diet "is not synonymous with serious hunger and malnutrition" and had warned against using these surveys to draw any conclusions such as those by Citizens Board.[53] The House Agriculture Committee response to the report noted that the Citizens Board had in fact made few visits to the 250 "hunger counties." According to the committee, most of the Citizens Board "evidence" of hunger came from its researchers applying mathematical formulas to uncover statistical correlations between various measure of food intake and income.[54]

Critics charged that the CBS program could hardly be considered a documentary; instead, they said, it was political agitation propaganda designed to inflame public passions. The child on his hospital deathbed not only did not die; the baby's poor medical condition was due to the fact that he had been born three months premature and weighed only three pounds at birth. He had been hospitalized following a car accident involving his mother.[55] President Johnson's agriculture secretary, Orville Freeman, who had long been a forceful advocate for expanding food and nutrition programs, charged that *Hunger in America* was a "travesty on objective reporting. It presented to millions of viewers a distorted, oversimplified, and misleading picture of domestic hunger and what is being done to combat it."[56] According to Secretary Freeman, the CBS-TV show was "shoddy journalism" laden with "gross errors of fact that were available to CBS weeks, and in some cases, months before the program was broadcast."[57] CBS's reporters had been briefed on the department's efforts to provide nutrition assistance to the needy, but none of the material was included in the CBS report.

The CBS report ignored the efforts that the Kennedy and Johnson administrations had made to increase federal nutrition assistance. In 1968, nearly 20 million school children were receiving federally subsidized lunches per month, up from 10 million a decade earlier. The food stamp program, which had not existed in 1958, was providing food assistance to 2.4 million people per month. Similarly, the two-year-old school breakfast program was providing meals to 165,000 children per month, and 6 million more children were receiving nutrition assistance from the government's surplus food commodities than there had been in 1958. In light of these trends, Daniel Patrick Moynihan aptly summed up the irony of the hunger lobby's charges: "The more government did to meet the nutrition needs of the poor, the more impassioned grew the insistence that it was not doing enough."[58]

The Democratic-controlled Senate formed a Select Committee on Hunger and Malnutrition, chaired by Senator George McGovern (D-SD), to be a public forum for nutrition advocates to disseminate information for expanding federal nutrition programs, and the committee regularly held hearings to publicize the extent of hunger in the United States. Congressional staff members worked hand-in-glove with reporters from the *New York Times* and the *Washington Post* to publicize hunger issues. Staff members regularly leaked documents to the press. Reporters, in turn, gave staff advance notice of major news stories so that timely hearings could be held. And then the hearings served as material for another round of press stories.[59] Experts who were sympathetic to the committee's cause regularly testified. Academicians and physicians from inside and outside government described widespread hunger throughout the country, the consequences of which included anemia, dental problems, goiter, and deficiencies of vitamins A, C, and D.

The Washington establishment was shocked to hear that widespread hunger and malnutrition could exist in a country with such extraordinary abundance. The hunger lobby had successfully given poverty a new face, and by the time Richard Nixon took office, proposals to expand federal nutrition programs were sweeping through Congress.

President Nixon declared on May 9 to Congress that the time had come "to put an end to hunger in America itself for all time." In a statement that matched the hunger lobby's hyperbole, the president asserted that "the honor of American democracy is at stake."[60] To preserve the nation's honor, the president proposed that food stamps be available to all low-income people, the able-bodied, as well as those who were unable to work. Eligibility was not to be conditioned on recipients' willingness to work.

The combination of the hunger lobby's extraordinary efforts and President Nixon's proposals produced a record-shattering legislative blitzkrieg of nutrition legislation over the next five years that transformed the food stamp and child nutrition programs into large-scale federal entitlements.

The food stamp program's transformation was achieved by acts of Congress in 1970 and 1973. The 1970 law established uniform standards, increased monthly food stamp benefits by 30 percent, and indexed them annually to the economy-wide growth in food prices. The 1973 law made the program national by requiring states to operate a food stamp program within their jurisdictions on an all-or-nothing basis; that is, if the program operated in one county, it must operate in all counties.[61] The 1973 law also indexed monthly benefits twice a year to inflation.[62]

The 1970 and 1973 laws were milestones that created the first national welfare entitlement program for individuals regardless of their demographic circumstances and established for the first time a nationally uniform floor on federal welfare aid. By relegating state governments to administrative agents for the program, the laws put the final nail in the New Deal welfare policy's coffin.

Congressman Richard Goodling (R-PA) had warned that the food stamp program was "on its way to becoming one of the largest welfare functions of the Federal Government."[63] His warning was prescient. Between 1970 and 1973, the number of food stamp recipients increased from 4.4 to 9.4 million, despite a significant improvement in the economy. By 1975, economic recession and the 1973 law's liberalizations caused the food stamp rolls to soar to a record-high 17 million people, exceeding the AFDC caseload by 6 million and making the program the nation's largest welfare program.[64]

The operation of the food stamp program in Puerto Rico following the 1973 law provides a stark example of the unintended consequences of the national entitlement standards. Puerto Rico's relatively low income in combination with a federal income-eligibility threshold at the U.S. poverty line resulted in more than half of the commonwealth's entire population on the food stamp rolls in mid-1976. By the end of the decade, food stamps were competing with U.S. currency as the commonwealth's medium of exchange as recipients used *coupanes* to buy all sorts of nonfood items.[65]

The transition of child nutrition programs to an entitlement began with the inclusion of an apparently minor provision in the 1970 School Lunch Amendments. The law's stated main purpose was to "clarify responsibilities related to providing free and reduced-price lunches and preventing discrimination against children."[66] Buried in section 6 of the law was a declaration that beginning on January 1, 1971, free or reduced-price lunches "shall be served" to all poor children.[67] The authorizing statute did not provide any funds to carry out the declaration. Those funds would be made available in a separate appropriations bill. The noncontroversial law passed the House by a voice vote and the Senate by a vote of 85–0.

The subsequent appropriations bill, however, failed to provide sufficient funds to serve all poor children. The Nixon administration, rather than request additional funds, issued regulations designed to limit the program's expenditures to the amount appropriated. The regulations restricted reimbursements to lunches served only to poor children.[68]

School food administrators, governors, members of Congress, and the hunger lobby cried foul. The major Washington newspapers piled on. The *New York Times*, noting President Nixon's earlier promise to end hunger, blasted the administration by saying, "Hungry children cannot eat promises." The *Washington Post* reported charges by school lunch officials that "the reduced federal payment would cripple their lunch programs."[69] The reality was, of course, quite different. Congress was equally to blame. It had approved a law with a costly mandate and then had failed to adequately fund it.

In response to the uproar, Congress overrode the administration's regulations and established statutory minimum federal school lunch reimbursement rates. The 1971 School Lunch Amendments also authorized the use of customs revenues to finance expenditures that were in excess of the amounts available from annual appropriations.[70]

These provisions transformed the program into an entitlement. The statutory reimbursement rates obligated the federal government to fixed payments per meal served. The economic characteristics of students, as attested to by their parents and the administrative actions of individual school districts, determined the number of meals served. The open-ended tap on a portion of customs revenues ensured that whatever funds were needed to meet the federal financial obligation were automatically available. The new entitlement law passed the House by a vote of 354–0 and in the Senate by a voice vote.

Laws transforming other child nutrition programs and the commodity assistance program into entitlements quickly followed. The entitlement laws enacted in 1974 and 1975 required that all eligible children be served meals, milk, or commodities at fixed federal reimbursement rates.[71]

National Health Insurance

Following the enactment of Medicare and Medicaid, health care costs soared. From 1965 to 1969, they rose 50 percent faster than overall consumer prices. The cost growth, itself partially the product of Medicare and Medicaid, caused President Nixon and many members of Congress to conclude that the nation faced a health care emergency. In a July 1969 message to Congress, President Nixon declared that U.S. health care markets faced a "massive crisis" and warned that if Congress did nothing, "we will have a breakdown in our medical care system."[72] Senator Edward Kennedy (D-MA), who along with organized labor was spearheading a campaign for national health insurance, echoed the president's sentiments, declaring that "doctor bills, hospital bills, the cost of drugs, nursing home care, and the like are out of control." Moreover, the senator charged, the high cost had produced an "obvious inequity of access to health care and the availability of health care."[73] Senator Frank Yarborough (D-TX), chairman of a key health care committee, joined in by saying, "The health care system in our nation now is in shambles," and warning that "only the wealthiest of us will be able to receive health treatment in the coming years."[74]

By mid-1971, more than a dozen major national health insurance plans had been introduced in Congress. The plans fell into three groups: single-payer plans modeled on Social Security, plans that required employers to provide their employees with health insurance, and subsidies in the form of tax credits to encourage individuals to voluntarily purchase private health insurance.

The single-payer approach would entitle all U.S. residents to a nationally uniform, comprehensive, health insurance plan.[75] The federal government would administer the plan and reimburse all health care providers for their services using government-determined prices.[76] Under the initial proposals, the federal government would offer insurance plans with no premium or copayments. Later proposals required modest copayments. Program administration would be carried out by a national health insurance board with vast regulatory authority. One indication of the extent of that authority was a provision that authorized the board to decertify health care facilities of its choosing upon a board finding that an excess supply existed in a geographic area. The plan would be financed by a new 4 percentage point payroll tax levied on top of the existing 10.4 percent Social Security payroll tax and an equal amount of general revenue.[77] This approach was led in Congress by Senator Kennedy with the support of the AFL-CIO and the United Auto Workers.

The employer mandate approach required employers to offer their employees a health insurance plan that met federally specified minimum benefits and maximum copayment standards.[78] Under the mandate, the costs of universal health insurance would not appear in the federal budget ledgers but would instead be paid for by workers and businesses in the form of lower money wages and lower business profits. To enforce the employer mandate, employees could bring lawsuits in federal court against employers who failed to provide health insurance. Nonworking people would be entitled to a federally provided, federally subsidized, and federally administered health insurance plan provided free to very poor families and subsidized on a declining scale to families with higher incomes. This program would replace most of the existing Medicaid program. The employer mandate approach was proposed by the Nixon administration and supported by moderate congressional Republicans.

The tax credit plan, called Medicredit, subsidized individual purchases of a private, federally approved health insurance plan. The credit would cover the full premium cost for poor people and a declining percentage of the premium cost for higher-income people. Those who owed no federal taxes would receive the "tax credit" as a government grant. Those whose tax credit exceeded their income tax liability would receive the excess credit as a government grant. Tax experts labeled this type of tax credit a "refundable credit," a policy that gave recipients a refund for tax payments that were never owed. This approach was sponsored by Republican conservatives and the American Medical Association.[79]

Significantly, none of the proposals contained any provisions that would appreciably contain rising health care costs.[80] Thus, while curtailing health care costs was the initial impetus for health care legislation, the main thrust of the proposals was to provide a universal entitlement to health insurance coverage.

Nevertheless, supporters claimed that their plan would reduce health care costs. Official estimates, however, showed the opposite.[81] According to official estimates at the time, the single-payer approach would increase aggregate U.S. health costs by 8 percent, the Nixon administration plan would reduce costs by 4 percent, and the Medicredit plan would lower costs by 2 percent. All are likely underestimates. Using modern assumptions that incorporate the expected increased use of health care services, the single-payer social insurance plan would have doubled aggregate U.S. health care spending, and the Nixon plan and Medicredit plan would have increased aggregate spending by as much as 12 percent and 18 percent, respectively.[82] In retrospect, had any of the national health insurance plans that Congress considered in the early 1970s been enacted, they would almost certainly have been self-defeating attempts to curtail the growth in national health care costs.

The national press treatment of the health insurance proposals was mixed, just as it was in the 1940s. The *Washington Post*, continuing its unwavering support for entitlement expansion, described the Kennedy/ UAW plan as "embodying an idea so natural, so reasonable, and so right that one wonders how the country would have floundered along for nearly two hundred years without it." Other newspapers vigorously opposed the idea. The *Tennessean*, for example, in an editorial entitled, "Thanks, But No Thanks, Senator Kennedy," opposed the Kennedy/ UAW plan by declaring that it was "fed up with the liberal oriented, spend-happy Congress."[83] The *New York Times* offered the more sober assessment that "there can be no disagreement with the goal of providing better medical care for more Americans at minimum cost, but experience with Medicare and Medicaid has demonstrated that radical change in medical practice can bring complications that had not been anticipated, particularly skyrocketing costs far beyond original estimates."[84]

The arguments employed during the early 1970s' debate were nearly a replay of the 1940s' debate over the Truman health care plan, as well as forerunners to the more recent debates on President Obama's Affordable Care Act.

National health insurance advocates argued, as they had in the 1940s, that individuals have a right to health care, and a federal entitlement program was the best way to provide it. Senator Edward Kennedy expressed this view when he introduced his Health Security Act in Congress by saying that his proposal "will enable our Nation to make the right to health care not merely a principle or a social goal, but a living and functioning reality."[85]

The advocates repeated the 1940s' assertion that the free enterprise system was incapable of ensuring sufficient access to health care. Senator Yarborough (D-TX), chairman of the Senate Labor and Public Welfare Committee, opened health care hearings with the statement that "Adam Smith's economic liberalism might have been appropriate for single-owned shops and English marketplaces in the 18th and 19th centuries. But, it simply will not do for our people's health needs."[86] Senator Kennedy echoed this sentiment by asserting that "our marketplace view of economics to govern our handling of people's health care needs" has produced high, rapidly rising health care costs and a declining quality of care. Senator Kennedy, citing infant mortality, death rates of mothers during childbirth, and life expectancy statistics, concluded, "Our rates of sickness, disability, and mortality already lag far behind the . . . reality" of medical care "in many foreign nations. . . . We know very well the dismal health record of the United States compared to the other major industrial nations of the world."[87] A Nixon administration task force report concluded, "The health-care delivery system cannot function effectively in response to consumer demand and provider self-interest but must be planned and managed so that the terms and conditions of payment shall have a powerful impact on the way the services are organized and delivered."[88]

National health insurance proponents viewed insurance not as a means of protection against financial risk from illness and injury but as a means of subsidizing individuals to offset the high cost of health care. According to this reasoning, too many Americans lacked health insurance. At the time, 20 percent of Americans lacked any hospital insurance, and 22 percent lacked coverage of surgery.[89]

Opponents of national health insurance pointed to the steady rise in health insurance coverage rates from 40 percent in the late 1940s to nearly 80 percent by the late 1960s as an indication that the private health insurance markets were working well. They also countered the claim that the U.S. health care system produced poor outcomes. Russell Roth, AMA president, asserted in testimony before the Ways and Means Committee "that more people are receiving more and better medical care from more and better trained physicians in more and better equipped facilities than ever before in history. These are not elements of crisis."[90] Opponents rejected the notion that poor-quality health care was responsible for relatively high U.S. infant mortality rates and relatively low U.S. life expectancies and instead were the result of lifestyle and nutrition factors.

By early 1974, a constellation of forces had lined up to make enactment of a national health insurance more likely than ever before. In February, President Nixon, who was under siege from the Watergate and abuse-of-office scandals, made another push for national health insurance. In April, the congressional leadership in both parties publicly affirmed their support for comprehensive health care legislation.[91] Senate Finance Committee chairman Russell Long and House Ways and Means chairman Wilbur Mills each introduced proposals. All of the major health care lobby groups, from the AFL to the AMA, supported one of the alternative national health insurance bills. Hearings held by the Ways and Means Committee that featured over five hundred witnesses provided a sure-fire indication of the high expectations for legislation. The *Washington Post* captured the growing momentum behind a bill: "The question being debated is not whether the United States should have national health insurance, but what kind should it have."[92]

President Nixon's August 8 resignation stunned the nation. President Gerald Ford entered office determined to demonstrate that the U.S. government could still function in times of great constitutional crisis. In his address to Congress and the nation four days after Richard Nixon's resignation, the new president declared that enacting a national health insurance plan should be part of that demonstration. He called on Congress to "sweat out a compromise." "Why," the new president asked Congress, "don't we write . . . a good health bill on the statute books, before this Congress adjourns?"[93]

The new effort to enact a health insurance bill ultimately foundered in the Ways and Means Committee in autumn 1974. Efforts to pass legislation would continue throughout the remainder of the 1970s, but no bill could garner enough votes to reach the floor of either chamber. The issue would then go dormant for the next twenty years until President Clinton revived it.

New Entitlements for the Unemployed

President Nixon's push for greater federal control over income transfer programs was not limited to welfare programs. His unemployment
insurance proposals included requiring that states broaden eligibility,
encouraging states to "voluntarily" adopt new federal minimum benefit
standards under the threat of a federal mandate, and creating a new
federally financed extended unemployment benefits program to provide an additional thirteen weeks of benefits during economic downturns.[94] These proposals were similar to previous attempts by the three
Democratic presidents, Harry Truman, John F. Kennedy, and Lyndon Johnson, and congressional liberals to impose minimum federal
standards for benefits and benefit durations. Congress had repeatedly
rejected these proposals on the grounds that state governments were
in a far better position to set benefit levels and benefit durations than a
distant federal government.

The extended benefits program proved to be the most important of
these changes. The president's proposal would provide thirteen additional weeks of federally financed unemployment benefits to workers
who had exhausted their regular unemployment insurance benefits
program in states with high unemployment rates. In both the 1957–
1958 and 1960–1961 recessions, Congress extended these benefits for
people who had exhausted their state benefits. However, due to the
lengthy process required to pass legislation, neither law was enacted
until these recessions were almost over.[95]

Timely provision of unemployment assistance during recessions was
a sound policy idea; however, the proposal did not take into account
Congress's long history of not only maintaining benefits once they are
provided but using existing benefits, regardless of their level, as a base
on which to build.

In August 1970, Congress overwhelmingly approved the new
extended benefits program by a vote of 77–0 in the Senate and 337–8
in the House.[96] But when the 1970 recession ended in November, Congress was unwilling to allow the extended benefits to expire. In December 1971, Congress extended the program for another six months. And

again in June 1972, eighteen months after the recession ended, Congress extended the program through March 1973.

When the next recession began in November 1973, the automatic extension of benefits quickly raised the duration of benefits to thirty-nine weeks in most states. But the longer duration proved to be a base for even longer benefit durations. Automatic extended benefits did little to obviate the need for congressional action. Pressure mounted on Congress to "do something" to alleviate the hardship of long-term unemployment. In December 1974, Congress bent to the pressures and lengthened the total duration of benefits from thirty-nine to fifty-two weeks.[97] Thirteen weeks later, in April 1975, Congress voted to give the same unemployed workers another thirteen weeks, increasing the total to sixty-five weeks.[98]

Benefits for Coal Miners

One additional new entitlement program created during Richard Nixon's presidency, black lung benefits for coal miners, warrants mention. The program is another extension of federal authority over income transfer functions that had been the province of state governments.[99]

A coal mine explosion in Farmington, West Virginia, in November 1968 killed an estimated seventy-eight miners and generated calls in Congress for federal oversight of mine safety and health. Coal state senators seized on the opportunity provided by a regulatory bill establishing federal oversight to create an entitlement for miners with black lung disease, a progressive respiratory disease that can lead to fibrosis, tuberculosis, and heart failure. The new benefit was justified, according to its advocates, because many state worker compensation programs did not cover coal miners with the disease. As Senator Robert Byrd (D-WV) put it, "We in Congress have a responsibility to work out some program whereby disabled miners would be given help when they are not eligible under State workmen's compensation programs."[100] The senator's justification was a variant of the equally worthy claim: Coal miners who were disabled by the disease were no less worthy of disability benefits than disabled workers in other industries. If state governments weren't willing to provide disability benefits, the federal government should.

The controversial bill passed both houses and was reluctantly signed by the president in December 1969. The law was a milestone on two fronts: It was the first other than veterans' benefits to single out a particular disease for compensation, and it brought the federal government squarely into the field of worker compensation.[101] The law's liberal provisions granted a lifetime entitlement to coal miners diagnosed with the disease. Taking a chapter out of the 1920s' World War I veterans' pension laws, the law established a presumption that coal miners who worked in the mines for at least ten years and had a respiratory or pulmonary impairment were entitled to benefits. When pressed about the liberal nature of these provisions, the law's supporters responded that the new entitlement was only a temporary emergency measure. It would cease paying new claims after January 1, 1972. By that time, states would include black lung disease in their worker compensation programs.

As so often happened in the past, the new law's actual cost far exceeded the estimates. The Nixon administration estimated that the new entitlement would cost between $150 million and $300 million per year. By 1972, actual costs were running in excess of $400 million.

After the law's enactment, the United Mine Workers union and other advocates for coal miners began pressing for liberalizations. Echoing assertions that had been made since the time of Revolutionary War pensions, they charged that proving disability based on long-ago events was too difficult. In addition, as the law's 1972 terminal date approached, no state had modified its worker compensation program to cover the disease in a manner consistent with the federal law. To do so would assume what was now a federal responsibility.

Congress responded with the Black Lung Amendments of 1972 that greatly liberalized the program. The amendments loosened medical requirements and extended eligibility to miners employed in surface mines. It also expanded eligibility to coal miners who worked in the mines for at least fifteen years and had any respiratory or pulmonary disease, regardless of whether the disease was a consequence of coal mine work. The statute expanded the benefit package to include dependent benefits and medical care benefits. Finally, the law allowed disabled black lung benefit recipients to work in other occupations without their earnings offsetting their black lung benefits. In the following year, black lung benefit outlays soared to just under $1 billion per year, exceeding the costs estimated at the time of the amendments by 25 percent.

Richard Nixon's Great Society II

Richard Nixon's presidency constitutes the second phase of the most rapid expansionary period for entitlements in U.S. history. From 1969 to 1974, six new entitlements were created, and a seventh, the earned income tax credit, was well on its way to becoming law. Congress, often at President Nixon's request and invariably with his support, granted new entitlements for disabled workers, coal miners, school districts, state and local governments, and the long-term unemployed. Congress increased Social Security benefits for retired people and disabled workers by 69 percent and raised benefits sharply for newly entitled food stamp and Supplement Security Income programs. Meanwhile, the AFDC program, the largest and most controversial welfare program, remained unreformed as its caseload doubled from the time Richard Nixon was elected president to 1975. The federal courts joined in with sweeping decisions granting new legal rights to welfare recipients at a speed unprecedented in judicial history.

As a result, from 1969 to 1975, inflation-adjusted federal entitlement spending grew annually at a remarkable 10 percent, registering an 86 percent increase in six years. By 1975, entitlements accounted for nearly half of all federal spending (48 percent) compared to 31 percent just six years earlier. In fact, the blistering pace of entitlement liberalizations during Nixon's presidency was as rapid as during Johnson's presidency. Total annual inflation-adjusted entitlement expenditures grew 20 percent faster under President Nixon than they had under President Johnson. While inflation-adjusted Social Security retirement expenditures grew at the same pace under the two presidents, disability insurance, food stamps, and AFDC expenditures registered more rapid increases. New entitlements, including Medicare for the disabled, federal unemployment benefits, black lung benefits, general revenue sharing, and a new Supplemental Security Income program added to the growth under President Nixon.

By 1975, the modern federal entitlement edifice was virtually complete. Nearly all of today's entitlement programs were on the federal statute books. In subsequent years, these entitlements would be repeatedly liberalized, sometimes significantly. But no new major entitlements would be enacted for another thirty-five years when Congress established the Affordable Care Act's health insurance subsidies.

Also by 1975, entitlement laws and legal decisions had put the federal government firmly in charge of who receives welfare benefits and how much they would receive. The signs of cracks in the New Deal welfare policy that had become apparent when Richard Nixon took office had caused the New Deal policy to collapse. The federal government now assumed control over most welfare eligibility and benefits decisions. For the most part, the state government welfare role was reduced to administering programs under federal rules and regulations. The federal government exclusively set eligibility rules and administered benefits for 28 million Social Security recipients, 25 million Medicare recipients, 6 million earned income tax recipients, and nearly 500,000 recipients of black lung benefits. The federal government determined benefits and eligibility rules and paid state and local governments to administer benefits for 17 million food stamp recipients, 4 million Social Security disability recipients, 2.5 million SSI recipients, and 25 million children who were receiving school lunches. State governments still retained control over benefit levels and eligibility rules for 11 million AFDC recipients and 22 million Medicaid recipients, but not without a heavy dose of federal administrative oversight.

A Brief Reflection on Post–World War II Entitlement Growth

The New Deal had broken new ground by extending federal entitlement programs to the U.S. population at large. Previously, entitlement programs had been limited to those who had performed services on behalf of the government, mainly wartime veterans. The explosive nature of these entitlements quickly became apparent as they grew rapidly to become major parts of the federal government's activities and its budget. But because entitlements were limited to veterans, their burden on the public had remained small. Veterans' pensions exceeded 1 percent of the nation's annual output of goods and services only twice between 1791 and 1940.

The fiscal impact of extending entitlements to the general population was profound. The impact is shown in Figure 2, which displays federal expenditures on entitlements, national defense, and all other federal programs (excluding net interest) as a percent of gross domestic product from 1947 to 1975.

In the years immediately following World War II, total entitlement spending (shown by the red line) equaled about 3 percent of GDP. Veterans' compensation and pension payments, mainly for World War II veterans, and GI Bill benefits accounted for three-fourths of federal entitlement spending. The New Deal entitlements for segments of the general population made up virtually all of the remainder but amounted to less than 1 percent of GDP.

Total entitlement spending grew steadily during the 1950s and reached 4 percent of GDP in 1960. Through the first half of the 1960s, entitlement spending increased at the same rate as the rapidly rising GDP. Over this twenty-year period, the composition of entitlement spending changed markedly as the rapidly growing New Deal entitlements offset the declining veterans' benefits share of GDP. By 1964, the New Deal entitlements accounted for three-fourths of all entitlement spending, an amount equal to about 3 percent of GDP.

The historic and unprecedented flurry of entitlement legislation from 1965 to 1975 produced a sharp upswing in entitlement expenditures. From 1965 to 1975, entitlement spending relative to GDP grew at a 6.9 percent annual rate, the second fastest ten-year growth rate during the entire post–World War II era before or since, exceeded only by the growth from 1966 to 1976. By 1975, only forty years since federal entitlements were first extended to the general population, entitlement spending reached 10 percent of GDP.

To the extent that government expenditures reflect government priorities, the growth of entitlements relative to national defense represents a historic reordering of federal priorities. As Figure 2 shows, throughout the 1950s and 1960s, national defense remained the federal government's highest expenditure category, just as it had been

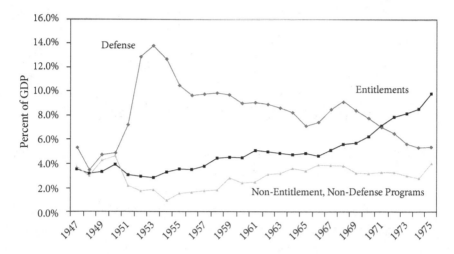

Figure 2. Federal Spending on Entitlements and Other Programs: 1947–1975.
Source: U.S. *Budget, Fiscal Year 2017,* Historical Tables, Tables 1.2, 3.1 and 13.1,
U.S. Budget, Fiscal Years 1942–2017.

throughout prior U.S. history. Defense spending surged during the
Korean and Vietnam wars, but even in peacetime while its relative
importance declined as entitlement spending grew, it retained its number one position. In the early 1970s, when the galloping entitlement
spending roared past national defense, entitlements replaced defense as
the federal budget's largest expenditure. From the early 1970s forward,
the federal government's highest priority, as measured by its expenditures, would be on income transfer programs for elderly, disabled, and
low-income people. National defense would stand second in line.

16 First Inklings of Fiscal Limits, 1975–1980

> The beneficial effect of State intervention, especially in the form of
> legislation, is direct, immediate, and, so to speak, visible, whilst its
> evil effects are gradual and indirect, and lie out of sight. . . . Hence the
> majority of mankind must almost of necessity look with undue favor upon
> government intervention.
>
> A. V. Dicey (1914)

PREVIOUS CHAPTERS DISCUSSED HOW BUDGET
surpluses throughout U.S. history created irresistible pressures for entitlement liberalizations. This chapter explores Congress's initial response to persistent federal budget deficits. From 1975 to 1980, deficits reached peacetime record highs that remain among the largest in history. The deficits were direct consequences of the prior decade's entitlement expansions that unleashed a torrent of federal spending. Congress had not only spent the overall federal budget into structural deficit, it had also, quite literally, spent the Social Security retirement and disability trust funds into a state of financial exhaustion.

Faced with large structural deficits, Congress dramatically slowed the pace of entitlement expansions. No new major entitlements were written onto the federal statute books during President Carter's term in office. To the contrary, the efforts of President Carter and the Democratic Party's liberal wing to establish legal rights to a guaranteed income and establish a national health insurance plan failed.

Expansions in existing entitlements were few, and, with the exception of the food stamp program, confined to relatively small entitlement programs. Most notable, to prevent Social Security's imminent bankruptcy and reduce its large unfunded long-term liability, Congress reduced benefits that future recipients were promised by the ill-advised 1972 Social Security law and raised payroll taxes dramatically. Following long-standing precedents that date back to Revolutionary War pensions, Congress did not change benefits to current recipients. Congress's unwillingness to reduce Social Security benefit levels for current recipients, even though these were the result of an admittedly flawed formula, is illustrative of the permanence Congress attaches to an existing entitlement benefit.

The Ford Presidency

When Gerald Ford assumed the presidency in August 1974, the combination of rapidly rising entitlement spending and a deep economic recession were producing record increases in federal spending and budget deficits. The fiscal year 1975 budget deficit set a new post–World War II record high, and the deficit for the next year, the nation's bicentennial year, broke that record. Budget projections by the new Congressional Budget Office made clear that budget deficits loomed as a permanent fixture. According to the office, budget deficits would persist for at least another five years even if the economy magically grew at an annual inflation-adjusted rate of 5 percent.[1]

President Gerald Ford took a tough-minded stance against higher spending, the first post–World War II president to do so. He began mildly as the nation was reeling from Richard Nixon's resignation. In September 1974, the new president called on Congress to hold spending to $300 billion, a generous 10 percent increase over the prior year's level. As the magnitude and growing certainty of deficits became clearer, however, President Ford's position hardened. In January, he announced that he was "proposing no new spending initiatives in this budget other than those for energy" and significant restraints on domestic programs, including entitlements.[2] The announcement effectively put national health insurance and comprehensive welfare reform legislation on indefinite hold. His proposed restraints included capping the cost-of-living adjustments in all entitlement programs. Later, he proposed legislation to require food stamp and Medicare recipients to pay more for their benefits, slow the growth in Social Security benefits, and cap federal spending on child nutrition, Medicaid, and social services programs.

The liberal post-Watergate Congress rejected all of President Ford's entitlement proposals. But still the president pressed on. After Congress rejected his legislative proposals to curtail food stamp and child nutrition subsidies, he proposed new regulations to achieve the same end. Congress and the federal courts then blocked these regulatory changes. President Ford also used his veto to thwart Congress's attempt to liberalize the child nutrition programs and used the threat of veto to deter Congress from expanding other entitlements.

The two-year battle between President Ford and Congress ended in a virtual draw preserving the entitlement status quo. Other than the earned income tax credit and the expansion of the Trade Adjustment Assistance program, there were no significant entitlement expansions or reductions during President Ford's brief term in office.

The Carter Years: 1977–1981

In the absence of legislation to curtail entitlements, their expenditures continued to grow rapidly. The result was the emergence of historically large deficits that persisted throughout President Carter's term in office and proved to be an important constraint on further entitlement expansions. Carter's signature initiative, comprehensive welfare reform, failed even more dismally than had President Nixon's, marking the end of a decade-long effort to establish a federally guaranteed annual income floor through a negative income tax. Liberals settled for an alternative, indirect, and less satisfactory method of using the food stamp program to establish a national income floor. This was achieved in 1977 when Congress eliminated the program's purchase requirement and thereby completed the program's transformation to an income maintenance program from a nutrition program. National health insurance, which Senator Ted Kennedy advocated on behalf of liberals but received only lukewarm support from President Carter, also failed in Congress. Its defeat signaled the end of major efforts for another decade and a half to pass national health insurance, the final prong in the Progressive era's long-term policy goals. The effort would be revived by President Clinton without success and would eventually succeed under President Obama. President Carter's much more modest proposals to expand college student loans to middle-income students did pass, as did his plan to make the black lung program a permanent fixture in the budget.

The most notable entitlement law during the Carter presidency was a historic change in Social Security retirement and disability benefits.

Social Security

When President Carter took office, the magnitude of Social Security's precarious financial future was well understood in Washington. For three years, Congress had held hearings on the flawed benefit formula, received reports filed by special expert Social Security panels, and weighed alternative assessments and recommendations, but it had taken no action. Meanwhile, Social Security expenditures had spiraled upward. From 1974 to 1977, Social Security retirement expenditures increased by 48 percent, and disability expenditures rose by an even more astounding 82 percent. The three-year 41 percent increase in Social Security revenues had not been nearly sufficient to finance either program's rapidly growing expenditures. The result was three consecutive years of Social Security deficits and a steady deterioration in both trust funds' financial position. Early in 1977, the Social Security trustees reported that the retirement fund's balance would be exhausted by early 1983, a scant six years away, and the disability program would be bankrupt in 1979. The trustees' long-term projections were equally bleak. They estimated that a permanent 70 percent tax increase was required to restore the retirement trust fund's solvency, three times their 1974 estimate. Similarly, a permanent 160 percent tax increase was immediately necessary to eliminate the disability trust fund's long-term deficit, six times the 1974 estimate.[3]

The causes of Social Security's bleak financial prospects were well understood. The poorly performing economy and the large benefit increases that had been granted earlier in the decade combined to create the short-term deficits. The long-term deficits were products of changing demographics and the flawed formula that Congress had adopted during the hectic days in late June 1972.[4]

The demographic problem was straightforward. The baby boomers, born between 1946 and 1964, would begin to retire starting around 2010. Longer life expectancies would raise the financial burden of this group even higher. The rapid decline in the U.S. birth rate since the 1960s, in full swing in the 1970s, meant that relatively few workers would be available to finance benefits promised to the baby boomers. Had Social Security operated like a private defined contribution retirement program by setting aside workers' contributions for their retirement, demographic change would not have created a problem. But under Social Security's defined-benefit, pay-as-you-go policy, the future financial shortfall could be eliminated only by some combination of reducing benefits for future retirees and increasing taxes on future workers.

The flawed indexing formula that Congress enacted in 1972 had not affected cost-of-living increases once a retiree began receiving benefits, but it had overindexed workers' initial Social Security benefits to inflation. Congress could not have written the error into the statute books at a worse time. Consumer prices were rising at peacetime record-high rates. As a result, new retirees in 1977 were receiving monthly benefits that were about 20 percent higher after adjusting for inflation than benefits new retirees just five years earlier had received. The flawed formula's generosity was expected to grow over time. According to projections in 1977, a 57-year-old typical worker who would retire in 1985 would receive an inflation-adjusted monthly benefit that was 48 percent greater than the amount received by a typical new retiree in 1975. A 37-year-old typical worker in 1977 could expect to receive an inflation-adjusted monthly benefit that was more than double the amount received by the typical new retiree in 1975. Under the flawed formula, benefits to new retirees would rise faster than workers' wages, causing Social Security benefits to replace an ever-increasing percentage of retirees' preretirement earnings. Low-wage workers who were in their 20s in 1977 could expect to receive monthly Social Security benefits that exceeded their monthly preretirement earnings.[5] The flawed formula had a similar effect on disability benefits: Monthly disability benefits would eventually exceed workers' after-tax take-home pay.

Commenting on the flawed formula, Senate Finance Committee chairman Russell Long (D-LA) aptly summarized the view of many members of Congress: "We never had any problem with Social Security financing, short-range or long-range, until we adopted this idea of an automatic increase whenever the cost of living goes up. . . . Looking back on it, it was a bad idea."[6]

With President Carter in the White House and large Democratic majorities in both houses of Congress, the time was ripe for change. Social Security's long roots were firmly planted in the Democratic Party's turf. Democrats were responsible for the creation of Social Security in 1935. They had preserved the program in the face of Republican efforts to limit its scope and generosity in the years immediately following World War II and created the disability program over Republican objections. They nurtured the retirement and disability programs to maturity throughout the post–World War II years. But Democrats had also been responsible for putting in place the flawed benefit formula that now threatened the program's future. The Speaker of the House of Representatives, Democrat Thomas P. "Tip" O'Neill (D-Massachusetts), summed up the need for his party to act: "If I've ever seen an issue that's a Democratic issue, it's this."[7]

President Carter proposed to replace the flawed-benefits formula with one that set initial monthly benefits for new retirees at a level that would, on average, replace the same percentage of preretirement earnings for all future cohorts of retirees. To achieve this target, initial monthly benefits would have to grow from one retirement cohort to the next at roughly the same rate as wages in the overall economy. To retain Social Security's redistributive nature, low-wage workers would receive a higher replacement rate, and high-wage workers would receive a lower replacement rate. As under the existing law, once a retiree began receiving benefits, the benefits would continue to be automatically adjusted to compensate for inflation.[8]

The new wage indexing policy corrected the flawed-benefits formula by eliminating the overindexing of initial benefits to inflation. Although the policy helped to reduce Social Security's long-term financing problem, it did little to alleviate the short-run problem.

The president, unwilling to reduce benefits for current retirees, proposed to address Social Security's short-run financial problem by sharply increasing payroll taxes and transferring funds from the Treasury's general fund and the Medicare trust fund. The higher payroll taxes and government transfers were highly controversial. Republicans, led by House Ways and Means Committee members, countered with a proposal to gradually increase the retirement age to 68 over an extended period and, along with Southern Democrats, opposed the use of general revenue.

After six months of intense debate and remarkably close votes on key items in both the House and Senate versions of the bill, Congress passed the 1977 Social Security Amendments into law. The law replaced the flawed-benefit formula with the new wage-indexed method for those who were under age 60 in 1977. The replacement was gradual. Those reaching retirement from 1982 to 1987 would receive benefits based on a blend of the two methods. Thus, it would be ten years before the new wage-indexing method would be fully effective. Benefits for current retirees and those nearing retirement were not changed.[9]

By design, when the new law was fully effective, Social Security benefits would replace, on average, about the same percentage of preretirement earnings as the average benefit new retirees in 1977 received. This amount was lower than benefits promised under the flawed formula, which allowed the replacement rate to rise over time. For example, the new law promised a typical 47-year-old worker a benefit that was 14 percent lower, after adjusting for inflation, than the benefit the worker would have received under the old law.[10]

The reduction in promised benefits shattered the mythology promoted by Social Security advocates that promised Social Security benefits, unlike private savings, were guaranteed by the federal government. Six years later, Congress would again lower benefits from their promised level when it was forced to address Social Security's insolvency a second time.

The new law's benefits, although lower than those promised by the flawed formula, were still generous relative to those retirees received in the late 1960s and early 1970s. A typical worker who retired in 1985 could expect to receive a monthly benefit that was 30 percent higher, after adjusting for inflation, than the typical worker who retired in 1975.[11] The new law's benefit promises to younger workers were even more generous. According to projections at the time, typical workers in their early 40s in 1977 who would retire in the year 2000 could expect to receive a monthly inflation-adjusted Social Security benefit that was 67 percent higher than the benefit received by typical 1975 retirees. Typical workers who were in their early 30s in 1977 could expect to receive inflation-adjusted benefits that were about double those of 1975 retirees.[12] That a law that granted such escalating benefits could nevertheless reduce Social Security's future expenditures stands as a testament to the magnitude of the flawed-indexing formula's generous promises.

During and leading up to the 1977 Social Security debate, experts warned Congress against adopting the wage-replacement policy. The principal argument was that the policy would lock in benefit increases that would inevitably require dramatically higher taxes. According to estimates at the time, wage indexing would require raising the payroll tax rate from its current rate of 11.7 percent to 18 percent to finance benefits to the baby boom generation.[13] An expert advisory panel registered its concern by saying that it "gravely doubts the fairness and wisdom of now promising benefits at such a level that we must commit our sons and daughters to a higher tax rate than we ourselves are willing to pay."[14] The panel believed that it would be preferable to instead preserve the inflation-adjusted value of benefits by allowing initial benefits to grow only by the rate of inflation. Such a policy would leave it "to future generations to decide what benefit increases are appropriate and what tax rates to finance them are acceptable."[15] The congressional liberals brushed these warnings aside and put in place the wage-indexing formula, one that was incompatible with demographic realities.

The use of general revenues to finance Social Security benefits generated the most significant debate. Liberal Democrats had long feared that the payroll tax would eventually constrain their ability to expand the program. The use of general revenues would remove this constraint. By 1977, there was growing bipartisan recognition in Congress that the payroll tax was approaching its upper limits. In the ten years since 1967, Congress had doubled the combined Social Security and Medicare payroll tax rate from 5.8 to 11.7 percent and increased wages on which the tax was levied from $6,600 to $16,500. The payroll tax now imposed a heavy burden on both lower- and middle-class workers. In the late 1970s, more than half of all taxpayers were paying more in payroll taxes than personal income taxes.[16]

Key Republicans and southern Democrats in Congress opposed general revenue financing, as they had since the early 1950s, because it would remove a constraint on the program's growth. Senator Russell Long (D-LA) criticized the use of general revenues as taking "the easy way out . . . by running off more printing press money."[17] Similarly, Senator Robert Byrd (D-WV) declared that arguments in favor of general revenue financing amounted to saying "that we can do all of this and no one has to pay for it."[18] The senators made a valid point. The administration's proposal would not actually transfer cash or any other financial resource to the Social Security Trust Fund. The transfer was merely a bookkeeping entry. The transfer would have no impact on the federal government's finances other than to appear to improve the trust fund's financial status, thereby permitting the Treasury to continue to send Social Security checks to 28 million beneficiaries. In a sense, general revenues were a free resource.

Other opponents charged that using general revenues to finance benefits would undermine Social Security's key founding principle. As Senator Paul Laxalt (R-NV) put it, "I cannot accept any diminution of the earned right principle."[19]

The Carter administration sought to avoid a philosophical fight that would put itself and congressional liberals in the unenviable position of arguing against the self-financing and earned-right principles that had been crucially important to President Franklin Roosevelt. So instead the administration tried to get a foot in the door by proposing a temporary transfer. The transfer, according to the administration, would merely offset payroll tax revenue losses from the high unemployment the country had experienced since 1975. The transfer would end, the administration promised, as soon as the unemployment rate fell from its level of over 7 percent to below 6 percent.

The proposal was criticized severely. Congressman Bill Archer (R-TX), the House Ways and Means Committee's ranking minority member, opened congressional hearings on the president's plan with the salutation: "Welcome to President Carter's Magic Show." Later, Russell Long (D-LA), Senate Finance Committee chairman, cut to the heart of the matter again by pointing out that in view of the federal government's budget deficit, "We do not have any general revenue to finance it [benefits] with."[20]

House liberals overrode these objections and included the temporary use of general revenues in its version of the 1977 Social Security Amendments. On the crucial vote, northern and western Democrats strongly favored general revenue financing by a margin of 171–22. Southern Democrats and Republicans opposed the measure by votes of 52–35 and 122–15, respectively. The vote totals demonstrate how far northern and western liberal Democrats had strayed from President Roosevelt's original vision of Social Security as a self-supporting program in which recipients earned rights to benefits based on their contributions. When a majority of the Senate opposed the measure, it was dropped from the final bill.

The absence of general revenues meant that payroll taxes had to be raised sharply. Congress complied with a payroll tax increase that was the largest tax increase in peacetime U.S. history. The law raised the current and future ceiling on taxable wages, moved forward in time the previously scheduled payroll tax rate increases, and raised the ultimate payroll rate to 15.3 percent in 1990 compared to its 11.7 percent level in 1977.

The record-breaking and highly controversial payroll tax increase averted Social Security's near-term insolvency. Nevertheless, the tax increase and new wage-indexing formula for benefits were not sufficient to fix Social Security's long-term problem. Projections immediately following the 1977 amendments showed that when the baby boomers began to retire, Social Security would again experience deficits.[21] Under the new benefit formula, higher economic growth could not be counted on to appreciably change this outcome. Rising GDP is inevitably accompanied by a corresponding rise in wages. Since Social Security benefits were now tied to wage growth, monthly benefits, and, hence, the program's cost to taxpayers would increase with the growth in wages.

The Carter administration declared that the new law made Social Security solvent for the next half-century. In signing the bill into law, President Carter proudly announced that "this legislation will guarantee that from 1980 to the year 2030, the social security fund will be sound."[22]

Reality quickly proved the projections profoundly wrong. Two years later, the Social Security trustees declared that owing to the poorly performing economy, the retirement program was once again in deep financial trouble. In spring 1980, they reversed their earlier projection and reported that the retirement fund would be bankrupt by 1982.[23] The massive tax increase contained in the 1977 amendments had done little to restore Social Security's short-term financial soundness, let alone its soundness for the remainder of the century.

Congress's decision to adopt the wage-indexing policy was a missed opportunity of extraordinary consequence. Since the program's inception in 1935, Social Security supporters had never clearly articulated its goals and objectives. Instead, they had continually relied on vague references to Social Security as a "safety net against old-age poverty" or a universal source of "economic security in old-age." Supporters had invariably argued for benefit increases on the grounds that existing benefits, whatever their level, were "inadequate" or "unrealistically low." They had assiduously avoided public debate over what these terms implied about the level and distribution of Social Security benefits. This purposeful vagueness, by allowing Social Security to appear to serve many different purposes to many different people, had served the program's supporters' expansionary interests well. But in 1977, with Social Security on the brink of financial bankruptcy and with foreknowledge of the enormous consequences of the demographic changes that were underway, the time had come to establish a clear, attainable goal for the program. No such debate occurred. Instead, Congress merely accepted the current level of benefits as a given, raised the necessary taxes to finance them, and set in place a long-term policy that the nation could not afford.

The job of fixing Social Security's financing problems would fall to the next president and Congress. As we will see in the next chapter, Congress and the Reagan administration, with the help of a special commission, would improve Social Security's finances, but only temporarily.

Welfare Reform

President Carter entered office with high hopes for welfare reform. Since the failure of President Nixon's reform plan, the welfare system's dysfunctional character had become even more apparent. Its cost burden, particularly for state and local governments, had become especially heavy, and public discontent had grown. President Carter had called the welfare system "an insult to those who pay the bill and those who honestly need help" and made welfare reform the centerpiece of his domestic policy agenda.[24]

After several fits and starts, the president introduced his plan in August 1977. In his special welfare message to Congress, he echoed the sentiments expressed earlier by Presidents Johnson and Nixon that "the welfare system is anti-work, anti-family, inequitable in its treatment of the poor and wasteful of taxpayers' dollars. . . . It treats people with similar needs in different fashion. . . . It provides incentives for family breakup. . . . It discourages work."[25]

The heart of President Carter's reform plan, like President Nixon's Family Assistance Plan, was a federally administered negative income tax that would replace the existing AFDC, SSI, and food stamp programs. The negative income tax included a guaranteed annual income between 65 and 45 percent of the poverty line for all households and individuals. The plan generously disregarded from the computation of benefits the first $3,800 of earnings for four-person households with people expected to work. Benefits were reduced by 50 percent for each dollar of income above this threshold. Assistance to families with children was further supplemented by an expansion of the earned income tax credit. The plan also included a public service jobs program to provide up to 1.4 million public sector jobs for people who were expected to work but were unable to obtain private sector employment.

The new welfare system, the president argued, would rectify the major problems that plagued the existing welfare system. The nationally uniform income guarantee and eligibility rules meant that within each category of household, benefits would be determined solely on the basis of need as measured by income. Welfare officials would no longer be required to distinguish between worthy and unworthy applicants based on claimants' personal behavior. All households with a given level of income would be equally worthy of the same amount of assistance regardless of where they lived. The president also argued that the reform plan's 50 percent benefit reduction rate would improve work incentives for current welfare recipients. The plan's uniform treatment of single-parent and intact households would not encourage divorce. Federal financing of benefits and coverage of single adults would alleviate state and local government welfare burdens.

Initially, most major newspapers greeted President Carter's reform plan warmly but with a certain wariness. The warmth stemmed from a recognition that the current welfare system was badly in need of reform. The wariness stemmed from recollections of how quickly the deep flaws in President Nixon's family assistance plan had been exposed and how their exposure had doomed a plan that seemed at first blush to be sound. According to the *Boston Globe*, "The Carter plan steers it [the welfare reform debate] in the right direction—toward a national income guarantee, greater Federal responsibility for welfare costs . . . and a sustained government commitment to ensuring jobs for all who can work."[26]

Welfare lobby groups heavily favored the Carter plan. The National Conference of Catholic Charities, the Association of Public Welfare Agencies, the National Conference of Social Workers, the AFL-CIO, the State Public Welfare Administrators, and the Local Public Welfare Administrators all lobbied in favor of a national uniform benefit level, an expansion of welfare eligibility, and greater federal funding. One noteworthy new lobby was the Children's Defense Fund (CDF). Declaring itself the representative of poor children, the CDF supported federalizing the welfare system: "Because children are citizens of the nation, providing for their welfare should not be left up to state discretion."[27]

The self-interest of the lobby groups was readily apparent, as it had been during the debate over the family assistance program. The American Public Welfare Association favored increased federal funding but sought to maintain state administration of welfare programs. The American Federation of State, County, and Municipal Employees supported the president's public service jobs program but demanded that Congress build in "some protection of the existing public sector workers." The AFL-CIO argued for a strong work training program that its members would help administer.[28]

The reform plan also received strong bipartisan support from the nation's governors, a lobby group that had grown more vocal and forceful.[29] Most governors had long been a force in opposing federal welfare mandates and requirements on the states. But the creation of the plethora of federal grants-to-states programs beginning in the 1960s had given the governors a common financial interest. Since then, the governors, acting through their National Governors Association, had become a powerful special interest lobby to protect a continued flow of federal grant funds to their states. Their interest in President Carter's reform plan was keen, but their interest in fiscal relief from a heavy welfare burden was keener. The governors, whom one senator disparagingly labeled the "Tin Cup Brigade," collectively stood to be relieved of a large annual $12 billion welfare burden.[30]

Arrayed against these lobbies were a handful of organizations, most notably the Chamber of Commerce and the National Taxpayers Union. The chamber's representative, Robert B. Carleson, made the conservative case for less federal involvement in welfare by arguing that "the States should have maximum freedom to create . . . and tailor their own welfare programs, because the closer the implementation of the programs to the people they are designed to serve, the more likely the programs will meet the needs of those individuals who cannot help themselves."[31]

Within Congress, the plan was greeted with bipartisan skepticism. Daniel Patrick Moynihan, who had been instrumental in developing President Nixon's reform plan and was now serving as a Democratic senator from New York, called the plan "grievously disappointing."[32] Finance Committee chairman Russell Long noted the plan's "laudable objectives" but said nevertheless that it would be "foolhardy" to enact the president's plan without first pilot-testing it "for a few years."[33]

As the program's details became more apparent, congressional skepticism turned to outright opposition. The objections centered on the large-scale expansion of assistance to nonpoor households and its costs. The Congressional Budget Office (CBO) showed that the plan would increase the number of households receiving federal assistance by 3.6 million, double the number of households receiving AFDC assistance at the time. The additional recipients would be accompanied by a hefty price tag for taxpayers. The CBO estimated the new welfare system would cost the federal government $17 billion per year more than the system it was replacing, a staggering 70 percent increase. Although a portion of the increase represented a shift in welfare costs from states to the federal government, the added costs raised the combined welfare costs at all levels of government by $14 billion. To make matters worse, only a little more than half of the additional expenditures would go to reducing the extent of poverty among the poor.[34] After reviewing the administration's plan, Congressman Skip Bafalis (R-FL) described it as "a massive new welfare program" that would produce "a heap of debt, default and red-ink."[35]

The higher cost was a consequence of well-intentioned efforts by the Carter administration to increase work incentives. Knowing that President Nixon's plan had foundered on the issue of work incentives, the Carter White House sought to improve incentives relative to President Nixon's plan. It had only three options: Lower the guaranteed income floor, lower the rate at which assistance is reduced as earnings rise, or increase the income disregard. The latter two options would move the cutoff point for assistance higher up the income ladder, adding to the plan's cost and caseload. President Carter, a Democrat, was unwilling to propose an income guarantee that was below the level proposed by a Republican president. Carter's choice of a large income disregard solved one problem, but it created two other insurmountable ones. Good intentions notwithstanding, President Carter had produced a welfare reform plan that was far more liberal than President Nixon's Family Assistance Plan and far too costly for Congress.[36]

Analysts questioned whether the Carter plan would actually improve work incentives. It undoubtedly did so for most AFDC recipients, but by how much was unclear. Most were also on Medicaid, which created its own obstacles to work. By extending assistance to millions of households ineligible for welfare assistance under the current system, the Carter plan created a new work disincentive for a large additional segment of the working population. Thus, whereas the existing system imposed a large work penalty on a relatively small group of people, the Carter plan spread a somewhat smaller work penalty to a relatively large group. Research from two major negative income tax social experiments that were released at the time welfare reform was being debated found that individuals covered by negative income tax programs, such as President Carter's, significantly reduced their hours of work.[37] Thus, the Carter plan would exacerbate existing work disincentives rather than encourage work.

Another factor contributed to the Carter plan's defeat. Analysts at the Stanford Research Institute released research at the time President Carter's plan was under congressional consideration that found that similarly structured negative income tax plans created even larger incentives for family breakup than the existing welfare system did. The similar negative income tax increased divorce rates among white couples by 194 percent, 68 percent among black couples, and 83 percent among Hispanic couples.[38] These results were the final blow to President Carter's welfare reform plan.

The marital dissolution findings had disturbing implications that went beyond President Carter's reform plan. Past and current members of Congress and presidential administrations had hoped that the optional AFDC program for two-parent families (AFDC-UP) would decrease incentives for divorce. The findings from the largest negative income tax experiment implied the opposite.

The CBO analysis and the analysis of labor supply and marriage responses from the negative income tax experiments were devastating. They showed that contrary to the president's promises, his reform plan would increase the number of welfare recipients, increase the welfare system's costs to taxpayers, reduce aggregate hours worked, and increase the divorce rate. In the face of the damaging assessments, President Carter walked away from his proposal.

A year later, the president proposed a scaled-down welfare plan with a national minimum benefit for the AFDC program and a requirement that all states adopt a two-parent AFDC program. The objective was to establish a national income floor for welfare households. Once the floor was established, liberals could count on the potent force of the equally worthy claim to expand the type of households covered until the income floor applied universally. The proposal, coming on the heels of the research findings that such a policy was likely to encourage divorce and discourage work, stands as a remarkable testimonial to the triumph of ideology over policy analysis. House Democrats cast aside these concerns and Republican objections that the plan was a significant step toward a "national income redistribution program" and passed the revised proposal. But the bill died in the Democratically controlled Senate.

Republicans countered with an alternative that would become an important policy many years later. They proposed a demonstration project to block-grant the AFDC program in eight states. Although judged too radical at the time, the AFDC block grant would become the law of the land two decades later when Republicans gained control of both houses of Congress.

The failure of President Carter's plan marked the end of efforts to enact comprehensive welfare reform. Senator Moynihan, who for ten years had been at the forefront of the major welfare reform efforts, upon hearing that President Carter's plan was doomed in Congress, exclaimed, "Oh, my God. Do you mean we are going to lose this again? We cannot lose it, again. If we lose it again, this will become a loser, instead of something that almost passed and was on the edge of enactment; it is going to be something that never passes."[39] The senator's assessment was astute. For nearly twenty years, as the welfare system continued to grow and as its deleterious effects on those it was designed to help became more manifest, presidents and Congresses would attempt to address the system's problems through piecemeal efforts.

The failure of President Carter's plan also marked the end of liberal efforts to enact a federally guaranteed annual income. They would have to settle for using the food stamp program as a distant second best way to achieve this objective.

Food Stamps

The raft of food and nutrition legislation during the first half of the decade produced a blisteringly fast growth in the food stamp rolls and school lunch programs. The number of food stamp recipients surged from under 3 million in 1969 to 17 million in 1977. Among welfare programs in 1977, only Medicaid with 23 million recipients had a larger caseload. Over the same eight years, the number of children receiving school lunches ballooned from 19 million to 26 million. Food stamp expenditures registered a tenfold increase and child nutrition program expenditures registered an eightfold increase over the same period of time.

The food stamp program had taken on a dual personality, having the characteristics of both a nutrition program and an income maintenance program. The purchase requirement, by requiring families to spend a certain fraction of its income to buy stamps and, thereby food, gave the program its nutrition character. The program's broad eligibility and the fact that food stamps could be used nearly as cash gave the program its income maintenance character. As an income maintenance program, food stamps served two distinct functions: It served as a "gap filler" that evened out differences across states in AFDC benefits, and since eligibility was not conditioned on marital status or other demographic characteristics and the program had only minimally effective work requirements, the program served as a quasi–income floor for all people.

The Carter administration proposed to eliminate the purchase requirement. Free food stamps had been a goal of the hunger lobby since the late 1960s. The president's proposal also lowered the recipient's total monthly allotment, so that the net benefit or bonus value remained unchanged. Supporters argued that the purchase requirement prevented many cash-poor individuals from obtaining needed food assistance, a position that seemed to be supported by the fact that only about half of all eligible people received food stamps despite court-ordered extensive outreach efforts by the Agriculture Department.

The Carter administration also argued that free stamps would reduce the fraud among food stamp vendors involved in cash transactions with recipients. By 1977, 17 million food stamp recipients were paying $3 billion a year to purchase stamps from fifteen thousand check-cashing firms, banks, post offices, churches, town clerks, welfare offices, corner stores, and even fire stations.[40] This unwieldy system had generated highly publicized cases of vendor fraud that exposed the tip of what was generally recognized as a large problem.[41] Eliminating cash transactions would eliminate the need for vendors and the fraud that went along with handling food stamp recipients' cash.

Supporters of retaining the purchase requirement argued that requiring recipients to put up some amount of cash, however modest, gave them a sense of responsibility for their food purchases. As Senator Herman Talmadge (D-GA), chairman of the Senate Agriculture Committee put it, a modest cash payment was "concrete evidence of the willingness of the participant to take a step toward self-improvement."[42] This view was echoed by Idaho congressman Steve Symms (R-ID), "Not only does it [the purchase requirement] re-enforce the idea of family responsibility, but it also places the Food Stamp recipient on an equal footing with his non-recipient counterpart who is forced by circumstances to commit a percentage of his income toward the feeding of his family."[43] Eliminating the purchase requirement would, in their view, remove the one remaining element that distinguished food stamps as a nutrition program.[44]

Other members believed that making food stamps free would make the program more susceptible to abuse. In particular, eliminating the purchase requirement would cause food stamps to be used to purchase all varieties of food and nonfood items, a prediction that proved to be prescient.

Both chambers of Congress approved eliminating the purchase requirement by overwhelming margins. Again, Congress grossly underestimated the cost of an entitlement expansion. Congress estimated that free food stamps would cost $540 million in fiscal year 1979, the provision's first full year in operation. The increase would raise total program expenditures to $5.8 billion. By spring 1979, it became clear that food stamp expenditures were up sharply. Unless Congress provided additional funds, monthly benefits would be automatically reduced. Instead, Congress appropriated the necessary additional funds. When the books were closed on the fiscal year, food stamp expenditures totaled $6.8 billion—$1 billion over the original estimate.

The next year repeated this scenario, except the magnitude was much greater. Food stamp expenditures, boosted by a mild recession, surged again. Early in the year, the administration warned Congress that expenditures were running far in excess of its $6.2 billion projection. Congress responded with an additional $2.6 billion of supplemental funds and then added another $200 million. This amount raised the total for the year to about $9 billion, nearly 50 percent more than the preceding year's cost estimate.

Black Lung Benefits and Trade Adjustment Assistance

The late 1970s witnessed skyrocketing expenditures in two entitlements with relatively narrow groups of eligible recipients: the black lung and trade adjustment assistance programs. Both entitlements followed an all-too-familiar path of liberalization to grow from relatively small programs in the early 1970s into billion-dollar programs by 1980.

Congress enacted the black lung program in 1969 as a temporary measure and then extended and liberalized the program in 1972. By 1977, owing to the federal law's generosity, not a single state had established a disability program for coal miners.[45] By then, it was clear that the original goal to have states and, ultimately, coal mine operators pick up the tab for black lung benefits had failed.

In 1977, Congress made the program a permanent federal responsibility. The 1977 Black Lung Amendments levied a permanent federal tonnage tax on all domestically produced coal. The tax proceeds were to be deposited into a new trust fund from which future benefits would be paid. But the law also relaxed the program's eligibility requirements by establishing additional presumptions under which miners and their survivors could qualify for benefits. The presumptions included eligibility for people who had worked in and around coal mines, including transportation and construction workers. The law also allowed survivors of deceased miners who had worked in the mines for at least fifteen years to collect black lung benefits regardless of the actual cause of the miner's death. Another provision allowed a mine worker's survivors, despite their obvious financial interest, to qualify for benefits merely by filing an affidavit testifying that the worker had suffered or died from black lung disease. The law precluded government agencies from using medical evidence, in the form of a chest X-ray, as a second opinion to deny claims. This provision effectively allowed claimants' private physicians the exclusive authority to make eligibility determinations. Finally, on the ground that previously denied claimants were no less worthy than new claimants, the 1977 law required federal officials to re-review all previously denied applicants under the new relaxed standards and to pay lump-sum retroactive benefits to applicants who were approved. The law had so liberalized the program, according to Congressman John Erlenborn (R-PA), "that compensation could be awarded to most miners and their dependents and survivors whether or not the miner had any medical evidence of the disease."[46]

The 1977 amendments produced another surge in the program's caseload and cost. In the next four years, the number of recipients of trust fund–financed benefits increased from fewer than 4,000 to 139,000.[47] Coal tax revenues quickly proved to be no match for the soaring costs. The trust fund was, for all practical purposes, bankrupt before it was started. From the fund's first full year of operation in 1979 to 1981, annual trust fund expenditures were three times its tax revenues. Congress covered these deficits with $1.5 billion of general fund "loans." The deficits continued for the next decade, despite a doubling of the coal tax in 1981 and another large increase in 1985. By 1985, the interest payments on the trust fund loans amounted to one dollar for every two dollars expended for benefit payments. Congress then forgave all interest due on prior loans and for all loans during the ensuing five years.[48]

The original Trade Adjustment Assistance program, enacted in 1962, provided only limited training, relocation, and related adjustment assistance to workers who were displaced from their jobs as a result of U.S. international trade policies.[49] In the Trade Reform Act of 1974, Congress had liberalized the program's benefits to include up to fifty-two weeks of cash assistance on top of state and federal unemployment benefits.[50] The law caused the benefit rolls to soar. The number of TAA recipients tripled from 1975 to 1978, rising from 54,000 to 164,000. Then the Carter administration further liberalized the program by relaxing eligibility standards. By 1980, the number of TAA recipients ballooned to 585,000. Program expenditures rose from a mere $79 million in 1976 to $1.6 billion in 1980.

The application process, which required a worker to demonstrate that he or she was *part of a group* of workers who had been displaced by import laws, was remarkably elaborate. Beneficiaries, as a result, were mainly unemployed union members who had their union's administrative support in navigating the program's complex qualifying procedures. In the late 1970s, three-fourths of all recipients were employees from the heavily unionized automobile, steel, or apparel and textile industries. Most recipients used the program as a source of cash assistance during a temporary spell of unemployment rather than a means to obtaining retraining. Only 3 percent of the recipients entered a training program. The rest were in it for the cash. Remarkably, 72 percent of all recipients eventually returned to their original jobs. Even more remarkable, more than half of all recipients had gone back to work before even applying for TAA benefits. Most of these recipients received a lump-sum retroactive payment back to the date of their application, a check that was often worth thousands of dollars.[51]

Entitlements at the End of the 1970s

By the end of the 1970s, the entitlement program edifice that constitutes the modern American welfare state was essentially complete. Virtually all of today's major entitlements, with the exception of the Medicare coverage of prescription drugs and the Affordable Care Act's health insurance subsidies, had been written into the statute books. The edifice was extensive, and it reached all segments of the population. In 1980, 49 percent of all U.S. households received cash or in-kind assistance from at least one federal entitlement program. Not surprisingly, virtually all households with people age 65 and older received assistance from Social Security or Medicare, or both. More noteworthy is the fact that one-third of the entire population of households without a member who was age 65 or older received benefits from at least one federal entitlement program. Among certain population subgroups, entitlement participation rates reached extraordinary dimensions. Seventy percent of all female-headed households with children were recipients of federal entitlement aid. Among households with children that were headed by black or Hispanic women, recipient rates exceeded 80 percent. Half of all school children were receiving federally subsidized school lunches. The labyrinth of overlapping entitlement programs, each with its own eligibility rules, resulted in millions of households simultaneously receiving assistance from two or more programs. Two-thirds of entitlement recipients (27 million households) collected benefits simultaneously from two or more programs. A quarter of entitlement recipients (11 million households) collected benefits simultaneously from three or more programs.[52]

The blistering growth in entitlements from the War on Poverty's launch in 1964 to 1980 is without parallel in U.S. history. The controversial AFDC program, which had defied reform attempts by two presidents, provided cash assistance to 10.8 million Americans, mostly women and children, up from 4.3 million in 1964. Almost half of all U.S. households headed by single women were on the AFDC rolls; 44 percent of recipient households were on the rolls because the mother was divorced or separated, and another 38 percent were on the rolls because the mother had a child out of wedlock. Enrollment in Medicaid stood at 22 million people, making it the nation's largest welfare program. In 1980, the food stamp program (which in 1964 operated in fewer than half the states and served only 360,000 individuals) provided assistance to 17 million individuals. The transformation of the Old-Age Assistance, Aid to the Blind, and Aid to the Permanently and Totally Disabled programs into the federal Supplemental Security Program (SSI) in 1972 caused the benefit rolls to surge. By 1980, 4 million people received SSI benefits. The only federal entitlement program that had failed to grow appreciably was the relatively young earned income tax credit program. Legislation in the 1980s and early 1990s would take care of that.

The much larger social insurance programs exhibited the same remarkable growth. Social Security provided monthly benefits to 31 million retirees and their spouses and survivors, up from just 18 million in 1964. Nearly all of these individuals also received Medicare assistance. The growth in the Social Security Disability Insurance rolls was even more spectacular. Between 1964 and 1980, recipients tripled to 4.7 million. Another 500,000 disabled coal miners were receiving black lung benefits. As the curtain descended on the 1970s, it can be said that the United States, through its entitlement programs, was providing assistance to alleviate poverty and economic hardship on a scale unparalleled in human history.

By 1980, the liberals' goal of making federal social insurance programs the primary vehicle for delivering assistance to the elderly, the disabled, and the unemployed had been achieved. It had been accomplished over initial resistance by congressional Republicans and southern Democrats who ultimately acquiesced.

Entitlement spending had transformed the federal government into a massive check-writing machine to support the lifestyles of middle-income households. In 1980, only 29 percent of all federal entitlement-based cash, nutrition, and health care services went to the poorest fifth of all households. The remaining 71 percent was distributed uniformly to higher-income groups: 29 percent went to households in the second lowest income quintile, 20 percent to households in the middle income quintile, and 22 percent to households in the two highest income quintile groups. Through five decades, entitlement expansions had invariably been rationalized on the ground that they would redistribute income to the poor. But their combined impact on the distribution of household income, as the numbers indicate, was modest.[53]

The avalanche of entitlement spending since the War on Poverty's launch appeared to have had little impact on poverty. The official poverty rate, which had declined sharply from 1964 to 1969, had remained stubbornly high thereafter. The reasons for continually high poverty rates are numerous and complex, and there is little consensus as to the relative importance of each. Certainly the rise in divorce rates and the corresponding prevalence of households consisting of single women with children played a role, as did the U.S. economy's poor performance during the 1970s. Previous research has shown that the official measure's failure to count in-kind benefits as income is important. In 1964, in-kind benefits constituted only 2 percent of total federal entitlement assistance. By 1980, 25 percent of federal entitlement aid was in the form of in-kind benefits.[54] But when all is said and done, the idea that the incentives created by entitlements were contributing to poverty needed to be reckoned with.

The prodigious growth of entitlement expenditures had also transformed the federal government's finances. From 1964 to 1980, entitlement outlays had grown at an annual compound rate of 13 percent. By the end of the period, entitlement spending accounted for over half of all federal government expenditures. So rapid was the growth that the federal government was spending more on entitlements in 1980 than it had on all government activities combined just six years earlier.

This extraordinary spending growth far outstripped the ability of both Congress and the nation's economy to generate the tax revenues necessary to finance it. The consequence was an unprecedented string of budget deficits. Between 1964 and 1980, the annual national budget was balanced only once, in 1969, despite a remarkable 10 percent annual growth rate in federal revenue over the sixteen-year period. By 1980, budget deficits had become a way of life in Washington. Ominously, the growth in budget deficits and debt began to accelerate in the latter half of the 1970s despite the concomitant acceleration of revenue growth. By the mid-1970s, the national debt was rising faster than the nation's output of goods and services, reversing the downward trend of the debt as a percentage of gross domestic product that had prevailed since the end of World War II.

Entitlement spending produced similar financial imbalances within the federal budget. With few exceptions, the main social insurance trust funds were experiencing severe financial difficulties. The Social Security retirement fund stood on the brink of bankruptcy in 1980, despite the massive increase in payroll taxes two years earlier. The Railroad Retirement Fund was running regular deficits. The Social Security Disability program was solvent only because it had been receiving regular transfers from the retirement fund. The three-year-old black lung trust fund was bankrupt, and without an immediate general fund bailout, the program would be able to pay beneficiaries only 55 cents on the dollar in 1980. Although the Medicare hospital trust fund's short-term financial prospects looked good, the Social Security trustees projected that the program's double-digit expenditure growth would create deficits by the end of the 1980s and make it insolvent within two decades.

The fiscal horizon looked even darker because there appeared to be no end in sight to galloping entitlement expenditures. Entitlement programs were on automatic pilot. Without the enactment of any liberalizing legislation during the last two years of the Carter administration, outlays for the Social Security retirement and disability programs, Medicare, Medicaid, Supplemental Security Income, and black lung benefits were all growing at double-digit rates. Federal AFDC expenditures, after pausing in 1979, began a two-year surge again that would take its expenditures to new record-high levels in 1981. The prospect of free food stamps promised continuing rapid growth in food stamp expenditures. Meanwhile, rapid inflation had pushed taxpayers into successively higher tax brackets, driving upward the federal government's claim on personal incomes. A revolt against rising tax burdens had begun in California and was about to spread across the country.

In 1980, public support for a strong safety net of assistance remained high, but public dissatisfaction with the existing welfare system had also grown large. That year, an ABC News/Harris Poll national poll found that 69 percent of Americans favored a reduction in welfare spending.[55]

One source of dissatisfaction was widespread reports of welfare fraud, abuse, lax administration, and legal loopholes that permitted middle-income people to receive benefits. Government investigators regularly reported that lax administration was causing eye-popping losses in welfare programs. Reports to Congress in 1980 estimated that AFDC and Medicaid were each losing over $1 billion per year due to errors in determining eligibility, errors in payments to recipients and improper payments to service providers. The investigative staff of the Senate Appropriations Committee estimated the overpayments of food stamps were well over $1 billion.[56] The Department of Health, Education and Welfare's inspector general estimated in 1978 that the department alone misspent $6 billion, mainly on entitlement programs.[57]

Lax administration accounted for most of the misspent taxpayer dollars, but welfare fraud captured newspaper headlines. News reports of fraud during the 1970s were every bit as sensational as those that had plagued the Civil War pension program. In one famous case, a Northeastern University professor of education and leisure studies who specialized in community recreation was charged with 170 counts of bilking the state of Massachusetts and the federal government out of $1 million in food stamp and Medicaid funds. The professor allegedly recruited more than one hundred students and nearby residents to help defraud the government in a scheme that the *Boston Globe* declared "may be the largest in Massachusetts history."[58] Another highly publicized investigation found that more than one hundred members of Jim Jones's People's Temple cult were receiving welfare benefits, half of them fraudulently, at the time of their mass suicide in Guyana.[59]

Perhaps the most famous of welfare fraud perpetrators were the so-called welfare queens. The original welfare queen, Linda Taylor, was arrested by Illinois authorities in 1974 on suspicion of defrauding the state of $154,000 in welfare benefits. She allegedly used twenty-seven aliases, thirty-one addresses, twenty-five phone numbers, and three Social Security numbers. At the same time, Taylor was also wanted for welfare fraud in Michigan and Arizona. The sheer scale of the charges, which were regularly headlined in the *Chicago Tribune* and widely reported in newspapers around the country, gave her instant notoriety. When she was arrested on a Chicago street sitting in her Cadillac that had been purchased with cashier's checks drawn on a Trinidad bank, she became a national symbol of welfare fraud and abuse.[60] She was eventually convicted on twenty-eight counts of fraud involving only $7,600. But by this time, the image of a welfare recipient driving around town in a Cadillac was firmly planted in the minds of many Americans.[61]

The food stamp program was particularly rife with fraud and legal loopholes. Newspapers during the 1970s are filled with reports of recipients using food stamps to purchase nonfood items including cars and guns. One Floridian used her food stamps to pay off a parking ticket. Strong and viable black markets for food stamps were operating in Chicago, New York, and Puerto Rico. Legal loopholes permitted college students and teachers during the summer vacations and union workers who were voluntarily on strike to receive food stamps.[62]

The fraud was by no means limited to welfare recipients. Fraud by service providers was especially rampant in Medicaid and Medicare.

The House Select Aging Committee's Subcommittee on Health and Long-Term Care estimated in 1979 that excess billing practices, payments for services to ineligible people, and outright fraud amounted to as much as 10 percent of Medicare and Medicaid costs—a whopping $4 billion. The FBI testified to Congress that "corruption has permeated virtually every area of the Medicare and Medicaid health care industry." An agent described Medicaid kickbacks as "a way of life," especially among nursing homes, clinical laboratories, X-ray operators, and oxygen providers.[63] A General Accounting Office investigation found that providers had marked up prices for 155 different Medicare and Medicaid services by as much as 133 percent.[64] Examples of Medicaid and Medicare fraud regularly received headline attention. A *Chicago Tribune* story headlined "Doctors 'Assembly Line' for Welfare Patients Bared" reported that Medicaid investigators had found that one doctor billed the program for seeing ten to twenty patients per hour and that another wrote prescriptions for thousands of sleeping pills for patients on welfare regardless of their diagnosis. Welfare workers and other public employees joined in to defraud federal, state, and local governments. Indictments for welfare fraud were handed down against public employees in cities across the nation.[65]

A more important and tragic source of public dissatisfaction came from mounting evidence that entitlement programs were encouraging recipients to engage in behaviors that were detrimental to their own and their family's long-run interests. The public debates over the Nixon and Carter welfare plans had brought to light the welfare system's disincentives. By the late 1970s, it was commonly understood that the welfare system erected high barriers to self-sufficiency.[66]

Academic research in the 1970s also found that recipients of Social Security retirement and disability programs were responding to the large work disincentives contained in those programs. Researchers found statistical evidence that Social Security's monthly benefit levels, its early retirement option, and its earnings test were inducing large numbers of older workers to opt for early retirement rather than continue working.[67] Highly influential studies published in 1980 concluded that the disability insurance program accounted for the large majority, if not all, of the unprecedented decline in the labor force participation rate of mature adult males during the 1960s and 1970s.[68]

Similarly, researchers found overwhelming evidence that the unemployment insurance program had increased the prevalence and duration of unemployment by sizable amounts. This research showed that the various extensions of unemployment benefits from twenty-six weeks in 1969 to sixty-five weeks in 1975 were large enough to significantly raise the national unemployment rate and, by extension, delay the recovery from the economic recession of 1974–1975.[69]

Far more controversial, but equally disturbing, were the research findings regarding the AFDC program's impact on marriage, divorce, and out-of-wedlock births. Throughout the post–World War II years, policymakers at all levels of government had expressed deep concern that AFDC was causing marriages to break up. But until the 1970s, there was little hard evidence to support the concern. The mid-1970s saw the publication of empirical studies showing a large impact of AFDC on divorce rates. Results from the largest negative income tax experiments added considerable weight to these findings. AFDC was, in fact, inducing mothers to, in the words of welfare rights activist Johnnie Tillman, "trade in a man for *the man* [emphasis added]."[70] Other research during these years found statistical significant evidence that AFDC was increasing the number of out-of-wedlock births. Still other research found that AFDC delayed marriage among young women with children born out of wedlock.[71]

By the end of the 1970s, the evidence of the adverse behavioral impacts of entitlement programs was still being hotly debated. Each of the findings noted was subsequently challenged by either methodology critiques or failures to corroborate the findings. Although there was no consensus, especially on the magnitude of the impacts, the evidence contributed to a change in public and congressional sentiment against further entitlement liberalizations. Facts were changing opinions.

17 A Temporary Slowdown, 1981–1989

The entitlement programs that make up our safety net for the truly needy have worthy goals and many deserving recipients. We will protect them. But there's only one way to see to it that these programs really help those whom they were designed to help. And that is to bring their spiraling costs under control.

President Ronald Reagan, 1982[1]

PRESIDENT REAGAN ENTERED OFFICE WITH POLIcies to create a noninflationary environment for economic growth and restore the nation's defense capacity. His program included sweeping personal income tax rate reductions, domestic spending restraint, regulatory relief, defense budget increases, and support for the Federal Reserve's anti-inflation policies. Entitlement restraint was part of the president's larger effort to curtail domestic spending and prevent the tax reductions and defense buildup from creating large budget deficits.

The economic conditions and budget trends of the latter half of the 1970s set the table for the president's policies. In the two years preceding his inauguration, consumer prices had increased by a staggering 27 percent and the number of unemployed people by 32 percent. Record-high interest rates, led by a 20 percent prime rate, had caused net domestic investment to decline by one-quarter over the same years. In January 1981, 19 percent of the nation's industrial capacity sat idle. In a televised address to the nation on February 5, the president described the economic situation as the "worst economic mess since the Great Depression."[2] It was hard to argue with his assessment.

The federal budget was similarly in bad straits. Federal expenditures had increased by 60 percent during the previous four years. All of the budget's main components contributed to the growth, but entitlement spending led the pack. The rapid upward pace of federal spending had produced annual federal budget deficits throughout President Carter's term in office despite a historic upward surge in federal revenues. From 1977 to 1981, inflation's "cruel tax," by pushing taxpayers into higher tax brackets, had caused the average federal personal income tax rate to climb by nearly 20 percent and had increased federal tax revenues relative to gross domestic product (GDP) to a then peacetime record high. Yet the federal budget deficit still equaled 2.6 percent of GDP in fiscal year 1980.[3]

Bipartisan recognition within Congress that defense spending had dropped below levels sufficient to ensure the nation's security added to upward budget pressures. The Carter administration and Congress had begun to reverse the nearly decade-long decline. In 1981, leaders in both parties were calling for more increases.

President Reagan's policy proposals, which constituted nothing less than a fundamental reordering of government priorities and a reversal of the budgetary trends of the three prior decades, produced a colossal battle between the two branches of government. The first two years of furious combat dominated the business of Congress and attracted national press attention like few other policy issues. During these initial years, Congress adopted the president's tax cuts and met him halfway on domestic spending reductions. As part of the historic domestic spending reductions, Congress subjected almost every major entitlement program to at least some retrenchment. Tax and spending battles continued for the next six years as the Reagan administration simultaneously fought a rearguard action to preserve its 1981–1982 spending reductions and achieve further reductions. Congress, in contrast, sought to return to its long-standing practice of incrementally expanding entitlements. But the administration's opposition and the constraining effects of large budget deficits severely limited entitlement liberalizations. In this way, the Reagan administration slowed, albeit temporarily, the growth of entitlement spending.

President Reagan's second term also produced two entitlement changes that deserve special consideration. In 1986, Congress repealed the general revenue-sharing entitlement to state and local governments. This marked only the third time in history, and the first time in fifty years, that Congress repealed a major entitlement program. In 1988, Congress enacted a new Medicare catastrophic health insurance benefit—and struck the law from the statute books the next year.

The President's 1981 Budget Program

The Reagan administration's economic program was built on four cornerstones: sharply reducing personal income tax rates, reining in federal spending, relieving businesses of heavy federal regulatory burdens, and supporting the Federal Reserve's pursuit of a stable monetary policy. "Taken together," the president promised, "these proposals will put the Nation on a fundamentally different course—a course leading to less inflation, more growth, and a brighter future for all of our citizens."[4]

The tax plan's central feature was an across-the-board 30 percent reduction in personal income tax rates that would reduce the annual growth in federal revenues from 14 percent to 8 percent.[5]

The administration's budget plan proposed to cut the annual growth in federal spending in half, from 12 percent to 6 percent. One-third of the budget savings were to come from reducing the annual growth in entitlement spending by a similar amount, from 12 percent to 7 percent. For the upcoming 1982 fiscal year, the entitlement proposals would shave $15 billion from the projected $363 billion of entitlement outlays. Although the large social insurance entitlements accounted for five of every six dollars spent on all entitlements, they accounted for only half of the proposed entitlement savings.[6] Welfare programs bore the brunt of the proposed reductions, accounting for the remaining half.

The remaining two-thirds of the administration's proposed spending savings were to come from sharp reductions in nondefense spending, which accounted for only about a fifth of federal program spending. The deep budget cutbacks would reduce nondefense discretionary expenditures to a level 15 percent below their fiscal year 1981 level. With these proposals, budget director David A. Stockman made good on his earlier boast that the president's domestic spending proposals would "reduce a thundering of sacred cows to just a handful."[7] Offsetting a portion of these reductions was a proposed acceleration of defense spending increases that had begun during the Carter administration's last two years.[8]

When the Reagan administration's entitlement proposals were being considered in Congress and since then, a myth has developed that the reductions, especially the welfare cutbacks, were deep and, in effect, amounted to shredding the nation's social safety net. To help give readers a proper understanding of the true nature and depth of these reductions, it is worthwhile to consider them in some detail.

The administration's welfare proposals sought to reverse what it called the fifteen-year "drift toward the universalization of social benefit programs."[9] The drift had occurred because the four previous presidents and seven previous Congresses, concerned about work incentives and possessed with a well-meaning desire to help the working poor, had steadily raised the income levels at which households qualified for various welfare programs. But the drift had spread welfare aid further up the income ladder to an increasing number of households. By 1981, one-quarter of all recipients of means-tested entitlements lived in nonpoor households, including 40 percent of all food stamp recipients. One-third of all Supplemental Security Income (SSI) recipients and 28 percent of all Medicaid recipients had household incomes above 150 percent of the poverty line.[10] Half of all U.S. federally subsidized meals were served to students in families with incomes near or above the median family income in the United States.

The welfare proposals sharpened the government's distinction between worthy and unworthy entitlement claims and shifted the boundary line between the two down the income ladder. Food stamp eligibility would be limited to individuals with incomes under 130 percent of the poverty line; Aid to Families with Dependent Children (AFDC) benefits would be restricted to households with incomes less than 150 percent of the need standard that state governments set for their programs, and free school meals to children would be available only to families with incomes under 125 percent of the poverty line.[11] Generous work expense, child care, and shelter deductions would be reduced, including the AFDC program's 1967 "thirty and a third" exemption. All sources of household income would be counted in determining welfare program benefits and eligibility.[12]

The administration's social insurance proposals were dictated by similar considerations, but also by a need to address the precarious financial positions of the trust funds through which social insurance programs were financed. The Social Security retirement program, despite the large payroll tax increase and the correction of the flawed indexing formula by the 1977 amendments, was again on the verge of bankruptcy. As budget director David Stockman explained in testimony to Congress, "Unless both the House and the Senate pass a bill . . . within the next 15 months, the most devastating bankruptcy in history will occur on or about November 3, 1982."[13] At that point, Social Security would be unable to pay full benefits to its 36 million retirees. Medicare was on a slower but equally sure road to bankruptcy by 1988. The black lung trust fund was being kept alive only by a steady infusion of taxpayer funds. The Social Security disability fund was running surpluses, but only because payroll taxes were being siphoned to it from the retirement fund.

The administration initially proposed only two significant changes to the Social Security retirement program, neither of which impinged on the program's earned-right principle. It proposed to eliminate benefits for college student children of Social Security recipients and to phase out the program's minimum benefit. The administration argued that the student benefit duplicated Pell grants and student loans. The Social Security minimum benefit, the administration argued, duplicated SSI benefits for some retirees with low lifetime wages or intermittent work histories and added to the already generous pension benefits of many federal, state, and local government workers.

The administration did not offer any significant proposals in 1981 for fundamentally altering the Medicare program. Its main Medicaid proposal, to cap Medicaid matching payments to states, was merely a placeholder to stem the program's rapid cost growth until a more permanent policy could be developed.

Thus, the initial round of administration proposals effectively exempted two-thirds of all entitlement expenditures that were accounted for then by Social Security, Medicare, and Medicaid. Significant proposals to address the Social Security retirement fund's imminent bankruptcy were proposed later in May, but with disastrous consequences. Major Medicare and Medicaid reform proposals would come in 1982 and 1983 as part of an incentive-based set of health care market reforms. The administration proposed to address the Social Security Disability Insurance program's problems mainly through administrative actions. We deal with these initiatives later in the chapter.

The administration proposed to eliminate the unemployment insurance program's extended benefit national trigger. Recall that the extended benefit program's original purpose was to provide additional weeks of unemployment benefits in states with high unemployment levels and reduced employment opportunities.[14] The national trigger allowed these benefits to be paid in states with low unemployment levels where employment opportunities were presumably plentiful. The administration also proposed to deny unemployment benefits to veterans who had volunteered for military service and had subsequently been voluntarily discharged. Under existing law, these veterans, in contrast to private sector workers who had voluntarily left their jobs, were entitled to receive twenty-six weeks of unemployment benefits. In the administration's view, voluntarily discharged veterans were no more worthy of assistance than similarly situated private sector workers.

The administration also proposed major legislative changes in the black lung and trade adjustment assistance (TAA) programs. As previously noted, the ballooning number of black lung recipients following the 1977 program liberalizations had required large general fund infusions into the black lung trust fund. By 1981, the bailout had already totaled $1 billion, and even larger future deficits were projected. A 1980 General Accounting Office review found that an astonishing 88 percent of all black lung benefit recipients had been certified for the program without adequate proof that they were disabled or that their disability was related to black lung disease.[15] The administration's main proposals included replacing the program's various presumptions of disability with a medical evidence requirement, requiring survivor affidavits to be supported by other evidence, and allowing government agencies to use chest X-rays as part of a second opinion. The new rules applied only to new applicants. The estimated 475,000 beneficiaries who were on the rolls without proper medical evidence of disability would not be affected.[16]

The administration also proposed to require TAA recipients to exhaust their unemployment insurance benefits before receiving benefits and to limit the combined number of weeks of receiving TAA and unemployment insurance to fifty-two. The two proposals would effectively eliminate the TAA entitlement to cash assistance.

The entitlement changes reflected President Reagan's long-held views about the proper federal government role in assisting individuals. Government, in the president's view, had a responsibility to maintain a safety net of assistance for people who were unable to provide for their own subsistence. He said, "Those who, through no fault of their own, must depend on the rest of us—the poverty stricken, the disabled, the elderly—all those with true need—can rest assured that the social safety net of programs they depend on are exempt from any cuts."[17] But the president also believed that government assistance, particularly welfare assistance, should be given with great care to avoid creating dependency and incentives for recipients to act in ways that were not in their best long-term interests. Indiscriminate welfare assistance, though it stemmed, in the president's words, from "well-intentioned" purposes, had too often "led to despair and dependency for the very people that needed genuine opportunity."[18] Furthermore, according to the president, state and local governments were best positioned to determine eligibility rules and the appropriate level of assistance and therefore should be free to administer their welfare programs. The federal government's welfare role should be limited mainly to providing financial assistance to these levels of government.

In these respects, President Reagan's views were not too dissimilar from President Franklin Roosevelt's. Both presidents recognized a governmental responsibility to maintain a social safety net, both expressed concern about the dangers to recipients of aid that was too liberally provided, and both believed that welfare policy was best made at the state and local levels. President Reagan accepted the legitimacy of the New Deal and its successor social insurance programs. Differences in the way historians view their entitlement policies stem from the fact that Presidents Roosevelt and Reagan were starting from different points in history. Franklin Roosevelt was launching the federal government into the social insurance and welfare assistance arena. Ronald Reagan was attempting to reduce the excesses that had been built into the system since the New Deal.

The Reagan administration accompanied its legislative proposals with a novel strategy to obtain congressional approval. President Reagan, like President Roosevelt, understood the importance of moving his legislative proposals quickly through Congress. History had shown that Congress gave considerable deference to a newly elected president's proposals. The passage of the Economy Act within two months of President Roosevelt's inauguration in 1933 served as an extraordinary but informative example. However, history had also shown that the deference lasted only for a brief period of time as the forces of the status quo quickly regrouped to preserve their programs.

Senior administration officials, most notably David Stockman, understood that the congressional committee system itself posed a significant obstacle to quickly enacting the president's budget plan, especially its entitlement proposals. David Stockman, like President Roosevelt's first budget director, Lewis Douglas, had served in Congress and understood its ways.

Under Congress's long-standing budget procedures, legislative responsibility for each entitlement program resides with a particular authorization committee. The proliferation of entitlements since the 1960s had spread this responsibility for entitlement programs, which in 1981 accounted for half of all federal expenditures, to more than a dozen congressional committees. With such divided jurisdiction, no individual committee had authority over the total amount of federal spending. Dispersed spending authority had created what is known in social science circles as a *tragedy of the commons*. Authorizing committees had little incentive to restrain their entitlement programs unless other committees also did so. As a result, entitlement restraint in 1981 was outside the experience of most committees, a fact that led Senator Orrin Hatch, the new chairman of the Senate Labor and Human Resources Committee, to remark, "I chair a committee that I don't think has ever made a cut in its existence."[19]

The landmark 1974 Budget Control and Impoundment Act had sought to address the problem by superimposing new budget expenditure and revenue targets on the traditional legislative process.[20] Newly created budget committees were responsible for preparing so-called budget resolution targets. These targets, established at the beginning of the legislative cycle, served as guidelines for the authorizing and appropriations committees as they carried out their unchanged legislative responsibilities. The Budget Act also included a provision that allowed the budget committees to include in the budget resolution so-called reconciliation instructions to require authorizing committees to produce legislation containing budget savings in entitlement programs under their respective jurisdictions.[21]

The Budget Act, however, failed to fulfill its promise. The budget resolution had become akin to a New Year's resolution, passed with great fanfare but with little follow-through to ensure that the resolution targets were met. Reconciliation instructions had been used only once, and only on a small scale, five months before President Reagan took office.

Mr. Stockman and Republican congressional leaders modified the Budget Act's machinery in an important way. Congress, at the beginning of the budget process, would vote to instruct various authorizing committees to produce legislative bills that contained specified savings amounts in their respective entitlement programs. The budget committees would then package these individual committee bills into a single omnibus budget reconciliation bill and send that bill for a vote by each chamber.[22]

This novel vehicle, the omnibus budget reconciliation bill, proved to be crucial to the administration's budget success in 1981. Since then, this vehicle has been used to enact entitlement reductions that have been included in virtually every congressional deficit reduction package. However, in President Reagan's second term and ever since, budget reconciliation bills have also become vehicles for legislatively expanding, and in some cases creating, new entitlements.

The First Two Years: Two Major
Successes and a Sharp Setback

Congress's reaction to the president's proposals was sharply divided.[23] While Republicans, as expected, supported his proposals, congressional liberals were appalled. Senator Ted Kennedy (D-MA), an ardent advocate for entitlement liberalizations, declared that he was "not prepared to see the social progress of a generation swept aside in a few short weeks."[24] House member Robert Garcia (D-NY), reflecting the prevailing liberal ideology that the private economy could not sustain rising living standards and that only government could, lamented that "supply side economics will just not put food on the table the way food stamps do."[25]

Moderate Democrats, including the party's congressional leadership, however, supported the broad outlines, if not the magnitude, of the president's budget plan. House Budget Committee chairman James Jones (D-OK) drafted an alternative budget plan that reduced income taxes, increased defense spending, and reduced nondefense spending, albeit by smaller amounts than the president proposed. House Speaker Tip O'Neill (D-MA) offered his view that "tax wise, all factions are in tune with the budget cuts."[26]

The phalanx of lobby groups that stood behind every line item in the entitlement budget were prepared to defend the entitlement edifice they had spent decades helping to construct. Senior citizens' lobbies, including the American Association of Retired People (AARP), the Gray Panthers, an umbrella group named Save Our Security, and the National Council of Senior Citizens, fought to protect Social Security benefits and prevent increases in Medicare copayments. The Alliance of Disability Insurance Recipients opposed disability cutbacks. The Welfare Recipients League defended AFDC against eligibility restrictions. The National Anti-Hunger Coalition resisted cuts in federal food assistance. The United Auto Workers fought trade adjustment assistance (TAA) benefit reductions, and the United Mine Workers battled against cuts in black lung benefits. A plethora of equally powerful lobbies representing entitlement service providers weighed in against the administration's budget. Medicare service provider lobbies representing physicians, psychiatrists, hospitals, outpatient clinics, home health agencies, nursing homes, durable medical equipment companies, and physical therapists fought to block Medicare reimbursement rate reductions. The American Food Service Workers and the National Milk Producers Association defended the school lunch and special milk programs. The National Association of Social Workers and the American Federation of State, County, and Municipal Workers pushed against reductions in social services for the poor. After observing the various efforts to protect entitlements from cutbacks, Congressman Phil Gramm (D-TX) observed, "Virtually all of the lobbying has come from people who are involved directly or indirectly in administering these programs."[27] The lobby groups countered that they were representing not their own financial interests but the interests of the poor, the elderly, and the disabled they served.

After initially being caught off guard by the depth and breadth of the administration's proposals, the lobbies quickly regrouped. By early spring, their power was on display. In March, nutrition advocates picketed the White House to protest food stamp and child nutrition cutbacks. In April ten thousand to eighteen thousand members of the Brotherhood of Railway and Airline Clerks, Railway Labor Executives' Association, and the United Transportation Union railroad workers marched on Washington to protest cuts in railroad retirement benefits, Amtrak, and the privatization of Conrail. In May, six thousand coal miners marched on the White House, and the United Mine Workers followed up with a two-day work stoppage to protest reductions in black lung benefits. The same month, beneficiaries of various entitlement programs held coordinated demonstrations in one hundred cities across the country. The demonstrations continued throughout the summer. In September, the AFL-CIO, along with two hundred other organizations, held a massive Solidarity Day in Washington to protest budget cuts.[28]

The Senate, under Republican control for the first time in twenty-five years, approved a partial budget resolution that contained many of the administration's proposals in early April. In the House, the budget resolution produced an extraordinary drama. The Democrat leadership put forward a resolution that contained a smaller reduction in nondefense spending, a smaller defense budget increase, and a smaller tax cut than the Reagan administration's budget. When the resolution came to the House floor, a bipartisan coalition of conservative Democrats and Republicans, led by Phil Gramm (D-TX) and Delbert Del Latta (R-OH), proposed a substitute budget plan, dubbed Gramm-Latta I, which more closely resembled the Reagan administration's budget. After a titanic struggle for votes, the House passed the Gramm-Latta budget resolution, 253–176.

Two weeks later, both chambers approved the budget resolution. The resolution instructed fourteen Senate and fifteen House entitlement committees to produce legislative bills by mid-June that would contain specified budget savings. The Budget Committee then was to bundle these bills into a single omnibus budget reconciliation bill for a vote by each chamber.

The Senate entitlement committees complied and the Senate version of the Omnibus Budget Reconciliation Act of 1981 passed overwhelmingly. The House entitlement committees were less compliant, and the House reconciliation bill fell well short of the savings targets. Once again Congressmen Gramm and Latta stepped forward with an alternative reconciliation bill, dubbed Gramm-Latta II, whose entitlement revisions provided the entitlement savings that had been promised by Gramm-Latta I.

The Gramm-Latta substitute set up a second monumental battle on the House floor that ultimately decided the fate of the Reagan administration's budget. The high stakes were summarized by House minority leader Robert H. Michel (R-IL): "Either we come to grips with the question of entitlement programs now, or we will have broken our compact with the American people."[29] Speaking in opposition, Richard Bolling (D-MO), who had stood with liberal Democrats in support of entitlement liberalizations since 1949, countered by asking members, "Do we have the guts to stand up for what we believe in?"[30]

Up to the time of the vote, the outcome was unclear. Liberal Democrats, who had spent decades building up the entitlement state, could be counted on to heavily oppose the bill. House Republicans, who had spent decades offering futile resistance to entitlement expansions, could be counted on to support the bill. Conservative southern Democrats, who for five decades had represented the swing vote on entitlement expansions, could go either way. After several days of strong rhetoric on both sides, the House passed the Gramm-Latta reconciliation bill, 217–111.[31]

The reconciliation bills put about 250 programs on the chopping block. Ironing out the differences between the House and Senate reconciliation bills was a gargantuan task for the conference committee with 184 House members and 72 senators.[32] But in less than five weeks, the committees resolved their differences. On July 31, the House approved the landmark 1981 Omnibus Budget Reconciliation Act by voice vote, and the Senate followed suit by approving the bill, 80–14.

Members of Congress from both sides of the aisle hailed the landmark law. Leading up to the final vote, Congressman Del Latta informed lawmakers that they were "about to adopt the largest package of spending cuts in the entire . . . history of the Congress." House Budget Committee chairman, James Jones (D-OK) concurred by saying that the law was "clearly the most monumental and historic turnaround in fiscal policy that has ever occurred." President Reagan echoed this sentiment in signing the bill, along with his sweeping tax reduction plan, into law, saying that the two bills "represent a turnaround of almost a half a century of a course this country's been on."[33]

At the time, the entitlement savings seemed draconian. Official Washington had not witnessed entitlement reductions of any consequence since President Franklin Roosevelt's first months in office. For the previous five decades, with few exceptions, the inexorable thrust of legislation had been expansionary. Contraction had not been part of the government's lexicon.

But as the numbers ultimately reveal, the 1981 Budget Reconciliation Act savings were hardly draconian. Congress shaved $11 billion from the more than $300 billion of entitlement spending that was projected to grow by $47 billion, a mere 3 percent from entitlements that were growing at 15 percent per year.[34]

With few exceptions, the entitlement savings were produced by marginal changes in eligibility rules. The law reduced the qualifying income levels for AFDC and food stamps to 150 and 130 percent of the poverty line, respectively. The law limited the AFDC program's thirty-and-a-third earnings disregard to a household's first four months on the rolls and reduced the food stamp program's earnings disregard to 18 percent from 20 percent. The law also required eligibility for AFDC, food stamps, and SSI to be determined by the applicant's actual income rather than likely future income. The law required a portion of a stepparent's income to be counted in determining AFDC eligibility and benefit levels.

The law temporarily reduced the Medicaid program's federal match rate and capped funding for the Social Services entitlement program at a level nearly $700 million below its current level.[35] It applied a means test for Guaranteed Student Loans to families with incomes of $30,000 or more and reduced both the income threshold for subsidized meals to 185 percent of the poverty line from 195 percent and the federal reimbursement rate for these lunches.

The Extended Unemployment Benefit program's national trigger was eliminated, and TAA recipients were required to exhaust unemployment insurance before receiving its benefits. This change effectively limited the number of weeks of TAA benefits to thirteen from twenty-six weeks and, for all practical purposes, ended the program's cash assistance entitlement.

The law also eliminated Social Security postsecondary student benefits, restricted lump-sum death benefits to widows and survivors, and terminated the Social Security minimum benefit.[36] Finally, the law increased Medicare deductibles and slightly reduced reimbursement rates on hospitals, nursing homes, and renal dialysis facilities.

Five days after passing the 1981 Budget Reconciliation Act, Congress passed the second major prong in the administration's economic program: the Economic Recovery Tax Act (ERTA), which provided a sweeping 25 percent reduction in personal income tax rates and large business income tax cuts.

A bruising battle over appropriation bills to fund government agencies followed passage of the Budget Reconciliation Act and the massive tax law. The battle, which lasted from September through mid-December, resulted in a presidential veto that shut down most government agencies in November and three temporary continuing resolutions.

When the dust finally settled on the 1981 fiscal year budget and the spending reductions were totaled up, the magnitude of their impact on federal spending became clear. The combination of entitlement reductions contained in the Budget Reconciliation Act and the nondefense discretionary program reductions achieved in the bitter late-year battle over appropriations bills had cut $28 billion from a $777 billion base of government spending that was projected to increase by $77 billion from 1981 to 1982. This restraint held the federal spending increase to the rate of inflation.

The lion's share of the budget savings came not from entitlements but from a historic reduction in nondefense discretionary programs. This category of programs accounted for only 20 percent of federal spending but 60 percent of the total 1982 savings. The $17 billion in savings from non-defense discretionary programs reduced their 1982 outlays below their level in 1980.

A Social Security Shellacking

In early 1981, the Social Security trustees reported that the Social Security retirement fund would be bankrupt in late 1982. The previous Congress, aware of the fund's serious financial condition, had nevertheless failed to act. Unless action was taken quickly, Social Security recipients would face an automatic reduction in monthly benefits. At that point, as budget director Stockman colorfully informed Congress, "The plug will be pulled on the great check-writing machine in Baltimore."[37] The shortness of time left policymakers with precious few options.[38]

In May 1981, the administration announced proposals to avert the program's bankruptcy. The centerpiece initiative would reduce the monthly benefits of workers who elected to take Social Security's early retirement benefits starting in January 1982, a scant eight months in the future.[39] Early-retiree benefit checks would be reduced 31 percent. The administration justified its proposal as necessary to ensure that full benefits could be paid to current retirees. Moreover, the administration argued, the proposal merely reduced an overly generous benefit. The benefit cut would have reduced the typical early retiree's inflation-adjusted rate of return on payroll tax contributions to 5.5 percent from

8 percent, still far more than the 3 percent workers would expect to earn on comparable private investments.

The proposal landed like a bombshell. Claude Pepper (D-FL), chairman of the House Aging Committee, immediately denounced the proposals as "nothing more than a wholesale assault on the economic security of America's elderly population."[40] Speaker of the House O'Neill called the proposal "a breach of faith, a rotten thing to do" and announced that he would "be fighting this thing every inch of the way."[41] Remarkably, some congressional leaders denied the need for legislation. House majority leader Jim Wright (D-TX) went so far as to declare to national news reporters that "Social Security is not broke or in any imminent danger of collapse."[42]

Interest groups representing Social Security recipients piled on. The AARP announced forming a grassroots campaign to defeat the initiative. Wilbur Cohen, a former secretary of Health, Education, and Welfare under Lyndon Johnson and now head of Save Our Security (SOS), a coalition of eighty-three groups opposed to program changes, called the proposed change "a calamity, a tragedy and a catastrophe." Earlier, Jacob Clayman, president of the National Council of Senior Citizens, anticipating the administration's proposed cuts, had expressed a sense of entitlement that had echoed through the halls of Congress from the time of Revolutionary War pensions, declaring that "all the [Social Security] benefits are legitimate and essential for this national social program and all are an earned right."[43]

Underlying the heated rhetoric was the objection that the benefit reduction, scheduled to occur only eight months away, was too abrupt. The policy gave older workers who had made important lifetime decisions based on the expectation of receiving a particular Social Security benefit at age 62 too little time to adjust.

Seizing the opportunity to deliver a blow to the president, Senate Democrats prepared a "sense of the Senate" resolution charging that the proposals were "a breach of faith with those aging Americans who have contributed to the Social Security system."[44] Senate Republicans, compelled to forestall the resolution, offered an alternative declaring that the Senate would not "precipitously and unfairly penalize early retirees." On May 20, just eight days after the administration had announced its proposal, the Senate passed the alternative resolution, 96–0.[45] The administration had overreached, and any substantive Social Security legislation was dead in the Ninety-Seventh Congress.

The administration and the deadlocked Congress finally agreed in December of 1981 to appoint a select commission to develop recommendations. The commission consisted of House and Senate members from both sides of the aisle, individuals appointed by the president, and chaired by the highly respected economist Alan Greenspan. Congress voted to keep Social Security afloat with transfers from the Medicare Hospital Insurance fund while the commission deliberated.

The Greenspan Commission delivered recommendations to President Reagan and Congress in January 1983. Congress passed the recommendations with some modifications, and the president signed them into law in April. The commission's work and the resulting Social Security Amendments of 1983 averted the trust fund's insolvency.

Solvency was achieved, however, mainly by adding federal revenues, both real and imaginary. Tax revenues were raised by moving forward in time previously scheduled payroll tax rate increases, requiring new federal workers to pay payroll taxes and subjecting Social Security benefits to higher-income retirees to federal income taxation. The additional tax revenues accounted for two-thirds of the trust fund's financial improvement attributable to the law.[46]

Imaginary revenues were created by immediately crediting the trust fund with $18 billion in general revenues, an amount equal to half of the remaining improvement in the fund. Congress and the administration rationalized the transfer as a reimbursement for the additional Social Security benefits that had been paid to former members of the armed forces. To avoid penalizing workers for their years of military service, Congress had granted former members of the military higher monthly Social Security benefits than they would have received but for their years of military service. The 1983 law reimbursed the fund for these additional payments since 1957 plus accumulated interest on these reimbursements. Couched in the language of military wage credits, the transfer was merely an accounting gimmick designed to improve the appearance of the financial position of the trust fund.

Setting aside the income tax on benefits that could arguably be treated as a benefit reduction, the law's only significant change to benefits was to delay cost-of-living increases (COLA). Starting in 1983, the COLA scheduled to take effect on July 1 was delayed for six months.

Although the focus of the 1983 amendments was on the near term, the law did begin to address Social Security's long-term problem. The law gradually increased the retirement age from 65 to 67 over a twenty-two-year period starting in the year 2000.[47] Workers could still retire at age 65, but under the new law, that age would be considered early retirement, and the worker would receive an initial monthly benefit that would be discounted accordingly. Thus, the policy had an effect similar to an across-the-board reduction in benefits for workers under age 46 in 1983. The reduction in monthly benefits amounted to about 13 percent.[48] With such long lead time, the policy generated little controversy. Remarkably, the slowly increasing retirement age since 2000 has occurred with little or no controversy.

The Reagan administration suffered a second serious Social Security setback when Congress rebelled against its review of Disability Insurance program recipients. In 1980 Congress had directed the Social Security administration to review the eligibility status of most people who were receiving disability insurance benefits once every three years.

The congressional directive was prompted by the high cost that had accompanied the rapidly rising number of workers on the disability rolls, which had grown from 1 million workers in 1965 to 2.9 million in 1980.[49] A 1981 General Accounting Office (GAO) study found that one in every five workers who were receiving Social Security disability benefits may not have met the disability criteria.[50] Lax administrative procedures by the Social Security administration and the state agencies that conducted the eligibility determinations had allowed individuals who were capable of working to gain entry to the disability insurance rolls. Once on the rolls, they tended to stay there because the Social Security administration reviewed only 3 percent of all people on the rolls each year. The lax administration was in part attributed to the unexpected flood of SSI claimants following the program's creation, responsibility for black lung disability determinations, and the surge in disability claimants after the extension of Medicare to the disabled, all of which had overwhelmed the Social Security administration and state disability agencies

Two other factors were at work. Hard-to-evaluate vocational considerations, as opposed to strictly medical factors, were playing an increasing role in initial disability determinations. In 1965, only one-sixth of newly approved claims were based on vocational factors. By 1980, one-fourth of all such claims were based on such nonmedical factors.[51] Four years earlier, former Social Security Administration chief medical director William Roemmich testified that the pervasive use of nonmedical factors had changed the eligibility standard from inability to perform any job in the economy by reason of disability to the "inability to engage in usual work by reason of age, education, and work experience providing any impairment is present."[52]

The failure of federally financed rehabilitative services also played a role. In 1978, the GAO reported that from 1967 to 1976, only 20,000 workers out of more than 3.5 million people who had joined the disability rolls during that time had been sufficiently rehabilitated to remove themselves from the disability rolls. Almost all of these recipients had medically recovered without the aid of government-financed rehabilitation services. Available data suggested that the effectiveness of rehabilitation had only deteriorated since then.[53]

The Reagan administration accelerated the reviews of the eligibility status of disability recipients in March 1981.[54] Only once before in the twentieth century, during Franklin Roosevelt's first year in office, had any presidential administration undertaken such a large-scale review of entitlement recipients. Within eighteen months, over 550,000 cases had been reviewed. Within three years, 1 million cases had been reevaluated, and benefits for 440,000 individuals had been terminated. The reviews had a brief but profound impact at all stages of the disability determination process. Between 1980 and 1982, approvals of new disability claims declined by 25 percent, to a low level not seen since the 1960s. Remarkably, new applications for disability claims also declined by 20 percent. This combination of factors caused the number of disabled workers on the rolls to decline by 10 percent between 1980 and 1983.[55] However, while President Roosevelt had been able to sustain his disability policy against a congressional backlash, President Reagan could not.

The reaction from the public, the press, federal courts, and Congress was fiercely negative. Newspapers described the reviews as "terrorization" and a "purge" of the rolls.[56] Press stories told of profoundly mentally and physically disabled people who lost their benefits despite disabilities that apparently prevented them from working. The *Chicago Tribune* reported that a man who was paralyzed in both arms and both legs had been terminated from the rolls because his disability was not judged to be sufficiently disabling. The *Washington Post* told the story of a mentally disturbed woman whose benefits had been cut off despite her doctor's diagnosis that she was "totally dependent" and unable to perform many activities of daily living. Ten months later, she was found dead of natural causes. The story was one of many that tied deaths and suicides of disability insurance recipients to their termination from the program.[57] Stories such as this led Congressman Silvio Conte (R-MA) to declare that "the overwhelming evidence is of individuals committing suicide when they learn that their benefits are ending."[58]

By late 1982, the disability insurance review policy was unraveling. In September, the Reagan administration temporarily halted disability reviews in a dozen states. In December, Congress voted to allow those whose continuing eligibility had been denied to continue receiving benefits during their appeals. In January 1983, Social Security administrative law judges, 540 agency employees who served as the arbiters on disability appeals, sued their own agency for its conduct.[59] During that year, a host of federal district court judges and several circuit courts ruled against the administration's review standards and ordered the administration to restore benefits to individuals who had been terminated. In June, the administration relaxed its standards, exempting an estimated 135,000 recipients from reviews.

The policy collapsed completely in 1984 as the disability review process descended into chaos. By midyear, about half of the states were refusing to conduct disability reviews. Disability cases swamped the federal courts. An astonishing 20 percent of all cases pending before all U.S. federal district courts in 1984 were appeals of disability determinations. Under siege, the Social Security Administration announced a moratorium on all reviews. The House of Representatives, after hearing Representative Jake Pickle (D-TX) describe the reviews as "horror story after horror story," voted 410–1 in March to end the disability reviews and legislate a new review standard for the program.[60] In May, the Senate voted 96–0 to end the reviews. The House and Senate agreed to a final bill, which the president signed on October 9.

The law imposed a new "medical improvement" standard for eligibility reviews. To remove a recipient from the rolls, the new standard required the administration to prove that a recipient's medical condition had improved to the point where the recipient was able to work. If the government could not produce the required evidence, a recipient would remain on the rolls regardless of whether he or she was capable of working.[61]

A separate provision of the 1984 law ordered the administration to develop new standards for mental impairment cases. All people who had been terminated from the rolls or had been denied initial benefits because they had failed to meet the administration's existing standards were allowed to reapply under the new standards.

The 1984 law put the disability program on an expansionary path once again. The number of workers on the disability rolls, after reaching a low point of 2.6 million in 1983, rose to 2.9 million by the decade's end. In the late 1980s, the percentage of reviews that resulted in eligibility termination fell to 60 percent of its level in the late 1970s, before the disability reviews had begun. The approval rate of new applicants, after declining to 31 percent in 1983, rose to 43 percent in 1989. The new mental impairment standards provided another avenue for growth. In 1981, only 10 percent of newly approved disability recipients claimed mental impairment. By 1991, 24 percent claimed to be suffering from mental illness.[62] So large was the reversal of the trend that by the late 1980s, the program was larger and more generous than it had been when the disability reviews started.

The administration's Social Security retirement proposals and its disability insurance reviews sought to abruptly reduce entitlement benefits for a large number of persons. The retirement proposals adversely affected millions of individuals who had made life-altering decisions based on the expectation of receiving a particular benefit. The disability reviews reversed previously granted entitlements to hundreds of thousands of recipients who, rightly or wrongly, had come to rely on these benefits for daily living. Congress's overwhelming rejection of these attempts serves as a vivid reminder of a general rule governing entitlement programs: Once granted, an entitlement can be taken away only under extraordinary circumstances.

Battling to a Stalemate, 1982–1988

Following passage of the landmark 1981 Budget Reconciliation Act, President Reagan told the American public that "this cannot be the last round of cuts. Holding down spending must be a continuing battle for several years to come."[63] Throughout his two terms, the president remained committed to staying the course he had charted in 1981. His annual budgets repeatedly pressed Congress to reduce nondefense discretionary appropriations and curtail the explosive growth in entitlements. These budgets invariably reproposed entitlement initiatives that Congress had failed to enact and added a few new entitlement initiatives that would trim the programs at their edges.[64] The president remained steadfast in his opposition to tax rate increases and his commitment to restoring the nation's defense capabilities was unwavering.

Congress greeted each of the president's budgets with bipartisan criticism. In an annual ritual, Democrats declared the budget dead on arrival. Republicans, for the most part, agreed.[65] Congress staged votes to reject the president's budget. The rejection was invariably followed by hand-to-hand combat over compromise plans. In most years, the contest dominated Congress's legislative calendar, often lasting the entire legislative session and always consuming most of its time and energy. The budget conflict seemed endless; on two occasions, it spilled over into the subsequent legislative session. In these annual battles, Republicans generally supported the administration's compromise plans. Many Republicans were willing to increase taxes, but only if it meant reducing the cavernous budget deficits. Democrats opposed the president on all fronts. They fought against any further nondefense spending reductions and battled to restore spending reductions that had been enacted in 1981 and further liberalize entitlements. Eventually, however, a compromise agreement was reached toward the end of the legislative session.

The negative congressional reaction in 1982 and 1983 was hardly surprising. By the beginning of 1982, the economy had fallen into a severe economic recession. Throughout 1983, although the economy was in recovery, the unemployment rate remained high. During these hard times, most members of Congress were loath to reduce social programs. Other members, unwilling to wait for the "riverboat gamble," as Senate majority leader Howard Baker (R-TN) had called President Reagan's economic program, to pay off, proposed to undo the 1981 reductions. They were unwilling to suffer through what former Secretary of State George Shultz has called the economists' lag—the long time between when an economic policy is enacted and when the policy manifestly affects the economy. So it was in 1982 and 1983, as both congressional chambers were filled with calls to reverse the president's economic program: to raise taxes, reduce his defense budget, and restore previously enacted budget cuts.

By mid-1984, the Reagan economic program was paying dividends. A strong economic recovery, which would continue throughout the remainder of the 1980s and the 1990s except for a brief downturn in 1990, was well underway. Employment was rising rapidly and inflation had been tamed. Yet the federal budget deficit stubbornly refused to decline. Large budget deficits constantly loomed on the fiscal horizon.

To reduce the budget deficit, the Reagan administration continued to put entitlement programs on the chopping block. With the notable exceptions of the Social Security retirement and disability programs, benefit reductions or eligibility restrictions were proposed for virtually every entitlement program at some point from 1982 to 1988.[66] In Congress, major tax bills and budget reconciliation bills enacted in 1982, 1984, 1986, 1987, and 1988, were the main legislative vehicles for entitlement changes. Each of these bills produced incremental changes in entitlement laws that, on net, only slightly lowered the upward trajectory of entitlement spending. None of these budget reduction measures came close to the matching entitlement changes contained in the landmark 1981 budget reconciliation bill. Two main 1982 budget bills combined shaved only $6 billion per year over the ensuing three years from a $330 billion base of entitlement spending that was growing by $40 billion per year. Three 1984 budget bills produced only $7 billion per year in three-year entitlement savings. Two 1986 budget bills contained only $8 billion per year. The 1987 bill was only $3 billion from the now larger $450 billion base of entitlement spending.[67]

The lion's share of entitlement savings in each of the budget reduction bills came from slowing the growth in Medicare expenditures. By the late 1970s, two decades of double-digit Medicare spending growth had propelled the program into position as the second largest entitlement program, behind only Social Security. By the mid-1980s, the federal government was already spending more on Medicare services than it was spending on all cash, nutrition, and health care means-tested entitlements combined to assist all poor and low-income households. Medicare's projected 10 percent per year spending growth provided a tempting target for budget savings.

After 1981, Congress had rejected all administration attempts to raise Medicare copayments as a means of dampening the increasing use of Medicare services. Medicare health maintenance organizations, which Congress had authorized in 1982, held promise but were too few in number to make a difference. Hence, the administration and Congress were left with squeezing savings from the Medicare program by limiting the annual increase in hospital and physician reimbursement rates below the medical care inflation rate. All of these deficit reduction bills, except for the 1983 Omnibus Budget Reconciliation Act, contained such limits.

A nontrivial portion of the Medicare savings eventually proved illusory as health care providers responded by offsetting the limits in various ways. Hospitals classified patients into more severe diagnostic groups, discharged and then readmitted patients, and transferred patients from inpatient to outpatient status. Physicians saw patients more frequently, ordered up more tests, and delivered more medical procedures. Thus, throughout the latter half of the 1980s, despite the budget savings measures, Medicare spending increased at a 9 percent annual rate, twice the growth in inflation and population.[68]

The budget-driven legislation produced some notable entitlement changes. In 1982, Congress changed the manner in which Medicare reimbursed hospitals from a cost per day to a cost per admission. The change paved the way for an entirely new Medicare hospital reimbursement system the following year: a prospectively determined payment for each patient discharged. Congress expanded the earned income tax credit program as an alternative to AFDC in 1984 and 1986. The tax credit program, in contrast to AFDC, contained positive work incentives for both household members in working-poor households with children. Congress also modernized the civil service retirement system in 1986 by allowing government employees to invest in 401k retirement plans as a replacement for a portion of their defined-benefit program that was partially financed by taxpayers. In 1988, Congress set the stage for the monumental 1996 welfare reform law by allowing states considerable flexibility to revise their AFDC programs to focus their efforts on moving recipients into self-sufficiency instead of simply maintaining recipients' income.[69]

Ominously, however, starting in 1984 Congress began reversing some of the 1981 entitlement reductions and further liberalizing exist ing entitlements. Reconciliation bills became the primary vehicle for these changes. In 1984, Congress raised the income threshold for AFDC eligibility and relaxed some AFDC work expense deductions that had been tightened in 1981. A year later, it liberalized food stamp benefits by reducing the benefit-reduction rate, increasing deductions allowed for work expenses, and adding a new child care expense deduction. In 1988, as part of that year's 1988 AFDC reform law, congressional liberals finally succeeded in permanently extending the AFDC program to two-parent households.[70]

The most significant and lasting liberalizations occurred in the Medicaid program. From 1984 to 1988, Congress liberalized Medicaid eligibility rules in no fewer than five legislative bills. Each set of liberalizations was attached to a large legislative bill whose primary purpose was not Medicaid. Three sets of expansions were inserted into budget reconciliation bills, another was attached to the Medicare Catastrophic Act of 1988, and the fifth set was attached to the 1988 welfare reform measure. The liberalizations continued into the George H. W. Bush administration with two sets that were included in budget reconciliation bills in 1989 and 1990.

The expansions began in 1984 when Congress restored Medicaid match rates to their 1981 levels. From that year through 1988, Congress required states to extend Medicaid eligibility to first-time pregnant women and to phase in coverage of young children in two-parent households who met the state's AFDC financial standards but were not receiving AFDC benefits. In 1988 and 1990, Congress followed the same pattern but changed the basis of income eligibility to the federal poverty line. Congress required states to cover first-time pregnant women and children age 6 and under who lived in families with incomes below 133 percent of the poverty line. Congress then required states to phase in Medicaid coverage of all children in all households with income below the poverty line. [71]

The seven-year Medicaid legislative blitzkrieg changed the nature of the program. Up to 1984, Medicaid had provided health care services as a supplement to cash assistance only for households that were already on welfare. Seven years later, Medicaid provided health care services as a basic benefit to all households with children who lived below the poverty line, including two-parent households, and to pregnant women with incomes as high as 133 percent of the poverty line. Taken together, by 1991 the incremental legislative expansions added more than 1 million new recipients to the Medicaid rolls. By the mid-1990s, 2 million recipients would be added.[72]

Enter the Grimm Reaper

The stubbornly high budget deficits and the inability to reduce them created a sense in the nation's capital that the federal government was incapable of performing one of its most basic functions: budgeting. The experience in 1984 and early 1985 in which reconciliation bills were used as vehicles to expand entitlements contributed importantly to this worry. In both bills, savings achieved by slowing the growth in one entitlement program were being used to finance another entitlement program's liberalizations. The palpable sense throughout Washington that extra budget mechanisms were needed led the administration and Congress to enact a new budget law in 1985.

The Gramm-Rudman-Hollings law, named after its three congressional architects, Phil Gramm who was now a Republican senator from

Texas, Senator Warren Rudman (R-NH), and Senator Ernst Hollings (D-SC), wrote numerical deficit targets into the statute books for the first time in U.S. history. The deficit targets were set to decline over five years to achieve a balanced budget by 1991. The law included an enforcement mechanism: If Congress did not take legislative action to meet the upcoming year's statutory deficit target, spending on all federal programs that were not specifically exempted would be automatically reduced by an amount necessary to meet the deficit target. A "grim reaper" would, in effect, sweep through the budget imposing equi-proportionate and indiscriminate reductions in all nonexempt programs regardless of any program's relative merits.[73]

The following year, after the Supreme Court declared certain provisions of the law unconstitutional, Congress passed a revised law that included higher deficit targets. Initially the law proved to be a modest success in restraining spending. A small 4 percent reduction was imposed on all nonexempt programs in 1986. But Congress soon found ways to circumvent the targets, so much so that an embarrassed Congress repealed the law altogether in 1990.

The law's importance for this book is that it demonstrates, once again, the special status of entitlement programs. The law fully or partially exempted almost all entitlement programs. It fully exempted the Social Security retirement and disability programs, railroad retirement, regular unemployment insurance benefits, veterans' compensation and pensions, federal civilian and military retirement programs, AFDC, SSI, Medicaid, and food stamps and child nutrition programs. The law limited reductions in Medicare to 2 percent. In contrast, among nonentitlement programs, Congress exempted only the Women, Infants and Children program and most Tennessee Valley Authority activities.[74]

An Eliminated Entitlement:
General Revenue Sharing

On September 30, 1986, Congress and the administration allowed the $4.6 billion general revenue sharing (GRS) program to expire. Its expiration marks only the third time in U.S. history that Congress had allowed a major entitlement to end.

President Nixon originally proposed the "no strings attached" (GRS) program to replace an existing array of discretionary federal grant programs for states and local governments. Following its enactment, Congress reauthorized the popular program three times. Remarkably, the program had remained free of congressional earmarks, except for a small grant to support Louisiana sheriffs, the handiwork of Louisiana senator and Finance Committee chairman Russell Long. Between 1973 and 1985, the program had transferred over $80 billion of federal funds to state and local governments. In 1985, the program dispensed federal funds to nearly thirty-nine thousand local governments.[75] During President Reagan's first term, his administration supported the program, as had the previous four presidential administrations. The program was in accord with President Reagan's federalism principles and had also served as a useful model for the administration's first-term proposals to consolidate existing education, health, and energy programs into block grants.

The program was not without its congressional critics. Government Affairs Committee chairman Jack Brooks (D-TX) spoke for the critics when he declared that the program "violates the cardinal principle of accountability—the simple but vital idea that those officials who spend money on government programs should be responsible for raising the revenues to pay for those programs."[76] Nevertheless, the program enjoyed considerable congressional support. As late as 1983, Congress voted overwhelmingly to reauthorize the program.

The deteriorating federal budget condition and rapidly improving state and local government budget situation changed the program's fortunes. In early 1985, the administration proposed to terminate the program as part of its sweeping postelection deficit reduction plan. The president explained his proposal's rationale by asking rhetorically, "How can we afford revenue sharing when we have no revenues to share?"[77] Juxtaposed against the large federal budget deficits was an estimated $50 billion of state and local budget surpluses that the two-year-old strong economic recovery had helped produce. Federal borrowing to finance even larger state and local government budget surpluses made little sense to the administration. These lower-level governments were, in some cases, using GRS funds to purchase the securities that the federal government was issuing to finance the GRS payments to them.

The proposed termination of such a large entitlement program was greeted with only modest opposition. The prevailing view was that the GRS program was a windfall to local governments that the federal government could no longer afford. One expert on government finance, Richard Nathan, expressed a common view of what the program's termination would mean for local governments: "Santa Claus Is Leaving Town."[78]

The program's end came swiftly. In early 1985, the Reagan administration proposed to terminate the program. Congress responded by sharply reducing the program's funding. In 1986, the administration reiterated its proposal. In March, when the budget reconciliation bill did not include provisions to reauthorize the program, the handwriting was on the wall. Congress then allowed GRS authorization to expire at the end of September.

The reasons for the program's demise are complex, as the causes of rare events are rarely understood. The coexistence of state and local budget surpluses seriously undermined its basic rationale. The contractionary pressures that accompanied the large and apparently permanent federal budget deficit also played a contributing role. These contractionary pressures were magnified by the newly established 1985 Gramm-Rudman-Hollings law's statutory deficit limits, which required any GRS expenditure to be offset, dollar for dollar, by a corresponding reduction in other federal program expenditures. This requirement forced Congress to weigh the relative merits of GRS against those of other government programs. In this weighing, GRS lost out.

The fact that GRS funds were an inconsequential part of most local government budgets also played a role. The funds, which on average constituted only 2.2 percent of local government revenues, merely added a fine layer of padding to most local government budgets.[79] Furthermore, because local governments comingled GRS funds with other local government revenues, the ultimate local recipients—police, fire, education, and transportation agencies—could not readily distinguish GRS funds from funds from other sources. As a general rule of political economy, the willingness of an interest group to lobby for a program increases in direct proportion to the program's financial importance to the group. Thus, local governments and representatives of local programs had little incentive to fight for the program's survival.

These latter two considerations and the fact that the program's reporting requirements were minimal combined to create a fourth factor. Because GRS funds were not earmarked, most members of Congress had little idea to what ends the thirty-nine thousand local governments were using the funds or how efficiently they were being spent. Congressional members were not involved in ribbon-cutting ceremonies or in other credit-claiming activities and hence had little attachment to the program. Although support in Congress was broad, it was only skin deep. In a sense, the program's structure and objectives made it vulnerable to its own elimination.

Enactment and Repeal: The Medicare Catastrophic Care Act

The end of the 1980s witnessed a remarkably rare event in the history of entitlements: Congress enacted a new entitlement, prescription drug coverage for Medicare beneficiaries, and then repealed it sixteen months later. The repeal came after the program's end was vocally demanded by many of the very persons it was designed to benefit.

The 1965 Medicare program afforded no protection against the high costs of catastrophic illness and provided no coverage for prescription drugs outside a hospital setting. In early 1987, President Reagan proposed to partially rectify these perceived shortcomings by establishing an overall limit on Medicare beneficiaries' out-of-pocket expenses for existing Medicare covered services. The proposal did not include prescription drug coverage due to concerns about its potentially high cost. The president's plan called for the costs of catastrophic coverage to be financed entirely by additional levies on Medicare beneficiaries.[80]

The president's plan was liberalized as it wound its way through Congress's committees. The most important expansion was the addition of a new Medicare prescription drug coverage program. The AARP, whose for-profit arm was one of the nation's largest dispensers of drugs and stood to make a considerable amount of money, lobbied heavily for the new drug benefit. Pharmaceutical companies, which feared price controls, and congressional conservatives, who feared the coverage's high cost, opposed the bill. But with President Reagan's support, Congress overwhelmingly passed the Medicare Catastrophic Care Act in July 1988. The law's catastrophic coverage limited the amount beneficiaries could pay out of pocket for Medicare covered services. The new prescription drug benefit initially required a $600 annual deductible and a 50 percent coinsurance rate.[81] The new coverage costs were financed exclusively by a two-part Medicare premium increase: a flat premium increase applicable to all Medicare enrollees and an additional income-related surcharge on all enrollees with an income tax liability of at least $150. Both increases were substantial. The flat premium increase was expected to add 36 percent to existing premiums in four years. The income-related surcharge, which was administered by the Internal Revenue Service, raised beneficiaries' income taxes by between 15 and 28 percent, up to a maximum of $800 per year.

The milestone law enacted the first major expansions in Medicare coverage since the program's inception in 1965. More important, for the first time in U.S. history, new entitlement benefits were exclusively financed by levies on the current beneficiaries.

Initially the law was hailed as a valuable and responsible piece of legislation. Coverage of catastrophic illness costs and prescription drugs was seen as an overdue modernization of Medicare's benefits. Requiring seniors and the disabled to finance the additional insurance coverage, instead of loading more taxes on workers, was considered proper in light of the already high payroll tax burden. Senator Lloyd Bentsen (D-TX) expressed the euphoria many members of Congress felt by declaring, "Let us allow Medicare beneficiaries to harvest the bounties of this catastrophic bill and give them and their children the peace of mind they deserve."[82]

The reverie did not last long. In autumn 1988, the first trickle of criticism of the landmark law began to flow into Congress. By early 1989, large numbers of senior citizens, upset by the higher premiums, were publicly denouncing it. At the time, 80 percent of all Medicare beneficiaries had already obtained prescription drug coverage from Medigap insurance, employer retiree insurance, or Medicaid coverage.[83] The law was requiring these seniors to pay for coverage that they already had. Moreover, because the law prohibited insurance companies from offering coverage that duplicated the new Medicare benefit, it forced seniors out of their existing prescription drug plans onto an untested new government program. Senator Phil Gramm likened the law's architects to the "Boy Scout who sees a little old lady standing on the corner . . . he decides he is taking her on across the street whether she wants to go or not."[84]

In addition, the premium surcharge was steeply progressive. The upper half of all income-earning seniors, those most likely to already have private insurance, financed 80 percent of the program's cost. The bottom 30 percent of earners paid only 8 percent. The premiums charged to the top 30 percent of income-earning seniors were four times the actuarial value of the coverage provided. The law, in effect, required these seniors to finance not only the cost of their own coverage under the law but the cost of coverage that law provided to three other seniors.

In August 1989, an extraordinary event sealed the law's demise. Congressman Dan Rostenkowski, the Ways and Means Committee chairman and one of the most powerful leaders of the House of Representatives, returned to his Chicago district. Following a speech, a group of irate senior citizens chased after him to let him know their views on the new Medicare law. The chairman dashed to his car and locked himself in as seniors surrounded his car and pounded it with their placards. With one elderly woman lying on the hood, the car couldn't leave. The chairman bolted from the car and ran down the street with dozens of seniors in hot pursuit yelling "coward," "recall," and "impeach." Congressman Rostenkowski cut through a gas station, jumped into a waiting car, and escaped.

The incident was widely reported by the print media, and videos of the incident were shown on the nightly news. From that point forward, with chairman Rostenkowski leading the charge, the law was on a fast track to oblivion. On November 2, 1989, Congress repealed the Medicare Catastrophic Care Act; only the third major entitlement law to be repealed in 147 years.

Conclusion

Ronald Reagan's success in reining in entitlements, though modest, is unmatched by any other presidential administration in U.S. history. Legislative actions reduced benefit levels or tightened eligibility rules in all but three entitlement programs: Medicaid, Social Security Disability program, and the earned income tax credit. One entitlement, general revenue sharing, was terminated, and only the remnants of another, the trade adjustment cash assistance program, remained on the statute books. A few statistics will help put the administration's results in perspective. Although entitlement spending continued to increase throughout the president's two terms in office, its growth slowed dramatically. Real per capita entitlement spending increased at an annual rate of just 1.4 percent from 1981 to 1989. With the exception of the early 1950s when GI Bill expenditures were winding down, the 1.4 percent growth is the slowest rate during any eight-year period from the New Deal through the first term of President Barack Obama's administration.

During Reagan's presidency, the percentage of U.S. households that received assistance from at least one federal entitlement program actually declined. Reductions in certain entitlement caseloads were quite sizable. The 16 percent decline in food stamps, the 3 percent decline in AFDC, and the 6 percent decline in child nutrition caseloads were the first significant reductions in each of their histories. The number of TAA recipients plunged from 600,000 in 1980 to a negligible 24,000 by 1989 and the black lung caseload plummeted from 376,000 to 226,000.[85]

The entitlement restraint and strong economic growth proved to be a valuable combination in lessening the burden of entitlements. While the restraint trimmed the benefit rolls, strong economic growth from 1983 on provided private sector employment alternatives to entitlement assistance. The growth also increased federal revenues, which lightened the burden of the expenditures. Together, restraint and growth caused entitlement spending's share of gross domestic product to decline by 11 percent from 1981 to 1989, reversing a thirty-year upward climb. Although the decline seems modest, today it would enable the federal government to finance entitlement spending with $1,000 less in income taxes per U.S. household.

Yet despite the Reagan administration's achievements, the entitlement state in 1989 remained largely intact. Its largest programs had defied retrenchment. Bipartisan majorities in Congress had repelled the administration's attempts to reduce Social Security's early retirement benefits and cull the Social Security Disability Insurance program roll. Congress had also rejected administration proposals to raise Medicare copayments, likely the single most effective means of constraining health care costs. Congress and the administration instead relied on limiting Medicare reimbursement rates to providers, an approach that, in view of the program's 10 percent annual expenditure growth rate, was a demonstrable failure.

The outlook for future control of entitlements was not good. The administration's successes had come early and had proven to be short-lived. By 1983, entitlement supporters in Congress and the well-entrenched phalanx of lobbies that obtained their sustenance from entitlements had regained the upper hand. With the Social Security retirement and disability trust funds out of near-term financial danger and the battle scars from attempts to rein in their expenditures now indelibly planted on the congressional DNA, the Social Security programs were off the table for the foreseeable future. Medicare and Medicaid expenditures were galloping along at near double-digit rates, and the policy options for slowing their growth were sorely limited. Although the administration's steadfast opposition to entitlement expansions and the existence of large budget deficits had prevented Congress from returning to the legislative excesses of the 1960s and 1970s, Congresses had begun incrementally liberalizing welfare programs.

The Reagan administration's success in restraining entitlement, though modest, demonstrates the crucial role of the presidency in restraining entitlements. Ronald Reagan's use of the presidency's power and prestige, along with his more than ample political skills, was essential to achieving the modest restraint, in much the same manner that Franklin Roosevelt's use of the office and political skills was in reducing veterans' pension rolls. The Reagan experience also reinforces the widely held view that in all policy areas, the prospects for a change in the status quo are highest during the president's first year when the office's power is at its peak.

Budget deficits proved helpful in producing pressures to curtail spending, just as surpluses had produced the opposite pressures. The large deficits that brought the Social Security trust fund to the brink of bankruptcy were the primary factors causing Congress to take action in 1983. At the other extreme, Social Security's annual surpluses during the latter half of the 1980s removed any near-term pressure to address Social Security's future financial shortfall. Similarly, the black lung trust fund's bankruptcy was instrumental in producing legislation to tighten the program's eligibility rules. At the unified federal budget level, the large deficits that persisted throughout the decade helped prevent the enactment of new major entitlements and put a damper on further existing entitlement liberalizations.

18 Recognition and Denial, 1989–2014

> We must not let our rulers load us with perpetual debt.
> *Thomas Jefferson*[1]

BY THE EARLY 1990S, CONGRESS HAD BEGUN TO recognize the true magnitude of the fiscal storm that loomed on the horizon. The leading edge of the baby boom generation would reach retirement age in less than twenty years. The fiscal problem they presented was no longer just a Social Security or just a Medicare problem; it was a problem that engulfed the entire federal budget. Starting in the early 1990s, the Congressional Budget Office, the General Accounting Office, the Office of Management and Budget, special congressional commissions, congressional study groups, and nongovernment research organizations began regularly issuing long-term budget projections that highlighted the future budgetary consequences of entitlement growth. Annual reports by the Social Security trustees increasingly focused on Social Security and Medicare's long-term financing problems. By the turn of the century, Congress was fully cognizant of the fact it faced a fiscal challenge unlike any other in U.S. history.

Yet both branches of government, as if in a continual state of denial, ignored the warnings. Congress held hearings on and vigorously debated Social Security retirement and disability reforms but took no action. Both branches of government resorted to manipulating budget accounting rules to create the appearance of restraining

Medicare spending. Throwing fiscal caution to the wind, policymakers then extended Medicare coverage to prescription drugs, the largest expansion in Medicare's fifty-year history. Both branches of government worked in concert to expand eligibility for Medicaid, the earned income tax credit, and food stamps to "worthy" claimants higher up the income ladder. President Obama and congressional Democrats capped off the period by extending the class of "worthy" individuals to a health insurance entitlement to the entire U.S. population under age 65.

In one striking departure from this legislative pattern, Congress enacted the landmark 1996 welfare reform law. The law reversed decades of federal welfare policy by eliminating an individual's entitlement to Aid to Families with Dependent Children (AFDC) benefits and transferring program policymaking authority to the states. The reform measure was motivated not so much by fiscal concerns but by a bipartisan realization that the AFDC program was encouraging recipients to act in ways that were harmful to the long-run interests of themselves and their families.

Debates on Social Security "Surplus"

Following the 1981–1983 recession, the U.S. economy entered a twenty-seven-year period of remarkably strong noninflationary economic growth. The growth, coupled with the 1983 Social Security law's acceleration of previously enacted payroll tax increases, generated a rapid rise in Social Security revenues. At the same time, a demographic dividend from a slowly growing age 65 and older population moderated the growth in Social Security outlays. This combination of economic and demographic forces generated a string of annually rising Social Security surpluses from the mid-1980s to the Great Recession in 2008.[2]

Meanwhile, the rest of the federal budget remained chronically in deficit, except for the four years from 1998 to 2001. The coexistence of large Social Security surpluses and large general fund deficits generated public concerns, reminiscent of those of the late 1930s, that Congress was using Social Security surpluses to finance other government programs. Defenders of the surpluses argued, as they had in the 1930s, that the surpluses were being invested in U.S. government securities that could be drawn on later to help finance future benefits. Critics countered that the trust fund contained no financial assets. It was merely a Treasury Department accounting ledger.[3] The high degree of public skepticism over the use of surplus funds is reflected in a widely cited poll in the early 1990s that found that nearly twice as many young Americans age 18 to 34 believed in extraterrestrial life than that Social Security would exist when they reached retirement age.[4]

Faced with growing skepticism, Congress responded by enacting two Social Security laws in 1994. The first created the physical appearance of a trust fund without altering the use of any federal funds. Public Law 103–296 authorized the Treasury Department to set aside a portion of a newly refurbished public debt building to house the trust fund.[5] The building was located in Parkersburg, West Virginia, which, by no small coincidence, was in the home state of the Appropriations Committee chairman, Robert C. Byrd (D). The building provided space for a government-issue, metallic file cabinet, complete with combination locks into which newly minted nonnegotiable U.S. Securities were, and currently are being, placed. These securities included facsimiles of those that the Social Security administration had allegedly purchased in prior years. One of those facsimiles, a fifteen-year, $5.9 billion Treasury bond, supposedly purchased in 1988, and carrying a 9.14 percent interest rate, is shown here (Photo 1).

The law was purely a cosmetic exercise. Authorization to use rooms in an existing federal building, furnish those rooms, and allow U.S. Treasury Department officials to print facsimiles of government securities that could be neither bought nor sold in public markets did not alter how the federal government actually used Social Security funds.

The second Social Security statute of 1994 was anything but cosmetic. In contrast to the retirement program's large annual surpluses, disability insurance had been experiencing financial difficulties. A 47 percent increase in the number of recipients since the enactment of the 1984 Social Security disability law had brought the disability fund to the brink of bankruptcy. In early 1994, the Social Security trustees projected that the fund would be depleted the following year.[6]

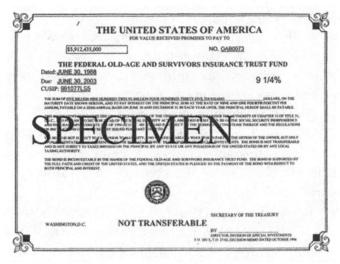

Photo 1. Treasury Bond Held by the Social Security Trust Fund.
Source: Social Security Trust Fund.

Instead of tightening the disability program's eligibility rules, Congress chose to permanently siphon off a portion of the retirement fund's revenues to the disability program by lowering the former program's payroll tax and raising the latter's in equal amounts.[7] The 1994 tax shift marked the sixth time that Congress had authorized such a permanent transfer. As of this writing, Congress has shifted nearly $500 billion (in today's dollars) from the former fund to the latter.[8] The 1994 action, taken at a time when Congress fully understood these ramifications, serves as a powerful example of Congress's short-term focus and its disregard for the long-term consequences of its actions.

Neither the trust fund in Parkersburg nor the diversion of funds quelled public concerns that surplus Social Security funds were being used to finance other government programs. In 1996 Senate majority leader Tom Daschle (D-SD) openly acknowledged what was widely understood to be true in Washington: "Right now, we are using Social Security trust funds to pay for other spending in the federal budget."[9]

As Social Security surpluses continued to mount, legislative bills were introduced to liberalize eligibility or increase benefits for almost every subgroup covered by the retirement program, including spouses, widows, children of retirees, and those whose benefits had been adversely affected by the 1977 Social Security law (so-called notch babies). Other bills would reestablish the Social Security's minimum benefit, restore the education benefit, increase cost-of-living adjustments above the Consumer Price Index, and raise the lump-sum death benefit. Still other bills would allow Social Security surpluses to be allocated to social investments for public infrastructure, housing, and education; to be invested in corporate equities. Another set of bills would allow young workers to invest a portion of their payroll taxes in personal private accounts.[10]

Years before, Senator Daniel Patrick Moynihan (D-NY) had explained the dangers of large surpluses by quoting the former Social Security chief actuary, Robert J. Myers: "Gentlemen, you are never going to save the surplus. . . . Temptation is never overcome. The flesh is weak the spirit notwithstanding. Give it back before [spending] it becomes a habit."[11] The myriad proposals confirmed Mr. Myers's and Senator Moynihan's keen understanding of Congress.

President Clinton and fiscally conservative members of Congress from both political parties countered these liberalizing plans with proposals that sought to ensure that Social Security surpluses were instead used to reduce the publicly held debt. These proposals took the form of creating procedural hurdles to prevent Congress from spending the surplus. In the 106th Congress alone, more than forty such legislative proposals were introduced. The case for these initiatives was strong. Neither the economy's torrid technology-fueled growth in the late 1990s nor the federal budget surpluses it generated could be expected to continue indefinitely. The economic laws governing the business cycle had not been repealed. Saving temporary surpluses to prefinance the benefits promised to the rapidly approaching baby boomer retirements was a sensible public finance plan. These proposals, besides serving as a counter to expanding Social Security benefits, also served as an alternative to efforts by liberal Democrats to use Social Security surpluses to finance additional domestic spending and plans by conservative Republicans for broad-based tax reductions.

Among these proposals, President Clinton's 1999 call for Congress to "save the surplus" attracted the most attention.[12] The president's plan was to use Social Security surpluses to reduce the publicly held debt and to credit Social Security for that debt reduction. The proposal's policy direction was sound, but it did not contain any new mechanism to ensure that surplus Social Security funds would actually be used for debt reduction. In fact, the proposal did not in any way affect the use of surplus Social Security funds.[13] It was merely a plea for Congress to do what it had been unwilling to do with Social Security surpluses for the prior sixty years.

President Clinton claimed that his proposal would improve Social Security's long-term financial health.[14] However, the accounting was false. As readers of this book know, Social Security's accounting treatment already assumed that the program's surpluses would be used to reduce the publicly held debt and already credited the Social Security trust fund with the assumed reduction. Remarkably, the president's plan proposed to double-count each dollar of surplus Social Security revenue and, on top of this, pay interest to the trust fund on these additional fictitious dollars. It was a more sophisticated version of the accounting gimmick that President Franklin Roosevelt had employed to double-count Social Security surpluses during World War II.

The president's plan was roundly criticized. The Congressional Budget Office concluded its assessment of the plan by saying that "plans that shift funds from one government pocket to another do nothing to address those programs' actual financing problem . . . and in fact could postpone corrective action."[15] Senator Susan Collins (R-ME) aptly called it "nothing but a shell game."[16] The president's plan and other similar "safe deposit box" proposals, including the "lock box" proposal made famous by Democratic presidential candidate Albert Gore, quickly became the subject of considerable ridicule inside and outside the nation's capital.[17]

Social Security surpluses continued to be an issue during the George W. Bush administration. President Bush proposed to dissipate the surpluses by allowing workers to voluntarily allocate a portion of their payroll taxes to investments in a broad-based portfolio of corporate stocks and bonds.[18] Workers who opted for these personal Social Security accounts would receive less in traditional Social Security benefits on retirement because they had contributed fewer taxes to the traditional program.

The aggregate amount of funds that could be allocated to personal accounts was projected to consume the lion's share of the Social Security surpluses for the next decade. Thus, at its core, Social Security personal accounts were simultaneously a means of using surplus to add an investment component to Social Security, lessen Social Security's long-term financial burden, and wall off Social Security's surpluses from Congress.

Democrats uniformly opposed the plan, arguing that it exposed workers to risky investments that could jeopardize their retirement security and that action to address Social Security's future was not needed. As Congressman (and now Senator) Charles Schumer (D-NY) said, "Social Security, if we don't do anything, is safe for approximately the next fifty years."[19] Republicans feared that without support from Democrats, a vote for the plan might jeopardize their own future. Perhaps more important, however, was the fact that allocating surplus payroll taxes to personal accounts would deprive the Treasury of about $70 billion in revenues per year. Both congressional Republicans and Democrats had come to rely too heavily on these surplus funds to finance federal activities unrelated to Social Security. Robert Myers's earlier warning that spending Social Security surpluses on other government programs would become a habit had proven prophetic. The plan eventually died in Congress without being reported out of committee.

In 2010, Congress further weakened Social Security's financial position. To combat the anemic recovery of the economy from the Great Recession, the Democratic-controlled Congress, with President Obama's support, temporarily reduced the employee share of the payroll tax rate by one-third.[20] The payroll tax cut was extended by the Republican-controlled Congress a year later.[21] The tax cut reduced payroll tax revenues below outlays for benefit payments, creating Social Security's first cash deficits in twenty-five years. To avoid creating any appearance that its actions worsened Social Security's already impaired financial condition, Congress credited the Social Security trust funds with general fund revenues to offset loss in payroll tax revenues. The two-year transfer of general revenues amounted to about $200 billion, 15 percent of Social Security's noninterest revenue.

These actions, reminiscent of Congress's 1867 decision to transfer general revenues to the navy trust fund to offset losses on the sale of trust fund securities, are an ominous harbinger for the future. President Roosevelt's self-financing principle has served as a constructive constraint on program benefits. Using general revenues in lieu of or in addition to payroll taxes removes this restraint.

Social Security: Concluding Thoughts

Throughout the post–Reagan years, Congress was fully aware of the inevitability, magnitude, and timing of the Social Security retirement program's coming financial shortfalls: the retirement program would begin running large cash deficits in this decade and would be insolvent within twenty years. Yet Congress on a bipartisan basis repeatedly failed to act to forestall these outcomes. It rejected entreaties by Presidents Clinton and George W. Bush to address the program's long-term funding problem. When unanticipated surpluses arose, Congress joined with the executive branch to regularly spend surplus funds on federal activities unrelated to Social Security while pretending to set the surpluses aside for the future. Even when payroll tax revenues were needed to finance current benefits, President Obama and the 111th and 112th Congresses reduced these taxes to serve other political purposes, pretending all the while that they had not done so. Similarly, when the 1984 Social Security Disability law's liberal excesses brought the trust fund to the brink of financial insolvency in the mid-1990s, the legislative and executive branches, rather than address the problem's source, agreed instead to siphon funds from the Social Security retirement trust. In the years since, both branches of government have sat idly by as the rolls have increased. Neither branch of government has proposed or otherwise acted to change benefits or eligibility rules to forestall this outcome. In 2015, the disability program was again facing financial insolvency. The Social Security trustees reported that the trust fund balance would be exhausted in 2016 and the program would be unable to pay the promised benefits. Rather than address the program's underlying problems and notwithstanding the fact that the retirement program's tax revenue is not sufficient to finance its benefit outlays,

Congress once again siphoned off funds from the retirement program into the disability program.[22]

Despite the absence of new laws to expand the Social Security retirement and disability programs, both grew substantially during the twenty-five-year period. In 2014, after adjusting for inflation, the Social Security retirement outlays were 70 percent higher than their 1989 level and the disability program's outlays were more than three times their 1989 outlays. The retirement program's outlay increases were driven primarily by the growth in the retiree population.

The source of the Disability Insurance program's growth is quite different: The number of recipients rose more than eight times faster than the U.S. population. Remarkably, this spectacular growth occurred at a time when technological advances, a shift to less physically demanding service sector jobs, and protective state and other federal laws created greater employment opportunities for disabled persons. The primary cause of the caseload increase can be traced to the 1984 Social Security disability law that relaxed eligibility standards and increased the difficulty of removing nondisabled persons from the rolls.[23] Since the law's enactment, disability awards for musculoskeletal system (e.g., back pain) and other difficult-to-diagnose medical conditions increased sharply. Approvals of claims based on nonmedical factors and mental disorders, both highly subjective, have doubled.[24] As in the 1970s, once a claimant gets on the disability rolls, the claimant usually stays on the rolls.

The law of unintended consequences has also been at work. Recall that the 1983 Social Security law gradually increased the retirement age, which made disability benefits more generous than retirement benefits for early retirees. In 1989, a worker's disability benefit at age 62 was 25 percent higher than the same worker's early retirement benefit. Today, it is 33 percent higher.[25] A third factor has been increasing health care costs that have made Medicare more financially valuable to disability recipient benefits. Today, the present value of the combination of disability cash and health care benefits is now $300,000 for the average new beneficiary.[26]

Incremental Expansions of Means-Tested Programs in the Early 1990s

In contrast to Social Security, Congress legislated often on welfare programs during the past twenty-five years. The general thrust of this legislation, with the exception of the landmark 1996 welfare reform law, was to extend the class of worthy claimants further up the income ladder. Food stamp liberalizations increased the amount of personal expenses applicants were permitted to deduct from their countable income, allowed certain types of income to be excluded from countable income, and increased the value of allowable assets. These liberalizations were designed primarily to allow a greater number of people with incomes between 100 and 130 percent of the poverty line to qualify for benefits. These liberalizations attracted little attention and passed Congress without much fanfare.[27] Earned income tax credit (EITC) expansions doubled the size the credit of to a maximum of 40 percent for each dollar earned and extended EITC payments to twice the poverty line. The law completed the job of severing the program's linkage to the Social Security payroll tax and reaffirmed its primary purpose of increasing the attractiveness of employment relative to welfare. Payments under the EITC, 80 percent of which were cash grants in excess of a family's income tax liability, quickly ballooned, rising from $13 billion in 1992 to $29 billion four years later.[28]

Medicaid expansions, designed to expand eligibility beyond those who received cash welfare, were far more consequential. The goal of the expansions was to extend the class of persons worthy of claimants beyond those who received cash federal welfare assistance. Legislation enacted during the five years from 1986 to 1990 achieved this goal. The first step had come in 1986 when Congress gave states the option of providing Medicaid coverage to families with children under age 6 and had incomes below the official poverty line. Three years later, Congress replaced the option with a mandate to cover such families and raised the mandated income threshold for these families to 133 percent of the poverty line. In 1990, Congress extended the required coverage to impoverished families with children ages 6 to 17. The 1990 law phased in the requirement by increasing the coverage age by one year each year until the year 2002, when children age 18 years were covered.[29] The 1990 law completed the job of severing the link between Medicaid eligibility and the AFDC and Supplemental Security Income (SSI) programs. The 1990 law and, to a lesser extent, its predecessors caused the Medicaid rolls to surge. By 1998, the Medicaid caseload was twice its 1990 level. In each law, Congress, with the executive branch's acquiescence, manipulated federal budget accounting rules to finance the actual Medicaid expansion with purported Medicare program savings. Medicaid expansions were financed in this way in 1984, 1986, 1987, 1989, 1988, and 1990. In 1997, Congress used a portion of Medicare "savings" to finance a new $4 billion per year federal health care entitlement to states to cover children in families with income under 200 percent of the poverty line.[30]

The 1990 liberalization serves to illustrate how the budget rules were manipulated to mask the cost of legislative expansions. Previous laws had required Medicare hospital and physician payment rates to be automatically updated each year to compensate for annual increases in the cost of medical care. Like Social Security's cost of living increases, the updates were scheduled to annually occur without any action by Congress. By making the payment rate increases automatic, Congress built automatic increases in Medicare expenditures into its budget baseline. Under budget accounting rules, if Congress increased an upcoming year's payment rate by less than the automatic update, the action was measured as budget savings regardless of how much the higher payment rate allowed Medicare spending to increase. In 1990, Medicare hospital and physician payment rates were scheduled to automatically increase the following year by 5.2 percent and 2.4 percent, respectively.[31] If these automatic payment rate increases took effect, Medicare outlays would increase by 12 percent, or $12 billion, in 1991. The health care committees under pressure to contribute Congress's deficit reduction efforts, included a 3.4 percent increase in hospital payment rates and froze physician payment rates in that year's budget reconciliation bill. This action allowed the committees to claim over $1.3 billion in budget savings in 1991, even though Medicare expenditures would still increase by 11 percent, nearly $11 billion. The committees also claimed

$25 billion in savings over the ensuing five years, even though they projected Medicare expenditures to rise by 70 percent.[32]

Budget changes of this magnitude were more than sufficient to cover the cost of expanding the much smaller Medicaid program, especially if the expansion was phased in slowly so that the bulk of its expenditures occurred beyond Congress's official five-year budget horizon. The budget cost of the 1990 Medicaid expansion was only $61 million in 1991 and only $337 million during the five-year budget horizon.[33]

The mandated Medicaid expansions imposed a heavy burden on state budgets. As the burden mounted, state governments, with Congress's acquiescence, employed creative ways to allow states to receive federal matching payments in excess of those permitted under the program's statutory payment formula.

States implemented three related types of schemes. In one, Medicaid hospitals voluntarily donated previously received Medicaid funds, which consisted of both state and federal matching monies, back to their state Medicaid programs. State governments then used these recycled funds to claim additional federal matching payments. Upon receipt of the additional federal payments, states returned the originally donated monies to the very same donor hospitals and used the remaining federal funds to finance additional Medicaid services or state programs unrelated to Medicaid.[34] The second scheme was the same, except that states used the proceeds of special taxes levied exclusively on Medicaid providers as the source for additional federal payments. In the third scheme, states agreed to pay county- and city-owned hospitals Medicaid reimbursement rates far in excess of rates paid to other hospitals. These hospitals then returned the excess funds to the state government through an intergovernmental transfer, whereupon the returned funds would generate federal matching payments.

The success of these schemes initially hinged on a 1981 law that allowed states to make special Medicaid payments to hospitals and other Medicaid providers, called disproportionate share (DSH) payments, which served a "disproportionate share" of Medicaid patients. Under the law's loose language, states could return, dollar for dollar, each medical provider's donations, taxes, and intergovernmental transfers after the state had collected the extra federal matching payments.[35]

As the impact of federal coverage mandates took effect, states used the schemes aggressively. By the early 1990s, the General Accounting Office reported that the schemes had become an "uncontrolled virus."[36] In West Virginia, hospitals donated $23 million to the state's indigent care fund, which allowed the state to receive $83 million in federal Medicaid matching payments. The state returned the donation to contributing hospitals and applied the remainder to other Medicaid services. A later General Accounting Office (GAO) report detailed how the scheme worked in Michigan: "On October 2, 1993, Michigan made a DSH payment of $489 million to the University of Michigan hospital. This included $276 million in federal matching funds and $213 million in state funds. Later that day, the hospital returned the entire payment to the state through an intergovernmental transfer. As a result, the state realized a net benefit from the federal share of the DSH payment equal to $276 million."[37]

Both the Reagan and George H. W. Bush administrations attempted to stop the abusive practices.[38] But Congress, at the behest of governors, prevented both administrations from doing so. Arkansas governor Bill Clinton typified the governors' argument to preserve the abusive schemes. In testimony against a Bush administration regulation to limit the schemes, the future president declared that the regulation "would severely hamper states' historic rights to raise revenue for the Medicaid program."[39] Henry Waxman, chairman of the House Energy and Commerce Committee's Subcommittee on Health, typified Congress's "ends justifies the means" rationale against eliminating the kickback schemes: "If this regulation goes into effect as scheduled on January 1, many States will be forced to make drastic cutbacks in eligibility, benefits, or reimbursement."[40]

Congress partially curtailed the abusive practices with laws enacted in 1991, 1993, 1997, and 2010. But the practice continues today, albeit on a limited scale compared to the 1900s.[41]

Welfare Reform

Soaring AFDC and SSI caseloads in the early 1990s renewed public concern about the damaging consequences of welfare for those it was seeking to help. The AFDC caseload, after holding steady at around 3.5 million households during the 1980s, rose sharply to a record-breaking level of over 5 million in 1993. This increase, the third great surge of the post–World War II era, was led by households headed by unwed teenage girls with children, who accounted for 70 percent of the increase. Nationwide, one in seven children received AFDC benefits in 1993. The percentage was much higher in major cities: two-thirds in Detroit, half in Philadelphia and Chicago, and nearly 40 percent in New York and Los Angeles.[42] For many of these families, AFDC had become a way of life. Although a large number of families experienced relatively short stays on AFDC, the typical recipient family at any point in time spent an average of twelve years on the rolls. Over half of those receiving AFDC benefits spent ten or more years on the rolls.[43] Additional data indicated that welfare dependency was being transmitted from one generation to the next.

In 1993, out-of-wedlock births accounted for one-fourth of all U.S births and two-thirds of all births among African American women. These rates were far higher than those that had led Daniel Patrick Moynihan to decry the breakdown of black families nearly thirty years earlier. New data showed that three-fourths of teenage mothers became welfare recipients within five years of giving birth to their first child. Nevertheless, analyses on the causal link between welfare and out-of-wedlock births were no more conclusive than they had been in the 1960s and 1970s.

The startling trends heightened long-standing concerns that the allure of welfare was leading young women into a lifetime welfare trap by penalizing work, encouraging out-of-wedlock births, and discouraging marriage. Welfare was also leading young fathers of children born out of wedlock to avoid their parental responsibilities. The data led former Secretary of Education William Bennett to conclude that "welfare is illegitimacy's economic life-support system."[44]

While the growing AFDC caseload generated national attention, out of the limelight the SSI rolls also soared. From 1988 to 1995, the number of recipients increased from 4.5 million to 6.5 million, and the program's expenditures ballooned from $11 billion to $24 billion. Disabled children and elderly legal immigrants accounted for more than half of the caseload increase.[45]

The SSI growth was due primarily to federal court decisions interpreting the poorly drafted 1972 SSI law. In 1990, the Supreme Court ruled that the SSI qualifying standard the Social Security administration had used for children since the program's beginning was "manifestly contrary to the statute."[46] In response, the agency issued regulations that entitled SSI benefits to children who, by reason of a physical or mental impairment, were unable to engage in "age-appropriate" behavior.[47]

The new standard, combined with existing eligibility standards that allowed children with behavioral disorders, including attention deficit disorders, learning disabilities, and hyperactivity to qualify, caused the number of child SSI recipients to soar from 265,000 in 1989 to 917,000 in 1995.[48] The sharp increase was accompanied by widespread reports of parents coaching children to display disruptive behaviors and to perform poorly in school to qualify for SSI benefits.[49] Other reports and a GAO investigation found that state and local welfare workers were helping AFDC mothers to qualify their children for higher and entirely federal-financed SSI benefits. By 1993, an astonishing 42 percent of children receiving SSI benefits were formerly receiving, or had siblings who were receiving, partially state and locally financed AFDC benefits.[50]

A similar story lay behind the growth in legal immigrants who received benefits from SSI and other welfare programs. The 1972 SSI law had granted eligibility to immigrants who were living in the United States "under the color of law."[51] In 1985, the Second Circuit Court ruled that this ill-defined phrase encompassed virtually all noncitizens whom the Immigration and Naturalization Service was not aggressively seeking to deport.[52] The ruling produced an avalanche of new SSI recipients. From 1986 to 1995, the number of legal immigrants receiving SSI more than tripled, increasing from 244,000 to 785,000.[53]

A large increase in the number of drug addicts and alcoholics on the SSI rolls also played a role, albeit a smaller one. Federal court decisions in the 1970s and 1980s gradually loosened eligibility requirements to allow alcoholics and drug addicts to qualify for SSI benefits regardless of whether recipients made any attempt at rehabilitation.[54] By 1994, SSI benefits paid to substance abusers were costing $1.4 billion annually. Only 10 percent of addicts and alcoholics receiving SSI were in treatment and only 1 percent of substance abusers on SSI ever recovered sufficiently to get a job.[55] In some instances, SSI had become an enabler of continued substance abuse rather than being a gateway to rehabilitation.

The "welfare crisis" and SSI abuses generated public demand for reform. The march to reform began simultaneously on two fronts. Bill Clinton opened up the first front during his 1992 presidential campaign by boldly promising to "end welfare as we know it."[56] After his election, the new president announced that his administration would immediately take steps "to encourage experimentation in the states."[57] The Family Support Act of 1988 had allowed states, with the federal government's approval, wide latitude to waive federal AFDC rules to explore alternative methods of moving individuals from welfare to work. President Clinton accelerated federal approval of AFDC waivers. By the spring of 1995, forty-five states were experimenting with a variety of reforms, including allowing recipients to retain a portion of their earnings and assets, providing child care and medical care to working welfare mothers, imposing time limits on the receipt of welfare payments, and limiting family benefits if an unwed recipient mother bore an additional child.[58] The successful results of these demonstrations, most notably in Wisconsin, New Jersey, Michigan, and California, greatly influenced the shape of federal welfare reform proposals.

President Clinton's welfare reform plan, delivered to Congress in June 1994, fell well short of his earlier bold promise. The plan would impose a two-year time limit on individuals' receipt of AFDC and a work requirement on AFDC recipients. But these provisions applied only to young women who were 13 years old or younger in 1994. Thus, the policies would not affect the vast majority of welfare mothers on the rolls at the time. In contrast, he proposed to provide states immediately with additional federal funds and considerable flexibility to use these funds for job training, education, child care, and public service jobs.

The proposal was too much reform for congressional liberals, who had spent the post–World War II years strengthening the AFDC entitlement and increasing federal control over the program. For congressional Republicans, the proposal was too little reform. Senate minority leader Robert Dole (R-KS), summed up the congressional response by quipping that the plan represented "the end of welfare reform as we know it."[59] Democrats agreed and, with large majorities in both houses of Congress, bottled up the proposal for the remainder of the 103rd Congress.

Congressional Republicans opened up the second front on welfare reform in 1992. That year, House Republicans introduced several AFDC reform bills that, like President Clinton's plan, imposed time limits on the receipt of AFDC assistance, required welfare recipients to work, and gave states more flexibility to design their own welfare-to-work programs. But Republicans were a minority in Congress, and these proposals went nowhere.

The political environment for welfare reform changed dramatically in 1994 when the midterm elections gave Republicans majorities in both houses of Congress for the first time in forty years. The "political earthquake" guaranteed that welfare reform would be a major issue for the 104th Congress.

The main Republican welfare reform bill proposed to make the most far-reaching changes in the nation's sixty-year-old welfare system, starting with radical changes in the AFDC program. In the words of Ways and Means chairman Bill Archer (R-TX), the bill would create "a new system that uplifts our Nation's poor, a new system that turns the social safety net from a trap into a trampoline, a new system that rewards work, personal responsibility in families, a new system that lifts a load off of working, tax-paying Americans."[60] The House bill proposed to eliminate the AFDC program's entitlement to recipients, create an AFDC block grant to states, establish a five-year lifetime limit on AFDC assistance to adults, require states to implement a work requirement for able-bodied adults, and deny welfare assistance to legal immigrants. The bill also proposed reforms of the SSI and food stamp programs. The ambitious bill set the terms of debate, which dominated Congress and the president for the next eighteen months.[61]

The floor debates presented a bipartisan indictment of the welfare system, in general, and the AFDC program in particular. Senator Phil Gramm (R-TX) concluded that after spending $5.4 trillion on income transfer programs since the Great Society, "we have made mothers more dependent, we have driven fathers out of the household, and we have denied people access to the American dream." Senator Joseph Lieberman (D-CT) offered a similar assessment, stating that "motivated by good intentions, charitable intentions at the outset, [welfare has become] a system that does not encourage work, that seems at times to reward the opposite, and that offends the great majority of people."[62]

But that was as far as agreement went. The ensuing harsh debate serves as a reminder of the old Washington adage that "politics is a contact sport." Liberal Democrats denounced Republicans for doing to the poor "close to what Adolph Hitler did to people," behaving like "Attila the Hun," depriving 1 million poor children of basic necessities, including "love," "taking food out of mouths of our kids," of orchestrating a "callous" and "coldhearted" attack on poor children, and of favoring "sterilization" and "castration."[63]

On the main issues, the individual entitlement to AFDC, the block grant, and welfare eligibility for legal immigrants, the large partisan divide that had separated the two political parties since World War II remained. Republicans viewed the AFDC entitlement as one of the principal causes of welfare dependency. The House Republican bill's architects, harkening back to Franklin Roosevelt's statement that "continued dependence upon relief induces a spiritual and moral disintegration fundamentally destructive to the national fiber," argued that "it is precisely the permanent guarantee of benefits that induces dependency."[64] Speaking for Democrats, Senator Claiborne Pell (D-RI) countered by saying that the entitlement meant "that this Nation will respond to anyone in great need—that we will not cut off people in need simply because there are too many people in line before them."[65]

Similarly, Republicans favored block grants on the ground that state and local governments were no less compassionate and were better able to set welfare policy than the federal government. Congressman Dave Camp (R-MI) made the case by saying, "The other side of the aisle holds tight to their belief that Federal bureaucrats based here in Washington are somehow more compassionate, and more capable of caring for the needy. To hear them tell it, our communities, local governments, and Governors will starve the children and give the money to the rich."[66] But to Democrats, the block grant meant that the federal government was washing its hands of difficult welfare issues. Senator John Breaux

(D-LA) argued that "block grants are like taking all the problems that we have with the welfare program and putting them in a box, then wrapping it all up, tying a bow around it, and then mailing that box of problems to the States, saying: Here, it is yours." Senator Moynihan warned that block grants would cause states to "rush to the bottom" as states reduced welfare benefits and curtailed eligibility relative to neighboring states to avoid becoming magnets for welfare recipients.[67]

Proposals to deny AFDC, SSI, and food stamp eligibility for legal immigrants until they became citizens produced even sharper exchanges.[68] The provision put the issue of worthy claims starkly before Congress. The architects of the Republican House bill stated their policy in straightforward terms: "Aliens are allowed to enter the U.S. and join our economy; in return, the nation asks that immigrants obey our laws, pay taxes if they earn sufficient income, and avoid welfare until they become citizens."[69] Congressional liberals took the contrary view that legal immigrants were no less worthy of welfare assistance than U.S. citizens. Congressman Jim McDermott (D-WA) said that an immigrant "who has been here for many years, who has worked, has paid their taxes, has raised their family and has been responsible" is no less worthy of aid in a time of need than a U.S. citizen.[70] *New York Times* columnist Anthony Lewis captured the essence of the liberal critique of the Republican plan by giving his editorial the title, "Some Are Less Equal."[71]

Following protracted and vigorous debate, the sharply divided House passed the Republican bill in March. An equally divided Senate followed suit in September with a similar but less extensive bill.[72] The final bill, which passed in December, abolished the individual entitlement right to AFDC, established the AFDC block grant, imposed time limits on the receipt of AFDC benefits, and mandated work requirements. The bill also gave states the option of denying benefits to unwed mothers under age 18 and denying additional payments to welfare families when the mother had an additional child. The SSI reforms replaced the "age-appropriate" behavior eligibility standard for disabled children with a strict requirement that a child's disability must be proven by medical techniques and disallowed disability benefits for drug addiction and alcoholism. The food stamp reforms canceled the upcoming cost-of-living increase and established new work requirements. The bill denied eligibility for all three welfare programs to almost all legal immigrants.

The reform bill set the stage for extraordinary battles with President Clinton. The battles included two presidential vetoes and finally ended in August 1996 when President Clinton signed welfare reform into law.

The first battle occurred in December 1995 when Republicans attached the welfare reform bill to a massive two-thousand-page deficit reduction bill. The budget bill also contained provisions to convert Medicaid and child nutrition programs to block grants and additional savings in other entitlements. President Clinton vetoed the bill, and the Republicans lacked the votes to override the veto.

Undeterred, congressional Republicans separated the welfare reform provisions from the deficit reduction bill. The revised reform bill, which retained the Medicaid block grant, was sent to the president, again on a largely party line vote. The president faced a conundrum. He had promised to "end welfare as we know it" and the Republicans had given him a bill to do just that. However, congressional Democrats pressured him not to sign the bill. Senator Moynihan declared his opposition by announcing, "If this administration wishes to go down in history as the one that abandoned, eagerly abandoned, the national commitment to dependent children, so be it. . . . [But], I would not want to be associated with such an enterprise."[73] Editorial boards of most major newspapers joined the opposition. The *New York Times* accused Republicans of "stripping parents of money they need to make life tenable for millions of destitute children."[74] The *Washington Post* described the House Republicans as having "Hard Hearts, (and) Soft Heads" and deemed the bill "a terrible piece of legislation."[75]

On January 9, 1996, the president vetoed the freestanding welfare reform bill. While he continued to believe that the "welfare system is broken and must be replaced," he objected to the Medicaid block grant and the magnitude of the reform plan's budget reductions.[76] Seven months later, in August, Republicans sent the welfare reform bill to the president for a third time, this time without the Medicaid block grant. President Clinton, to liberals' dismay and outrage, signed the bill into law.[77]

The law immediately accelerated the transfer of policymaking authority for the renamed Temporary Assistance for Needy Families

(TANF) to state governments. By 1999, all states, in conformity with federal law, established limits to time on welfare and required adult welfare recipients to work within two years. Forty-two states had relaxed their AFDC rules to permit welfare recipients to keep more of their benefits while working. Forty states had allowed welfare recipients to keep more of their assets. Thirty-four states instituted diversion plans that provided emergency assistance to families in temporary need instead of formally enrolling them in the state's welfare program. Most states provided an array of employment services, including child care, education and tuition assistance, transportation, peer counseling and employment assistance such as arranging contacts with employers, making job phone banks available, and offering courses in résumé building and job interviewing techniques.[78]

Most important, the waivers and the 1996 law produced a revolutionary change in the culture and role of state and local welfare offices. Their new mission became helping welfare recipients become self-sufficient and preventing others from becoming dependent. Thus, instead of processing eligibility paperwork and ensuring that AFDC recipients complied with government eligibility rules, welfare offices were now designing plans to help individuals get back on their feet. In 1962, John F. Kennedy had declared that "public welfare . . . must be more than a salvage operation, picking up the debris from the wreckage of human lives. Its emphasis must be directed increasingly toward prevention and rehabilitation."[79] The cultural change in welfare offices went a long way toward realizing the former president's aspiration.

Following enactment of the 1996 law, the AFDC rolls declined precipitously. As Figure 3 shows, prior to 1994, the year the federal waivers had their first significant aggregate impact, the number of households on the AFDC rolls rose inexorably. By 2001, the number had plummeted to 2.2 million from its peak of 5 million in 1994. By the middle of the next decade, the number of AFDC households had stabilized at about 1.8 million, where it remains today.[80] This remarkable reduction is unprecedented among major entitlement programs in U.S. history.

Studies of welfare reform have found that between 60 and 70 percent of adults who left AFDC became employed. One study found that the percentage of young unmarried women who were working within two

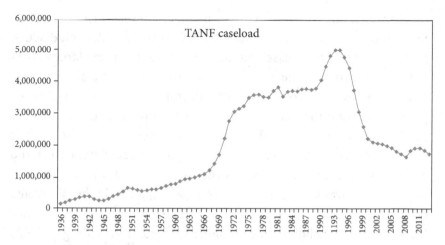

Figure 3. TANF Recipients (in 1,000s). Source: *Annual Statistical Supplement to the Social Security Bulletin* 1992 and 2005, Table 9.G1 for 1936 to 2000; https:// www.acf.hhs.gov/ofa/programs/tanf/data-reports, for 2001–2016.

years after having a child increased by 50 percent, from 44 percent to 66 percent.[81] The shift from welfare to work among adult AFDC recipients was sufficiently large to produce important changes in the aggregate labor force behavior of single female heads of household. From the late 1970s to the mid-1990s, the percentage of single mothers who worked at all during the year had remained constant at below 80 percent. By the mid-2000s, the percentage had risen to 87 percent, where it remains today.[82] President Ronald Reagan once described the proper objective of welfare by saying, "The only true measure of a welfare program's success is how many people it makes independent of welfare."[83] By this standard alone, the 1996 law was a remarkable success.

The decline in AFDC caseloads and the corresponding rise in employment was accompanied by a significant decline in poverty rates of female-headed families with children and in all children. By 2007, the poverty rate of both groups was about 20 percent below their respective rates in the mid-1990s. Among African American single heads of households, the results have been even more striking. Prior to 1994, their poverty rate had never fallen below 50 percent. By 2001, their poverty rate had declined to 41 percent and has remained below 50 percent every year since, including during the Great Recession.

Certainly, not all of the changes noted can be ascribed to the welfare reform law alone. Academic scholars continue to dissect, discuss, and debate the AFDC caseload and poverty data for explanations of the observed trends. The exceptionally strong economic growth from 1994 to 2007, which was only briefly interrupted by the 2001 recession, played a contributing role. But the fact that neither the AFDC caseload nor the poverty rate of single female-headed households rose to their pre–welfare reform law levels during the Great Recession of 2008 and 2009 suggests that the economy's role was not a dominant one. Perhaps the best way to characterize the economy's role is that it created employment opportunities for welfare mothers who, with the new law's incentives, responsibilities, and support services, were willing and able to seize them.

Other governmental policies, especially expansions in the EITC, also are likely to have contributed to the beneficial changes. By 2007, legislation enacted in 1994 and 2001 increased by 33 percent both the maximum credit and the program's maximum earnings. The well-documented incentives of the EITC to increase work among very low-income recipients suggest that the program's expansion played a role in lowering the TANF caseload and raising employment levels among single mothers, but the magnitude of its role is yet unclear.

With one exception, any identifiable negative impacts of the 1996 AFDC reforms have been minor. The exception is that a relatively small group of former adult AFDC recipients, in the neighborhood of 10 percent of all adult recipients, have suffered significant income losses following their exit from welfare. Nevertheless, the dire predictions by the law's opponents that it would throw millions of people into poverty, including 1 million children, have been proven wrong. Similarly, assertions that states would rush to the bottom by curtailing AFDC eligibility and cutting benefits have also been shown to be without merit.

The SSI reforms were far less consequential. The number of children qualifying for SSI declined rapidly following the tightening of the eligibility standard. However, a decade later, despite the absence of any major legislative changes, the number of children recipients began to rise again.[84] As of December 2013, 1.3 million children were on the SSI rolls, 43 percent more than in 1996 just prior to the law's enactment.[85]

The attempt to deny welfare eligibility to noncitizens also had limited success. Under the 1996 welfare reform law, SSI, food stamps, and AFDC benefits for noncitizens were to be terminated a year following the law's enactment. But before the termination date arrived, Congress extended the deadline. Later, Congress allowed everyone who was on the welfare rolls when the welfare reform measure was enacted to remain on the rolls.

Academic researchers will continue to assess the impact of the landmark law. But as it stands now, the 1996 welfare reform law is a milestone in U.S. welfare policy. The law marks only the second time in the twentieth century that an entitlement to individuals has been ended. The first time was in 1933 when President Roosevelt abolished veterans' compensation benefits for nonservice-connected disabilities. The legislative transfer of AFDC policymaking authority from the federal government to the states reversed a five-decade trend of increasing federal controls. The reduction in the AFDC caseload and its costs to taxpayers, the rise in employment rates of female heads of households with children, and the decline in poverty rates of these women and children that followed the law's enactment make the 1996 law the twentieth century's most successful entitlement reform.

The Return to Incremental Welfare Expansions

The ink was barely dry on the landmark welfare reform law when Congress reversed course and returned to its pattern of incrementally liberalizing entitlements. In 1997, it reversed the welfare reform law's policy of denying new legal immigrants eligibility for Medicaid benefits. A year later, it did the same for eligibility for food stamps, SSI, and AFDC. Starting in 2001, Congress embarked on a policy of eliminating the limits on assets an individual could own and still qualify for welfare program eligibility. That year, Congress increased the values of housing and motor vehicles that food stamp recipients were allowed to keep. The following year, Congress enacted a broad-based categorical eligibility policy that allowed states to waive food stamps and Medicaid asset limits. In 2008, in states unaffected by the broad-based categorical eligibility policy, Congress indexed the asset limit for food stamp eligibility to inflation and exempted individual retirement accounts and educational savings accounts from the program's asset limit. Also in 2008, Congress suspended restrictions on the amount of time an able-bodied person could spend on the food stamp rolls without working. In 2009, in response to the Great Recession, Congress waived the food stamp work search requirement. The 2010 Affordable Care Act (discussed later in this chapter) allowed states to extend the Medicaid entitlement to adults without children.

The eligibility liberalizations from 1997 to 2008 produced sharp increases in the food stamp and Medicaid rolls. From 1998 to 2008, the food stamp rolls increased to 28 million people from 20 million and the Medicaid rolls increased to 59 million from 40 million people. The liberalizations enacted during the Great Recession have lasted well beyond the recession's end in 2010. In 2016, the number of food stamp recipients ballooned to 44 million, and the number of Medicaid recipients rose to 73 million in 2016.[86]

Medicare Shifts from Cost Reimbursement to Price Controls

Congress had begun to take action in the 1980s to rein in Medicare's double-digit fifteen-year annual expenditure growth rate. At the time, policymakers recognized that the rising overall health care costs that invariably accompanied steady advances in medical treatments, diagnostic and surgical procedures, and technology contributed to Medicare's cost growth. But they also had come to understand that Medicare's payment system was at fault. Reimbursing hospitals for all "reasonable" costs of care and paying doctors their "customary" charges without any effective limits on amount of services provided was a recipe of soaring costs. The payment system, especially given Medicare's low beneficiary copayments, was not sustainable.

Congress and the Reagan administration began by focusing on hospital inpatient care, which accounted for two-thirds of Medicare expenditures at the time. In 1983, Congress established the prospective payment system (PPS) to replace Medicare's hospital cost reimbursement policy. The PPS paid hospitals a fixed amount per inpatient admission, which varied depending on the severity of the patient's diagnosis. The law precluded hospitals from charging patients in excess of Medicare's statutory deductible and coinsurance rates. Thus, the PPS system operated as a de facto system of price controls on Medicare hospital inpatient services. The following year, Congress turned its attention to physician payments, Medicare's second largest expenditure category. In 1984, Congress temporarily froze physician fees, and in 1987 it limited the amount that physicians could increase their Medicare fees.[87] Despite these actions, Medicare physician payments continued to grow at double-digit rates.

In 1989, Congress and the George H. W. Bush administration established a nationwide Medicare fee schedule for all Medicare physician services.[88] The fee schedule consisted of a set of relative prices Medicare would pay physicians for their services. The gargantuan undertaking established prices for each of more than seven thousand medical procedures that were performed by over 500,000 physicians who submitted over 400 million medical bills annually. Federal authorities could, in principle, use the fee schedule to slow the growth in physician payments by limiting the increases in the fee from one year to the next. Concerned that physicians would pass on any higher costs of care to patients, the 1989 law also limited the amount that physicians could charge patients over and above the amount that Medicare paid. The combination of the fee schedule and the limits doctors could charge their patients constituted a system of price controls.[89]

The fee schedule represented a historic shift in Medicare physician reimbursement policy. Since its enactment through the mid-1980s, Medicare had paid physicians 80 percent of their customary charges for Medicare services as long as those charges were deemed reasonable. Medicare had also allowed physicians to set the remaining balance of the medical bill that the patient was required to pay, a practice known as "balanced" billing. Those policies had lasted twenty-five years. Under the new policy, federal authorities would set the amount physicians would receive for their services, and physicians were no longer free to determine the amount they could charge Medicare patients for their services.

The hospital PPS and the physician fee schedule failed to put Medicare on a sound financial footing. During the first half of the 1990s, the growth in Medicare outlays for hospital services slowed to a 6.1 percent annual rate. But by the mid-1990s, the hospital insurance trust fund was in deficit. Despite the removal of the ceiling on Medicare taxable wages, the trust fund was headed for exhaustion in 2001. Outlays for physician services had also slowed to a 5.9 percent annual rate, but they were still growing at a rate 10 percent faster than gross domestic product.[90] As a result, by the mid-1990s, Medicare had become the federal budget's third largest program expenditure, behind Social Security and defense.

In 1994, the newly elected Republican majority pledged to balance the federal budget. Medicare was too large not to be part of any deficit reduction plan.

Republicans proposed sweeping Medicare changes, including limiting increases in existing reimbursement rates, gradually increasing Medicare's eligibility age to 67, a means test for Medicare deductibles, higher Medicare premiums, and a new high-deductible Medicare option plan that allowed enrollees to deposit any Medicare savings into a medical savings account. Democrats countered a nationwide publicity campaign to block the initiatives. The so-called "Mediscare" campaign frightened senior citizens and scared the daylights out of congressional Republicans. After the 1996 elections, which returned President Clinton to the White House and Republican majorities in both houses of Congress, Republicans dropped most of their reform plans. House Ways and Means Committee chairman Bill Archer (R-TX) explained their change of heart with classic understatement by saying, "I just think the entire environment is different this time."[91]

Republicans included major Medicare changes in the Balanced Budget Act of 1997. The law extended price controls to three Medicare post-acute care services: home health, outpatient, and skilled nursing care. Outlays for all three services had soared in the decade leading up to the 1997 law. Home health outlays grew at a remarkable 31 percent annual rate, outlays for skilled nursing facilities at a 22 percent annual rate, and outlays for outpatient care at a 9 percent annual rate.[92]

As with other health care services, the rise in post–acute care services was due importantly to advances in treatment methods, medical procedures, and technology. But legislative, regulatory, and judicial liberalizations fueled further increases.

The home health benefit had originally been designed as a limited benefit for patients following their discharge from a hospital. The 1965 Medicare law had required a three-day prior hospital stay and allowed only a limited number of visits by home health care aides for most beneficiaries. The law had also required a 20 percent coinsurance payment. Congress eliminated the coinsurance requirement in 1973. It also repealed the hospitalization requirement, the limit on the number of home health aide visits, and the payment of a deductible in 1980.[93] These changes transformed the home health benefit into a free and virtually unlimited Medicare benefit for chronically ill enrollees, as well as for patients requiring post-acute care. The settlement in 1988 of a class action lawsuit that allowed home health agencies to be reimbursed for continuous, as opposed to intermittent, care caused outlays to grow even more rapidly.[94] Federal regulations in 1988 that allowed nursing homes to be reimbursed for care regardless of whether the patient's condition was expected to improve played a key role in the growth in nursing home outlays

Incentives created by the Medicare PPS for hospitals also fueled the growth in post–acute care outlays. The PPS gave hospitals an incentive to shorten the length of an inpatient hospital stay and to shift patients to post–acute care settings. Outpatient departments, skilled nursing facilities, and home health services, all of which Medicare reimbursed on a cost basis, served as alternatives for discharged hospital patients who were still in need of care. By transferring patients from an inpatient setting to a post–acute care setting, hospitals could simultaneously reduce inpatient care expenses and increase Medicare reimbursements.

The 1997 law replaced Medicare's existing retrospective cost reimbursements for the three post–acute care services with separate fee schedules.[95] For outpatient services, Congress combined the fee schedule with a reduction in coinsurance payments to a maximum of 20 percent.[96] There was no need for similar coinsurance reductions for home health care, since Medicare did not permit copayments for these services. The fee schedules combined with limits on coinsurance amounted to a system of price controls.

The 1997 law also superimposed a global Medicare budget for physician payments on top of its network of price controls. The 1989 price control policy had done little to correct the incentives to overuse Medicare physician services, as physicians continued to be reimbursed regardless of the volume of services they provided. The law may have in fact exacerbated these incentives by eliminating balanced billing, a step that further insulated patients from cost.[97]

The global budget policy sought to restrain Medicare physician payments by setting an overall annual expenditure target for Medicare physician payments. The annual target allowed payments to grow from one year to the next at a "sustainable growth rate", which was approximately the growth in GDP.[98] If, in any year, total Medicare physician payments exceeded its target, physician reimbursement rates would be automatically lowered the following year by an amount sufficient to offset the excess. The percentage reduction would be applied equally to all physician services.[99] So if expenditures exceeded target by 10 percent in one year, physician reimbursement rates would be automatically reduced by 10 percent the following year.

Congress proved unwilling to enforce the global budget. Only in 2002, when physician expenditures exceeded the sustainable growth target, did Congress permit an automatic reduction to take effect. Every year thereafter, and sometimes more than once a year, sixteen times in all from 2003 to 2014, Congress overrode the law's automatic reductions. On eight occasions, Congress increased reimbursement rates. Congress regarded each override as merely a temporary one-year deferral. Each deferral therefore added to the total reduction that was scheduled to occur the following year. By 2010, the automatic reduction had grown to 21 percent. By then, the sustainable growth rate policy had become a farce. Congress had no intention of allowing a reduction of such a magnitude to take effect. Nevertheless, Congress continued to enact "temporary" deferrals of the automatic rate reductions until 2015, when it finally repealed the sustainable growth rate limit altogether.[100]

The price controls and global budget policies may have slowed the growth in Medicare expenditures, but they failed to put the program on a financially sustainable basis. From 2000 to 2015, Medicare expenditures have grown at about a 6 percent annual compound rate, about 50 percent faster than GDP over the same period.[101]

The expenditure growth is largely attributable to increases in the volume and intensity of services provided, not in the number of patients served. Medicare price controls gave physicians, home health care agencies, skilled nursing facilities, and hospital outpatient departments incentives to increase the volume and sophistication of services they provide, and they responded accordingly. According to the Medicare Payment Advisory Commission, the price-adjusted volume of physician services provided to the typical Medicare patient grew 58 percent from 2000 to 2015. Within this total, the volume of imaging services increased by 71 percent, relatively minor medical procedures increased by 73 percent, and tests grew by 88 percent.[102] The price controls and the responses they generated have been likened to squeezing down on a balloon. Applying pressure to one portion merely causes another part to expand.

The 1997 Balanced Budget Act contained one additional important change that was potentially beneficial to reining in Medicare costs. The law expanded Medicare coverage of managed care plans. These plans are reimbursed on a per enrollee basis, a feature that eliminates the incentive to overuse services that is present among fee-for-service plans. The bundled payment per enrollee also obviates the need for federal authorities to set Medicare prices for each medical service provided.

Congress had allowed managed care plans to operate on an experimental basis since 1982, and the results had been encouraging.[103] These plans had not delivered inferior care, as its critics had warned. Instead, substantial cost savings had been used to finance additional benefits for enrollees, including prescription drugs, dental care, and vision care. However, by 1995 only 4 percent of all Medicare beneficiaries were enrolled in managed care plans. In contrast, more than half of all privately insured individuals were enrolled in managed care plans as opposed to fee-for-service plans.[104]

Since 1997, participation by Medicare beneficiaries in managed care plans has grown steadily, reaching 32 percent of all beneficiaries by 2016. However, Medicare's reimbursement system has negated managed care's potential to reduce Medicare's expenditure growth. Medicare managed care payment rates have been tied to the average cost of Medicare services in the fee-for-service program. Thus, as Medicare fee-for-service costs per beneficiary have increased, Medicare managed care payments have grown at an equal rate.

A New Medicare Prescription Drug Benefit

The expansion of Medicare coverage to prescription drugs, the most significant liberalization in the program's history, came in 2003. The original 1965 Medicare law had covered only medicines provided in a hospital setting and injectable drugs that were not self-administered. It had not covered outpatient prescription drugs.[105] For at least a decade, congressional liberals had sought to add prescription drug coverage to Medicare. Democrats had succeeded in adding a drug benefit to President Reagan's Medicare catastrophic plan in 1988 "as a way of putting a Democratic stamp on the plan."[106] The benefit was enacted, only to be repealed a year later. In 1993, President Clinton had included Medicare drug coverage in his 1993 national health insurance proposal, but that coverage died along with his larger proposal.

Concerns about rising prescription drug costs had been growing for two decades. Pharmaceutical expenditures, spurred by the introduction of new and more efficacious drugs and increases in drug prices, rose rapidly throughout the 1980s and 1990s. Most senior citizens had made provision for financing these higher expenses. By the late 1990s, nearly three-fourths of Medicare beneficiaries had some prescription drug coverage. Most had purchased private insurance as a supplement to Medicare or had obtained coverage through an employer retirement plan. Others were covered by Medicare managed care plans that had begun offering prescription drug coverage in the 1980s as an inducement for seniors to enroll in their plans. Largely because Medicaid provided prescription drugs free of charge, prescription drug coverage among poor elderly persons was nearly as high as it was for the entire population of seniors.[107]

The coverage insulated most seniors from high drug costs. Sixty percent of Medicare beneficiaries spent less than $250 annually on prescription drugs. However, 8 percent spent more than $2,000.[108] Thus, if a case could be made for adding a drug benefit to Medicare, it would be for a catastrophic benefit.

The efforts that led to the 2003 law began with the emergence of large budget surpluses in the late 1990s. The surpluses were fueled by an extraordinary growth in revenues from the dot-com boom. The federal revenue increase from 1995 to 2000 was large enough to finance a 50 percent increase in spending on every federal program, project, and activity. The revenue surge created budget surpluses unlike any other that the federal government had experienced in decades. By the end of President Clinton's second term, the budget was experiencing the third of four consecutive annual surpluses. So bright were the revenue forecasts that federal officials openly talked about the possibility of paying off the national debt in a decade.[109]

As had happened so often before, the surpluses created upward pressure on federal spending. This time, the Medicare prescription drug coverage became the major focal point. President Clinton proposed to spend a portion of the budget surplus on a new prescription drug plan for seniors. In 2001, when President George W. Bush proposed his own plan, the battle between the political parties was joined.[110]

Republican plans called for private insurers, pharmacy benefit managers, and health plans to offer a menu of alternative drug benefit plans from which seniors could choose. These private sector entities would deliver benefits and negotiate prices with drug manufacturers. The plans also called for higher, income-related Medicare premiums to finance a portion of the new entitlement's cost. Democratic plans proposed a single drug plan for all seniors. The federal government would administer the plan and set drug prices. The plans were debated extensively, and the Republican-controlled House passed bills in both 2000 and 2002. Both bills died in the Democratic-controlled Senate.

In 2003, the political climate changed. The midterm elections gave Republicans control over both houses of Congress and the White House for the first time in five decades. Medicare prescription drugs put the party at an entitlement crossroad. Since the New Deal, the Republican

Party, with the exception of Richard Nixon, had resisted entitlement liberalizations. However, enactment of a prescription drug benefit would allow Republicans to put their stamp on the Medicare program.

The changed fiscal climate created an obstacle. The 2001 economic recession had significantly reduced federal revenues. The terrorist attacks on September 11, 2001, brought wars with Afghanistan and Iraq that guaranteed a large increase in military spending. Together, these events caused the surpluses to vanish. Budget deficits were, once again, a current reality and a likely fixture on the budget horizon.

Nevertheless, at President Bush's urging, a divided Republican congressional caucus moved forward to enact a Medicare prescription drug plan. The path to enactment was not easy. Fiscally conservative members objected to adding a new Medicare entitlement. In their view, Congress had shown that it was demonstrably incapable of controlling the existing health care entitlements: Medicare and Medicaid. The support of some members was conditioned on coupling the drug benefit with fundamental cost-reducing Medicare reforms. The Bush administration had included some reforms in its proposal. But when these reforms were dropped from consideration, support among reform-minded Republicans turned to opposition. Echoing Congressman John Byrnes's sentiment fifty years earlier against imposing a future Social Security financing burden on future generations, Senator Judd Gregg (R-NH) made the case against a stand-alone drug benefit on the Senate floor:

> It is a massive tax increase being placed on working, young Americans and Americans who have not yet been born in order to support a drug benefit for retired Americans and Americans who are about to retire, without any underlying reform to try to control the cost. . . . It seems incredibly unfair for one generation to do this to another generation, for us to use our political clout because we are in office to benefit our generation at the expense of our children and our children's children.[111]

Democrats vehemently opposed the Republican plan. The plan's reliance on beneficiary choice among prescription drug plans and competition among insurers, health plans, and pharmacy benefit managers lay at the heart of their opposition. Energy and Commerce Committee

Democrats expressed their opposition in philosophical terms: "For the first time, seniors and individuals with disabilities would not be permitted to get a benefit through Medicare but would have to enter the private insurance market to do so."[112] House Ways and Means Committee Democrats regarded a plan that relied on choice and competition as "not an entitlement at all."[113]

Democrats also strenuously objected to charging higher Medicare premiums to high-income Medicare enrollees compared to low-income enrollees. As Ways and Means Committee member Benjamin L. Cardin (D-MD) put it, "Medicare is not a welfare program. If basic benefits are denied based on income, you're compromising the philosophy of Medicare." According to Cardin, income-related premiums would set "a dangerous precedent for a social insurance policy in which all Americans participate."[114]

The final version of the Medicare drug bill passed the Senate with room to spare: 54–44. But in the House, opposition among a cadre of fiscally conservative Republicans and the vast majority of Democrats put the bill in jeopardy. Its passage required the Republican leadership to go to extraordinary lengths, reminiscent of Lyndon Johnson's efforts in 1956 to pass the Social Security Disability Insurance program, to secure enough votes for enactment. The House vote began at 3:00 a.m. on November 22. Fifteen minutes later, after the normal amount of time allowed for a vote had elapsed, the bill lacked the necessary votes. House Republican leaders then held the vote open for an unprecedented three hours to arm-twist, cajole, and offer special benefits to Republican members who had withheld their votes. Only when the leaders had secured the required votes nearly three hours later did they allow the voting to end.[115]

The final bill was a curious mixture of a catastrophic and a routine care benefit. The basic benefit covered all major prescription drugs. Most Medicare beneficiaries were required to pay a modest monthly premium and a $250 per year deductible. The federal government would pay 75 percent of drug costs for people with routine drug expenses and 95 percent of the costs for those with catastrophic care expenses.[116] In an intermediate-expense range, referred to as the "doughnut hole," the federal government would pay nothing and the beneficiary would bear the entire expense burden. Poor and near-poor Medicare beneficiaries would receive substantial subsidies to eliminate or reduce their out-of-pocket drug expenses.

In a departure from prior Medicare policy, private insurers, health plans, and pharmacy benefit managers would provide the new drug benefit. These providers could offer Medicare beneficiaries a variety of alternative drug plans so long as those plans met government-specified actuarial and coverage requirements. The federal government would pay prescription drug providers an amount per enrollee. The variety of plans would give Medicare beneficiaries the ability to choose a plan that best suited their needs and allow competition among plans to hold costs down. The payment per enrollee would obviate the need for the federal government to set drug prices, and the federal government would be prohibited from negotiating premiums. In another important departure, the statute charged higher-income seniors higher prescription drug premiums (and Medicare Part B premiums). The new law was a costly measure. Government officials estimated that the drug benefit would add about 20 percent to the level of the projected Medicare prescription drug spending over the next ten years.[117]

The prescription drug benefit is a political milestone in entitlement policy. Prior to its enactment, Republicans had been in a minority in Congress for most of the post–World War II years. Throughout these years, with the exception of the Nixon administration, they had resisted efforts of congressional Democrats and presidents to liberalize entitlements. From the 1930s to the 1970s, they sought to limit increases in Social Security benefits. In the 1950s and 1960s, they had opposed the enactment of disability insurance and Medicare and used congressional rules and procedures to block or slow down these liberalizing laws. They offered alternatives and more limited bills. Only when passage of an entitlement liberalization bill appeared unavoidable did they join with their Democratic counterparts in a "Hurrah!" vote for the bill. In the more recent past, they had supported President Reagan's efforts to trim the growth of entitlement spending and had eliminated the entitlement to AFDC benefits.

In 2003, having achieved control over both the executive and legislative branches for the first time in five decades, they had a unique opportunity to restrain entitlement. Instead, they passed the largest Medicare expansion in the program's history. They did so despite knowing that the avalanche of spending on baby boomers' entitlements was less than two decades away and that the new benefit would add significantly to the existing expenditure burden. And they did so despite knowing that neither the current Congress nor any of its predecessors had been able or willing to adopt federal health care entitlement reforms to slow their growth.

The Affordable Care Act

National health insurance became a major issue in 2008. During the presidential campaign, all major candidates offered universal health insurance plans. Although all plans claimed reducing health care costs as a goal, the overriding objective of each was universal health insurance coverage. Democratic Party candidate Hillary Clinton proposed a federal mandate to compel all individuals to obtain health insurance coverage. Barack Obama argued that health care "should be a right for every American" and proposed a new "public insurance program" for uninsured persons.[118] Republican candidate Senator John McCain, taking a chapter from George McGovern's 1972 campaign playbook, proposed to entitle all individuals to a $5,000 refundable health insurance tax credit.[119] Former Massachusetts governor Mitt Romney campaigned on his comprehensive state-level health care program, which would eventually serve as the model for the Affordable Care Act (ACA). Thus, each of the major candidates embraced the view that all individuals were worthy of government health care assistance.

The election's outcome guaranteed that national health insurance would be high on Congress's agenda. Voters gave Democrats the White House and large congressional majorities. Barack Obama was a strong ideological liberal. The large Democratic majorities in both houses of Congress were also vastly more liberal than their predecessors. Gone were southern Democrats who had previously exerted a restraining influence on the party's liberal instincts. They had been replaced by liberal Democrats from New England and the northern urban centers.

The highly partisan battle to pass a national health insurance program began in early 2009 and lasted fourteen months. Early signs of bipartisanship quickly evaporated as the outlines of the main bills became known. The Democratic consensus included a federal mandate that employers provide health insurance plans that met federal "essential benefit" standards, a federal mandate that all individuals were required to have such a plan, federal and state-government-run health care exchanges for individuals who did not have employer-provided insurance, and subsidies to assist individuals purchase insurance in these exchanges.

Liberal members also pressed for a public option that would establish a federally financed and federally administered national health insurance plan to compete directly with existing private insurance plans. The public option was eventually dropped from consideration due to concerns among moderate Democrats that federal authorities, by subsidizing and conferring other benefits on its own health plan, would establish the federal government as a single payer for all health care services.

The terms of the debate were the same as those that had governed the national health insurance debates of the 1940s, the 1970s, and the 1990s. President Obama made the moral case to a joint session of Congress by reading from a letter that Edward Kennedy had written soon after the senator had been diagnosed with a terminal illness: "What we face . . . is above all a moral issue; at stake are not just the details of policy, but fundamental principles of social justice and the character of our country."[120] The president and congressional advocates for universal coverage charged that the private market system was too costly, that it left too many people without access to medical care, and that it failed to improve health outcomes. The advocates pointed to the fact that rising medical costs were driving up insurance premiums more rapidly than employee compensation, thereby dampening the growth in money wages. They asserted that health care providers were shifting the cost of care to the uninsured onto privately insured medical bills, thereby driving insurance premiums even higher. Equating a lack of insurance to a lack of health care access, they pointed to the large uninsured population (46 million in 2008) as evidence that too many people lacked access to health care. News reports that insurers were denying coverage for preexisting conditions and were dropping covered individuals bolstered their lack-of-access claims. Advocates pointed to the relatively low U.S. life expectancy and relatively U.S. high infant mortality rates compared to other nations as evidence of the U.S. health care system's inferiority.

Universal coverage, advocates claimed, was the solution to the twin problems of rising costs and a lack of access. In their view, an entitlement to health insurance would provide equal health care access to all individuals. The federal government could "bend the cost curve" downward by using its broad regulatory powers to force competition among health providers and insurers in government-managed markets.

Opponents of mandatory universal coverage plans agreed that health care costs were rising too rapidly, but they argued that cost increases were primarily driven by important medical care quality improvements and ill-conceived government policies. Advances in medical technology, diagnostic and surgical procedures, and lifesaving medicines were extending lives and improving quality of life. Americans were better off, they asserted, with today's medical care at today's cost than they were with 1960s medical care at 1960s costs. Counterproductive government tax and health care entitlement policies had contributed to the high cost of health care by insulating patients from the true cost of that care.[121] Opponents also agreed that too many individuals lacked health insurance, but, they said, this did not mean they lacked access to health care. Nor was the fact that U.S. life expectancy was lower and the U.S. infant mortality rate higher than other countries evidence that U.S. health care outcomes were inferior to those of other countries. Life expectancy and infant mortality were due to a multitude of factors other than a country's medical care system.[122] As for cost shifting, opponents pointed to peer-reviewed research that found that the cost shift added less than 2 percent to private health insurance premiums.[123]

Opponents further argued that the federal government had demonstrated that it possessed no ability to control the two existing major federal health care entitlements, Medicare and Medicaid. The idea that adding a third major health care entitlement would reduce the growth in costs was, in their view, sheer folly. They argued that the increased aggregate demand for health care from providing insurance subsidies to upward of 40 million persons would bend the cost curve upward.

Few members of Congress on either side of the debate questioned the ACA's fundamental premise: that providing health insurance to the general population would in fact improve health outcomes. Some studies have found a positive impact on particular subgroups of the population. Others have found a positive statistical association between health insurance and health outcomes in larger populations. But these studies suffer from various methodological deficiencies that have prevented researchers from drawing any strong conclusions about the existence of a causal relationship between health insurance and health outcomes. An equally large and impressive body of research suggests that health insurance does not necessarily improve health outcomes.

This body of research includes one of the most remarkable government experiments in U.S. history, one that is generally regarded as the gold standard for academic medical research. The 1970s Rand National Health Insurance Experiment randomly assigned over twenty thousand individuals to various insurance plans with varying deductibles and copayments. Analysis of the data found that low copayments led individuals to increase their use of health care services by large amounts. For example, persons enrolled in a free care plan, one in which the insurance plan paid all health care expenses and the patient paid none, were estimated to spend 31 percent more than people enrolled in a plan in which insurance paid half the costs. Similarly, persons enrolled in a free care plan spent 18 percent more than persons enrolled in a plan with a deductible of $1,100.[124] The Rand study also found that the increase in health care spending was, for the most part, not associated with an overall improvement in health outcomes.[125] This basic finding has been bolstered over the years by subsequent analysis, most recently by a randomized, controlled experiment involving the Oregon Medicaid program. Analyses of twelve thousand individuals, which were completed after the ACA's enactment, found that Medicaid enrollees showed no improvement in health outcomes compared to uninsured people after two years.[126] At the time of the debate over the ACA, the fairest assessment of the state of knowledge about the relationship between health insurance and health outcomes was given by scholars Helen Levy and David Meltzer. Writing in 2008, the two health experts concluded that "the central question of how health insurance affects health, for whom it matters, and how much, remains largely unanswered at the level of detail needed to inform policy decisions."[127]

The law's partisan path to enactment contained several twists and turns that made its enactment unique among U.S. entitlements. The 2008 election had given Senate Democrats fifty-eight seats, not enough to prevent a filibuster. In March, Pennsylvania Republican Arlen Spector switched parties, and in July, Minnesota resolved its contested election in favor of Democrat Al Franken. The two changes gave Democrats a filibuster-proof majority. When Senator Ted Kennedy died in August, the health care bill lost a strong and valuable advocate, but there was little concern that the normally reliable Massachusetts electorate would not send a Democrat to replace the legendary liberal senator.

In December, before the Massachusetts special election, the Senate passed its version of the health care bill with the sixtieth vote provided by Senator Kennedy's temporary replacement. The House had passed its bill the month before, so it remained only for a House-Senate conference committee to work out the differences between their respective bills. Remarkably, not a single Republican member in either chamber cast a vote in favor of either version. No other major entitlement in U.S. history had ever been passed on such a partisan basis.

In January 2010, Massachusetts voters shocked Washington by electing a Republican senator. Suddenly and unexpectedly, Democrats had lost their filibuster-proof majority. Now only one legislative path was available: the House could pass the Senate bill, and it could become law without another Senate vote. Provisions that were unacceptable to House Democrats could be addressed in a separate corrections bill. Classifying such a corrections bill as a budget reconciliation bill would prevent the bill from a filibuster under the Senate's rules. But this path required House Democrats to trust the Senate to pass their corrections bill after they approved the Senate health care bill. Mutual trust, however, has never been a hallmark of House-Senate relations.

After considerable deliberation, House Democrats followed this strategy. On March 21, the House passed the Senate version of the Affordable Care Act by a 219–212 vote and sent the bill to the president. The House then passed its corrections bill 220–211 and sent that bill to the Senate. On March 25, the Senate passed the reconciliation bill. President Obama signed the two separate bills into law, which together have become known as the Affordable Care Act.[128] Ironically, the budget reconciliation process, initially a means of restraining federal spending had been used to create the largest new entitlement since the New Deal.

The landmark law's key entitlement provisions included mandates that individuals obtain and employers provide health insurance that meets federal "essential benefits" standards; the establishment of federally regulated exchanges, or regulated marketplaces, within which individuals purchase such insurance plans; the creation of an entitlement to a sliding scale of health insurance subsidies to individuals with incomes between 133 percent and 400 percent poverty; and Medicaid coverage (now at state option) to everyone with an income below 138 percent of the poverty line. In addition, the law required insurers to guarantee coverage to all individuals at community-rated premiums, prohibited insurers from charging premiums based on preexisting conditions, and imposed limits on health plan deductibles. Finally, the law temporarily entitled health insurers that offer plans in the health insurance exchanges to subsidies for losses incurred.[129]

The law immediately faced legal challenges on the ground that the individual mandate was unconstitutional, that the financial penalty on states that did not expand Medicaid coverage was unconstitutional, and that the law did not allow subsidies to be paid in states with federally run exchanges. The legal challenges eventually reached the Supreme Court.

The stakes for the individual mandate were high. The mandate was crucial to achieving the law's universal coverage goal, and without it, the program might unravel. The mandate also had more important ramifications that went far beyond health insurance. A government that could command its citizens to purchase health insurance could also compel its citizens to purchase any privately produced product.

The Obama administration made its case for the mandate in part on the Constitution's commerce clause. Prior Supreme Court decisions had given the federal government broad latitude to regulate commercial activities. The Supreme Court narrowly rejected the administration's commerce clause argument by a 5–4 vote. The Court drew a line for the commerce clause at the regulation of "inactivity." Writing for the Court's majority, Chief Justice Roberts warned that "construing the Commerce Clause to permit Congress to regulate individuals precisely because they are doing nothing would open a new and potentially vast domain to congressional authority."[130]

The administration also made the case for the individual mandate by appealing to the Constitution's tax power. Here, it struck pay dirt. The issue turned on whether the penalty the law imposed on individuals who failed to purchase insurance was a "fine" or a "tax." The Supreme Court had previously developed a commonsense distinction between the two. A tax, the Court had declared, "is an enforced contribution to provide for the support of government. A penalty "is an exaction imposed by statute as punishment for an unlawful act." The ACA seemed to describe the payment for persons violating the mandate as a penalty. The statutory language used the term *penalty* repeatedly to describe the payment for failing to obtain insurance and never once used the term *tax*.[131]

A Court 5–4 majority, with Chief Justice Roberts casting the deciding vote, ruled that the payment for noncompliance was a tax. Therefore, the individual mandate was constitutional.

In the same ruling, the Court decided that the law's Medicaid mandate was unconstitutional. The administration argued that the law's penalty for noncompliance, the loss of all Medicaid funds, was a method of "persuasion," not a method of "coercion." The Court disagreed. It refused to draw a bright line between persuasion and coercion but concluded that the threatened loss of funds was "a gun to the head" and therefore constituted coercion.[132]

In 1937, the Supreme Court had ruled that imposing a federal payroll tax on businesses within a state that failed to establish a federally approved unemployment insurance program did not constitute federal coercion of states but instead was an "inducement" and was therefore constitutional.[133] In its ACA ruling, the Court did not say what distinguished the payroll tax penalty from the loss of Medicaid funding penalty.

In a subsequent decision, the Court ruled 6–3 that the federal government could legally pay subsidies to individuals in federal health insurance exchanges. Here again, the statutory language seemed to state the opposite. The law stipulates that subsidies "shall be allowed," but only to those who obtained an insurance plan through "an Exchange established by the State."[134] The Court's majority deemed this language to be ambiguous and that it had resulted from "inartful drafting."[135] When statutory language is ambiguous, the Court ruled, the words should be read "with a view to their place in the overall statutory scheme."[136] In the majority's view, Congress could have not meant to deny subsidies in federal exchanges, for if it did, the statutory scheme could not produce the desired universal coverage outcome.

Justices Antonin Scalia, Samuel Alito, and Clarence Thomas dissented. In their view, the statute's plain language was not ambiguous. Justice Scalia wrote, "Words no longer have meaning if an Exchange that is not established by a state is 'established by the State.'"[137] The justices opined that it was plausible that the statutory scheme was to encourage states to take on the financial and administrative burdens of running an exchange. Limiting subsidies to state exchanges was one way to accomplish this.

The ACA stands as the most significant advance in the long march of entitlements since the New Deal. The law's underlying premise, that all individuals have a right to health insurance, extends the "equally worthy" claim far beyond its previous confines. The law's mandate that individuals purchase health insurance extends the federal government's authority over individuals beyond its previous boundaries. Its mandate that employers must provide insurance is a similar extension of federal authority over business enterprises. The law's Medicaid mandate, which the Supreme Court has since ruled unconstitutional, extends the idea even further that state governments are administrative agents of federal policy dictates. Finally, its rules and regulations on insurers and health care providers extend the federal government's intrusions to all segments of the U.S. health care market, which currently accounts for one-sixth of all U.S. goods and services.

The law's mandates mark an important change in the means of financing federal entitlements that are a harbinger for the future. A significant portion of the law's entitlement costs is financed outside the federal budget through mandates on employers, employees, and insurers. The use of mandates in lieu of taxes is a likely indication that the federal government has reached an upper limit on the use of payroll and other taxes to finance new entitlements. If so, future entitlement expansions will be established by similar mandates rather than by taxes.

The law has succeeded reasonably well in expanding health insurance coverage. By March 2016, the number of Medicaid recipients totaled 73 million persons, up from about 55 million in 2011. A large, but unknown number of this increase is due to the ACA. As of March 2016, thirty one states had responded to the ACA's financial incentives to expand their Medicaid programs to newly cover 14 million adults.[138] Eligibility expansions and outreach efforts that have been part of the ACA have added an undetermined number of families with children. In addition, by early 2017, 12 million people had enrolled in the ACA's health insurance exchanges.[139]

However, important cracks in the ACA's exchanges have emerged. Premiums of health insurance available on the exchanges, after rising slowly during the law's first two years in operation, have begun recently to rise sharply. Preliminary analysis by the Kaiser Foundation indicates that premiums will rise 20 percent in 2017 over the prior year. In six states, premiums will increase by more than 50 percent.[140] Equally concerning, as insurance companies have withdrawn from the exchanges, the number of health plans available has markedly declined. In early 2017, only a single insurer offers insurance to individuals who purchase insurance on one-third of all the health care exchanges.[141] As of this writing in early 2017, the fate of the ACA is uncertain. Republican majorities in both chambers and President Trump have promised to repeal the law, and a bill that repeals major portions of the ACA is working its way through the House of Representatives. The bill would transform the Medicaid program into a block grant, thereby reducing the liberalizing incentives the federal matching formula creates and freeing the states to set their own Medicaid policies. The bill would also establish a new entitlement to private health insurance subsidies to replace the ACA's entitlement. The replacement of one entitlement with another, coming after seven years of stiff Republican opposition to the ACA, demonstrates a bipartisan denial of the entitlement problem the country faces.

Conclusion

The years 1989 to 2016 represent a period of recognition and denial. At the outset, Congress and the executive branch recognized that the fiscal challenge presented by the baby boomers' retirement was only a generation away. Yet elected officials failed to prepare to meet the challenge. Policymakers refused to address the Social Security retirement and disability programs' looming financial shortfalls and proved incapable of addressing Medicare's rising cost. With the exception of the historic AFDC reform in 1996, they continued to incrementally enlarge the food stamps, Medicaid, and the EITC programs by extending eligibility higher up the income ladder.

Neither the storm that lay on the fiscal horizon nor the large annual budget deficits that dominated the fiscal landscape during most of the twenty-five years were sufficient to overcome the seemingly relentless pressures to expand the class of worthy entitlement beneficiaries. Perhaps nowhere is this clearer than in health care legislation. After spending the first half of the period fruitlessly attempting to control the costs of existing federal health care entitlements, Congress and the executive enacted two major health entitlement expansions. Medicare coverage of prescription drugs was extended to all seniors and disabled persons regardless of income and regardless of whether they had provided for their own coverage. Similarly, government-subsidized health insurance coverage was expanded to a group that could potentially encompass two-thirds of all the nonelderly lower- and middle-class persons.

19 A Challenge Unlike Any Other in U.S. History

They say the world has become too complex for simple answers. They are wrong. There are no easy answers, but there are simple answers.
  Ronald Reagan[1]

FEDERAL ENTITLEMENT PROGRAMS SINCE THEIR inception in the late eighteenth century have occupied a special place among federal government programs. As the primary vehicle for delivering federal aid to individuals, entitlements have served a crucially important role in alleviating poverty and economic hardship among poor, disabled, elderly persons. Under the banners of providing economic security, reducing poverty, and pursuing economic fairness, entitlement eligibility rules have been loosened and benefits have been raised to ensure they meet constantly evolving perceptions of "adequacy" and "worthiness." The ever-higher benefits to ever-larger groups of claimants have transformed the various programs to a point where the original noble goals of poverty mitigation and economic security are hardly recognizable.

Persistent forces have been evident from the earliest days of the Republic. The Revolutionary War and Civil War disability pension programs initially limited eligibility to soldiers and seamen injured in wartime and their widows. Over time, eligibility for both programs was gradually liberalized until benefits had been extended to virtually all wartime veterans. World War I legislation repeated this pattern. Pensions were routinely expanded during the 1920s, and by 1931, they were granted to veterans with disabilities unrelated to wartime service. In the twentieth century, Social Security was conceived with the well-intentioned purpose of providing retired industrial workers a measure of financial protection against poverty in old age. Today, the program's nearly universal cash benefits, along with Medicare's health benefits, far exceed a level necessary for poverty protection. Together these now massive entitlements can, by themselves, afford many retirees a middle-class standard of living, often supplanting other meaningful sources of retirement wealth that retirees would have accumulated in the absence of these entitlements. The Social Security disability program originally limited cash assistance to permanently disabled older workers who were unable to perform any job in the economy. Today it extends benefits to a large number of workers who are temporarily and partially disabled. Welfare assistance in the form of cash, nutrition aid, and health care was originally limited to impoverished persons who were unable to provide for themselves: the elderly, the disabled, and children of mothers who had been widowed or deserted. A first wave of liberalizations, which took place from 1950 to the mid-1970s, extended means-tested assistance to all poor people regardless of their ability to work. After a decade-long pause, a second wave, spanning the late 1980s to the 2009 Great Recession, extended assistance to households higher up on the income ladder to large numbers of middle-class families.

The emergence of federal budget surplus from time to time has only served to magnify existing pressures to liberalize entitlements. The heightened pressures have been sufficiently powerful to invariably overcome reasoned concerns about the long-term fiscal consequences of liberalizations. All of the major nineteenth-century veterans' pension liberalizations occurred during economic good times when the U.S. Treasury was temporarily flush with revenue. The massive 1924 Bonus Bill for World War I veterans was enacted in the midst of a decade of large budget surpluses. Similar pressures generated by accounting surpluses in government trust funds have produced program liberalizations regardless of the federal budget's overall fiscal health. The transient navy pension fund surpluses regularly produced legislative liberalizations, the last of which in 1837 ended in bank-rupting the fund. In the modern era, President Roosevelt's attempt to build a large Social Security reserve to finance future benefits collapsed under similar pressures when Congress voted to raise benefits, grant survivors' benefits, and move forward by one year the date at which benefits would begin to be paid. Since then all of the major expansions in Social Security have occurred during times when the Social Security trust fund has been flush with large accounting surpluses and without regard for whether the federal budget overall was in surplus or deficit. The last of these expansions in 1972 put the trust fund on its own long road toward bankruptcy.

A second pattern of modern expansions emerged from the New Deal and Great Society after entitlements were created for the unemployed and the poor. During recessionary periods when general economic hardship has spread among the population, pressure has mounted on Congress to expand entitlement programs to meet the rising economic need. Congress has invariably responded with program liberalizations. As a result, entitlements are expanded during recessions that bring hard times to the general population, as well as during economic good times when federal revenues are plentiful. The large swings in the business cycle, as in the 1970s, produced large legislative expansions.

As the preceding chapters of this book have shown, electoral politics have been an important driver of entitlement expansions since the latter part of the nineteenth century. Because entitlement programs distribute cash assistance directly to large numbers of voters and reimbursements directly to sizable numbers of service providers, they are an efficient vehicle for gaining electoral advantage. As we have seen, the Republican Party was the first to recognize the political power of entitlements by joining with the nation's first great lobbying organization, the Grand Army of the Republic, to promote Civil War pensions. These pensions played a central role in the national electorate's realignment behind the Republican Party in the 1890s. Following World War II, Congresses led by Democrats developed the practice of raising Social Security benefits to gain electoral advantage into a finely honed skill. Six of the ten post–World War II legislative increases in Social Security benefits prior to Congress's decision to tie Social Security benefit increases to inflation took effect during an election year. Four of these increases first appeared in Social Security monthly checks in October, one month before federal elections.

Large-scale liberalizations are rare. They usually occur in the midst of major wars, extraordinary economic events, or social upheavals. Typically, legislative responses to the ever-present pressures for expansion have been incremental. The incremental expansion of Revolutionary War widows' pensions provides a clear early example. Pensions, originally reserved for the widows of Continental Army soldiers and seamen during the war, were extended first to spouses who were widowed before 1794, then to widows of all wartime veterans who had been married before 1800, and finally to widows regardless of when they were married. The incrementalism is also evident from 1950 to 1975 when Congress and the executive branch were building the modern entitlement state. During these years, every president proposed to expand at least one existing entitlement or create additional ones. Every Congress, from the Eighty-First, which convened in 1949, to the Ninety-Fifth, which was seated in 1975, enacted at least one such expansion. Social Security was significantly liberalized in no fewer than fifteen separate legislative acts. Aid to Families with Dependent Children (AFDC) and the Old Age Assistance program were markedly expanded four times, Social Security disability eight times, and Medicare and food stamps twice. From the mid-1970s until the Great Recession of 2007–2009, the incremental liberalizations continued, though at a diminished pace. Chronic federal budget deficits have dampened but not stopped the incremental pattern of expansion. The series of Medicaid expansions from 1984 to 1990, the periodic liberalizations of food stamps and the earned income tax credit (EITC) serve as vivid illustrations of this incremental pattern during a time of federal budget deficits. The incremental liberalizations, coupled with the degree of permanence Congress attaches to entitlement benefits, have created a step-wise process by which entitlements are expanded over time. In this process, each expansion creates a new base on which future liberalizations are built.

With their actions, Congress and the executive branch have conferred a degree of permanence on entitlement benefits that it has not bestowed on most other programs. Once granted, these benefits are rarely subject to retrenchment. When economic good times have turned bad, as they inevitably do, liberalized entitlement programs have typically been kept intact in the face of revenue reductions, while other worthy federal programs have been placed on the chopping block. The special status of entitlement benefits is evident in Congress's behavior during the nineteenth-century recessions of 1808, 1819, and 1837.[2] In each instance, veterans' pensions were left intact while other government spending was reduced significantly. When the navy pension fund went bankrupt in 1841, Congress continued to pay navy pensions but financed them with general revenues.

The same pattern is evident during twentieth-century recessions. Significant entitlement cutbacks among existing recipients have been rare. The notable exceptions are President Franklin Roosevelt's removal of hundreds of thousands of veterans from the pension rolls in 1933, President Ronald Reagan's welfare eligibility restrictions, and the 1996 welfare reform law. Congressional and judicial reversals of President Reagan's Social Security Disability Insurance reviews serve as an important reminder of the sacrosanct nature of entitlement benefits to existing recipients.

The product of these powerful forces on the growth of modern entitlements is depicted in Figure 4, which compares entitlement spending to expenditures on the two other major federal programs categories: national defense and all other programs (mainly discretionary programs). Expenditures are measured as a percent of GDP.[3] The upward trajectory of entitlement spending since the end of World War II is clearly evident. Since 1946, entitlement spending has grown at an average annual rate 33 percent faster than the growth in GDP. The rapid growth has caused entitlement programs' claims on national income to rise from 4 percent in 1947 to 16 percent in 2015. Alternatively, after adjusting for inflation, federal spending on entitlements per U.S. resident increased from about $500 in 1947 to over $7,500 (in 2015 dollars).

Incredible as it may seem, entitlements have accounted for all of the growth federal spending as a percent of GDP during the post–World War II era. By 1972, entitlement spending soared higher than defense spending; by 1987 entitlement spending exceeded the expenditures on defense and all other federal programs combined.

Entitlements have also been the prime mover of the relentless post–World War II rise in the national debt. Federal outlays have exceeded federal revenues in all but eleven of the seventy years since the war's end. The chronic deficits produced by these excesses have caused the outstanding public debt to rise to about $40,000 per U.S. resident in 2015; up from $20,000 (in today's dollars) just after World War II and from $10,000 in 1965 (in today's dollars).

Federal entitlements now distribute government aid on a scale that is unprecedented in history. Each year since the beginning of the Great Recession in 2009, the federal government has distributed over $2 trillion in entitlement benefits, an all-time U.S. high. It now redistributes 16 percent of all U.S. personal income from some members of society to others.[4]

In recent years following the Great Recession, the reach of each major entitlement program into the population has also risen to unprecedented levels. In 2015, the number of Social Security retirement and Medicare recipients reached record levels. Likewise, the number of Medicaid recipients, spurred by the Affordable Care Act, hit its peak. Recipients of Social Security Disability Insurance, Supplemental Security Income, the EITC, food stamps, and school lunches, whether expressed as an absolute number or as a percentage of the population, are down only slightly from their all-time highs reached during or immediately after the Great Recession. The caseloads of only the Temporary Assistance for Needy Families program, the cyclically sensitive state-run unemployment insurance programs, and the black lung program, are well below their record highs.

Taking all major entitlements together, the entitlement system's reach is even more striking. Estimates prepared for this book using the Current Population Survey (CPS) show that by 2015, the last year for which CPS data are available, the number of households receiving entitlement assistance swelled to well over half of the U.S. population. Fifty-five percent of all households, which includes more than 170 million persons, received cash or in-kind benefits from at least one major federal entitlement program. Perhaps even more noteworthy, given that virtually all senior citizens receive Social Security benefits, is the high recipient rate among households that are headed by people under age

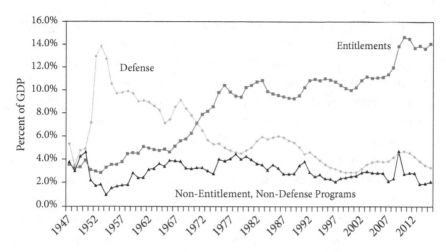

Figure 4. Federal Spending on Entitlements and Other Programs: 1947–2015.
Source: *U.S. Budget, Fiscal Year 2017*, Historical Tables, Tables 1.2, 3.1 and 13.1,
U.S. Budget, Fiscal Years 1942–2017.

65. In 2015, 41 percent of the nation's nonelderly-headed households
received entitlement benefits. More than 80 percent of all households
headed by single mothers received benefits from at least one entitlement program, and 58 percent of all children were growing up in families that received entitlement assistance.[5] These numbers, remarkable as
they appear, are likely to understate the true extent of the entitlement
system's reach. It is well known that the CPS significantly underestimates program participation, particularly among means-tested entitlement programs.[6]

The data reveal just how far entitlements have departed from their
original purpose of providing a measure of security from economic
destitution among the elderly, the disabled, and the unemployed and
to alleviate poverty among the general population. In 2015, 62 percent
of recipient households, encompassing over 100 million U.S. residents,
had incomes that were above the poverty line prior to the receipt of
assistance. Thirty-one percent, nearly 60 million persons, were in the
upper half of the U.S. income distribution. The distribution of entitlement dollars is similarly striking. Nonpoor households received 48
percent of the $2.4 trillion that was distributed in federal cash and in-
kind entitlement benefits. Households in the upper half of the income

distribution received $725 billion of this assistance; households in the top fifth received $225 billion.[7]

Most entitlement spending serves purposes other than reducing the degree of poverty among the poor. The degree is best measured by the percentage of assistance needed to bring the income of the nation's poor households up to the poverty line. This number excludes the portion of assistance to poor households that raises their income over and above the poverty line. In 2015, only 26 percent of all cash entitlement assistance was spent to reduce the extent of poverty. Including the market value of in-kind benefits, only 21 percent of entitlement assistance went to alleviating poverty.[8] Sixty-three percent of all cash and in-kind benefits distributed to poor persons was over and above the amount necessary to lift them from poverty.

The main reason that such a large percentage of entitlement spending is received by nonpoor households is that the vast majority of assistance is delivered through social insurance programs. These programs, which by design provide assistance largely independent of financial need, distribute four dollars of assistance for every dollar of entitlement aid delivered through means-tested programs.

Over 90 percent of social insurance assistance consists of cash and medical benefits for a single demographic group: those age 65 and older. This assistance far exceeds that amount required to provide a measure of economic security against impoverishment. It now supports the lifestyles of middle- and upper-income senior citizens. The federal government distributes about $50,000 annually in Social Security and Medicare benefits to the typical married couple who retired at age 66 in 2015. This amount is nearly equal to the $56,000 median income among all U.S. households.[9] Put another way, upon reaching age 66, the typical married couple, who have had a lifetime to prepare for their retirement, can now expect to receive over $1 million in Social Security and Medicare benefits over their remaining life spans, after adjusting for inflation. Although retirees have contributed payroll taxes to partially finance these benefits, the proceeds of those taxes were spent long ago on previous retirees. The burden now falls on the nation's younger workers who must simultaneously meet their own families' needs. The massive transfer does not end there. For the typical worker who qualifies for Social Security disability insurance benefits, the present value of those benefits plus the Medicare benefits the person also qualifies for is about $300,000. This is equivalent to writing each new disability recipient a check for $300,000 at the time the initial disability award is made.[10]

The departure of entitlements from their original purposes is not confined to social insurance programs. In 2015, only 60 percent of means-tested entitlements benefits were distributed to poor people, down from 80 percent 25 years earlier. The remainder was spread widely across the income distribution. One-fifth (22 percent) was received by households in the upper half of the income distribution. The surprisingly low percentage of means-tested benefits received by poor households is the product of legislative acts over the past two and a half decades that have steadily extended the universe of worthy claims higher up the income ladder.

The extension of entitlement benefits to a large number of nonpoor households has created a new and growing economic problem. As entitlement assistance has been extended up the income ladder, so have the harmful incentives that necessarily accompany this assistance. Work disincentives, especially those created by means-tested programs, are especially acute. The phase-out or termination of benefits as household income rises acts much like a tax on earnings. The food stamp program's phase-out imposes an effective 24 percent marginal tax on earnings. Supplemental Security Income most often imposes an 80 to 100 percent marginal tax rate. Most state-run TANF programs impose a marginal tax in the neighborhood of 50 percent. The EITC offsets the lion's share of these work penalties for poor recipients. But the price of this offset is another 21 percent tax in the form of a phase-out of benefits to recipient households higher up the income ladder. In addition, the Medicaid program abruptly terminates eligibility when a family's earnings rise above a threshold that extends up to 100 percent of the poverty line in some states and 138 percent of the poverty line in other states. The loss of medical benefits, the value of which can easily exceed income that could be earned from several months of work, also acts as an effective tax on work, and a sizable one. The ACA's health insurance subsidies can reduce the magnitude of the work penalty for those in poor or low-income households who work their way off Medicaid eligibility. But the phase-out of ACA subsidies has created an additional 10 to 15 percent effective tax rate that affects lower- and middle-class recipients with incomes that can range up to 400 percent of the poverty line—nearly $100,000 for a family of four in 2015.[11] The extension of means-tested entitlements higher up the income ladder, particularly the EITC and other tax credits, Medicaid, and the ACA, means that the tax on earnings from these programs increasingly comes on top of income and payroll taxes.

The disincentives for work and human capital formation are not limited to means-tested entitlements. They are also present in the federal disability programs and unemployment insurance. The relaxation of their eligibility rules has further contributed to the growing work incentive problem among middle-income workers.

In 2015, the most recent year for which data are available, 68 million working-age persons lived in households that received benefits from at least one means-tested entitlement. They constitute nearly 40 percent of all people age 21 to 64.[12] Half of this large group faced a marginal tax rate greater than 31 percent, excluding the additional impact from the potential loss of their Medicaid eligibility and the ACA phase-out as their income increases. So for these individuals, each additional dollar of earnings increases their disposable income by less than 70 cents. Twenty million people in this group faced marginal tax rates greater than 40 percent, again excluding the additional impact from a loss of Medicaid and the ACA phase-out. These high effective tax rates are present among all groups of workers, including young adults age 21 to 24, prime-age men and women age 25 to 54, and secondary workers of all ages.

The large prevalence of high marginal tax rates on earnings among such a significant segment of the working-age population has adverse consequences for the economy at large. The incentives for less labor force attachment, lower productivity, and less human capital formation inevitably produce slower economic growth. Recent analyses indicate that the harmful economic incentives created by entitlement programs have contributed to both the decline in U.S. labor force participation and the slow economic growth that characterizes today's economy.[13]

The Fiscal Challenge

The soaring growth in entitlement spending creates a fiscal challenge unlike any other in U.S. history. The leading edge of the baby boom generation has already reached retirement age. In the coming years, their numbers will accelerate far faster than working-age population. In twenty years, there will be 79 million persons age 65 and older compared to 48 million today, a 31 million increase. The working-age population (ages 18–64), however, is projected to increase by only 14 million. Demographic imbalance will continue to grow for decades beyond that point.[14]

The financial burden that social insurance programs will impose on the nation's finances will be extraordinary as senior citizens claim their promised Social Security checks and health care benefits. Absent any legislative change in spending or taxes between now and 2024, rising entitlement spending is projected to drive real per capita federal expenditures to a level nearly 50 percent higher than it is today, far outstripping the growth in real per capita income. By that time, according to official government projections, annual federal budget deficits will regularly exceed $1 trillion.[15] In fifteen years, official forecasts project that entitlement expenditures plus interest on the national debt will consume all government tax revenues, leaving no tax revenues to finance all of the federal government's other national security and domestic activities.

Financing this expenditure burden will require either massive borrowing or economically crippling taxes. Reliance on borrowed funds would cause the national debt to soar past 100 percent of the nation's output of goods and services by 2032. Reliance on higher taxes would require a 33 percent increase in every federal tax. Middle-class households would face combined federal income and payroll taxes of nearly 40 percent, and the top federal income tax rate would exceed 50 percent.[16]

The harsh reality is that entitlement programs, originally established to "promote the general welfare," have become a clear and present danger to the nation's future welfare. Basic economics teaches us that high tax rates, broadly imposed, reduce economic activity and impair economic growth. History teaches us that high levels of public sector debt threaten prosperity by reducing economic growth, raising economic volatility, and making a country's financial system more fragile.[17] But just how large the damaging consequences might be is not known with any significant degree of certainty because the nation has never experienced a prolonged period of public debt or taxes at these extraordinary levels. Entitlements are marching the country into economically uncharted and turbulent waters.

Readers might be tempted to regard these economic concerns as overblown. After all, there are apparently few signs in current financial markets that a tax- or debt-induced fiscal calamity is on the horizon. But the absence of signs should provide no comfort. Throughout history, warning signs of a coming financial crisis, public or private, are rarely seen in bond and financial futures markets. It is only after a crisis has hit and damage has been done that reviews of earlier events, conducted with the benefit of hindsight, reveal the presence of ominous warning signs that were missed. These reviews usually reveal a pattern of profligacy, of unrealistic expectations about the sustainability of existing trends, and a denial of their likely consequences. These patterns are invariably accompanied by a breakdown of financial discipline and a general loosening of fiduciary standards, compromised ethics, and the scandalous use of improper budget and accounting rules to mask unpleasant financial realities. In sum, the reviews reveal a widespread degradation of budgeting standards. As we look across today's political landscape, many of these toxic warning signs are manifest.

Rethinking Social Insurance Dogma and the Role of Entitlements

This book is a work of history, not a vehicle for offering specific policy prescriptions. This history makes clear the magnitude of the challenge that lies before the nation. Changing entitlements to avoid the risk of fiscal calamity, while maintaining the entitlement goals of a compassionate society, is a herculean task. The powerful forces that have caused entitlements to expand and proliferate have been operating nearly continuously for more than two centuries. The forces are still at work, as evidenced by legislative bills that have recently been introduced in Congresses to increase Social Security benefits, expand unemployment insurance, lower the eligibility age for Medicare, and provide universal health insurance coverage. These omnipresent forces, as this book has emphasized, are inseparable from the entitlement itself.

But this history also provides a few observations that may help guide policymakers toward meeting the entitlement challenge. In considering policy changes to reduce benefits or restrict eligibility, focus should be placed on the policy's long-term consequences. Proposals that impose abrupt and significant benefit or eligibility cutbacks to achieve immediate budget savings are rarely enacted; if they become law, they are rarely sustained. The backlash by the federal government and the federal courts to the state of Louisiana's action to immediately terminate AFDC benefits for twenty-three thousand children in 1960 serves as a stark illustration of the ineffectiveness of abrupt, large-scale entitlement reductions. The unanimous Senate rejection of the Reagan administration's 1981 proposal to substantially reduce Social Security's early retirement benefits is another vivid example. The revolt by states, the federal courts, and ultimately Congress to the Reagan administration's accelerated eligibility reviews of disability recipients provides further counsel against abruptly terminating benefits for large numbers of entitlement recipients. In contrast, the Reagan administration's black lung program initiatives, which left benefits for existing recipients unaffected but tightened eligibility for future claimants, stands in contrast as a striking example of a successful policy. Fortunately, policies that focus on the long term are complementary to the fiscal problem that entitlements have created. The costs of entitlements may be high now, but their future costs are unaffordable.

Closely related is the observation that achieving long-term policy goals is best accomplished through incremental changes. The Carter administration's Social Security policy of reducing the program's long-term costs by gradually reducing the growth in promised benefits for future retirees in incrementally larger amounts for each successive cohort of retirees is a clear example of this lesson in action. Although the first reductions occurred for people who were only five years away from Social Security's normal retirement age at the time, the policy was sustained. Similarly, the sustainability of the 1983 Social Security Amendment's policy of increasing the retirement age is attributable to its long-term focus and incremental nature. Although neither reform was sufficiently large to forestall future cost problems, each policy dealt with a long-term problem by avoiding abrupt benefit reductions for those on the rolls at the time and instead focused on reducing benefits promised to future retirees.

The adverse incentive effects of well-intentioned entitlement policies need to be recognized and accounted for in assessing their efficacy. John Quincy Adams's statement that Revolutionary War soldiers "seemed to multiply with time" occurred after a flood of applicants responded to the incentives created by the Universal Service Pension law. Congress has badly misjudged the consequences of similar incentive effects in subsequent laws time and again. The explosion in Civil War pension rolls following the grant of retroactive benefits by the Arrears Law in 1879 and following the Dependent Pension Act of 1890 were responses to incentives created by these laws. In modern times, the incentives created by generous benefits and court decisions contributed to the rapid increase in children on the disability rolls in the early 1990s and the continual growth in the adult disability rolls since the 1960s. The long length of time many welfare mothers spent on the welfare rolls was partly a consequence of the AFDC program's harmful incentives. The soaring costs of Medicare and Medicaid since their enactment are largely a consequence of incentives the programs created for excess use of health services. In a slightly different way, the large number of powerful service provider lobby groups, from hospitals and doctors to professional social service workers, is in response to incentives for economic gain created by in-kind entitlement benefits.

As this book has emphasized, fairness and worthiness have been powerful concepts driving the upward growth of entitlements. These concepts have also proven crucially important in the rare retrenchment of entitlements. President Franklin Roosevelt's actions in 1933 to immediately terminate the disability benefits of over 400,000 veterans stands out as the single most important entitlement reduction in U.S. history. The president's overarching rationale was fairness.

In his view, all citizens had an obligation to serve their country in wartime, so wartime service alone did not make veterans a special class of citizens worthy of government assistance. Therefore, veterans who suffered from disabling injuries that were unrelated to wartime service were no more worthy of assistance than individuals who worked in wartime munitions factories or shipyards and later suffered from disabilities that were also unrelated to their wartime service. Since the latter group of individuals had never been eligible for disability benefits, neither should veterans with nonservice-connected disabilities. President Roosevelt's strong case carried the day in Congress.

Similarly, but on a much smaller scale, fairness concepts were important in other entitlement reductions. The excessive retroactive benefits awarded to widows of navy sailors and seamen by the 1837 Jarvis bill, amounting to $100,000 or more (in today's dollars), were repealed. One of the principal arguments for President Carter's Social Security reform was that requiring workers to pay payroll taxes to finance Social Security benefits that would exceed a retiree's preretirement earnings was unfair. President Reagan's efforts to trim the welfare rolls was based on the view that it was unfair for working persons to support benefits to people with incomes above the poverty line who were capable of providing for themselves. The historic 1996 reform of the ADFC program was predicated on the view that in return for financial aid, it was only fair to ask welfare recipients to take responsibility for making themselves ultimately independent of government aid.

Fairness considerations can be as important in stemming the growth in entitlements as they have previously been in expanding entitlements. The heavy financial burden that entitlements will impose on younger workers and their children when they enter the workforce comes in several forms. First, rising federal expenditures will require some combination of steeply higher taxes and a heavy federal debt burden on younger individuals. The higher taxes will reduce their disposable income and, hence, their standard of living. Second, higher taxes and a heavy public debt, by impairing the ability of the economy to grow, will further impair the growth in living standards. Third, the large work disincentives that are part of entitlement programs and their extension to large segments of the working-age population will also inhibit economic growth, and thereby further weaken the advancement of living standards. This is profoundly unfair. Younger workers and their children are no less worthy of reaping the rewards of their hard work and successes than past generations.

Finally, the entitlement system's present and future high cost, its inefficiencies, and its maldistribution of benefits raise fundamental questions about what role government should play in the economy and in the lives of individuals. In our market system, individuals are free to seek economic advancement. They are able to make choices about their careers, their family life, and their lifestyles. They reap the rewards of their successes and suffer the consequences of their failures.

The modern entitlement system, in contrast, appears to be based on the premise that a large portion of the population is not capable of providing for their own basic economic needs and that government must step in and do their job. According to this premise, a majority of individuals are not capable of saving sufficiently for their retirement needs, a large number of individuals are unable to properly choose their health care or satisfy their basic nutritional needs, and a majority of able-bodied low-wage workers are unable to adequately provide for their families. Accordingly, the government must provide retirement benefits and medical care to senior citizens and the disabled regardless of financial need, subsidize health care and nutritional assistance to middle-class households as well as the poor, and supplement the earnings of low- and middle-income workers.

The basic purposes of entitlements, their structure, and the level of government that operates them need to be thoroughly restructured. The current system's generosity and incentives are too destructive of individual initiative and pose too much harm to economic advancement. Its promises are no longer affordable. The system needs to be restructured to become a safety net that preserves the dignity of recipients and rewards self-reliance. It must be kept in mind that providing assistance to individuals who are impoverished through no fault of their own is not only consistent with widely held public goals, it is a hallmark of a compassionate society.

Readers may be inclined to conclude that there is little that can be done to alter the course we are on: The forces behind entitlement liberalization are too powerful and too embedded in our governing institutions to overcome. Such a conclusion would be wrong.

Nearly thirty years ago, Milton and Rose Friedman described how major changes in social and economic policy take place. They described policy change as a series of ocean tides—in their words, "the tide in the affairs" of a society. The "tides begin in the minds of men, spread to the conduct of public policy, often generate their own reversal, and are succeeded by another tide."[18] The change starts with intellectual ideas that are usually developed in reaction to the failure of earlier ideas to live up to their promises. The new intellectual climate, a countercurrent, gradually gains acceptance in the general population as dissatisfaction with existing policies grows.[19] The dissatisfaction eventually turns into public pressure on governing institutions for policy change. Ultimately this pressure overwhelms the forces maintaining the status quo and major policy changes that are in accord with the new intellectual climate occur. This process is a gradual one, often taking place over decades and often spurred forward by a societal or economic crisis.

The Friedmans' main elements for a change in entitlement policy are falling into place. Decades-old countercurrents contained in the writings of Friedrich von Hayek, Robert Nozick, Milton and Rose Friedman, and Charles Murray have been gaining acceptance among the public for some time.[20] Although their acceptance is far from universal, they have begun to form a new tide, one that stresses individual responsibility and self-reliance over government entitlements. As the tide of entitlement approaches its crest, public dissatisfaction with the entitlement state is mounting. The public is coming to realize that the utopian ideas of the Progressive era tide have not lived up to their promise. Their costs, measured in terms of a loss of personal freedom and individual initiative, burdensome taxes, and a crushing national debt are outweighing their benefits.

The shift in the intellectual tide is producing a gradual convergence within the body politic for policy change. There is widespread public skepticism that entitlements are delivering on their promises. There is even more skepticism among the public at large that the country can afford to deliver on future promises. As yet, this convergence has not reached elected representatives. Hence, gridlock in Congress prevails. But as entitlement costs continue to grow and their harmful consequences become more apparent, public pressure will grow and will ultimately force government to change policies.

Notes on Major Data Sources

Federal Budget and Entitlement Data

All aggregate federal expenditure, revenue, and public debt data, except veterans' pension expenditures from 1791 to 1940, are taken from one of two sources. Total federal government expenditures and receipts from 1791 to 1899 are from the U.S. Treasury Department, *Annual Report of the Secretary of the Treasury*, Statistical Appendix (Washington, D.C.: U.S. Government Printing Office), Table 2. Public debt numbers from 1791 to 1939 are also taken from this document, Table 6. Total federal revenue and expenditure data from 1900 to the present are from the U.S. Budget for Fiscal Year 2017, Historical Tables, Table 1.1. Debt numbers from 1940 to 2015 are from this document, Table 7.1.

The U.S. Budget for Fiscal Year 2017, Historical Tables, Table 13.1 provides historically consistent expenditures and end-of-year balances for the Social Security Retirement and Disability funds and the Medicare trust funds. Social Security Trustee Reports contain estimates of projected outlays, revenues, and trust fund balances just prior to the enactment of legislation. Social Security Actuary Reports published following the enactment of Social Security legislation provide projections of outlays, revenues, and trust fund balances following the enactment of legislation. Annual expenditures on all other entitlement programs are taken from annual issues of the U.S. Federal Budget. Budgets back to 1996 are available at https://www.gpo.gov/fdsys/browse/collection-GPO.action?collectionCode=BUDGET. Budgets for these and prior years are available at https://fraser.stlouisfed.org.

Veterans Pension Data from 1791 to 1940

The Report of the Commissioner of Pensions for 1873, House Exec. Doc. 1601, 43rd Congress, 1st Session contains total annual pension expenditures from 1791 to 1873 (334–336). The report also contains the number of recipients of veterans' pensions for intermittent years from 1791 to 1853 and continuously for all years from 1853 to 1873 (pp. 334–336). The Report of the Commissioner of Pensions for 1917, House Doc. 915 part 3, 65th Congress, 1st Session contains total annual pensions from 1866 to 1917 (pp. 319–320). The two reports give different estimates of pension expenditures from 1866 to 1873. I have used the data contained in the 1917 Report. The Annual Report of the Administrator of Veterans Affairs, 1932, House Doc. 415, 72nd Congress, 2nd Session (Table 30, p. 94) provides data on the annual number of pensioners by war from 1866 to 1832. The data include the annual number of pension recipients of the Revolutionary War and the War of 1812 for all years, Mexican American from 1887 to 1932, Indian Wars from 1893 to 1932, and the War with Spain from 1899 to 1932. Civil War pension recipients are combined with recipients from other wars and with "unclassified" pension recipients, 1866 to 1886. The Annual Report of the Administrator of Veterans Affairs, 1940, House Doc. 11, 77nd Congress, 1st Session contains the annual number of pension recipients and expenditures on each by war from 1910 to 1940. I have used the number of pension recipients and expenditures in the 1940 report for these latter years.

Annual Pension Office reports distinguish expenditures for Civil War pensions from those paid to veterans of other wars starting only in 1910. The use of total pension expenditures as a proxy for Civil War pension expenditures in prior years is not likely to distort the picture presented in the text. In 1910, Civil War veterans and their survivors still accounted for 94 percent of all pension payments. Twenty-two years earlier, when Pension Office Annual

Reports first provide the number of pension recipients by war, 93 percent of all pension recipients were Civil War veterans and their survivors. During the intervening years, Civil War pension recipients remained above 93 percent.

The Annual Report of the Administrator of Veterans Affairs, 1932, House Doc. 415, 72nd Congress, 2nd Session provides the annual number of Revolutionary War and War of 1812 pension recipients from 1866 to 1932 and the number of Mexican-American War pension recipients from 1885 to 1932 (p. 94). Prior to 1886, Mexican-American and Civil War pensioners are combined, along with pensioners who are unclassified by war. The Annual Report of the Administrator of Veterans Affairs, 1940, House Doc. 11, 77nd Congress, 1st Session contains the number of veterans and survivors receiving pensions, and the expenditures on each, by war, from 1910 to 1940.

Entitlement Recipients

Data on the number of entitlement recipients are administrative data reported by federal agencies that administer these programs. Useful sources for data from the 1940s to the 1990s are annual issues of the Social Security Bulletin, Annual Statistical Appendix. Annual issues of the House Committee on Ways and Means' *Green Book*, particularly issues published in the 1980s and 1990s, is a valuable source of data on caseloads for smaller entitlement programs, such as trade adjustment assistance and black lung benefits. It also provides useful data on various attributes of individual entitlement programs, including the size and characteristics of program recipients. Information on the number of program beneficiaries in more recent years is reported on each administering agency's website.

Distribution of Entitlement Benefits

The source for data presented in Chapters 1, 16, 17, and 19 on the aggregate distribution of entitlement benefits and the number and distribution of households that receive benefits from at least one entitlement program is the *Current Population Survey*. A detailed description and user file for the March 2016 *Current Population Survey* can be found at http://www.nber.org/data/current-population-survey-data. The entitlement programs included in the analysis are Social Security retirement and disability, railroad retirement, federal retirement, black lung, unemployment insurance, veterans' compensation and pensions, Temporary Assistance to Needy Families, the earned income and child care (EITC) tax credits (refundable credits only), Medicare, Medicaid, food stamps, child nutrition programs, and SSI. The data do not include estimates of subsidies of health insurance premiums and copayments under the Affordable Care Act. Program participation data are obtained directly from the survey for these entitlement programs, except the earned income tax credit. The amount of assistance payments for entitlement programs, except the EITC, Medicare, and Medicaid, is obtained directly from the Current Population Survey (CPS).

The number of recipients of refundable EITC tax credits and the amount received by each are imputed to CPS households using the National Bureau of Economic Research's TAXIM model (see http://users.nber.org/~taxsim/ and Feenberg and Coutts, 1993). Only households that receive the refundable portion of the EITC are recorded as program participants.

The value of Medicare and Medicaid is imputed to persons identified in the survey as enrolled or receiving assistance from either program. Prior to 2015, the CPS included imputed insurance values for both programs. The Census Bureau assigned Medicare valuations for all recipients on the basis of the respondent's state of residency and whether the recipient qualified for the program because of age or disability status. Medicaid valuations varied by state, age (under 21, 21–64, and over 65), disability status, and whether the respondent was also enrolled in Medicare. Beginning with the March 2015 CPS, the Census Bureau ceased imputing these values. The calculations in the text for 2014 and 2015 use the valuations of the 2014 survey updated for medical inflation. That is, recipients were grouped by factors already listed (e.g., state, age, and disability) and then assigned the inflation-adjusted 2014 valuation of their particular group (using the average growth rate in the Medical CPI-U for each calendar year).

In rare cases, Medicaid valuations were unavailable for certain groups in certain states. Earlier survey years (going as far back as 2011) were used to fill most of these voids. In very rare cases (3 out of more than 100,000), no valuation was available for any recent survey year. In these cases, respondents were assigned a valuation equal to the average cost for respondents in the particular group from all other states multiplied by the average Medicaid cost in the particular state divided by the average Medicaid cost across all states. This procedure was only necessary for three respondents.

Marginal Tax Rates

Marginal tax rates reported in Chapter 19 are imputed to CPS households by use of TAXIM (http://users.nber.org/~taxsim/). Tax rates for federal payroll taxes, personal income taxes, the EITC, the child tax credit, and state income taxes used to estimate marginal income tax rates are included in the analysis. Food stamp recipients are obtained by applying the National Bureau of Economic Research's TAXSIM9 to the 2015 Current Population Survey. Information on the TAXSIM model is provided by Feenberg and Coutts (1993). Respondents with reported family incomes below the annual amount for the standard deduction receive a SNAP effective tax rate of 0 percent (details concerning the standard deduction are available here: https://www.fns.usda.gov/snap/eligibility). TANF recipients are assumed to face a 50 percent marginal tax rate for TANF benefits. In reality, marginal tax rates for TANF programs vary by state, family composition, and length of time on assistance. State welfare program specifications can be found at https://www.acf.hhs.gov/sites/default/files/opre/welfare_rules_databook_final_v2.pdf.

Key Websites for Economic, Congressional, and Presidential Materials

Proquest Congressional (www.congressional.proquest.com) is an excellent source for congressional and executive branch documents, including Congressional Research Service papers. I have also relied heavily on

Proquest's extensive newspaper archive for all newspaper articles and editorials: http://www.proquest.com/products-services/pq-hist-news.html.

I used the American Presidency Project at the University of California at Santa Barbara as my principal source for presidential messages and party platforms. The project's website (http://www.presidency.ucsb.edu/ws/index.php) provides easy access to an extraordinarily comprehensive set of public papers of the presidents, including presidential addresses, messages to Congress, and proclamations. The website also contains party platform documents and transcripts of presidential press conferences.

Economic data, including gross domestic product, consumer prices, unemployment and employment, production and business activity published by the Bureau of Economic Analysis, labor market and price-level data published by the Bureau of Labor Statistics, Industrial Production are from the St. Louis Federal Reserve (https://fred.stlouisfed.org/categories).

Notes

Chapter 1

1. President Ronald Reagan, Address to the Nation on the Program for Economic Recovery, September 24, 1981.

2. This central idea is the outgrowth of informal discussions more than thirty years ago with David A. Stockman, then the director of the U.S. Office of Management and Budget. Mr. Stockman does not recall discussions about the notion of "worthy claimants," but I do. A similar description of the process by which entitlements are liberalized is provided by Murray (1984).

3. Dewey (1931), 431.

4. Federal government documents provide several similar but not identical definitions of entitlements. The definition provided in the text is from Executive Office of the President, Office of Management and Budget, "Circular A-11, Preparation, Submission, and Execution of the Budget," July 2010, sec. 20, 5. Federal Budget for FY2016, "Analytical Perspectives, Budget Concepts, 108, defines an entitlement as "a program in which the Federal Government is legally obligated to make payments or provide services to any person who, or State or local government that, meets the legal criteria for eligibility."

5. The programs covered in this work account for 94 percent of all federal spending classified as mandatory program spending during the past twenty years.

Chapter 2

This chapter draws heavily on the seminal work of Glasson (1918). The discussion of the 1818 law draws on Resch (1999).

1. Annals of Cong., vol. 31, January 29, 1818, 158.

2. *U.S. Statutes at Large*, vol. 1, September 29, 1789, 95. See Glasson (1918) for a complete discussion of the origins of Revolutionary War pensions.

3. *U.S. Statutes at Large*, vol. 2, April 10, 1806, 376. Prior to the 1806 law, Congress had passed several less important laws (see Glasson, 1918, 58–62).

4. Federal budget spending and revenue numbers are taken from U.S. Treasury (1980), Table 2.

5. Annals of Cong., vol. 15, December 18, 1805, 296.

6. Ibid.

7. Receipts and Expenditures—1789 to 1829, H. Doc. No. 90, 21st Cong., 1st Sess., 1830. Appropriations exclude those for debt service.

8. *Report of the Commissioner of Pensions for 1873*, 334–336, and U.S. Treasury (1980), Table 2.

9. David and Solar (1977), 16.

10. *U.S. Statutes at Large*, vol. 3, April 24, 1816, 296–297.

11. Annals of Cong., vol. 3, December 2, 1817, 19.

12. *U.S. Statutes at Large*, vol. 3, March 18, 1818, 410.

13. H. Rep. No. 17, 16th Cong., 1st Sess., December 28, 1819 (reported in Glasson, 1918, 68).

14. Reported in Resch (1999), 104; Annals of Cong., vol. 31, December 19, 1817, 492.

15. Annals of Cong., vol. 31, January 29, 1818, 156.

16. Resch (1999), 113.

17. H. Rep. No. 17 (reported in Glasson, 1918, 68).

18. Annals of Cong., vol. 31, December 24, 1817, 510.

19. Ibid., February 12, 1818, 491.

20. The amendment to include members of the militia was defeated on the House floor. Annals of Cong., vol. 31, March 5, 1818, 1110–1111. The new law also did not apply to veterans of the War of 1812. Since the war had ended only four years earlier, the veterans of that war were in a far better position than the Revolutionary War veterans to document that the disabilities were connected to wartime service. Eligibility for the War of 1812 veterans continued to require the soldier to have been injured in battle during the war.

21. *Report of the Commissioner of Pensions for 1873*, 334–336, and U.S. Treasury (1980), Table 2.

22. In 1820, Revolutionary War pensions totaled $2.8 million. From 1791 to 1817, pension outlays totaled $2.6 million. *Report of the Commissioner of Pensions for 1873*, 334–336.

23. The simultaneous occurrence of government borrowing and widespread allegations of fraud led many in the public to causally connect the two. One of the era's major newspapers, the *National Intelligencer*, for example, attributed the budget deficit to the cost of the 1818 law. It editorialized that

the pension law would not have passed "could the extent and inequality of its operation have been foreseen" (Glasson, 1918, 71). The secretary of war and the official charged with administering the pension program, John C. Calhoun, also laid the blame on the pension law. Calhoun remarked to John Quincy Adams, "The present embarrassments in the Administration all originated in two measures of the first session of Congress under it—the repeal of the internal taxes, and the profuse Pension Act."

24. Resch (1999), 148.

25. Statement of Representative Marvin, Register of Debates, House of Representatives, 20th Cong., 2nd Sess., 373, 1829.

26. *American State Papers*, Claims, vol. 1, February 10, 1823, 885.

27. *U.S. Statutes at Large*, vol. 3, March 1, 1823, 782.

28. Claims, *American State Papers*, vol. 1, December 30, 1819, 677–678.

29. Ibid., March 12, 1818, 591.

30. House of Representatives, *Register of Debates*, 20th Cong., 1st Sess., 2659, May 12, 1828.

31. There were 235 surviving Revolutionary War officers eligible for the 1828 act (ibid.). The law also provided full pay-for-life plus two years back pay to non-commissioned officers and soldiers who had enlisted, served to the war's end, and were not already receiving pensions under the provisions of the 1818 law. This provision added another 615 soldiers to the pension rolls. Glasson's estimate (1918, 51) that at the end of 1828, 850 Revolutionary War veterans had been granted full-pay pensions by the law is apparently the sum of the two provisions.

32. *U.S. Statutes at Large*, vol. 4, June 4, 1832, 529.

33. House of Representatives, *Register of Debates*, 21st Cong., 2nd Sess., February 16, 1831, 727–728.

34. Ibid., 22nd Cong., 1st Sess., February 29, 1832, 1920.

35. Ibid., February 29, 1832, 1935.

36. Ibid., March 29, 1832, 2294.

37. Ibid., February 29, 1832, 1924.

38. Ibid., April 12, 1832, 2490.

39. Ibid., 21st Cong., 2nd Sess., February 16, 1831, 744.

40 Ibid., April 4, 1832, 2393.

41. Reported in Glasson (1918), 85, and taken from H. Doc. No. 33, 22nd Cong., 2nd Sess., 1832–1833.

42. Ibid.

43. Senate Doc. No. 33, 22nd Cong., 1st Sess., 1831–1832. Glasson (1918), 80. Representative Ellsworth provided an estimate of 9,762 veterans. *Register of Debates*, 22nd Cong., 1st Sess., March 28, 1832.

44. *Report of the Commissioner of Pensions* (1873), 334–336; U.S. Treasury (1980), Table 2.

45. *U.S. Statutes at Large*, vol. 9, May 13, 1846, 9.

46. *Report of the Commissioner of Pensions*, 334–336; U.S. Treasury Department (1980), Table 2.

Chapter 3

1. Annals of Cong., vol. 41, December 23, 1823, 880.

2. This chapter draws heavily on the excellent work on the pension fund's history by Clark, Craig, and Wilson (2003).

3. Paullin (1906); *U.S. Statutes at Large*, vol. 1, March 2, 1789, 709, and April 23, 1800, 45.

4. Clark, Craig, and Wilson (2003), 68 (trust fund balances) 55 (outlays).

5. Naval Affairs, *American State Papers*, no. 125, January 24, 1815. Note that the fund balance and outlays differ slightly from those reported in Clark, Craig, and Wilson (2003).

6. *U.S. Statutes at Large*, vol. 3, March 4, 1814, 103.

7. Ibid., March 3, 1817, 369, 373.

8. Ibid., vol. 4, January 22, 1824, 4.

9. The laws are as follows, all from *U.S. Statutes at Large*: 1818, vol. 3, April 16, 1818, 427–428; 1819, vol. 3, March 3, 1819, 502; 1824, vol. 4, January 22, 1824, 4; 1828, vol. 4, May 23, 1828, 288; 1832, vol. 4, June 28, 1832, 550; 1834, vol. 4, June 30, 1834, 714–715; 1837, vol. 5, March 3, 1837, 187.

10. See Clark, Craig, and Wilson's (2003) detailed summary of the pension fund's finances, 68–69.

11. Navy fund records indicate that the Bank of Columbia paid 10 percent dividends in 1814, 1815, and 1818. The Union Bank and the Bank of Washington paid 12 percent dividends in 1814, 1815, 1817, and 1819. It is unclear as to whether the banks paid dividends in other years. Clark et al. (2003) note the fund's poor record keeping.

12. Clark et al. (2003), 81, 106, and Walsh (1940), 73–74, 85–86.

13. Starting in 1823, the bank maintained only a skeleton staff to collect accounts receivable (Walsh, 1940, 90). Naval Affairs, H. Doc. No. 529, *American State Papers*, January 17, 1834, 490.

14. Clark et al. (2003), 96. Congress also restricted the fund's ability to purchase private securities to only those issued by the Second Bank of the United States.

15. Naval Affairs, *American State Papers*, 490.

16. H.R. Doc. 531, 28th Cong., 1st Sess., June 7, 1844.

17. H. R. Doc. 236, 27th Cong., 2nd Sess., May 26, 1842.

18. Adams (1840), 1.

19. *U.S. Statutes at Large*, vol. 13, July 1, 1884, 414.

20. Cong. Globe., 40th Cong., 2nd Sess., February 22, 1868, 1335.

21. Ibid.

22. Ibid., 1721.

23. *U.S. Statutes at Large*, vol. 15, July 23, 1868, 170.

Chapter 4

This chapter draws liberally on a century of research on Civil War pensions; in particular Oliver (1917) and Glasson (1918), who separately traced the legislative history of veterans' pensions through the Civil War; Dearing (1952) and W. Davies (1955), who documented the activities of the Grand Army of the Republic; Skocpol (1992), who established the central role of Civil War pensions in the development of the modern U.S. welfare state; Costa (1998), who documented the role of Civil War pensions in the evolution of the U.S. retirement system; and Holcombe (1999), who documented the key role Civil War pensions played in setting precedents for the subsequent growth of federal spending.

1. Ransdell (1916), 50.

2. Pension expenditures are from *Report of the Commissioner of Pensions, 1917*, 319–320. Total pension expenditures are displayed instead of Civil War pension expenditures because the latter are not available from Pension Office and Veterans Administration Annual Reports until 1910. The use of total pension expenditures should not appreciably distort the pattern of Civil War expenditures. The number of Revolutionary War and Indian War pensioners is always less than 1 percent of the total; the number of War of 1812 pensioners is generally around 10 percent of total pensioners at its peak percentage during the 1870s; the number of Mexican-American War pensioners is around 3 percent of the total during its peak years in 1890s; and the number of Spanish-American War pensioners is also around 3 percent of the total during the first decade of the twenty-first century. The number of pensioners reported in the text also overstates the number of Civil War pensioners for years prior to 1888. But the overstatement is not likely to be quantitatively important. Pension Office and Veterans Administration Annual Reports distinguish pensioners from the Revolutionary War, the Indian Wars, the War of 1812, and the Spanish-American War from Civil War pensioners. But the reports do not distinguish Mexican-American War pensioners from Civil War pensioners prior to 1887. The number of Mexican-American War pensioners in 1887, the first year the number is separately reported, is small relative to the number of Civil War pensioners. That year, only 8,398 persons received Mexican-American War pensions compared to 384,655 Civil War pensioners. See Veterans Administration, *Annual Report* (1932) 94. Note that in all years, Civil War pensioners are combined with a presumably small number of "unclassified" pensioners.

3. Costa (1998), 197.

4. The number of Civil War pension recipients is from Veterans Administration, *Annual Report* (1932), 94. The number of Civil War veterans and population of white males are from the 1890 U.S. Census of Population and Housing, Table 123. Federal program expenditures exclude interest payments on the publicly held debt and are from U.S. Treasury Department (1980), Table 2. Social Security, Medicare and total federal expenditures are taken from the U.S. Budget for Fiscal Year 2017.

5. See "Notes on Major Data Sources" for federal budget and veterans' expenditures and GNP. Veterans' pension expenditures peaked as a percent of GDP in 1893 and 1894, two years when a severe economic recession reduced GDP.

6. A draft law would not be enacted until 1862.

7. An Act to Grant Pensions, 37th Cong., 2nd Sess., chap. 166, July 14, 1962.

8. Glasson (1918), 128.

9. *Report of the Commissioner of Pensions* (1873), Table I. The number includes pensioners from prior wars; see Notes on Major Data Sources.

10. Oliver (1917), 17–28

11. *Report of the Commissioner of Pensions* (1873), Table I.

12. Glasson (1918), 148.

13. *Report of the Commissioner of Pensions* (1873), Table I.

14. *U.S. Statutes at Large*, vol. 15, chap. 264, July 27, 1868, 235.

15. Indiana senator Daniel Voorhees made the case for extending the application period by asking whether it was fair and just for a disabled veteran who, because of "ignorance, obscurity, poverty, or any other cause," to be denied a pension. Cong. Rec., vol. 8, part 1, January 16, 1879, 488.

16. Oliver (1917), 53.

17. Cong. Rec., vol. 8, part 1, December 2, 1878. For this calculation, the Southern states include the states of the Confederacy and the border states of Kentucky, Tennessee, and Missouri.

18. The Senate followed suit with an even more lopsided vote, 44–4 with 26 abstentions. All votes against came from Southern and border state Democrats. Cong. Rec., vol. 8, part 1, January 16, 1879.

19. The only significant dispute during the date was over whether the law provided benefits retroactive to the date of discharge or to the date of the disability. See ibid., 484–494.

20. The $3,900 assumes that the soldier was disabled at the beginning of 1862 and filed for arrears payments in June 1879. This amount was updated by the growth in consumer prices using the series constructed by David and Solar (1977) up to 1913 and the official Consumer Price Index from that year to 2013. The average annual manufacturing wage in 1880 is from the U.S. Census of Population for 1880, vol. 2, 5, Table 1 multiplied by fifty weeks.

21. Glasson (1918), 76.

22. Williams and Smith (1914), 2:338.

23. Oliver (1917), 79.

24. Ibid., 72.

25. Glasson (1918), 76.

26. For Senator Ingals's estimate, see Cong. Rec., vol. 8, part 1, January 16, 1879, 484. The Hayes administration estimate is reported in Oliver (1917), 58.

27. President Arthur, First Annual Message, December 1881.

28. Had annual pension outlays remained at their 1878 level during the 1880s, pension outlays would have been $383 billion below their actual level during the 1880s.

29. Cong. Globe, 41st Cong., 2nd Sess., July 3, 1870, 5533.

30. Glasson (1918), 160–165.

31. The story is told in Oliver (1917), 100–101.

32. Davies (1955), 139.

33. See Dearing (1952) and Davies (1955) for an extensive documentation of the GAR's political activities.

34. Oliver (1917), 93.

35. Party platforms can be found at http://www.presidency.ucsb.edu/platforms.php.

36. Oliver (1917), 95; Dearing (1952), 269–270

37. Nevins (1933), 326.

38. Ibid., 326–227.

39. Richardson (1910), 7:4945.

40. Keller (1977), 311.

41. See Nevins (1933), 327, for a description of the process.

42. Richardson (1910), 50:200.

43. Glasson (1918), 278.

44. The specifics of the case are as follows. In 1880, the Pension Office had rejected Mrs. Elisha Griswold's claim alleging that her husband had died from wounds while serving in the military in 1866. The Pension Office investigation showed that at the time of his death, Mr. Griswold was in fact serving time in a San Antonio, Texas, prison. He died when he fell from a swing that he and a few of his fellow inmates had erected. Congress was well aware of these facts, noting in the bill's committee report that soldier Griswold had been killed "while engaged in recreation." It nevertheless approved the bill on the grounds that "such recreation is a necessary part of a soldier's life." Richardson (1910), 5256.

45. The case involved Ann Kinney, the widow of a soldier who had served for eight months during the Civil War and, according to her claim, had recently died from a gunshot wound. But according to the local marshal's sworn testimony, the soldier had been arrested on the day of his death for being drunk and died an hour later in jail. Richardson (1910), 5065.

46. Bensel (1984).

47. Skocpol (1952), 64.

48. Dearing (1952), 331.

49. Ibid., 425.

50. See Skocpol (1992), 127, and Dearing (1952). Nevins (1933), however, downplays the importance of the "soldiers' vote" and instead attributes Cleveland's defeat primarily to the tariff issue.

51. Dearing (1952), 389.

52. Ibid., 389.

53. McMurry (1922), 31.

54. Dearing (1952), 390.

55. Ibid., 391.

56. Election results and population are from Leip (2012) and 1890 Federal Population Census, respectively. Veterans data are from Special Schedules of the Eleventh Census (1890) Enumerating Union Veterans and Widows of Union Veterans of the Civil War.

57. Ransdell (1916), 50.

58. In a Chicago speech, Tanner, who had served on the GAR Pension Committee and had worked as a claims agent, announced, "I tell you frankly that I am for 'the old flag and an appropriation' for every old comrade who needs it" (reported in McMurry, 1926).

59. McMurry (1926), 352. The reviews were conducted in violation of Interior Department policy. The re-rated pensioners included Pension Bureau employees.

60. *New York Times*, August 25, 1889, reported in McMurry (1926).

61. McMurry (1926), 360–361.

62. Dewey (1931), 428.

63. President Benjamin Harrison, First Annual Message, December 3, 1889.

64. *U.S. Statutes at Large*, vol. 26, June 27, 1890, 182–183.

65. Ibid.

66. The number of pensioners is from Veterans Administration, *Annual Report* (1932), 94. Expenditures on Civil War pensions are not separately available from Pension Office annual reports prior to 1910. The numbers reported in the text are total pension expenditures, including those for veterans of prior wars, and are taken from *Report of the Pension Office* (1917), 319–320. The use of total pension expenditures is not likely to distort the impact of the 1890 law since 93 percent and 97 percent of all pensioners were Civil War pensioners in, respectively, 1889 and 1893.

67. U.S. Office of Management and Budget, Historical Tables (2017), Tables 13.1 and 1.1.

68. H. Rep. No. 1160, 51st Cong., 1st Sess. (1890), 13.

69. *Tribune Almanac and Political Register for 1895,* 29.

70. *New York Herald,* June 14, 1862, reported in Dearing (1952), 428.

71. The platform merely stated, "We pledge anew to the veterans of the soldiers of the Republic a watchful care and a just recognition of their claims upon a grateful people." Party Platforms, http://www.presidency.ucsb.edu/platforms.php.

72. Voters returned Cleveland to office by the widest electoral margin since President Lincoln's reelection in 1864. The Populist and Temperance parties, fueled by the growing importance of the silver and temperance issues, played a central role in Cleveland's win. The two third parties received 17 percent of the popular vote nation-wide and one-third of the vote in the states from Kansas to the west.

73. Dearing (1952), 430–433. It appears that Democrats had also learned to use pensions for electoral purposes. Dearing reports, for example, that the party located its state headquarters in rooms directly below the Pension Bureau Office in Indiana.

74. *Report of the Commissioner of Pensions* (1894), 7.

75. Dearing (1952), 436.

76. Ibid., 452–453.

77. Ibid., 437.

78. Party platforms at http://www.presidency.ucsb.edu/platforms.php.

79. *Chicago Tribune,* June 15, 1896. reported in Dearing (1952), 455.

80. *Report of the Commissioner of Pensions* (1899), 56th Cong., 1st Sess., 46.

81. Ibid., 1900, H. Doc. 5/6, 39. The Act of May 9, 1900, took another step by raising the allowable amount of nonwage income a widow could receive and still qualify for pension to $250.

82. Ibid., 1906, H. Doc 5/3, 547.

83. *U.S. Statutes at Large,* vol. 34, chap. 1862, April 24, 1906, 133.

84. Ibid., February 6, 1907, 879.

85. Ibid., 37, chap. 123, May 11, 1912 at 112. The law also raised benefits for Mexican-American War veterans.

86. Glasson (1918), 256.

87. See Mayer (1968), Brady (1973), and Keller (1977).

88. See Sanders's (1980) study of Ohio voters and Cogan's (2015) study of national elections.

89. The evidence is reviewed in more detail in Cogan (2015).

90. *Report of the Commissioner of Pensions* (1921), Exhibit 18, 26; Act of May 1, 1920, 66th Cong., 2nd Sess., chap. 165.

91. Consumer prices rose by 38 percent between 1916 and 1918 and by another 35 percent between 1918 and 1920. Federal Reserve Bank of St. Louis, Consumer Price Index, Series, Consumer Price Index, All Urban Consumers, Not Seasonally Adjusted.

92. Pub. L. 71-323, June 9, 1930.

93. Pub. L. 85-425, May 23, 1958.

94. Ransdell (1916), 43–45.

95. The *Chicago Tribune* article appeared on April 29, 1916. Congressman Ransdell's quotes are from Ransdell (1916), 52.

96. For data prior to 1940, see Veterans Administration, *Annual Report* (1932), 94–95. Data for 1940 are from ibid., 64.

97. Veterans Administration, *Annual Report* (1940), 64, and Historical Tables, Table 1.1.

Chapter 5

1. Gebhart (1918), 13.

2. Pub. L. 65-90, October 6, 1917.

3. Dillingham (1952), 27.

4. Pencak (1989), 177.

5. Gebhart (1918), 13.

6. Dillingham (1952), 30.

7. President's Commission on Veterans' Pensions, "Historical Development of Veterans' Benefit in the U.S. Staff Report No. 1," House Committee Print, No. 244, 94th Cong., 2nd Sess., 1956, 37.

8. U.S. Federal Budget for 2017, Historical Tables, Table 1.1.

9. Committee on World War Veterans' Legislation, *Hearings on World War Veterans' Legislation,* 71st Cong., 2nd Sess., February 4, 1930, 3.

10. President Herbert Hoover, Veto of the World War I Pensions Bill, June 26, 1930.

11. The income threshold was set at the income level that generated a federal income tax liability. At the time, about 90 percent of all families fell below this threshold. Internal Revenue Service, Statistics of Income (1930), reported 2,036,345 taxable returns on p. 4. The population that year was 29,904,653 (*Statistical Abstract for 1930*).

12. Veterans Administration, *Annual Report for Fiscal Year Ending June 20, 1931*, 5.

13. Ibid., 37.

14. Dillingham (1952), 50.

15. Veterans Administration, *Annual Report for Fiscal Year Ending June 20, 1932*, Table 86.

16. Pencak (1989), 74.

17. S. Rep. No. 403, Part 2, 68th Cong., 1st Sess., 2.

18. The average manufacturing wage is from "Hourly Money Earnings in Payroll Manufacturing Industries, 1890–1926, NBER, Macrohistory, vol. VIII. Income and Employment. The growth in wages is from the U.S. Index of

Composite Wages, 01/1910–12/1920. The increase in prices is from U.S. Index of General Price Level, 01/1860–11/1939.

19. Pencak (1989), 117.

20. H. R. Report No. 313, 66th Cong., 1st Sess.

21. Surpluses are from Federal Budget for 2017, Historical Tables, Table 1.1. Debt reduction is from *Annual Report of the Secretary of the Treasury*, 1980, Statistical Appendix, Table 19.

22. S. Rep. No. 403, 68th Cong., 1st Sess., 6, 7.

23. Pub. L. 68-120, May 19, 1924, sec. 505, 506.

24. See H. R. Doc. No. 313, 68th Cong., 1st Sess., 7, for President Calvin Coolidge's veto message.

25. Ibid.

26. Ibid.

27. Veterans Administration, *Annual Report for 1932*, 37.

28. Committee on Ways and Means, H. Rep. No. 2670, 71st Cong., 3rd Sess., 3.

29. Dickson and Allen (2004), 36.

30. Ibid., 52.

31. President Herbert Hoover, Statement on Bonus Legislation for World War Veterans, March 29, 1932.

32. I have drawn heavily on Dickson and Allen (2004) for a description of the Bonus March. The quotes are from Waters (1969), 8–9.

33. Dickson and Allen (2004), 136

34. The *New York Times* headline on July 31, 1932, read: "Reds Accept Blame for Bonus Rioting; Communist Party Here Declares It Also Plans New March on Capital Next December."

Chapter 6

1. The vetoes were of the following bills: H.R. 3896, H. R. 8729, H. R. 6898, H. R. 9870, S4026, and S. 3257. The overrides were of the last three of these bills.

2. Browder and Smith (1986), 67.

3. Ibid.

4. President's Message on Reduction of Expenditures, H. R. Doc. No. 2, 73rd Cong., 1st Sess.

5. The president's actions are described in Freidel (1973). The quote is from 245.

6. The bill maintained benefits for widows of veterans of the Spanish-American War who had service-connected disabilities.

7. Pub. L. 73-2, March 20, 1933, sec. 1. The statutory language reads, "That subject to such requirements and limitations as shall be contained in

regulations to be issued by the President, and within the limits of appropriations made by Cong., the following classes of persons *may* be paid a pension" (italics added).

8. Ibid., sec. 1-4, 18.

9. Ibid., sec. 5.

10. Ibid., sec. 19.

11. The June 6 regulations restored eligibility to nonservice-connected Spanish-American War veterans age 62 and older and partially restored benefits for totally and permanently disabled veterans. Ortiz (2006).

12. Pub. L. 73-78, June 16, 1933. The law also permitted veterans to continue to receive pensions at a 75 percent rate until final determination of their appeals or October 31, 1933, whichever came sooner.

13. Pub. L. 73-141, March 28, 1934, sec. 28–33. The generous treatment of Spanish-American, Boxer Rebellion, and Philippine Insurrection veterans stems from the fact that under the Act of June 5, 1920, higher pensions could be received under laws granting pensions for service than under laws granting benefits for disabilities related to wartime. As a result, proof that a veteran's disabilities were due to wartime service was not necessary and, hence, not collected by the Veterans Administration at the time of the veteran's initial application. The absence of records and the lapse of time since these wars led Congress to restore their eligibility. Veterans Administration, *Annual Report for FY1934*, 20. The law also restored benefit levels of totally blind World War I veterans.

14. See Ortiz (2006) for a comprehensive review of the Economy Act. The quote is from 436.

15. Ibid., 436.

16. Veterans Affairs, *Annual Report for FY1934*, 63–65. These reductions reversed the trend of rising pension outlays during the years leading up to the 1933 Economy Act.

17. This number includes 42,686 Spanish-American War veterans who were restored to the rolls as a result of Pub. L. 73-141, March 28, 1934, sec. 28–33; 21,955 World War I nonservice-connected disability veterans who were restored as a result of being reclassified by review boards as having disabilities that were service-connected cases. Veterans Affairs, *Annual Report for FY1934*, 20–22; Ortiz (2006), citing Sargent (1981), reports an estimate of 501,777.

18. Veterans Affairs, *Annual Report for FY1940*, 63–65.

19. In 1939, Congress did restore benefits to veterans who had contracted a venereal disease during the war and had been removed from the rolls in 1933 because their disease had resulted from "moral misconduct." Significantly, the law affected only those who had been on the rolls in March 1933. No claimants after that point in time were granted eligibility. Also, the law

did not provide retroactive benefits to those who had been removed from the rolls in 1933.

20. Veterans Affairs, *Annual Report for FY1940*, 63–65.

21. H. R. Doc. No. 197, 74th Cong., 1st Sess., 8.

22. Ibid.

23. Ibid., 5-6.

24. Ernest Hemingway, who was on the scene, wrote, "The veterans in those camps were practically murdered. The Florida East Coast [Railroad] had a train ready for nearly twenty four hours to take them off the Keys. The people in charge are said to have wired Washington for orders. Washington wired the Miami Weather Bureau which is said to have replied there was no danger and it would be a useless expense." Myers (1985), 288.

Chapter 7

1. President Franklin Roosevelt, Statement on Signing the Social Security Act, August 14, 1935.

2. President James Madison, Veto Message of March 3, 1817. The Court has retained a role as guardian of the boundary line in cases involving federal requirements on states as conditions for the receipt of federal funds. It has allowed the federal government to attach conditions to the receipt of federal funds by state and local governments to states. See Dole v. South Dakota, 483 U.S. 203 (1987). But the conditions are permissible only up to a point where the conditions no longer serve as "inducements" and instead become coercive. See National Federation of Independent Business v. Sebellius, 567 U.S. 1 (2012).

3. Brown (1940), 1–9.

4. Trattner (1989), 92.

5. Two highly influential state government reports issued in the 1820s, the Quincy Report in Massachusetts in 1821 and the Yates Report in New York in 1824, were important to this change. Both reports criticized outdoor relief as costly and harmful to the persons it was designed to help. Trattner (1989), 53. See Lubove (1968).

6. Trattner (1989), 86.

7. Cong. Globe, 33rd Cong., 1st Sess., May 3, 1854, 1061–1063.

8. Douglass (1881), 385.

9. For rations, see Keller (1977), 209. For the number of students, see H. R. Exec. Doc. No. 1446, 41st Cong., 3rd Sess., 1870, 322. For persons receiving medical care, see Foner (1988), 151. For a more detailed history of the Freedman's Bureau, see Bentley (1955) and Gray (1994).

10. Trattner (1989), 104.

11. Report of the White House Conference on the Care of Dependent Children, 1909 (cited in Bell, 1965, 4).

12. Ibid. (cited in Bell, 3).

13. Trattner (1989), 194.

14. Douglas (1939), 187.

15. Lubove (1968), 101.

16. Ibid., 102.

17. New York State Commission on Relief for Widowed Mothers, Report, March 27, 1914, 21.

18. Bell (1965), 8–9. Bell reports that an additional eight states had statutes that were broad enough to include children of unmarried women.

19. Ibid., 7–8.

20. Rubinow (1916), 404.

21. See Lubove (1968), 135–144, for a discussion of the early development of state old-age assistance programs.

22. Peters and Whoolley, www.presidency.ucsb.edu, Democratic Party Platform of 1932.

23. https://www.ssa.gov/history/townsendproblems.

24. The act also created smaller nonentitlement federal matching programs for state programs for maternal and child health services and services for crippled children, vocational rehabilitation, child welfare, and public health.

25. President Franklin Roosevelt, Message to Congress on the Objectives and Accomplishments of the Administration, June 8, 1934.

26. Ibid.

27. The payroll tax rate was initially set at 1 percentage point each on employers and employees on the first $3,000 of earnings received by the worker.

28. Mr. Justice Black, dissenting remarks in Flemming v. Nestor, 363 U.S. 603 (1960).

29. Perkins (1946), 281.

30. President Franklin Roosevelt, Message to Congress on Social Security, January 17, 1935.

31. Perkins (1946), 268.

32. S. Rep. No. 628, 74th Cong., 1st Sess., 26.

33. Derthick (1979), 285 quoting Justice Douglas Brown.

34 Whitman and Shoffner (2011).

35. In 1937, the employee share of Social Security payroll tax collections totaled $132.5 million (Federal Budget, Historical Statistics, Table 13.1), of which 90 percent was paid by workers with earnings of $3,000 or less (Corson, 1939). Hence, $119 million came from these workers. That year, according to IRS Statistics of Income (1937, 118), tax filers with incomes below $3,000 paid $33 million in personal income taxes.

36. The benefit amount assumes that the worker earned $100 per month, about the average for a covered worker in the late 1930s.

37. S. Rep. No. 628, Committee on Finance, 74th Cong., 1st Sess., 7.

38. My calculation. Assumes the worker earns $100 per month in covered employment. The calculation is adjusted for the probability of death based on 1940 life tables from Centers for Disease Control.

39. H. Rep. No. 615, 74th Cong., 1st Sess., 4.

40. Internal Revenue Service, Statistics of Income, 1937, 118.

41. House of Representatives, Committee on Ways and Means, statement of Henry Morgenthau, *Hearings on Social Security,* 1935, 899.

42. House Ways and Means Committee, statement of J. Douglas Brown, *Hearings on the Economic Security Act,* 74th Cong., 1st Sess., January 25, 1935, 243–244.

43. Cong. Rec., vol. 79, part 9, June 17, 1935, 9419.

44. Ibid., part 5, April 12, 1935, 5533.

45. Geddes (1937) reports the number of Old-Age Assistance programs in operation in 1934 and the number of Aid to the Blind programs operating in 1935. See Douglas (1939), 187, for the number of states operating mothers' aid programs in 1934.

46. Both the Ways and Means and Senate Finance committees reserved Title I for the Old-Age Assistance program.

47. The statutory entitlement language requires that "the Secretary of the Treasury shall pay to each State which has an approved plan for old-age assistance . . . an amount . . . equal to one-half of the total of the sums expended" (Pub. L. 742-71, sec. 3).

48. More precisely, the Old-Age Assistance program limited the requirement to five of the previous nine years. States could, of course, maintain residence requirements for a period longer than the specified federal maximums, but they would receive no federal matching payments.

49. Epstein (1938), 630.

50. The Social Security Act's matching programs were not the federal government's first such programs. The 1914 Smith-Lever Act provided matching payments for state agriculture extension programs; the 1917 Smith-Hughes Act did the same for agriculture teacher training programs; and two programs in the 1920s provided federal support for state disability rehabilitation services and state maternal and child health services. These forerunner programs were small, accounting for only $11 million in 1937 compared to the $125 million for old-age assistance matching payments. Only a small portion of the agriculture extension program (Pub. L. 63-95, May 8, 1914), $480,000, provided federal payments on an entitlement basis.

51. House of Representatives, Committee on Labor, *Hearings on House Joint Resolution 159,* 64th Cong., 1st Sess., April 11, 1916, 155.

52. S. Rep. No. 629, Individual Views., 72nd Cong., 1st Sess., April 29, 1932, 24.

53. S. Rep. No. 964, 72nd Cong., 1st Sess., June 30, 1932, 48.

54. A portion of the grants was also used to finance the federal-state employment service.

55. In 1800, Madison wrote: "Money cannot be applied to the General Welfare, otherwise than by an application of it to some particular measure conducive to the General Welfare. Whenever, therefore, money has been raised by the General Authority, and is to be applied to a particular measure, a question arises whether the particular measure be within the enumerated authorities vested in Congress. If it be, the money requisite for it may be applied to it; if it be not, no such application can be made." Virginia Resolution of 8th of January 1800.

56. Lodge (1904), vol. 4, 70, 151.

57. Story (1833), 649.

58. This discussion draws heavily on the comprehensive critique of the Hamilton-Story view by Warren (1923), 9–29.

59 See Warren (1923) for a thorough treatment of this issue.

60. Under the ruling, a citizen's case did not have standing unless the person could show that a court decision would have an effect on his or her taxes. The ruling, in effect, precluded a citizen from challenging all programs financed by the large pool of general funds. Thirty-one years later, the Court did hear a case challenging a provision in the Elementary and Secondary School Act of 1965 that allowed school districts to use federal grants to purchase religious school books the constitutionality of a general fund program (Flast v. Cohen, 392 U.S. 83, 1968).

61. United States v. Butler, 297 U.S. 1 (1936).

62. Justice Roberts, writing for the Court's majority, concluded "that the act is one regulating agricultural production [and] that the tax is a mere incident of such regulation" (United States v. Butler, 297 U.S. 1 (1936).

63. This point is also made by Levy and Mellor (2009), 26. The Court appears to recognize this fact and applies it to the scope of the spending power. In its decision, the Court determined that it need not "ascertain the scope of the phrase 'general welfare of the United States' or determine whether an appropriation in aid of agriculture falls within it. Wholly apart from that question, another principle embedded in our Constitution prohibits the enforcement of AAA" (United States v. Butler, 297 U.S. 1 [1936]).

64. In the Court's words, "The Congress is expressly empowered to lay taxes to provide for the general welfare . . . [and]. . . . the power to appropriate is as broad as the power to tax. Ibid.

65. Ibid.

66. Helvering v. Davis, 301 U.S. 319 (1937), 641.

67. Ibid.

68. Steward Machine Company v. Davis, 301 U.S. 548 (1937), 587.

69. The endeavor was, in fact, hardly cooperative. By the time of the Court decision in *Steward*, forty-three states had enacted unemployment insurance programs in response to the new law, and thirty-five of them contained a provision for automatic termination of the program in the event the federal law was declared unconstitutional.

70. Steward Machine Company v. Davis, 589.

71. Ibid., 588.

72. Ibid., 591.

73. Ibid.

74. In South Dakota v. Dole, 483 U.S. 203 (1987), the Court ruled that any conditions attached to a federal expenditure must be reasonably related to the basic purpose the expenditure seeks to accomplish.

75. President James Madison, Veto Message of March 3, 1817.

Chapter 8

1. Cong. Rec., vol. 81, part 2, March 17, 1937, 2326.

2. Mills (1937) titled his article, "The Social Security Hoax."

3. Linton (1936), 372.

4. Ibid., 482. The Republican Party called for abandoning the reserve plan in its 1936 party platform. Republican Party National Convention, June 9, 1936.

5. Cong. Rec., vol. 81, part 1, January 29, 1937, 548.

6. Ibid., part 2, March 17, 1937, 2324.

7. Ibid., March 17, 1937, 2326.

8. Flynn (1939) called the reserve "a swindle" and "a solemn and cruel farce," the *New York Times* labeled it financial "hocus pocus" (Berkowitz, 1991, 59), and the editors of the *American Mercury* (December 1937, 393) labeled the reserve a scheme of "hollowness and humbuggery." Congressmen Knutson and Gearhart were among those who charged that the surplus funds were "misappropriated" and "embezzled." House Ways and Means Committee, *Hearings Relative to the Social Security Act Amendments of 1939*, 384.

9. Epstein (1938), 806.

10. Ibid., 807.

11. In a rare meeting of the minds, business groups, including the Chamber of Commerce, the National Association of Manufacturers, and the National Dry Goods Association, were joined by labor groups, including the American Federation of Labor and the Workers Alliance of America, in recommending that the large reserve policy be abandoned. House of Representatives, Ways and Means Committee, *Hearings Relative to the Social Security Act Amendments of 1939*, p. 2041 for the National Association of Manufacturers, p. 1329 for the National Dry Goods Association, and p. 1182 for the Workers Alliance of America. Opposition by the

Chamber of Commerce and the American Federation of Labor is reported by Berkowitz (1987), 59.

12. Social Security Advisory Council Report, 1939.

13. S. Doc. No. 4, 76th Cong., 1st Sess., December 1938.

14. Pub. L. 76-379.

15. The monthly survivor benefit replaced lump-sum death benefits.

16. This amount, according to Morgenthau, would be limited to "not more than three times the highest prospective annual benefit in the ensuing five years." House of Representatives, Ways and Means Committee, *Hearings Relative to the Social Security Act Amendments of 1939*, 2113.

17. As DeWitt (2008) has pointed out, actuarial estimates of Social Security's long-term financing were showing by 1939 that even with the large reserve, the Social Security program would not be self-financing.

18. House of Representatives, Ways and Means Committee, statement of Henry Morgenthau, *Hearings Relative to the Social Security Act Amendments of 1939*, 2112.

19. The 1939 law changed the interest rate on trust fund surpluses from the 1935 statute's 3 percent to the average rate of interest paid on outstanding Treasury debt.

20. President Franklin Roosevelt, State of the Union Message to Congress, January 11, 1944.

21. War expenditures are from Historical Tables, Table 3.1. GDP is from Historical Tables, Table 10.1.

22. U.S. budget for 1942 and 1945, respectively.

23. For a thorough discussion of the tax freeze, see DeWitt (2008). See Table 3, 58, for a summary of congressional inaction on payroll taxes during the years 1941 to 1947.

24. DeWitt (2008), 10.

25. The Roosevelt administration, despite having proposed the pay-as-you-go policy, tried unsuccessfully to argue that it had not agreed to the policy. President Roosevelt wrote to Congress, "In 1939, in a period of underemployment we departed temporarily from the original schedule of contributions, with the understanding that the original schedule would be resumed on January 1, 1943. There is no sound reason for departing again under present circumstances." Cong. Rec., vol. 88, part 6, October 9, 1942, 8005–8006.

26. U.S. Budget for FY 1943, "Message Transmitting the Budget," 13.

27. Seven billion dollars would be raised by higher personal corporate income taxes. Annual Budget Message, U.S. Budget for FY 1943.

28. U.S. Budget for FY 1943, "Message Transmitting the Budget," 15.

29. Testimony of Henry Morgenthau to the House Ways and Means Committee, "Revenue Revision of 1942, Volume I," 77th Cong., 2nd Sess., March 3, 1942, 2.

30. Ibid.

Chapter 9

1. *New York Times*, January 26, 1943.

2. U.S. House of Representatives, House Committee Print No. 289, Staff Report No. IX, Part A., 2, 84th Cong., 2nd Sess., September 1956.

3. Pub. L. 77-772.

4. Franklin D. Roosevelt, "Fireside Chat on Progress of War and Plans for Peace," July 28, 1943.

5. Testimony of Harry W. Colmery, *Hearings before the Committee on World War Veterans' Legislation*, 78th Cong., 2nd Sess., 1944, 396.

6. Olson (1974), 20.

7. Ross (1969), 80.

8. Cong. Rec., vol. 90, part 3, March 24, 1944, 3081.

9. Altschuler and Blumin (2009), 58.

10. Ross (1969), 42.

11. Cong. Rec., vol. 90, part 3, May 17, 1944, 4446.

12. Ibid., 4620.

13. Cong. Rec., vol. 90, part 4, May 12, 1944, 4449.

14. Servicemen's Readjustment Act of 1944, Pub. L. 78-346, part VIII, sec. 8, June 22, 1944.

15. A further indication of the bill's lack of controversy was that forty-six Senate members were absent for the final vote.

16. There are two principal versions of the story—one reported in Frydl (2009), the other by Camelon (1969). The version in the text follows Frydl's.

17. Camelon (1969).

18. The story of the police finding Gibson at a truck stop comes from Frydl (2009). Camelon's story has Gibson returning home to hear his phone ringing.

19. Pub. L. 78-346, June 22, 1944.

20. Cong. Rec., vol. 90, part 4, May 11, 1944, 4339.

21 Administrator of Veterans Affairs, *Annual Report* (1959), Table 60.

22. Cong. Rec., vol. 90, part 4, July 18, 1944, 7712.

23. The number of discharged World War II veterans reached its peak in 1950 at 15.4 million.

24. Pub. L. 79-268, December 28, 1945.

25. Administrator of Veterans Affairs, *Annual Report* (1959), Table 60.

26. Ibid. (1947), Table 84.

27. Ibid. (1955), Table 64, and *Statistical Abstract for 1950*, Table 274, respectively

28. U.S. Budget for 1950, Table 8.

29. Administrator of Veterans Affairs, *Annual Report* (1956). Data on the number of veterans receiving assistance are from Table 66. Expenditure data are from U.S. Budget for Fiscal Year 1957, 184. The data exclude recipients of Korean War benefits.

30. In 1956, only 1,169 veterans received educational assistance (Olson, 1974, 44).

31. *Statistical Abstract 1957*, Table 312.

32. Data on participating educational institutions and business firms are from Committee on Veterans Affairs, *Report on Education and Training*, 3.

33. Mettler (2005), 62.

34. Altschuler and Blumin (2009), 161.

35. Committee on Veterans Affairs, *Report on Education and Training*, 69 and 68, respectively. One radio school that had operated in 1945 and 1946 with a requirement that students complete one hundred hours suddenly increased its requirement to eight hundred hours in 1947. The school raised its tuition accordingly. Similarly, a photography course that had required forty-eight weeks in 1945 increased its course to ninety-six weeks a year later. Ibid., 75 and 76, respectively.

36. Ibid., 63. Congress eventually clamped down on colleges, but not too hard, by imposing a cap on increases in nonresident fees at 25 percent above the college's 1944 fee.

37. Korean War veterans were given twenty-six weeks of unemployment benefits as opposed to the fifty-two weeks given under the GI Bill. Korean War veterans were also given a maximum of three years of educational assistance rather than the four years provided to World War II veterans.

38. Frydl (2009), 358.

Chapter 10

1. *Annual Statistical Supplement to the Social Security Bulletin*, 1965, 26 (for workers covered) and 15 and 21 (for number of recipients). For 65 and older population, see U.S. Census of Population, 1950, General Characteristics, Table 38.

2. *Statistical Abstract* (1952). The number of workers paying payroll taxes is from Table 269. The number of employed people is from Table 207. The number of Social Security recipients and the number of people age 65 and over (for 1950) are from Tables 271 and 20, respectively. The number of public assistance recipients is from Table 292. The number of unemployment insurance recipients is from Table 269, and the number of unemployed persons is from Table 200 of the *Statistical Abstract* for 1948.

3. President Harry S. Truman, Special Message to Congress Presenting a 21-Point Program for the Reconversion Period, September 6, 1945.

4. President Harry S. Truman, Special Message to Congress Recommending a National Health Program, November 19, 1945.

5. U.S. Budget for FY1950, 33. The preference for social insurance was widely shared by New Deal advocates. Elizabeth Wickenden, for example,

described welfare "as the safety-net, the court of last resort, for those who fall through the insurances. " Cited in Coll (1995), 159. See Steiner (1966) for a comprehensive treatment of this issue.

6. See Steiner (1966) for a particularly thoughtful discussion of the New Deal's views.

7. President Harry S. Truman, remarks at a campaign rally in San Diego, California, September 24, 1948.

8. President Harry S. Truman, Special Message to the Congress on the Nation's Health Care Needs, April 22, 1949. The president's plan also included grants to medical schools to increase the supply of physicians, an extension of hospital construction subsidies, grants to state and local governments for disease control, grants to public health activities and crippled children's services, and additional grants for maternal and child programs.

9. Ibid.

10. Ibid.

11. O. Anderson (1968), 61.

12. Thompson (1916), 315.

13. The president kept the idea alive through speeches, special messages to Congress, and the appointment of a medical care committee. Senator Robert F. Wagner introduced legislation calling for federal health care grants to states in 1939. In 1943 and again in 1945, Senators Wagner and Murray and Congressman John Dingell introduced national health insurance legislation.

14. The legislation also called for federal funding of hospital construction, an expansion in public health services and maternal and child health services, a national institute for medical research and education, and a program for disability and sickness insurance.

15. Laurence (1949)

16. President Harry S. Truman, Special Message to the Congress on the Nation's Health Care Needs, April 22, 1949.

17. Ewing (1948), 88. A similar sentiment is contained in Senator Claude Pepper's Report to the Senate Committee on Education and Labor, April 24, 1948. According to the report, "Millions of people are not eligible for any [health insurance] plan. To prevent adverse selection of risk, they [insurance companies] adopt such rigid eligibility requirements that they exclude the very people who need care most."

18. Ewing (1948), 85.

19. Senate, Committee on Labor and Public Welfare, testimony of John H. Hayes, president, American Hospital Association, *Hearings on S.545 and S.1320*, 1947, National Health Program, part 1, 252.

20. President Harry S. Truman, "Special Message to the Congress on the Nation's Health Care Needs," April 22, 1949.

21. "Federal Health Insurance Urged by Truman, Ewing," *New York Times*, September 3, 1948.

22. I have drawn heavily on Kelley (1956), 73–86, for a description of the AMA's campaign.

23. President Truman's successor, Dwight Eisenhower, opposed national health insurance and instead supported private health care markets along with modest support of state-run health programs for the indigent. President Dwight Eisenhower, Special Message to the Congress on the Health Needs of the American People, January, 18, 1953.

24. *Annual Statistical Supplement to the Social Security Bulletin*, 1952, 44.

25. *Statistical Abstract* (1952), 250, for Social Security recipients (excluding children); 269 for Old Age Assistance recipients. Average payments are computed by dividing total payments (pp. 249 and 269) by the number of recipients.

26. President Harry S. Truman, Special Message to Congress on Social Security, May 24, 1948.

27. Since benefits were tied to earnings, Social Security did allow initial benefits to rise as wages increased from one retiree cohort to another.

28. President Truman, in Special Message to Congress on Social Security, May 24, 1948, termed the benefits "seriously inadequate." House Ways and Means Committee chairman Robert Doughton asserted that while he did not know what a realistic level of benefits was, he did know that "social security benefits certainly did not have a very realistic level in . . . 1948." Cong. Rec., vol. 95, part 10, October 4, 1949, 13820.

29. The conclusion for a typical married couple is the same. The average benefit for a retired worker who also received a spousal benefit amounted to only about one-third of the poverty line for a two-person household.

30. Historical Tables, Table 13.1.The trust fund balance, at ten times the program's highest annual outlays during the next five years, was three times the level required to satisfy the Morgenthau Rule.

31. The wage and salary data are from the BEA, National Income and product Accounts, Interactive Table 2.1. The number of covered workers and recipients is taken from the *Social Security Bulletin*, Statistical Appendix, 2011, Tables 4B.1 and 6.1, respectively.

32. *Tenth Annual Report of the Board of Trustees of the Federal Old-Age and Survivors Insurance Trust Fund* (1950), 12.

33. The increase ranged from 100 percent for retirees with the lowest benefit levels to 50 percent for retirees receiving the maximum benefit.

34. The New Start policy, effective in July 1951, required six quarters of coverage starting in 1950. So a person 63 years old in a newly covered occupation who worked for six quarters would start collecting benefits by mid-1951. For future beneficiaries, the law excluded covered wages earned prior to 1950

from the calculation of monthly benefits if their inclusion lowered the level of benefits payable.

35. "Social Security Act," *Congressional Quarterly Almanac 1950*, 165–177.

36. President Harry S. Truman, Special Message to the Congress on Social Security, May 24, 1948.

37. Douglas's statement was made in reference to the Senate Finance Committee version of the bill. Cong. Rec., vol. 95, part 7, July 6, 1949, 8897.

38. House, Ways and Means Committee, Social Security Act Amendments of 1949, H. Rep. No. 1300, 81st Cong., 1st Sess., August 22, 1949.

39. The Actuarial Report on the 1950 Amendments, issued by the Ways and Means Committee following the law's enactment, did not provide an estimate of the impact of the law on Social Security outlays. The estimate is calculated by taking the difference between actual Social Security outlays and those projected by the trustees just prior to the enactment of the 1950 law. Public assistance payments are from *Statistical Abstract* (1954), 284.

40. Pub. L. 81-734, August 28, 1950.

41. Cong. Rec., vol. 95, part 10, September 28, 1949, 13490 (quoted in Derthick, 1979, 241–242).

42. The Actuarial Report on the 1950 Amendments states, "The proposed tax schedule is not quite self-supporting but is sufficiently close for all practical purposes considering the uncertainties and variations possible in the cost estimates." House Ways and Means Committee, Actuarial Cost Estimates (1950), 18.

43. The House report on the 1950 Amendments declared that the "program should be on a completely self-supporting basis." H. Rep. No. 1300, 81st Cong., 1st Sess., 31. The Senate report contained nearly identical language.

44. The 1935 law's self-financing principle did allow for the use of general revenue–financed interest payments earned on surplus payroll tax revenues. In 1943, an amendment sponsored by Republican senator Arthur Vandenberg and Democratic senator James Murray allowed general revenues to be used if future payroll tax revenues proved insufficient to meet benefit payments. Another chink in the self-supporting principle occurred in 1947 when Congress established Social Security credits for World War II military service. Finally, in 1950 key congressional Republicans supported a general revenue–financed alternative Social Security program that was similar to the Townsend movement's program.

45. *Annual Statistical Supplement to the Social Security Bulletin* (1952), Table 36.

46. The remaining 25 percent consisted of children in households in which the father was incapacitated due to a physical or mental disability.

47. Abrahamson (1998), 146.

48. U.S. Census Bureau (1975), Chap. B, 64 and 52, respectively.

49. See Bucklin and Lynch (1938) and Berman (1947, 1949).

Chapter 11

1. Cong. Rec., vol. 104, part 12, July 31, 1958, 15744.

2. *Social Security Trustees Report* (1958), 18–19.

3. U.S. House of Representatives. Cong. Rec., vol. 104, part 12, July 31, 1958, 15744.

4. Senate Finance Committee Report, Social Security Amendments of 1958.

5. Pub. L. 85-840, August 28, 1958, contained eighteen other incremental changes to benefits levels and eligibility rules.

6. Congress increased the taxable wage base to $4,800 from $4,200, effective in January 1959, and raised the payroll tax rate by ¼ of 1 percent starting in 1959.

7. U.S. House of Representatives, Cong. Rec., vol. 104, part 12, July 31, 1958. 15746.

8. Estimates are from the testimony of Robert J. Myers, Committee on Finance, *Social Security Amendments of 1955, Hearings before the Committee on Finance, United States Senate on H.R. 7225*, 84th Cong., 2nd Sess., 13–62. The actual number of early retirees is from Table 95 of the *Annual Statistical Supplement to the Social Security Bulletin* (1975).

9. Roper Commercial Survey, August 1952.

10. The calculation assumes the worker received the average covered wage in each year worked and had paid Social Security taxes since 1937. The months-worth calculation assumes a 3 percent real interest rate. The monthly benefit is based on the 1950 Social Security Amendment formula.

11. The full *Washington Post* editorial against the early retirement benefit for women on July 19, 1956, reads: "There may have been some degree of Southern chivalry and sentiment behind the Senate's adoption of Senator Kerr's amendment to the Social Security Act permitting women to collect benefits at the age of 62. The merits of this discrimination in favor of the distaff side are not altogether clear, and there was a good deal of force, we think, to the Administration's opposition." *Washington Post* editorials on other Social Security legislation during the decade include the following: September 10, 1950, praising the "long step toward that universal coverage"; May 21, 1952, lauding Congress for a "long overdue" benefit increase; January 15, 1954, imploring Congress to "broaden and improve" Social Security; June 7, 1956, urging the Senate to "restore the amendment . . . providing benefits for persons 50 years of age or older who are totally disabled"; August 25, 1958, approving that year's 7 percent increase in benefits; December 7, 1959, calling for the "elimination of the arbitrary 50-year age limit" for disability benefits; February 3, 1961, in favor of improvements in Social Security benefits in the interest of "economic justice to the old, the widowed and the disabled."

12. Key Republican leaders in the House had supported a program that would provide a basic floor of economic protection only. But they had objected to providing Social Security benefits to individuals who had sufficient resources to provide for their own support during retirement. House Republican leaders on Social Security had gone so far as to say, "A form of compulsory social insurance which unnecessarily takes from the individual funds which he would invest or otherwise use for building his own security is incompatible with our free enterprise system." Committee on Ways and Means, "The 1950 Social Security Amendments, Views of the Minority on H.R. 1300," H. Rep. 1300, House of Representatives, 81st Cong., 1st Sess., 157.

13. 1952 Republican Party platform.

14. See Lubove (1968), 45–66, for a discussion of the early development of workman's compensation laws.

15. The story of the disability "freeze" is taken from Derthick (1979), 300–304.

16. Robert Doughton, Cong. Rec., vol. 98, part 4, May 19, 1952, 5470.

17. The Federal Security Agency could not overrule state agency denials of applicants but could overrule approvals.

18. Berkowitz and McQuaid (1988), 172.

19. Derthick (1979), 301.

20. See H. Rep. No. 84-1189, 84th Congress, 1st Sess., 2–6.

21. U.S. Senate, "Social Security Amendments of 1956," S. Rep. No. 2133, 84th Cong., 2nd Sess., 3.

22. Cong. Rec., vol. 95, part 11, October 5, 1949, 13970.

23. Senator George, who five years later would sponsor the Social Security Disability Insurance program, argued against the 1950 proposal by saying, "When we insure against disability . . . then it is opening up an avenue for the expenditure of vast sums of money, which will certainly embarrass us." Cong. Rec., vol. 96, part 3, March 7, 1950, 2950.

24. The quote from Senator Byrd is from Cong. Rec., vol. 102, July 17, 1956, 13046. The quote from Senator Dirksen is from the *Congressional Quarterly Almanac 1956*.

25. Cong. Rec., vol. 102, July 17, 1956, 13050.

26. Ibid., 13038.

27. Ibid., 13051.

28. *Annual Statistical Supplement to the Social Security Bulletin* (1958), 7.

29. Cong. Rec., vol. 102, July 17, 1956, 13051.

30. "Social Security," *Congressional Quarterly Almanac 1956*, 392–397.

31. Caro (2002), 678–681.

32. Ibid., 680.

33. Ibid., 681.

34. Ibid.

35. The dependent benefits increase was effective in October 1958.

Chapter 12

1. Special Message to Congress on Public Welfare Programs, February 1, 1962.

2. President Truman did propose to raise the federal match rate in 1948 (Special Message to Congress on Social Security, May 24, 1948), but thereafter opposed congressional efforts to do so. For Eisenhower's statement, see his Annual Budget Message for FY61 (January 18, 1960).

3. Most notably in 1952 and 1956, Congress raised the federal match rate in all four federal-state public assistance programs. In 1956, Congress established separate open-ended matching payments for state medical expenditures on behalf of welfare recipients. In 1958, Congress overhauled its federal matching formulas to allocate federal welfare funds on the basis of state fiscal capacities.

4. Bell (1965), 86.

5. Ibid., 48.

6. Coll (1995) reports that in 1940, of the forty-three states with Aid to Dependent Children programs, thirty-one had suitable home provisions.

7. Bell (1965), 29.

8. Ibid., 35–36. Bell reports that the Federal Security Administration opposition prevented seventeen states from enacting new or continuing existing suitable home laws during the 1950s. Only Mississippi in 1958 went ahead with its law despite FSA's threat to withhold federal funds.

9. Ibid., 58.

10. Ibid., 68.

11. Ibid., 50.

12. Ibid., 44.

13. Federal Security Administration, "Public Assistance Goals for 1947: Recommendations for Improving State Legislation," vol. 9, no. 12 (December 1946), 11.

14. See Bell (1965), 51–56.

15. "Louisiana Drops 23,000 Children on Relief Rolls as Illegitimate," *New York Times*, August 28, 1960.

16 Coll (1995), 209.

17. "Louisiana Fighting to Stay on Federal Welfare Aid Books" (1960).

18. Bell (1965), 58.

19. Ibid., 99.

20. House Ways and Means Committee, Public Welfare Amendments of 1962, H. Rep. No. 1414, 87th Cong., 2nd Sess., March 10, 1962.

21. The discussion of the Newburgh crisis is taken from Coll (1995) and Levenstein (2000), 10–33.

22. *Los Angeles Times*, August 10, 1961; Ritz (1966), 51–54.

23. *New York Times*, June 24, 1961; Coll (1995), 210; *Chicago Tribune*, July 16, 1961; *Los Angeles Times*, August 19, 1961; *Washington Post*, August 6, 1961; *Raleigh News and Observer*, July 18, 1961; and *Louisville Courier-Journal*, July 16, 1961. A *Washington Post* story, for example, was titled, "Newburgh Is a Mirror Reflecting On Us All." Similarly, the *Raleigh News and Observer* story said "Not Only in Newburg." The *Los Angeles Times* wrote "Crackdown on Welfare . . . Could Hit Entire U.S."

24. Coll (1995), 215.

25. "Most of U.S. Favors Newburgh Plan" (1961).

26. Coll (1995), 215.

27. Ibid.

28. Department of Health, Education, and Welfare, Division of Program Statistics and Analysis, *Characteristics of Families Receiving Aid to Families with Dependent Children*, November–December 1961, Tables 26, 27.

29. Mugge (1963), 8.

30. The *Boston Globe* informed its readers that in 1961, "one out of every 16 people" in the city was on the welfare rolls. *Boston Globe*, October 27, 1961. The *Los Angeles Times* ran a series of six articles on the welfare system's high cost. One article, "County Welfare Inspires 2nd Gold Rush for Relief," pointed out that public relief expenditures now accounted for one-third of Los Angeles County taxes. Similarly, the *Chicago Daily Tribune* ran a dozen or more stories on welfare beginning in early 1960. One headline read: "ADC Rolls Hit All-Time Peak in Lake County"; another reported that welfare costs in Cook County had increased by 33 percent from 1959 to 1961. The Lake County headline is from June 5, 1960; the Cook County story is from March 6, 1961.

31. *Los Angeles Times*, February 7, 11, 1960, respectively. The $50,000 of funds would be worth $400,000 if measured by the CPI increase from 1960, and by a larger amount if measured from the time she received the funds.

32. Steiner (1966), 26.

33. Harrington (1962).

34. Special Message to Congress on Public Welfare Programs, February 1, 1962. President Kennedy shared the concern of many that the AFDC program was encouraging broken homes. Two years before he was elected president, Senator Kennedy testified before the Committee on Finance that "the Federal [AFDC] thus puts a premium on desertion. I believe this is immoral and unsound." Committee on Finance, *Hearings H.R. 1354, the Social Security Amendments of 1958*, 85th Cong., 2nd Sess., 1958, 415.

35. The bill passed the House of Representatives by a 320–69 vote and by voice vote in the Senate. "Major Public Welfare Changes Enacted," *Congressional Quarterly Almanac 1962*, 205–212. Republicans did object to the bill's increase in federal matching payments for public assistance programs other than ADC on the ground that it represented an "ever-increasing federalization of what should be inherently state programs." Public Welfare Amendments of 1962, Report of the Committee on Finance, S. Rep. No. 1549, 87th Cong., 2nd Sess., 1962, 7.

36. Pub. L. 87-543, July 25, 1962.

37 Public Welfare Amendments of 1962, Report of the Committee on Finance, S. Rep. No. 1589, 87th Cong., 2nd Sess., 7. June 14, 1962.

38 Pub. L. 87-543, July 25, 1962.

39 House of Representatives, Ways and Means Committee, Hearings on Public Welfare Amendments of 1962, 12.

40 Murray (1985), 23.

41 President Lyndon Johnson, Annual Message to Congress on the State of the Union, January 8, 1964.

42 Pub. L. 88-452, August 20, 1964.

43. Ibid., Title II.

44. Martin (1972), 50.

45. President Lyndon Johnson, Remarks upon Signing the Economic Opportunity Act, August 20, 1964.

46. The program was established under the Potato Control Act of 1935. The program, which began operations in 1939, allowed participants to use food stamps only to buy foodstuffs that had been designated as "surplus commodities." The program reached a peak in 1943 when it was operating in 1,741 counties. Congress ended the program that year as agricultural surpluses diminished during the war. The Food Stamp program was renamed the Supplemental Nutrition Assistance Program in 2008. Throughout the text, I refer to the program by its original and more popular name.

47. See Ripley (1969) for a discussion of the logroll. Research (see Ferejohn 1986) has shown that the trade mainly benefited the farm price support program, which at the time faced considerable opposition in the House outside of the Agriculture Committee.

48. Steiner (1971), 196.

Chapter 13

1. "Marchers Protest Welfare Program," *Washington Post*, July 1, 1966, B1.

2. Marmor (1973), 37. In a related matter, Congress in 1959 enacted a health insurance program for federal workers. The Federal Employees Health Benefits plan allowed federal workers and retirees to choose from one of several federally approved and privately administered health plans. Government workers

and retirees were initially required to pay 50 percent of the premiums, with the remainder financed by taxpayers. Six years later, the plan became a model for the congressional Republican alternative to President Johnson's Medicare plan.

3. Ibid., 50.

4. Pratt (1976), 91.

5. "The Decline of Congress" (1963).

6. "Medicare Shenanigans" (1964).

7. "Balancing the Ways and Means" (1964).

8. "Medicare Merry-Go-Round" (1964).

9. "One-Man Veto on Medicare" (1964).

10. The Senate rejected attempts to add the health plan to a welfare bill on the Senate floor in 1962 and 1963.

11. The Republican plan was modeled on the existing health plan available to federal workers and retirees.

12. The name was given to the plan by Wilbur Cohen (see Marmor, 1970, 68).

13. Newhouse and Taylor (1970), 3.

14. See Finkelstein (2007).

15. President Lyndon Johnson, Special Message to Congress Proposing Programs for Older Americans, January 13, 1967.

16. On three additional occasions from 1966 to 1973, Congress shifted a portion of the Social Security tax to the disability insurance program. By 1974, Congress had shifted 0.65 percentage points of the payroll tax from the retirement program to the disability insurance program, more than doubling the disability insurance tax rate and reducing the tax rate applicable to the retirement program by 7 percent. Congress also delayed the previously scheduled Social Security payroll tax rate increase to make room for the increase necessary to finance Medicare Part A program.

17. U.S. Department of Health, Education and Welfare, Social and Rehabilitation Services, National Center for Social Statistics, "Public Assistance Statistics" (December 1969).

18. Moynihan (1967), 31.

19. Moynihan (1973), 54–55.

20. "Anti-Poverty Programs Doubled," *Congressional Quarterly Almanac 1965*, 405–420.

21. Ibid.

22. West (1981), 22.

23. Kornbluh (2007), 58.

24. Bailis (1974), 11. West (1981, 295) provides a somewhat higher estimate of twenty-five thousand. Membership was concentrated among welfare recipients in major industrial cities, including New York, Boston, Detroit, Los Angeles, and Chicago (West, 1981, 11). The estimate of the number of local

welfare rights organizations is from Reisch and Andrews (2002), 146. See also Trattner (1989), 344.

25. West (1981), 27.

26. The *New York Times* headline read, "Welfare Protest Made at City Hall: 1,500 Demand More Help and End to 'Indignities.'" In the nation's capital, the *Washington Post* reported, "18 Poor Marchers Arrested at Capitol." In Los Angeles, the *Los Angeles Times* reported, "100 Recipients March against Welfare Setup."

27. Kornbluh (2007), 47.

28. *National Welfare Leaders Newsletter,* vol. 1, no. 14 (1967). The document contains no specific date.

29 Bailis (1974), 39

30. See Chapter 12. The grants were authorized by the Public Welfare Amendments of 1962 (Pub. L. 87-543).

31. Kornbluh (2007), 43–44, and Bailis (1974), 157.

32. Bailis (1974), 28.

33. Kornbluh (2007), 84.

34. Bailis (1974), 59.

35. Kornbluh, 47.

36. Ibid., 56.

37. "Marchers Protest Welfare Program," *Washington Post,* July 1, 1966, B1.

38. Tillmon (1972).

39. The figure is computed from data provided in Department of Health, Education and Welfare (1967). Medicaid reimbursements totaled $18.4 million for services to nondisabled adults and $4.6 million for services to children. There were 121,000 adults and 77,100 children served by the Medicaid program. The federal minimum wage in late 1967 was $1.15 per hour.

40. The earnings disregard had been used for the Aid to the Blind program and Old-Age Program recipients.

41. Senate Committee on Finance, *Hearings on the Social Security Amendments of 1967,* 90th Cong., 1st Sess., August 29, 1967, 776.

42. Burke and Burke (1974), 35.

43. "Social Security Aid Raised; Welfare Pay Restricted," *Congressional Quarterly Almanac 1967,* 13-892–13-916.

44. The breakeven level of income can be approximated by the formula G/t, where G is the amount of money the family received if it had no other source of income, and t is the rate at which benefits are reduced when other income rises. In most states prior to the 1967 Amendments, t equaled 100 percent. Following the 1967 Amendments, t equaled .67 in most states. The increase in the breakeven level of income equals the ratio of $G/1$ to $G/.67$, or 1.50. The $30 income disregard raised the breakeven level of income further.

Chapter 14

1. Goldberg v. Kelley, 397 U.S. 254 (1970), n. 8

2. For example, the Revolutionary War pension law of March 19, 1792, stipulated that all disabled veterans who met the law's qualifying requirements "shall be entitled to be placed on the pension list of the United States" (U.S. Statutes at Large, vol. 1, Chap. 11, sec. 1, March 19, 1792, 243). Similarly, the 1862 law authorizing Civil War disability pensions stated that all eligible veterans' pension applicants "shall be placed on the lists of invalid pensions . . . and be entitled to receive . . . such pensions as is hereinafter provided" (Chap. 166, 73th Cong., 2nd Sess., July 14, 1862). The 1917 law authorizing World War I disability compensation benefits stipulated "that for death or disability resulting from personal injury suffered or disease contracted in the line of duty . . . the United States shall pay compensation as hereinafter provided" (see Chap. 105, sec. 300, 65th Cong., 1st Sess., October 6, 1917).

3. See Frisbie v. United States, 157 U.S. 160 (1895), and Lynch v. United States, 292 U.S. 571 (1934).

4. Decatur v. Paulding, 39 U.S. 497 (1840), 498.

5. Silberschein v. United States, 266 U.S. 221 (1934). Similarly, the Court of Claims resisted interfering (Snyder et al., 1992, 52).

6. Lynch v. United States, 292 U.S. 571 (1934).

7. Ibid.

8. Ibid.

9. Nestor v. Flemming, 363 U.S. 603 (1960).

10. The Court noted, "Of special importance in this case is the fact that eligibility for benefits, and the amount of such benefits, do not in any true sense depend on contribution to the program through the payment of taxes, but rather on the earnings record of the primary beneficiary." Ibid.

11. Davis (1993), 34.

12. Lawrence (1990), 28.

13. Melnick (1994), 83.

14. Ibid.

15. King v. Smith, 392 U.S. 392 (1968).

16. Melnick (1994), 88.

17. Committee on Finance, S. Rep. No. 74-628. 74th Cong., 1st Sess., May 14, 1935.

18. Davis (1979), 68.

19. King v. Smith(1968), 309.

20. Subsequent decisions, including Van Lare v. Hurley, 421 U.S. 338 (1975), Townsend v. Swank, 404, U.S. 282 (1971), and Carleson v. Remillard, 406 U.S. 598 (1972), reaffirmed the Court's conclusion in King v. Smith, 392 U.S. 309 (1968) .

21. Melnick (1994), 101.

22. Shapiro v. Thompson, 394 U.S. 618 (1969).

23. Ibid. Two years later, in Pease v. Hansen, 404 U.S. 70 (1971), the Court extended its ban on residency requirements to welfare programs that do not receive federal funds (Lawrence, 1990, 142).

24. "Welfare Proposals Studied, Oasdi Benefits Raised," *Congressional Quarterly Almanac* (1969), 833–840.

25. Starns v. Malkerson, 401 U.S. 985 (1971); Lawrence (1990), 142.

26. See U.S. Senate, Committee on Finance, *Hearings on H.R. 6000*, 81st Cong., 2nd Sess., 1950, 142–143.

27. John F. Kennedy, Special Message to the Congress on Public Welfare Programs, February 1, 1962. The effort to repeal state residency requirements that began in 1957 was led by the National Social Welfare Assembly. By the early 1960s, the assembly had within its umbrella thirty organizations. For examples of their arguments, see House of Representatives, Committee on Ways and Means, *Hearings on H.R. 10032*, 87th Cong., 2nd Sess., 385–395.

28. When New York terminated Mr. Kelly, the claimant in the lead case, the state regulations did not require a notice of termination or inform a welfare recipient that he or she had a right to appeal. After suits were brought against New York procedures, including Mr. Kelly's, the state modified its regulations to include face-to-face hearings and written notification that the recipient could appeal the termination before benefits were actually terminated.

29. Goldberg v. Kelly, 397 U.S. 254 (1971).

30. Ibid.

31. Ibid.

32. Davis (1993), 104.

33. Dandridge v. Williams, 397 U.S. 471 (1970).

34. Court rulings in Rosado v. Wyman, 397 U.S. 397 (1970), and Jefferson v. Hackney, 406 U.S. 535 (1972) reaffirmed its conclusion that AFDC recipients did not have a constitutional right to a minimum level of welfare benefits (Melnick, 1994, 96).

35. Matthews v. Eldridge, 424 U.S. 319 (1976).

Chapter 15

1. The FY1969 unified budget registered a scant $3 billion surplus, a mere 2 percent excess of revenues over expenditures.

2. The citations in order of the quotes are: President Richard Nixon, Special Message to the Congress Recommending a Program to End Hunger in America, May 6, 1969; Special Message to the Congress on the Unemployment Insurance System, July 8, 1969; Remarks at a Briefing on the Nation's Health System, July 10, 1969; Address to the Nation on Domestic Programs, August 8, 1969; Special Message to Congress on the Reform of the Nation's Welfare

System, August 11, 1969; and Special Message to the Congress on Social Security, September 25, 1969. The final quote is from the president's Address to the Nation on Domestic Programs, August 8, 1969.

3. Stein (1984), 198.

4. The CPI rose 44 percent from January 1968 to June 1974: http://research.stlouisfed.org/fred2/.

5. Leimer (2007), Table C-1.

6. McGovern's announcement is reported in the *Washington Post*, February 3, 1972; Mills's in Cong. Rec., vol. 118, part 5, February 23, 1972; Muskie's in *New York Times*, March 4, 1972; and Humphrey's in *New York Times*, March 28, 1972.

7. U.S. Senate, Committee on Finance, *Hearings on the $450 Billion Debt Limit*, 92nd Cong., 2nd Sess., February 28, 1972, 62.

8. If a debt ceiling bill failed to pass, the existing temporary ceiling would revert to its old level of $400 billion. In late June, the outstanding debt stood at $426 billion. Thus, in the absence of legislation, the Treasury would have to find sufficient cash to retire $26 billion of outstanding debt.

9. Cong. Rec., vol. 118, part 18, June 29, 1972, 23286.

10. Congressional Research Service, "The Social Security Benefit Increase Provided by Pub. L. 92-336," H. Doc. No. 7094, 92nd Cong., 2nd Sess., 1972, 9.

11. The basis for this claim is that at the time, 21.6 percent of elderly people lived below the poverty line. Hence, if benefit levels were uniformly distributed among elderly individuals in all income groups, slightly more than 20 percent of Social Security benefits would have been received by poor people. However, because benefits are related to lifetime earnings, benefit levels are higher among nonpoor retirees than poor retirees.

12. Cong. Rec., vol. 118, part 18, June 29, 1972, 22684.

13. The new actuarial method had been blessed by the Social Security Administration, its Advisory Council, and its trustees.

14. Cong. Rec., vol. 118, part 18, June 29, 1972, 23733.

15. Ibid., 2373, cited in Schieber and Shoven (1999), 162.

16. Ibid., 2372.

17. Congressional Research Service, "The Social Security Benefit Increase Provided by Pub. L. 92-336," 7.

18. "Manna from Big Daddy," *New York Times*, October 4, 1972.

19. The retirement program would require a 27 percent increase. The disability program would require a 26 percent increase. *Social Security Trustees Report*, 1975, 35, 37, resp.

20. Ibid., 44.

21. This discussion draws heavily on two excellent books on Nixon's reform plan: Burke and Burke (1974) and Moynihan (1973).

22. President Richard Nixon, "Address to the Nation on Domestic Programs," August 8, 1969.

23. Ibid.

24. Ibid.

25. Moynihan (1973), 65.

26. The president promised that "in no case, would anyone's present level of benefits be lowered." "Address to the Nation on Domestic Programs."

27. The net cost of the bill was estimated to be $4.3 billion. In FY1971, federal outlays on the federal-state public assistance programs (Aid to Families with Dependent Children, Old Age Assistance, Aid to the Blind, Aid to the Permanently and Totally Disabled) totaled $3.6 billion. Committee on Finance, S. Rep. No. 91-1431, 91st Cong., 2nd Sess., December 11, 1970, 421422.

28. "Away from Welfare's Morass," *New York Times*, August 10, 1969.

29. "Needed Welfare Changes," *Los Angeles Times*, August 12, 1969.

30. Burke and Burke (1974), 128.

31. Ibid., 177. Federal spending in FY1972 totaled $230 billion.

32. Moynihan (1973), 336.

33. Nadasen, Mittelstadt, and Chappell (2009) contains a useful description of the NWROs activities.

34. House of Representatives, Ways and Means Committee, *Hearings on Social Security and Welfare Proposals*, 91st Cong., 1st Sess., September 1969, 2375.

35. Moynihan (1974), 325.

36. The program announced in August proposed to abolish food stamps. After criticism that the proposal ran contrary to the president's pledge to eliminate hunger in America, the administration quickly dropped the proposal.

37. The national average per person Medicaid benefit in 1970 was $330 (*Statistical Abstract of the United States*, 1985, xxii). The minimum wage in 1970 was $1.45 an hour.

38. Moynihan (1974), 370.

39. Burke and Burke (1974), 154.

40. Moynihan (1974), 407.

41. Patterson (2000), 170.

42. The Senate Finance Committee rejected the FAP plan in autumn 1970 and again in April 1972.

43. U.S. Senate, Committee on Finance, S. Rep. No. 92-1230, 92nd Cong., 2nd Sess., 1972, 1.

44. See Steiner (1971) for a comprehensive discussion of the hunger issue.

45. Kornbluh (2007), 133–134.

46. See Jones (1983) for a legislative history. Modest program liberalizations in 1962 and 1966 increased program participation among low-income children. The 1962 law (Pub. L. 87-82, October 15, 1962) added funding for

schools located in low-income areas. The 1966 law (Pub. L. 89-642, October 11, 1966) provided funds for schools to purchase food preparation equipment to enable wider participation of schools in low-income neighborhoods.

47. The School Breakfast Program was initially authorized for two years by the Child Nutrition Amendments of 1966 Pub. L. 89-642 and extended in 1968 by Pub. L. 90-302. The Summer Feeding and Child Day Care programs were initially authorized for three years in 1968 by Pub. L. 90-302. The much smaller and temporary Special Milk program was enacted in 1955 to supplement school lunches and to help prop up dairy prices. The 1954 law, Pub. L. 83-690, established a two-year program in which the secretary of agriculture would purchase $50 million of milk from the Commodity Credit Corporation for distribution to schools. In 1956, the program was continued for another two years, and funding was increased to $75 million per year (Pub. L. 84-465 and Pub. L. 84-752). In total, the program was reauthorized five times between 1955 and 1969.

48. Citizens, Board of Inquiry into Hunger and Malnutrition in the United States (1968), 4.

49. Ibid., 9.

50. "Hunger in America," *CBS News*, May 21, 1968, https://www.youtube.com/watch?v=h94bq4JfMAA.

51. "Hunger in America," *Washington Post*, April 24, 1968.

52. "Starvation in Mississippi," *New York Times*, March 26, 1968. Like the *Washington Post*, it called for greater federal spending. According to the *Times*, "None of the programs from Head Start to hot school lunches to farm housing to manpower training is big enough or working well enough. A greater investment of money . . . [is] urgently needed."

53. USDA, *Handbook of Agricultural Charts* (1968), 63.

54. U.S. House, Committee on Agriculture, *Hunger Study*, 90th Cong., 2nd Sess., June 11, 1968, 1.

55. Melnick (1994), 321.

56. Letter from Secretary Orville Freeman to Frank Stanton, May 27, 1968, reported in Committee on Agriculture, *Hunger Study*, 72.

57. Ibid., 74.

58. Moynihan (1973), 117.

59. Melnick (1994), 199.

60. President Richard Nixon, Special Message to Congress, May 9, 1969.

61. Pub. L. 93-326, enacted in 1974, granted automatic eligibility to recipients of the newly created Supplemental Security Income program.

62. Much like the Old-Age, Aid-to-the-Blind, and AFDC programs and veterans' pensions before and since, Congress continued to fund the food stamp program with annual appropriations. The Appropriation Committees regarded the annual food stamp appropriation as a pro forma exercise; that

is, it would appropriate whatever funds were required to finance benefit payments to all claimants. For example, see H. Rep. No. 94-346, July 10, 1975.

63. "Food Stamps," *Congressional Quarterly Almanac 1970.*

64. The 1970 and 1973 laws were only part of the reason for the soaring number of food stamp recipients. From 1970 to 1976, federal courts also played a significant role, as they had in the AFDC program's expansion. See Melnick (1994), 185-231.

65. General Accounting Office, "Problems Persist in the Puerto Rico Food Stamp Program, the Nation's Largest," CED-78-84, April 27, 1978, 15.

66. Preamble, Pub. L. 91-248, May 14, 1970. The full title of the act is "An Act to Amend the National School Lunch Act and the Child Nutrition Act of 1966" to clarify responsibilities related to providing free and reduced-price meals and preventing discrimination against children, revise the program-matching requirements, strengthen the nutrition training and educational benefits of the programs, and otherwise strengthen the food service programs for children in schools and service institutions.

67. Section 6 of Pub. L. 91-248 stipulated that "any child who is a member of a household which has an annual income not above the applicable family income level set forth in the income poverty guidelines shall be served meals free or at reduced cost."

68. These regulations revised an initial regulation that would have reduced reimbursements for all meals served, including those provided to poor children. Those earlier regulations generated a firestorm of criticism that was not quelled by the later regulations.

69. "Food, Not Promises," *New York Times*, October 21, 1971; "Taking Back the Lunch Money," *Washington Post*, October 9, 1971.

70. Pub. L. 92-153, November 5, 1971.

71. The school breakfast entitlement was created by Pub. L. 93-150 in 1974. The Child and Adult Care Feeding Program entitlement was created by Pub. L. 94-105 in 1975. The Special Milk entitlement was created by Pub. L. 93-347 in 1974. Congress authorized the use of section 32 funds in Pub. L. 93-86 and Pub. L. 93-86 in 1973 for the purchase of commodities for donation to schools. In 1974, Congress mandated that 10 cents worth of commodities be donated to schools for each lunch served in Pub. L. 93-326. A 1975 law, Pub. L.94-105, required that no less than 75 percent of the so-called commodity entitlement be provided in the form of commodities rather than cash (Jones, 1983).

72. President Richard M. Nixon, Message to Congress, July 10, 1969.

73. U.S. Senate, Committee on Labor and Public Welfare, Subcommittee on Health, *Hearings, Health Care Crisis in America,"* 92nd Cong., 1st Sess., February 22, 23, 1971, 1, 2.

74. U.S. Senate, Committee on Labor and Public Welfare *Hearings, National Health Insurance,* 91st Cong., 2nd Sess., September 23, 1970.

75. The insurance would cover nearly all medical and mental benefits, including hospital inpatient and psychiatric care, outpatient services, skilled nursing and home health services, physician medical and psychiatric care services, eye care, dental care for children, rehabilitation services, and prescription drugs. That bill also covered personal health care services, such as social work, health education, nutrition aids, and psychological services.

76. The early version contained no deductibles, no coinsurance, and no waiting periods for coverage to begin. Later versions included a modest deductible and coinsurance payments. Initial versions also called for federal price controls and a fixed national health care budget to be set annually by Congress.

77. Cavalier (1970), 3–4.

78. The main bills with employer mandates introduced in the 91st Congress were H. R. 7741 and S. 1623.

79. The main tax credit bills introduced in the 91st Congress were H.R. 4960 and S. 987.

80. The proposals did include provisions that would expand the availability of the health maintenance organizations plans. But in the early 1970s, cost savings from this form of reimbursement was merely a theoretical proposition that had little empirical support.

81. Cavalier (1972).

82. The official estimates were based on an assumption that a 10 percent reduction in coinsurance rates would increase the demand for health care services by about 1 percent. Modern research has showed that the response is in the range of 4.5 percent.

83. *Washington Post*, August 30, 1970; *Tennessean*, August 28, 1970.

84. "National Health Insurance Plan," *New York Times*, July 9, 1970.

85. Cong. Rec., vol. 116, part 22, August 27, 1970, 30142.

86. Senate Committee on Labor and Public Welfare, *Hearings, National Health Insurance*, 2.

87. Cong. Rec., vol. 116, part 22, August 27, 1970, 30142–30143.

88. Senate Committee on Labor and Public Welfare, *Hearings, National Health Insurance*, 6.

89. Cong. Rec., vol. 116, part 22, August 27, 1970, 30143.

90. "Health Plans Opposed by AMA President," *National Journal*, May 11, 1974, 707.

91. Wainess (1974), 9.

92. "The Health Insurance Debate," *Washington Post*, May 26 1974.

93. "Ford's Message Omitted Poverty," *National Journal*, August 24, 1974, 1267.

94. President Richard Nixon, Special Message to Congress on the Unemployment Insurance System, July 8, 1969. Nixon made the case for his

minimum benefits plan by saying, "Up to now, the responsibility for determining benefits amounts has been the responsibility of the states. . . . However, the overriding consideration is that the objective of adequate benefits be
achieved."

95. In 1958, Congress encouraged states to offer up to thirteen weeks of
extended benefits by offering federal loans to state unemployment insurance programs. In 1961, Congress did the same by offering states interest-free
advances to their programs. In both instances, the additional costs were ultimately financed by state unemployment taxes. The 1958 law had been enacted
two months after the recession had formally ended and the 1961 law only one
month before the recession's end.

96. The law, Pub. L. 91-373, established national and individual triggers
that would automatically provide additional weeks of unemployment benefits if insured unemployment rates reached particular thresholds. Congress
financed the benefits jointly with the states on a 50–50 basis as opposed to the
100 percent federal benefit the president had proposed.

97. Pub. L. 93-572.

98. The law, Pub. L. 94-45, passed the House by voice vote and the Senate,
83–3.

99. McClure (1981), which I have heavily relied on, provides an excellent
legislative history of the black lung program through 1981.

100. Cong. Rec., vol. 115, part 20, September 26, 1969, 27291.

101. Previously, the federal government's role in workers' compensation
was limited. The 1916 Federal Employees Compensation Act covered federal
employees. The 1927 Longshore and Harbor Workers' Compensation Act covered longshoremen and harbor workers for injuries incurred while working
on U.S. navigable waters. Subsequently, Congress extended the law to include
workers employed on outer continental shelf natural resource exploration
projects and civilian employees employed on military installations.

Chapter 16

1. Congressional Budget Office, "Five-Year Budget Projections Fiscal Years
1977–81," January 26, 1976, 7.

2. President Ford, Fiscal 1976 Budget Message to Congress, February 3,
1975.

3. 1977 Social Security Trustees Report. The OASI trust fund's exhaustion
date is from p. 59; the DI trust fund's date is from p. 29. The tax increases are
calculated from long-run actuarial data on p. 54.

4. See, for example, Senate Committee on Finance, *Report of the Panel
on Social Security Financing to the Committee on Finance*(Committee Print),
94th Cong., 1st Sess., February 1975, and Senate Committee on Finance and

the Ways and Means Committee, *Report of the Consultant Panel of Social Security to the Congressional Research Service* (Committee Print) , 94th Cong., 2nd Sess., August 1976.

5. All of the projections are from the Committee on Finance, Social Security Amendments of 1977, S. Rep. No. 95-526, 95th Cong., 1st Sess., November 1, 1977, 20.

6. *Los Angeles Times*, September 26, 1976.

7. "Congress Clears Social Security Tax Increase," *Congressional Quarterly Almanac 1977*, 161–172.

8. The administration embraced the wage-indexing policy that had been recommended in 1975 by the Social Security Advisory Council and by President Ford in June 1976.

9. To be more precise, the law applied only to those who were born in 1917 or later. The new wage-indexing formula was phased in for those born between 1917 and 1922. They would receive benefits based on a blend between the new and old formulas.

10. Committee on Finance, Social Security Amendments of 1977, S. Rep. No. 95-526, 95th Cong., 1st Sess., October 29, 1977, 20, 21. The actual reduction turned out to be much larger: 34 percent (Commission on the Social Security Notch Issue 1993).

11. Committee on Finance, Social Security Amendments of 1977, 20, 21. The inflation-adjusted value of benefits was projected to rise because U.S. productivity improvements would continued to cause wages to rise faster than prices, as they had for most of U.S. history.

12. Ibid.

13. Ibid., 61. The projected expenditures as a percent of payroll of 17.86 in 2030 is used for this calculation.

14. Congressional Research Service (1976), 8.

15. Ibid., 5–8.

16. Author's calculations using data from the 1980 Current Population Survey and the NBER TAXIM model.

17 U.S. Senate, Committee on Finance, *Hearings on Social Security Financing Proposals*, 95th Cong., 1st Sess., June–July 1977, 22.

18. Ibid, 24.

19. Ibid, 5.

20. Congressmen Archer's quote is from House of Representatives, Ways and Means Committee, Subcommittee on Social Security, *Hearings on President Carter's Social Security Proposals, Part 1*, May 10, 1977, 15. Senator Long's quote is from U.S. Senate, Committee on Finance, *Hearings on Social Security Financing Proposals*, 95th Cong., 1st Sess., June–July 1977, 21.

21. *Social Security Trustees Report* (1978), 2.

22. President Carter, The Social Security Amendments of 1977, Remarks as the Signing Ceremony, December 20, 1977.

23. *Social Security Trustees Report* (1980), 3.

24. "Carter, Congress and Welfare: A Long Road," *Congressional Quarterly Almanac 1977*, 471–478.

25. President Carter's Message on Welfare Reform, August 8, 1977.

26. *New York Times* (August 9, 1977) gave its support by saying, "Mr. Carter has offered us the good and it deserves our support." Similarly, the *Washington Post* (August 7, 1977) opined that "the administration has done its work well: It has come out at the right place." In the same vein, the *Los Angeles Times* (August 10, 1977) wrote, "Carter's program wouldn't solve all . . . of the country's problems of poverty and deprivation. But it is going in the right direction."

27. Committee on Finance, Subcommittee on Public Assistance, statement of the Children's Defense Fund, *Hearings on Welfare Reform Proposals*, 95th Cong., 2nd Sess., 1978, 1319.

28. Ibid. The quote is from the statement of William Welsh of the American Federation of State, County, and Municipal Employees, 1196.

29. Committee on Finance, Subcommittee on Public Assistance, *Hearings on Welfare Reform Proposals*. Representing NGA, Governor Hugh Carey testified that the NGA supported a "national minimum benefit to promote equity among recipients and states . . . and . . . fiscal relief for state and local governments," 888. See also David Broder, "Governors Support Welfare Reform Plan," *Washington Post*, September 9, 1977.

30. The label was provided by Congressman Steve Symms (R-ID): House Subcommittee on Welfare Reform, *Hearings on the Administration's Welfare Reform Proposal, Part 1*, September 19–21, 1977, 112.

31. Committee on Finance, Subcommittee on Public Assistance, statement of Robert B. Carelson, *Hearings on Welfare Reform Proposals*, 665.

32. "One FAP Fiasco Is Enough," *Washington Post*, October 7, 1977.

33. *Los Angeles Times*, August 15, 1977.

34. Congressional Budget Office (1978), 83.

35. House of Representatives, Subcommittee on Welfare Reform, *Hearings on the Administration's Welfare Reform Proposal, Part 1*, 112.

36. The Nixon plan set the cutoff income level for assistance for a family of four at about $6,000, after adjusting for inflation to 1979 dollars. The Carter plan's cutoff was set at $8,400, and the earned income tax credit extended the cutoff to $9,600.

37. See Keeley et al. (1977) for results from the Seattle-Denver negative income tax experiment and Cogan (1978) for results from the New Jersey–Pennsylvania negative income tax experiment.

38. House of Representatives, Subcommittee on Welfare Reform, *Hearings on the Administration's Welfare Reform Proposal*, 59.

39. Ibid., 1330.

40. House of Representatives, Agriculture Committee, *Hearings on 1977 Amendments*, 94th Cong., 1st Sess., 1975, 893.

41. New York investigators uncovered a million-dollar scheme involving cash purchases of food stamps by a White Plains check-cashing firm. "A $1 Million Food-Stamp Embezzlement Laid to Head of White Plains Check Firm," *New York Times*, September 9, 1976. Investigators in the District of Columbia reported that more than $300,000 in cash used to purchase food stamps was missing from the Friendship House Community Federal Credit Union. *Washington Post*, March 24, 1977.

42. Herman Talmadge to Secretary Bergland, February 24, 1977; U.S. Senate, Agriculture Committee, *Hearings on Food Stamps*, 95th Cong., 1st Sess., 1977, 178.

43. U.S. Senate, Agriculture Committee, *Hearings on Food Stamps*, 181.

44. Senator Steve Symms (ID) expressed this view by saying that free food stamps would "all but eliminate the nutritional focus of the Food Stamp program and substantially transform [it] into an all-purpose income supplement."

45. The 1972 law allowed the federal government to assign claims to coal mine operators. But only 25 to 30 percent of all claims had been assigned. McClure (1981), 10.

46. U.S. Senate, Committee on Labor and Human Resources, Subcommittee on Labor, statement of John Erlenborn, *Hearings: Black Lung Benefits and Revenue Amendments of 1981*, 97th Cong., 1st Sess., December 1981, 35.

47. House, Ways and Means Committee, *Green Book* (1991), 1479.

48. Ibid., 1482. Pub. L. 99-272 (1985) forgave interest payments.

49. The following discussion is taken from the *Green Book* (1991), 452–460.

50. Pub. L. 93-618, January 3, 1975.

51. The union percentage is from ibid., 460. The percent of persons who entered training, the percent of recipients who returned to their original employer, and the percent who applied after returning to work are from the U.S. Office of Management and Budget, Fiscal Year 1982 Budget Revisions, Additional Details on Budget Savings, April 1981, 241.

52. The statistics are my calculations from the March 1981 Current Population Survey.

53. My calculation from the Current Population Survey (see "Notes on Major Data Sources"). If only cash assistance is counted, the poorest fifth of the population receives 33 percent of all entitlement assistance, the second quintile receives 28 percent, the middle quintile receives 18 percent, and the two highest quintiles receive 21 percent.

54. See Paglin (1980). For a valuable summary of the issues involved in calculating poverty, see National Research Council (1995).

55. Harris (1980).

56. The AFDC erroneous payments are reported in "ADC Overpayments Top Billion in Year, U.S. Says," *Chicago Tribune*, March 13, 1980. The Medicaid estimate is obtained from U.S. House, Committee on Appropriations Departments of Labor, Health and Human Services, *Hearings on Education and Related Agencies Appropriations FY 81, part 2*, February 19–22, 25–27, March 3, 1980. The billion-dollar figure is obtained by applying the reported 9 percent error rate to the $12 billion of Medicaid spending in FY1979. Investigators estimated that food stamp overpayments were as high as $1.8 billion. U.S. Senate, Committee on Appropriations, "Need for an Overall Strategy to Combat Fraud, Worker Errors, and Regulation Loopholes in the Department of Agriculture's Food Stamp Program," November 1980, 4.

57. U.S. Senate, Committee on Governmental Affairs, Inspector General, Department of Health, Education and Welfare, statement of Thomas Morris, *Hearings before the Permanent Subcommittee on Investigations*, 95th Cong., 2nd Sess., July 20, 1978, 19.

58. "NU Professor Held in Welfare Scheme," *Boston Globe*, May 14, 1980.

59. "Half of 913 Guyana Temple Victims Had Received Calif Welfare Checks," *Washington Post*, December 7, 1979.

60. Taylor's story was told in a series of *Chicago Tribune* articles, including "Welfare Queen Quiz Goes Abroad," February 3, 1975; "Welfare Queen Is Under New Probe," April 10, 1975; "Welfare Queen's Role: Was It Voodoo Spell?" June 29; "Medical 'Practice' Just That for Welfare Queen," July 14, 1975; "Welfare 'Queen' Indicted Again; 2 Kin Also Named," September 18, 1975.

61. Reports of other "welfare queens" further ingrained this image. In 1979, the *Chicago Tribune* ("City's Reigning Welfare Aid Queen Gets Four Years for Fraud," January 9, 1979) labeled Arlene Otis, a mother of four children, the "city's reigning welfare aid queen" when she was convicted of bilking state welfare programs out of $150,000 in funds over six years. In Los Angeles, Barbara Williams, a 33-year-old mother of four, was charged with using fake drivers' licenses, Social Security cards, and birth certificates to defraud the government of over $100,000. Bill Hazlett, "'Welfare Queen,' 5 Others Charged in New Fraud Case," *Los Angeles Times*, August 18, 1979, B1.

62. The use of food stamps to purchase the car and the gun is from "Probe of Food Stamp Abuses Leads to Arrest of Floridian," *Washington Post*, February 17, 1975. The example of the woman who used her stamps to pay off her parking ticket is from "USDA under Fire in Food Stamp Probe," *Chicago Tribune*, November 17, 1975. Examples of other newspaper stories are "Food Stamp Fraud Reported in Florida," *Los Angeles Times*, February 16, 1975;

"Food Stamp Fraud Costing State Millions," *Chicago Tribune*, February 15, 1975.

63. Senate Committee on Finance, Subcommittee on Health, statement of Oliver Revell, *Hearing on Medicare and Medicaid Fraud*, July 22, 1980, 7–8.

64. General Accounting Office, "Tighter Controls Needed over Payments for Laboratory Services under Medicare and Medicaid," HRD-76-121, August 4, 1976.

65. "Doctors' 'Assembly Line' for Welfare Patients Bared," *Chicago Tribune*, January 23, 1975. Examples of welfare worker fraud are: "Three in Welfare Fraud Sentenced," *Los Angeles Times*, January 25, 1975; "Employees of City Found on Relief: 1,388 Workers Suspected of Getting Aid," *New York Times*, January 11, 1975"; Woman Jailed for Welfare Fraud," *Los Angeles Times*, October 24, 1975; "10 Former Aid Workers Indicted in Stamp Theft," *Chicago Tribune*, May 30, 1979; "75 Indicted in Welfare Fraud Netting More Than $1 Million," *Chicago Tribune*, June 29, 1979; "5 Ex-Welfare Workers Indicted," *Chicago Tribune*, March 30, 1979; "57 Indicted in Welfare Fraud," *New York Times*, May 31, 1979.

66. One of the early studies of AFDC and work incentives is an examination of AFDC by Durbin (1973). The major study of work incentives from the Seattle–Denver negative income tax experiment is Keeley et al. (1978). Levy (1979) finds that the "thirty-and-a-third" provision enacted in the 1967 Public Assistance Amendments reduced overall labor supply.

67. An example of early research is Long (1958). An early survey is Palmore (1964). The first important study finding that Social Security induced retirement is Boskin (1977). Later research found similar but much smaller effects. See, for example, Burtless (1986). More recent research has found effects as large as, or larger than, Boskin's.

68. See Parsons (1980a, 1980b).

69. Classen (1977); Moffitt and Nicholson (1982).

70. Tillmon (1972).

71. The most influential study of this period is Hannan, Tuma, and Groeneveld (1977). Valuable reviews of the evidence provided by Bishop (1980), Hutchens (1979), and Honig (1974) find compelling evidence that AFDC reduces the probability of remarriage. For a critique of Honig, see Minarik and Goldfarb (1976) and Honig (1976) for a reply.

Chapter 17

1. President Ronald Reagan, Address before a Joint Session of the Congress Reporting on the State of the Union, January 26, 1982.

2. President Ronald Reagan, Address to the Nation on the Economy, February 6, 1981. The increase in consumer prices (as measured by the CPI for

All Urban Consumers) and the number of unemployed persons are measured from January 1979 to January 1981. Net domestic investment is expressed in inflation-adjusted terms using the GDP deflator. Industrial capacity is measured by "Capacity Utilization: Total Industry" (https://fred.stlouisfed.org/).

3. In the late 1970s, none of the federal income tax code's sixteen separate tax brackets were indexed to inflation. With only $4,000 to $5,000 separating one tax bracket from the next, middle-income taxpayers were quickly pushed into higher personal income tax brackets as their incomes rose with inflation.

4. President Ronald Reagan, Message to the Congress Transmitting the Proposed Package on the Program for Economic Recovery, February 18, 1981.

5. Congressional Budget Office, "An Analysis of President Reagan's Budget Revisions for Fiscal Year 1982," March 1981, Table 4.

6. My calculations from Office of Management and Budget, "Additional Details on Budget Savings, Fiscal Year 1982 Budget Revisions," April 1981.

7. Of the $49 billion in proposed savings from the budget baseline, $16 billion came from rapidly growing entitlements. The lion's share of remaining $29 billion in nondefense budget reductions would be taken from nondefense discretionary programs.

8. The Reagan revisions to the 1982 budget proposed to increase defense spending relative to its estimated baseline by $28 billion in 1982. Neither the president's budget revisions nor CBO provided a defense budget baseline for defense. The baseline estimate is constructed by increasing the 1980 outlays by the Reagan administration's projected rate of inflation for 1981 and 1982. For inflation assumptions, see Office of Management and Budget, "Additional Details on Budget Savings, Fiscal Year 1982 Budget Revisions," April 1981, 13. Defense outlays for 1980 are provided in the same document on p. 34.

9. Fiscal Year 1982 Budget Revisions, February 1981, 8–9.

10. U.S. Office of Management and Budget, "Major Themes and Additional Details," FY1984, 27.

11. The administration proposed to reduce child nutrition subsidies to children with family incomes above 185 percent of poverty, eliminate subsidies for lunches served in high-tuition private schools, and limit the number of subsidized snacks to children in day care programs.

12. The proposals included eliminating welfare agency use of estimated "prospective," rather than actual, income, to determine AFDC, food stamp, and Supplemental Security Income program eligibility; requiring benefits to new recipients to be prorated over their first month on the rolls instead of providing an entire month of benefits regardless of when during the month the new recipients became eligible; and eliminating nutrition education and nutrition equipment subsidies. The administration also proposed to eliminate the Special Milk program and the fraud-ridden Summer Feeding program. House of Representatives, Committee on Education and Labor, Subcommittee

on Elementary, Secondary, and Vocational Education, statement of Richard Lyng, *Hearings on the Administration's Fiscal Year 1982 budget Authorizing for Child Nutrition*, 1981, 5.

13. House of Representatives, Subcommittee on Social Security, testimony of David A. Stockman *Hearing*, 40–41, May 28, 1981.

14. The measure of unemployment was the state's insured unemployment rate. The administration also proposed to revise the calculation of the unemployment rate used for the state triggers to exclude EB recipients.

15. General Accounting Office, "Legislation Allows Black Lung Benefits to Be Awarded without Adequate Evidence of Disability," Report HRD-80-81 (1980), 13–14.

16. Senate, Committee on Labor and Human Resources, Subcommittee on Labor, statement of Robert Collyer, *Hearings, Black Lung Benefits and Revenue Amendments of 1981*, 97th Cong., 1st Sess., December 1981, 17–19. The administration proposed to double the coal tonnage tax, require earnings and other disability benefits to offset black lung benefits, and limit assistance to widows of miners who had actually died of black lung disease

17. President Reagan, Message on the Budget, February 18, 1981.

18. President Ronald Reagan, Remarks at a Meeting with Chief Executive Officers of National Organizations to Discuss Private Sector Initiatives, March 24, 1982.

19. *Congressional Quarterly Weekly Report*, May 16, 1981.

20. See Schick (1980) for a comprehensive treatment of the act. The act also limited the president's power to impound federal funds that Congress had previously appropriated. The presidential use of impoundments had been confined to nonentitlement programs.

21. A vote by the full chamber in favor of instructions constituted a strong expression of the will of Congress to each of the committees affected. If an entitlement committee failed to comply with the instructions, the process permitted the budget committee to develop its own legislative proposal to achieve the specified restraint.

22. Importantly, the special rules governing debate over a budget reconciliation bill precluded a Senate filibuster.

23. See White and Wildavsky (1989) for a comprehensive treatment of the 1981 and 1982 budget battles.

24. *Congressional Quarterly Weekly Report*, February 21, 1981.

25. Ibid., March 14, 1981.

26. Ibid., February 21, 1981.

27. Ibid., April 11, 1981, 662.

28. Nutrition picketing was reported in *Congressional Quarterly Weekly Report*, March 14, 1981; railroad workers' marches in "Railroad Workers Protest Proposal to Cut U.S. Subsidies," *Washington Post*, April 30, 1981; the

UMW demonstration and the nationwide demonstrations in "Black Lung Program Cuts Protested," *Washington Post*, May 10, 1981; the AFL-CIO rally in David Broder, The Rising Opposition to Reagan . . . ," *Washington Post*, September 23, 1981.

29. "Fiscal 1982 Reconciliation Cuts: $35.2 Billion," *Congressional Quarterly Almanac 1981*, 256–266.

30. Ibid.

31. Ibid.

32. White and Wildavsky (1989), 153.

33. The quotes by Representatives Latta and Jones are from "Fiscal 1982 Reconciliation Cuts: $35.2 Billion," *Congressional Quarterly Almanac 1981*, 255–266. President Reagan's quote is from Ronald Reagan, Remarks on Signing the Economic Recovery Tax Act of 1981 and the Omnibus Budget Reconciliation Act of 1981, August 13, 1981.

34. My calculation. Entitlement savings are contained in U.S. Budget for FY1983, Part 3, 6. Entitlement outlays and their projected growth are contained in FY1982 Budget Revisions, Additional Details on Budget Savings, April 1981.

35. The law reduced the federal match rate by 3 percent reduction in 1982, 4 percent in 1983, and 4.5 percent in 1984.

36. Congress restored the minimum benefit later in December of that year in Pub. L. 97-123.

37. U.S. House, Ways and Means Committee, Subcommittee on Social Security, *Hearings on Social Security Financing Recommendations*, 97th Cong., 1st Sess., May 28, 1981, 41.

38. Congress had little desire to enact additional payroll increases. It had raised the payroll tax rate by 10 percent and the ceiling on taxable wages by 80 percent in 1977.

39. The administration proposed to reduce early retirement benefits to 55 percent from 80 percent of the normal retirement age benefit. Other proposals included ending the children's benefit for early retirees, capping family benefits to prevent the total for any family from exceeding the worker's net take-home pay, taxing the first six months of sick pay, phasing out the earnings test, delaying for three months the following year's cost-of-living increase, and slowing the growth in initial monthly Social Security benefits paid to future retirees.

40. "President Faces Potentially Divisive Battle," *Washington Post*, May 13, 1981.

41. "Coalition Plans Drive against Move to Trim Social Security," *New York Times*, May 14, 1981. Clayman's quote is from *Congressional Quarterly*, February 21, 1981.

42. *Congressional Quarterly,* May 30, 1981. Democratic Social Security Committee members refrained from joining the attack. Under Democratic control, the House Ways and Means Committee's Social Security Subcommittee had recently given tentative agreement to a plan to increase Social Security's retirement age from 65 to 68.

43. The Cohen and Clayman quotes are from "Coalition Plans Drive against Move to Trim Social Security," *New York Times,* May 14, 1981.

44. "Congress Votes Fiscal 1981 Funds, Rescissions," *Congressional Quarterly Almanac 1981,* 281–285.

45. "Senate Resolves to Safeguard Social Security," *Wall Street Journal,* May 21, 1981.

46. My calculation from House Ways and Means Committee, "Actuarial Cost Estimates of the Effects of Public Law 9821 on the Old-age, Survivors, and Disability Insurance and Hospital Insurance Program," September 8, 1983. If the income taxation of benefits is counted as a benefit reduction rather than as a revenue increase, the remaining payroll tax increases were projected to account for 51 percent of the trust fund's improvement.

47. Starting in the year 2000, the law raised the retirement age for workers reaching age 62 by two months each year until the retirement age reached 66 years. The increases then paused for a period of twelve years and then began at the same rate until the retirement age reaches 67 in 2022.

48. See Social Security Trustees, *Report* (2015), Table V, 7C.

49. *Annual Statistical Supplement to the Social Security Bulletin* (2008), Table 5.D3.

50. General Accounting Office, "More Diligent Followup Needed to Weed Out Ineligible SSA Disability Beneficiaries," HRD-81-48, March 1981.

51. House, Committee on Ways and Means, *Green Book* (1984), 94.

52. House of Representatives, Ways and Means Subcommittee on Social Security, memorandum from William Roemmich, *Hearings on the Disability Insurance Program,* 94th Cong., 2nd Sess., May 17, 1976.

53. See Koitz (1980), 40–44. General Accounting Office, statement of Gregory J. Ahart before the Subcommittee on Social Security, Committee on Ways and Means, 5 (http://www.gao.gov/assets/100/98687.pdf).

54. The administration proposed to require disability recipients to have worked in the recent past and to limit monthly disability benefits to a worker's prior after-tax earnings.

55. The fact that such reductions occurred during a severe economic recession, when disability claims invariably increase, makes it all the more remarkable. During the 1970–71 recession, new awards had risen by 19 percent and in the 1974–75 recession by 21 percent. House, Committee on Ways and Means, *Green Book* (1983).

56. See, for example, "Social Security Disability Cutoffs Assailed at Congressional Hearing," *New York Times*, May 22, 1982.

57. Examples include a September 17, 1982, *Los Angeles Times* story, "11 Denied Disability Benefits Die of Illness," that detailed the tragic consequences of unfair benefit terminations of various individuals. Another *Los Angeles Times*, November 7, 1981, story chronicled the shotgun suicide of a 46-year-old man who suffered from a back injury that, upon review, no longer qualified him for continued benefits. A May 27, 1982, *Washington Post* story, "In the Rush for Budget Savings, a Life Is Trampled," told the story of a man who died of a heart attack after receiving notice that his benefits had been terminated.

58. "Bill on Pension Appeal Passes," *New York Times*, December 22, 1982.

59. The court ultimately rejected the suit.

60. "House Votes to Ease Review of Disability Benefits," *New York Times*, March 27, 1984.

61. Pub. L. 98-460.

62. *Annual Statistical Supplement to the Social Security Bulletin* (1983), Table 48, and ibid. (1992), Table 5. D5.

63. President Ronald Reagan, Televised Address to the Nation on the Program for Economic Recovery, September 24, 1981.

64. The administration proposed to eliminate all federal matching payments for erroneous welfare benefits; to require all able-bodied AFDC and food stamp recipients to work, and to reduce the food stamps earnings disregard. It also proposed to reduce the federal match rate for optional medical services and to allow states to charge modest Medicaid copayments. And it proposed limits on cost-of-living increases for federal civilian and military retirees and reduced veterans' compensation payments for veterans with partial disabilities. The main Medicare proposals included lowering permissible upper limits on hospital and physician reimbursement rates.

65. Representative Leon Panetta (D-CA), a fiscal leader among Democrats, declared, "I don't think there's any question up here that this budget isn't going to fly " (*CQ Weekly Report*, February 20, 1982). The Senate Budget Committee chairman, Pete Domenici (R-NM), opined that "only something like a miracle will allow this plan to be adopted this year " (*CQ Weekly Report*, November 13, 1981).

66. The only exception was the Social Security Disability Insurance program, which after the bloodletting and the 1984 disability legislation, neither the administration nor congressional Republicans wanted to reconsider.

67. Two major budget reduction bills were enacted in 1982: OBRA of 1982 (Pub. L. 97-253) and the Tax Equity and Fiscal Responsibility Act (Pub. L. 97-248). Savings from these laws are provided in H. Rep. No. 72-350, 82, and H. Rep. No. 97-760, 464. Two major budget reduction laws enacted in 1984

were OBRA of 1984 (Pub. L. 98-258) and the Deficit Reduction Act of 1984 (Pub. L. 98-369). Savings from the 1984 laws are contained in CBO, "The Economic and Budget Outlook, an Update," FY1984, August 1984, 56, and H. Rep. No. 98-673, 98th Cong., 2nd Sess., 8. Two major budget reduction bills were enacted in 1986: the Consolidated Budget Reconciliation Act of 1985 (COBRA) (Pub. L. 99-272) and the OBRA of 1986 (Pub. L. 99-509). Savings from COBRA are provided in House, Committee on Ways and Means, *Green Book* (1987), 849. Savings include those from changes in entitlement programs and exclude receipts from asset sales. Savings from OBRA of 1986 are provided in S. Doc. No. 99-46, 160. One major budget reduction bill was enacted in 1987: OBRA of 1987 (Pub. L. 100-203). The 1987 savings are contained in House, Committee on Ways and Means, *Green Book* (1988), 967. The savings from the 1987 legislation are an average over two years and do not include asset sales and offsetting receipts. They are reported in CBO, "The Economic and Budget Outlook: Fiscal Years 1989–93," February 1988, 59.

68. The increase is measured over the years 1985 to 1990.

69. The 1982 Medicare changes were contained in Pub. L. 97-248. The 1983 Medicare prospective payment system was enacted in Pub. L. 98-21. The EITC changes were made in Pub. L. 98-369 and Pub. L. 99-514. The new civil service retirement program was added in Pub. L. 99-335. The AFDC changes were contained in Pub. L. 100-485.

70. The 1984 AFDC changes were contained in Pub. L. 98-369, which also included twenty other relatively minor changes; the most significant was to extend the $30 per month income disregard to twelve months. The food stamp program changes were made in Pub. L. 99-198.

71. The 1984 Deficit Reduction Act (Pub. L. 98-369) allowed federal matching rates to return to their 1981 levels. The law also extended the period of Medicaid eligibility of households that had earned their way off AFDC from four to eight months. A third provision of the law required states to phase in coverage of children up to 5 years of age who were born after September 30, 1983, and first-time pregnant women in two-parent households who met the qualifying standards for AFDC, regardless of whether they were enrolled in the program. In 1986, Congress required state Medicaid programs to cover all pregnant women in two-parent households if the main breadwinner was unemployed (Pub. L. 99-272). In a separate 1986 law (Pub. L. 100-203), Congress extended coverage for children newly covered under the 1984 law to age 7. In the 1988 Medicare Catastrophic Coverage Act (Pub. L. 100-360), Congress required all states to cover pregnant women and infants up to age 1 in households with income under the poverty line. The same year, in the Family Support Act (Pub. L. 100-485), which required all states to adopt AFDC-UP programs, Congress also required all states to cover families enrolled in the AFDC-UP program. In 1989, Congress required all states to cover pregnant

women and children on a phased-in basis up to age 6 who lived in households with incomes below 133 percent of poverty (Pub. L. 191-239). In 1990, Congress required all states to cover children on a phased-in basis up to age 19 who lived in households with incomes less than the poverty line.

72. Langlois (2014), 31.

73. Pub. L. 99-177, December 12, 1985.

74. The law also exempted several mandatory programs, including payments for legal claims against the government, the Postal Service Fund, the Foreign Military Sales Trust Fund, and legal obligations of insurance and loan guarantee funds. Similar limitations were imposed on reductions in veterans medical care, community health centers, migrant health centers, and Indian health facilities and services. Allen Schick, "Explanation of the Balanced Budget and Emergency Deficit Control Act of 1985," Congressional Research Service, February 1986.

75. Congressional Research Service, General Revenue Sharing, Action in the 99th Cong., December 17, 1986.

76. "Mayors Back Revenue-Sharing Fight," *Washington Post*, March 11, 1986.

77. Ronald Reagan, Remarks at the Annual Legislative Conference of the National Association of Counties, March 4, 1985.

78. "Reagan Cutbacks Worry Cities and States," *Los Angeles Times*, March 31, 1985.

79. Committee on Appropriations, Subcommittee on HUD and Independent Agencies Appropriations, Department of Housing and Urban Development, and Certain Independent Agencies Appropriations, March 27–28, 1985, 454.

80. Ronald Reagan, Statement on Proposed Catastrophic Health Insurance Legislation, February 12, 1987.

81. The deductible was slated to rise to over $1,000 and the coinsurance rate to decline to 20 percent in four years. The law, Pub. L. 100-360, also required state Medicaid programs to pay all Medicare premiums and deductibles for poor persons, regardless of whether they were enrolled in Medicaid. CBO, "Medicare Catastrophic Coverage Act of 1988," Staff Working Paper, October 1988.

82. "Catastrophic Health Insurance Bill Enacted," *Congressional Quarterly Almanac 1988*, 281–292.

83. Congressional Budget Office, "Updated Estimates of Medicare's Catastrophic Drug Insurance Program," October 1989, 48.

84. "Catastrophic Coverage Law Is Repealed," *Congressional Quarterly Almanac 1989*, 149.

85. My calculation of the change in the number of households receiving benefits from at least one entitlement program is from the Current Population

Survey (see notes on sources). With the exception of the black lung recipients, the source for the caseload numbers is House, Committee on Ways and Means, *Green Book* (1991). The black lung caseload is taken from the *Annual Statistical Supplement to the Social Security Bulletin* (2013), Table 9D.

Chapter 18

1. Letter from Thomas Jefferson to Samuel Kerchevel, July 12, 1816.

2. Annual Social Security accounting surpluses reached $50 billion in the 1990s and more than $150 billion in the next decade. Although lawmakers regularly claimed that the surpluses were due to their foresighted actions in 1983, the surpluses were entirely unintended. See *Report of the National Commission on Social Security Reform* (1983) for a statement of the commission's intent and Blahous (2010) for a thorough discussion of the issue.

3. Representative Bill Thomas (R-CA), for example, argued that the trust fund merely contained "IOUs represented by notations on the federal books." See House of Representatives, Ways and Means Committee, Social Security Subcommittee *Hearings, Proposals for Alternative Investment of Social Security Trust Fund Reserves*, 103rd Cong., 2nd Sess., October 1994, 9.

4. Ibid., 8.

5. See Pub. L. 103-296, sec. 301, August 15, 1994.

6. See Trustees Report (1994), 18, for a discussion of the importance of the 1984 disability insurance law's provisions.

7. Pub. L. 103-387, October 22, 1994, lowered the OASI tax rate and raised the DI tax rate by .68 percentage points from 1994 to 1996, .5 percentage points from 1997 to 1999, and .6 percentage points thereafter. Congress did make one change in disability benefits in 1994. Pub. L. 103-296 limited the duration of benefits paid to addicts and alcoholics to thirty-six months. All but the 1981 tax shifts were permanent. The 1981 tax shift was for only one year.

8. Previous tax shifts occurred in 1965, 1967, 1969, 1977 and 1981. The $500 billion estimate is computed by multiplying the changes, plus the changes enacted in 1994 by each year's taxable wages. *Annual Statistical Supplement to the Social Security Bulletin* (2014).

9. , Robert D. Novak, "What Social Security Trust Fund?" *Washington Post*, December 6, 1996.

10. Bills introduced in the 102nd Congress (1991–92) include House Reports 56, 210, 437, 439, 1641, and 3812. Bills introduced in the 103th Congress include House Reports 306, 316, and 2539. Bills introduced in the 104th Congress include House Reports 2928 and 3098. Bills introduced in the 105th Congress include House Reports 3207 and 3822

11. Quoted in Blahous (2010), 80. Similarly, Representative Andy Jacobs (D-IN), when asked about the wisdom of allowing large Social Security surpluses to build, had responded, "It'll be like walking through a bad

neighborhood with a diamond ring." Quoted in Lee Smith, "Trim That Social Security Surplus," *Fortune Magazine*, August 29, 1989.

12. For a description of the plan, see the Federal Budget for Fiscal Year 2000, 41.

13. The Government Accounting Office summarized the proposal as follows: "The changes to the Social Security program will thus be more perceived than real. . . . The President's proposal does not alter the projected cash flows . . . even [by] 1 cent." Blahous (2010), 99.

14. Budget of the U.S. Government, 2001, 41.

15. U.S. House of Representatives, Committee on Ways and Means, statement of Dan L. Crippen, director of the Congressional Budget Office, *Hearings on the President's Social Security Legislation*, 106th Cong., 1st Sess., November 8, 1999, 81.

16. Cong. Rec., vol. 145, part 4, March 23, 1999, S3185.

17. The president also proposed to invest a portion of Social Security surpluses in corporate stocks and bonds. The Senate voted down the proposal, 96–0. Koitz (2000).

18. The president initially proposed personal accounts in his Address before a Joint Session of the Congress, February 27, 2001.

19. Blanhous (2010), 245.

20. Pub. L. 111-312, December 17, 2010.

21. Pub. L. 112-78, December 23, 2011, and Pub. L. 112-96, February 22, 2012.

22 Pub. L. 114-74, November 2, 2015, raised the disability payroll tax rate by .57 percentage points and lowered the retirement program payroll tax rate by the same amount through 2018.

23. Recall that the law liberalized medical eligibility standards, allowed greater use of nonmedical, or vocational factors in the disability determination process, and shifted the burden of proof onto the government to show a recipient's "medical improvement" before it could terminate benefits. See Gokhale (2014).

24. Gokhale (2014). Data are from 1975 to 2010.

25. Duggan (2015), 4. Duggan also notes that disability benefits will be 43 percent higher than early retirement benefits for persons reaching age 62 in 2022.

26. Ibid.

27. The main food stamp extensions of this period were enacted in Pub. L. 101-508 and Pub. L. 103-66.

28. Ways and Means Committee, *Green Book* (2000), 809–813.

29. The 1986 law, Pub. L. 99-272, also allowed states to use Medicaid funds to pay for premiums and copayments of impoverished Medicare enrollees. In 1987, Congress gave states the option of providing Medicaid coverage to

impoverished children up to age 8. The law also raised the income thresh-old for optional coverage to 185 percent of the poverty line for families with children under age 6 (Pub. L. 100-203). In 1989, Congress raised the income threshold to states to cover children under age 6 in families with incomes less than 133 percent of the poverty line (Pub. L.101-239). The 1990 law, Pub. L. 101-508, also replaced the state option of using Medicaid funds to premiums and copayments for impoverished Medicare enrollees with a mandate and gradually raised the income threshold to 120 percent of poverty.

30. Pub. L. 105-33, August 5, 1997.

31. Ways and Means Committee, *Green Book* (2004), Table 2–16.

32. Bill report on Pub. L. 101-508, Energy and Commerce Reconciliation Provisions, 67–70.

33. Ibid.

34. See Senate, Finance Committee, testimony of Michael F. Mangano, *Hearings on Upper Payment Limits: Federal Medicaid Spending for Non-Medicaid Purposes*, 106th Cong., 2nd Sess., September 6, 2000.

35. The Reagan administration, concerned that such payments would become a source of abuse, issued regulations to limit the provision of DSH payments. Wynn et al. (2002).

36. U.S. General Accounting Office (1994).

37. Ibid.

38. In 1986, Congress overturned the Reagan administration's regula-tions. Two years later imposed a moratorium on the administration's new regulations.

39. House of Representatives, Committee on Energy and Commerce, Sub-committee on Health and the Environment, *Hearings on State Financing of Medicaid*, 102nd Cong., 1st Sess., September 30, 63.

40. Ibid., 162.

41. The 1991 law capped the state share of Medicaid expenses that could be financed through provider taxes and donations and imposed aggregate state limits on DSH payments from taxes and donations. Pub. L. 103-66 (1993) limited the amount of DSH payments that could be made to any individual hospital. Pub. L. 105-33 (1997) capped total federal DSH payments to states on a declining basis from 1998 to 2002. But when budget surpluses emerged in 2001 and 2002, Congress lifted the caps. Pub. L. 111-148, sec. 3133 of the Affordable Care Act. See Hearne (2005), 6–7.

42. Cong. Rec., vol. 141, part 17, September 6, 1995, S12683.

43. Bane and Ellwood (1994), 39.

44. The Bennett quote is from Weaver (2000), 151. These conclusions received widespread public attention by the 1984 publication of Charles Mur-ray's seminal book, *Losing Ground*.

45. House, Committee on Ways and Means, *Green Book* (2000), 247, 268.

46. Sullivan v. Zebley, 493 U.S. 521 (1990).

47. CRS, Disabled and Blind Child Recipients of Supplemental Security Income (SSI): Background and Concerns, October 12, 1993. Until the 1972 Supplemental Security Income law, disabled children were not covered by federal or federal-state disability programs. Children were covered by a parenthetical phrase inserted into the 1972 law that granted an entitlement to children who suffered from "any medically determinable physical or mental impairment of *comparable severity*." See Justice White's dissent, with Justice Rehnquist joining, in Sullivan v. Zebley (1990).

48. Carolyn Weaver, testimony before the Senate Finance Committee, "Growth of the Supplemental Security Income Program," 104th Cong., 1st Sess., March 27, 1995, 56.

49. See, for example, Bob Woodward and Benjamin Weiser, "Cost Soar for Children's Disability Programs," *Washington Post*, February 4, 1994.

50. Solomon (1983), 5.

51. The phrase "under the color of law," was inserted into the statute as a Senate floor amendment in 1972. The federal SSI law ran contrary to long-standing immigration law that barred immigrants who were unable to provide for themselves. The SSI law was quickly followed by laws granting immigrants eligibility for food stamps, Medicaid and AFDC.

52. Berger v. Heckler, 771 F.2d 1556 (1985).

53. House, Committee on Ways and Means, *Green Book* (2000), 1382–1383.

54. States had not allowed drug addicts or alcoholics to qualify for benefits under their SSI predecessor disability program. The 1972 SSI law allowed alcoholics and drug addicts to qualify for assistance, but only if they were receiving treatment and only if they allowed "representative payees" to receive their SSI checks and oversee the use of their funds. Subsequent key Court decisions include Badicheck v. Secretary of H.E.W, 374 F. Supp. 940 (1974); Griffis v. Weinberger, 509 F.2d 837 (1975); Cooper v. Bowen, 815 F.2d 557 (1987); Johnson v. Harris, 612 F.2d 993 (1980); Gerst v. Secretary of HHS, 709 F.2d 1075 (1983); Rutter v. Secretary of HHS, 914 F.2d 1495 (1990); McShea v. Schweiker, 700 F.2d 117 (1983); Purter v. Heckler, 771 F.2d 682 (1985); and Wilkerson v. Sullivan, 727 F. Supp. 925 (1989). See Hunt and Baumohl (2003).

55. "Addicts and Disability," *Washington Post*, November 16, 1994.

56. President William Jefferson Clinton, Address before a Joint Session of Congress on Administration Goals, February 17, 1993.

57. President William J. Clinton, Remarks before the National Governor's Association, February 2, 1993.

58. A dozen states required young recipients to attend school or older recipients to work to participate in job training programs. Eleven states allowed recipients to keep more of their welfare benefits if they worked, and ten states allowed recipients to build up larger amounts of assets, including

four states that permitted recipients to build modest savings accounts. Six states imposed limits on the amount of time adults could spend on the welfare rolls. A few states used their newly granted authority to reduce incentives for bearing children out of wedlock. Three states, including New Jersey, chose to no longer provide additional welfare benefits to mothers who had another child out of wedlock while on the rolls.

59. *CQ Weekly Report*, June 18, 1994.

60. Cong. Rec., vol. 141, part 6, March 21, 1995, H3352.

61. Committee on Ways and Means, H. Rep. 104-81, March 15, 1995.

62. Cong. Rec., vol. 141, part 17, September 6, 1995.

63. Representative William Clay (MO) denounced his Republican colleagues on the House floor by saying, "They ought to be ashamed, and they ought to go back into history and look and if [what they are doing] is close to what Adolph Hitler did to people. . . . "What's next? Castration? Sterilization?" Hasking (2006), 188. Cardiss Collins (D-IL): "If Attila the Hun were alive today and elected to Congress, he would be delighted with this bill that is before us today and proud to cast his vote for [the bill] it." Cong. Rec., vol. 141, part 6, March 22, 1995. Sam Gibbons (D-FL): "[The bill] will deprive them [children] of the basic necessities for food, of clothing, of housing, of education, of love." Cong. Rec., vol. 141, part 6, March 21, 1995. Representative Stupak (D-MI): "And their bill literally takes food out of the mouths of our kids." Cong. Rec., vol. 141, part 6, March 23, 1995.

64. House of Representatives, Ways and Means, 1995, Welfare Transformation Act of 1995, H. Rep. No. 104-81, Part 1, March 1995, 5.

65. Cong. Rec., vol. 142, no. 110, July 24, 1996. S8672.

66. Ibid., vol. 141, part 6, March 21, 1995, H3357.

67. The quote is from Senator Breaux, ibid., vol. 141, part 17, September 6, 1995, 23646.

68. The bill granted exceptions for certain elderly people, veterans, and refugees.

69. House of Representatives Ways and Means Committee, Welfare and Medicaid Reform Act of 1996, H. Rep. 104-65 (1996).

70. Cong. Rec., vol. 141, part 6, March 22, 1995.

71. Lewis (1995). The House Republican bill's illegitimacy provisions were another flash point for Democrats and pro-life Republicans. See Cong. Rec., vol. 141, part 6, March 21, 23, 1995.

72. Only nine House Democrats and five Senate Democrats voted in favor of the Republican bills that passed each chamber.

73. *CQ Weekly*, September 16, 1995.

74. "Welfare Unreformed," *New York Times*, December 21, 1995.

75. "Hard Hearts, Soft Heads," *Washington Post*, December 22, 1995.

76. President William Jefferson Clinton, Message to the House of Representatives Returning without Approval Legislation on the Welfare System, January 9, 1996.

77. A *New York Times* (August 1, 1996) editorial, "A Sad Day for Poor Children," cited a recently released study projecting that the bill would "throw a million more children into poverty," and declared, "This is not reform, it is punishment." The *Washington Post* ("The Welfare Decision," August 1, 1996) attacked President Clinton's motives by saying it was dictated by "political expediency and opportunism."

78. U.S. Department of Health and Human Services, Temporary Assistance to Needy Families Program, *Third Annual Report* (August 2000). Also see Weaver (2000), 348.

79. President John F. Kennedy, Special Message to Congress on Public Welfare Programs, February 1, 1962.

80. House, Committee on Ways and Means, *Green Book* (2014), Table 7–9.

81. See Haskins (2006) for a comprehensive review of analyses of the welfare reform law.

82. My calculation from the Current Population March Surveys from 2004 to 2006. The measure of work is positive weeks worked during the year.

83. President Ronald Reagan, Radio Address to the Nation on Welfare Reform, February 7, 1987.

84. From 1997 to 2012, Congress passed no fewer than fifteen laws making substantive changes to the SSI program. For a summary of SSI laws since 1996, see House, Committee on Ways and Means, *Green Book* (2012).

85. *Annual Statistical Supplement, Supplemental Security Income* (2014), Table 3.7A.

86. Food stamp recipients are from Supplemental Nutrition Assistance Program Participation and Costs, www.fns.usda.gov. Medicaid recipients are from Medicare/Medicaid Statistical Supplement (2013), Table 13.4 and http://kff.org/health-reform/state-indicator/medicaid-expansion-enrollment.

87. Recall that Medicare's allowable, or reasonable, charge was limited to the lowest of (1) the physician's actual charge for a service, (2) the physician's customary charge for that service, or (3) the prevailing charge for that service in the physician's locality. Prior to the 1984 law, annual increases in the prevailing charge had been limited to the Medical Economic Index, which reflects annual changes in the level of wages and physician practice costs. The 1984 law provided inducements, including a higher prevailing charge and more rapid payment of claims, for physicians to accept Medicare as payment in full for their services, that is, to limit the amount patients were billed to Medicare's deductible and coinsurance rates. The 1987 law imposed maximum allowable actual charges to 1 percent per year.

88. Previously, Congress had established fee schedules for clinical lab tests and durable medical equipment.

89. The law barred the practice of balanced billing for services provided to all Medicare patients who were also eligible for Medicaid.

90. The period is 1991 to 1895. Data are from the Medicare and Medicaid Statistical Supplement (2003), Table 55.

91. "Big Medicare, Medicaid Changes Enacted in Budget Bills," *Congressional Quarterly Almanac 1997*, 6-3–6-12.

92. House, Committee on Ways and Means, *Green Book* (2004), 2–80, for home health outlays. *Green Book* (2004), 2–70, 2–106 for skilled nursing and outpatient outlays in 1997, respectively. *Green Book* (2000), 135, 157 for 1987 skilled nursing and outpatient outlays in 1997, respectively.

93. Pub. L. 96-499, December 5, 1980.

94. See Duggan v. Bowen, 691 F. Supp. 1487 (1988). House Committee on Ways and Means, *Green Book* (2004), 2–78.

95. The new prospective payment system established a fee schedule for over five hundred individual medical procedures, tests, and services that are provided in hospital outpatient departments; reimbursed home health agencies on the basis of a sixty-day visit; and reimbursed skilled nursing facilities on a per diem basis that varies with the severity of the patient's condition and the type of services provided. House, Committee on Ways and Means, *Green Book* (2004).

96. Under this policy, cost-sharing amounts paid by outpatients declined from around 40 percent in 2001 to 22 percent in 2014. MedPac, *Health Care Spending and the Medicare Program: A Data Book*, June 2015, 101.

97. *Medicare and Medicaid Statistical Supplement*, 2003, Table 55.

98. Hahn (2014), 2. The SGR replaced a voluntary performance standards approach that had attempted, but failed, to achieve the same outcome.

99. The global budget had the unintended consequence of further exacerbating physician incentives to increase the volume of services provided. The global budget created a prisoners' dilemma, which works as follows. A physician who increases the volume of services receives a higher income if all other physicians do not and suffers no loss of income if all other physicians also increase their volume of services. A physician who does not increase his or her volume of services to patients runs the risk of a reduction in income if all other physicians increase their volumes. Under these circumstances, the rational physician will seek to protect his or her income by increasing the volume of services provided.

100. Hahn (2014), 6–8. The provision was repealed in Pub. L. 114-10, April 5, 2015.

101. MEDPAC (2016), 90, reports that physician payments per beneficiary were 70 percent higher in 2015 than in 2000. MEDPAC (2016), 112, reports

that physician payments were 1.6 percent higher in 2015 than in 2014. CMS (2016), 2, reports that were 39 percent more enrollees in 2015 than in 2000.

102. MEDPAC (2016), 91, provides the cumulative growth in each category from 2000 to 2014. MEDPAC (2017), 112, provides the growth in each category from 2014 to 2015.

103. In 1972, Congress had first authorized Medicare HMOs. But by 1979, only a few HMOs had been approved. The 1982 Tax Equity and Responsibility Act expanded HMOs by relaxing some of the prior law's restrictive requirements, but enrollment remained low. In 1994, only 5 percent of Medicare beneficiaries were enrolled in managed care plans.

104. Medicare/Medicaid Statistical Supplement (2003), Table 74.

105. In the ensuing years, coverage had been expanded to particular medicines, including immunosuppressive drugs. O'Sullivan (2002).

106. Oliver et al. (2004), 298. The quote is attributable to House majority leader Jim Wright (D-TX).

107. Seventy-one percent of Medicare beneficiaries with incomes below the poverty line had coverage, and 73 percent of all Medicare beneficiaries had coverage. Morgan (2001), 2.

108. Morgan (2001), 3.

109. *CBO Budget and Economic Outlook*, 1999, 2000, and 2001.

110. President Clinton proposed to spend $230 billion over the next ten years. President George W. Bush's more modest plan carried a $153 billion ten-year price tag. In 2002, House and Senate Republicans proposed to spend $350 billion. Senate Democrats then upped the ante to $800 billion.

111. Cong. Rec., vol. 149, November 24, 2003, S15673.

112. House, Energy and Commerce Committee Bill Report, H. Rep. No. 108-178, pt. 1, 239, June 25, 2003.

113. House, Ways and Means Bill Report, Medicare Prescription Drug and Modernization Act of 2003, H. Rep. No. 108–178, 296.

114. "Medicare Revamp Cuts It Close," *Congressional Quarterly Almanac 2003*, 11-3–11-8.

115. The final vote on the bill was 220–215. For a discussion of the House action on the law, see Oliver, Lee, and Lipton (2004), 321–322, and Starr (2011), 149.

116. The government paid 75 percent of the expenses up to $2,250 per year and 95 percent of expenses over $5,100.

117. Congressional Budget Office Testimony, statement of Dan L. Crippen, Projections of Medicare and Prescription Drug Spending before the Committee on Finance, March 7, 2002, 9.

118. Starr (2011), 248. Candidate Obama criticized Hillary Clinton's individual mandate proposal and instead proposed an employer mandate that

required employers to contribute an unspecified minimum contribution toward employees' insurance.

119. The refundable credit, which had first been proposed by congressional Republicans during the early 1970s' debate over national health insurance and subsequently by George H. W. Bush, had become a Republican staple by 2008.

120. President Barack Obama, Address to a Joint Session of the Congress on Health Care Reform, September 9, 2009.

121. On the impact of the tax exclusion, see Phelps (2003). For the impact of Medicare, see Finkelstein (2007).

122. As Atlas (2011) and others have argued, such factors include genetic differences, cigarette smoking, prevalence of obesity, homicide rates, nutritional choices, and differences across countries in basic definitions of birth and death.

123. Hadley et al. (2008).

124. The estimate of the impact of coinsurance and deductibles is reported in Phelps (2003), 140 (Table 5.1), 148 (Table 5.6). Phelps reports results for an annual deductible of $500 in 1984 dollars. The $1,100 is that amount increased by the growth in the CPI from 1984 to 2014.

125. Ibid., 67. An important caveat is the limited duration of the experiment (three to five years). This may not have allowed sufficient time for all health outcomes to fully manifest themselves.

126. See Baicker and Finkelstein (2011); Baicker et al. (2013).

127. Levy and Meltzer (2008), 399–409.

128. The Senate made two modifications to the House "corrections" bill, which required sending the bill back to the House. The House then passed the modified version. "Health Care Overhaul Makes History for Obama, Democratic Congress," Congressional Quarterly Almanac 2010, 9-3-9-5.

129. A useful summary of the law's provisions is provided by the Kaiser Family Foundation at//kff.org/health-reform/fact-sheet/summary-of-the-affordable-care-act/.

130. See NFIB v. Sebellius (2012), 3.

131. For example, immediately following the provision requiring individuals to have insurance, the law states that if "an applicable individual . . . fails to meet the requirement . . . there is hereby imposed . . . a penalty" (sec. 5000 A[b]). The statute uses the word penalty no fewer than eighteen times.

132. NFIB v. Sebellius, 567 U.S.1 51 (2012).

133 Steward Machine v. Davis, 301 U.S. 548 (1937).

134 Pub. L. 111-148, sec. 36B, May 23, 2010.

135 King v. Burwell 576 U.S.___ (2015), 3.

136. Ibid.

137. Ibid. Scalia, dissenting, was joined by Justices Thomas and Alito.

138 http://kff.org/health-reform/state-indicator/medicaid-expansion-enrollment. In July 2017, Louisiana became the thirty second state to expand Medicaid. Data on 2011 Medicaid enrollment from CMS (2012), 28.

139. http://kff.org/health-reform/state-indicator/total-marketplace-enroll-ment.

140. http://kff.org/health-reform/state-indicator/marketplace-average-benchmark-premiums.

141. http://kff.org/slideshow/insurer-participation-in-the-2017-individual-marketplace/.

Chapter 19

1. Ronald Reagan, "A Time for Choosing," nationally televised address on behalf of Barry Goldwater for president. October 27, 1964.

2. The benefit rolls were reduced in 1820 by the War Department, pursuant to legislation passed by Congress during the depths of the economic recession of 1819. But as I noted in Chapter 2, this legislation was motivated primarily by fraud perpetrated by veterans who were feigning impoverishment. Most of these veterans were subsequently restored to the benefit rolls when economic good times returned in 1823.

3. The programs included in the entitlement category are: Social Security retirement and disability, railroad retirement and unemployment insurance, federal-state unemployment insurance, Medicare, federal and military retirement, black lung, general revenue sharing, veterans compensation, pensions, readjustment, and insurance benefits, Medicaid, food stamps, child nutrition programs, SSI, Temporary Assistance for Needy Families, the earned income tax credit (refundable credits only), the child tax credits (refundable credits only), guaranteed student loans, and the social services block grant. Outlays for these programs account for 95 percent of all noninterest outlays of programs classified by the federal government as mandatory. Interest on the publicly held federal debt, which currently accounts for about 7 percent of outlays, is excluded from the numbers.

4. In fiscal year 2015, outlays by the major entitlement programs totaled $2.5 trillion (my calculation from the federal budget for 201, Analytical Perspectives, "Federal Budget by Agency and Program"). Personal income is for the comparable period, October 2015 to September 2016, and is from https://fred.stlouisfed.org.

5. A detailed description and user file for March 2016 Current Population Survey can be found at http://www.nber.org/data/current-population-survey-data. The entitlement programs included in the analysis are Social Security retirement and disability, railroad retirement, federal retirement, black lung, unemployment insurance, veterans insurance, veterans' compensation and pensions, TANF, the earned income and child care tax credits (refundable

credits only), Medicare, Medicaid, food stamps, child nutrition programs, and SSI. The data do not include estimates of subsidies of health insurance premiums and copayments under the Affordable Care Act. Entitlement program participation data are obtained directly from the CPS. Estimates of the receipt of earned income and child care tax credits are imputed to CPS households by use of TAXIM (http://users.nber.org/~taxsim/).

6. Numerous studies have compared program participation and expenditure data obtained from the CPS with official U.S. government administrative data for each of the major entitlement programs. The studies have consistently shown that the CPS significantly undercounts both the number of recipients and the amount of assistance received in virtually all major entitlement programs. The exception to this finding is the EITC. The CPS does not report individuals' receipt of earned income tax credits. Our imputation of these tax credits assumes that all households that are eligible for tax credits receive them and overstates both the number of recipients and the amount of refundable credits.

7. The estimates are calculated from the March 2016 Current Population Survey (http://www.nber.org/data/current-population-survey-data). The estimates are derived by multiplying actual federal outlays for cash assistance and in-kind benefits from major federal entitlement programs in 2015 by estimates of the distribution of these benefits from the 2016 Current Population Survey.

8. In addition to this maldistribution, improper payments and outright fraud permeate the entitlement system. The Government Accountability Office estimates that such payments totaled $114 billion in 2014. The EITC, Medicare, and Medicaid accounted for 60 percent of all improper payments. Fraud and otherwise improper payments accounted for an astonishing 27 percent of all EITCs. Yet despite the inability of federal authorities to ensure that payments are properly made, Congress continues to use the tax code as a means of distributing federal entitlement benefits to low- and middle-income families. Government Accountability Office, "Improper Payments, Government-Wide Estimates and Use of Death Data to Help Prevent Payments to Deceased Individuals," statement of Daniel Bertoni and Beryl H. Davis, before the Committee on Homeland Security and Governmental Affairs, U.S. Senate, March 16, 2015.

9. My calculation of Social Security and Medicare benefits. In 2015, a newly retired 66-year-old male worker received an average monthly retirement benefit of $1,781 (*Social Security Bulletin*, 2016, Table 6.B4). The worker's annual benefit plus a spousal benefit totals $32,058. In 2012, the latest year Medicare expenditures for elderly persons are available, Medicare spent $6,534 per elderly enrollee Total expenditures from *Medicare Statistical Bulletin* (2013), Table 3.2. Enrollment is from Medicare Enrollment Statistics, Medicare Enrollment in Parts A and B (MDCR ENROLL AB), Table 3. The

amount is updated to 2015 by multiplying the 2012 amount by the growth in total Medicare expenditures per enrollee (*Medicare Trustees Report*, 2013, 200). Median household income is from www.census.gov/data/tables /2016/ demo/income-poverty/p60-250.html.

10. Duggan (2015), 9.

11. The ACA poverty line for a family of four in 2015 is $23,850 (https:// obamacare.net/2015-federal-poverty-level/).

12. My estimates derived from applying TAXIM to the 2016 Current Population Survey data. As a check on the accuracy of the estimates, I compared my estimated marginal tax rates to those published by the Congressional Budget Office average tax rate (CBO, "Effective Marginal Tax Rates for Low and Moderate-Income Workers in 2016," November 2015). Using the same sample of persons, individuals ages 21 to 64, I obtained the same overall average marginal tax rate as CBO (31.6 versus 31.3) and a similar distribution of tax rates, with one exception.

13. See Mulligan (2012).

14. U.S. Census Population Projections, Table 9, December 2014.

15. CBO, "An Update to the Budget and Economic Outlook, 2016–2026," Table 1–1.

16. My calculations from U.S. Census Population Projections, Table 3, December 2014, and CBO, 2016 Long-Term Budget Outlook, July 2016, Table 1.

17. See Reinhart and Rogoff (2013) and Cecchetti, Mohanty, and Zampolli (2011) for a discussion of the impact of government debt on economic activity.

18. Friedman and Friedman (1989), 1.

19. Friedman and Friedman attribute the term *countercurrent* to Dicey (1914)

20. These works include *The Road to Serfdom* by Hayek (1944); *Free to Choose* by Friedman and Friedman (1980); *Anarchy, State and Utopia* by Nozick (1974); *Losing Ground* by Murray (1984).

Bibliography

Aaron, Henry J. 1978. *Politics and the Professors: The Great Society in Perspective*. Washington, DC: Brookings Institution.

Abrahamson, Mark. 1998. *Out-of-Wedlock Births: The United States in Comparative Perspective*. Westport, CT: Praeger.

Achenbaum, Andrew W. 1983. *Shades of Gray: Old Age, American Values, and Federal Policies since 1920*. Boston: Little, Brown.

Adams, John Quincy. 1840. "Speech of the Hon. John Quincy Adams: In Relation to the Navy Pension Fund." galenet.galegroup.com.

"Addicts and Disability," *Washington Post*, November 16, 1994.

Altschuler, Glen C., and Stuart M. Blumin. 2009. *The G.I. Bill: A New Deal for Veterans*. New York: Oxford University Press.

American Council on Education. 1941. *The History and Activities of the American Council on Education, 1941–42*. Washington, DC: American Council on Education.

Anderson, Barry, and James Sheppard. 2009. "Fiscal Futures, Institutional Budget Reforms, and Their Effects: What Can Be Learned?" *OECD Journal on Budgeting* 2009:7–117.

Anderson, Martin. 1978. *Welfare*. Stanford, CA: Hoover Institution Press.

Anderson, Odin W. 1968. *The Uneasy Equilibrium: Private and Public Financing of Health Services in the United States, 1875–1965*. New Haven, CT: College of University Press.

Atlas, Scott. 2011. *In Excellent Health: Setting the Record Straight on America's Health Care*. Stanford, CA: Hoover Institution Press.

Baicker, Katherine, and Amy Finkelstein. 2011. "The Effects of Medicaid

Coverage: Learning from the Oregon Experiment." *New England Journal of Medicine* 365:683–685.

Baicker, Katherine, Sarah L. Taubman, Heidi L. Allen, Mira Bernstein, Jonathan H. Gruber, Joseph P. Newhouse, Eric C. Schneider Bill J. Wright, Alan M. Zaslavsky, and Amy N. Finkelstein, for the Oregon Health Study Group. 2013. "The Oregon Experiment: Effects of Medicaid on Clinical Outcomes." *New England Journal of Medicine* 368:1713–1722.

Bailis, Lawrence Neil. 1974. *Bread of Justice: Grassroots Organization in the Welfare Rights Movement.* Lexington, MA: Lexington Books.

"Balancing the Ways and Means." 1964. *Washington Post,* November 7.

Bane, Mary Jo, and David T. Ellwood. 1983. "The Dynamics of Poverty Dependence: The Routes to Self-Sufficiency." Report prepared for the U.S. Department of Health and Human Services, Office of the Assistant Secretary for Planning and Evaluation. Cambridge, MA: Urban Systems Research and Engineering.

Bane Mary Jo, and David T. Ellwood.. 1994. *Welfare Realities: From Rhetoric to Reform.* Cambridge, MA: Harvard University Press.

Beath, Robert B. 1889. *History of the Grand Army of the Republic.* New York: Bryan, Taylor.

Bell, Winifred. 1965. *Aid to Dependent Children.* New York: Columbia University Press.

Bensel, Richard. 1984. *Sectionalism and American Political Development, 1880–1980.* Madison: University of Wisconsin Press.

Bentley, George, R. 1955. *A History of the Freedman's Bureau.* Philadelphia: University of Pennsylvania,

Berkowitz, Edward D. 1991. *America's Welfare State from Roosevelt to Reagan.* Baltimore: John Hopkins University Press.

Berkowitz, Edward, and Kim McQuaid. 1988. *Creating the Welfare State: The Political Economy of Twentieth-Century Reform.* New York: Praeger.

Berman, Jules. 1947. "State Public Assistance Legislation, 1947." *Social Security Bulletin* 10:7–15.

———. 1949. "State Public Assistance Legislation, 1949." *Social Security Bulletin* 12:3–10.

Bishop John, H. 1980. "Jobs, Cash Transfers, and Marital Instability: A Review and Synthesis of the Evidence." *Journal of Human Resources* 15:301–334.

Blahous, Charles. 2010. *Social Security: The Unfinished Work.* Stanford, CA: Hoover Institution Press.

Boskin, M. J. 1977. "Social Security and Retirement Decisions." *Economic Inquiry* 15:1–25.

Brady, David W. 1973. *Congressional Voting in a Partisan Era: A Study of the McKinley Houses and a Comparison to the Modern House of Representatives.* Lawrence: University Press of Kansas.

Bremner, Robert H. 1956. *From the Depths: The Discovery of Poverty in the United States*. New York: New York University Press.

Broder, David. 1981. "The Rising Opposition to Reagan . . . ," *Washington Post*, September 23, 1981.

Browder, Robert Paul, and Thomas G. Smith. 1986. *Independent: A Biography of Lewis W. Douglas*. New York: Knopf.

Brown, Josephine Chapin. 1940. *Public Relief, 1929–1939*. New York: Holt.

Bruce, Maurice. 1968. *The Coming of the Welfare State*. London: B. T. Batsford.

Bucklin, Dorothy, and John M. Lynch. 1938. "Aid to Dependent Children and Mothers' Aid in December 1937." *Social Security Bulletin* 1(12): 19–26.

Burke, Vee, and J. Vincent Burke. 1974. *Nixon's Good Deed*. New York: Columbia University Press.

Burnham, Walter D. 1965. "The Changing Scope of the American Political Universe." *American Political Science Review* 59:7–29.

Burtless, Gary. 1986. "Social Security, Unanticipated Benefit Increases, and the Timing of Retirement." *Review of Economic Studies* 53:781–805.

Bushnell Hart, Albert, ed. 1907. *The American Nation: A History*, vol. 26: *National Ideals Historically Traced, 1607–1907*. New York: Harper.

Camelon, David. (1949). 1969. "How the First GI Bill Was Written: A Wild Ride from Georgia." *American Legion Magazine* 47 (February 9): 22–51.

Cannon, Lou. 1991. *President Reagan: The Role of a Lifetime*. New York: Simon & Schuster.

Caro, Robert A. 2002. *The Years of Lyndon Johnson: Master of the Senate*. New York: Knopf.

———. 2012. *The Passage of Power*. New York: Knopf.

Cavalier, Kathleen. 1970. "National Health Insurance Proposals and Their Alternatives." Congressional Research Service, May 5.

———. 1972. "National Health Insurance: A Summary of Program Costs." Congressional Research Service, April 12.

Cecchetti, S., M. Mohanty, and F. Zampolli. 2011. "The Real Effect of Debt." BIS Working Papers 352. Basel: Bank of International Settlements.

Centers for Medicare & Medicaid. 2011. *Brief Summaries of Medicare & Medicaid*, November 1, 2011.

———. 2016. *CMS Statistics Booklet*. https://www.cms.gov.

Citizens' Board of Inquiry into Hunger and Malnutrition in the United States. 1968. *Hunger U.S.A.* Boston: Beacon Press, 1968.

Clark, Robert L., Lee A. Craig, and Jack W. Wilson. 2003. *A History of Public Sector Pensions in the United States*. Philadelphia: University of Pennsylvania Press.

Classen, K. P. 1977. "The Effect of Unemployment Insurance on the Duration of Unemployment and Subsequent Earnings." *Industrial and Labor Relations Review* 30 (4): 438–444.

Cleaveland, Frederic N. 1969. *Congress and Urban Problems*. Washington, DC: Brookings Institution.

Cogan, John, F. 1978. *Negative Income Taxation and Labor Supply: New Evidence from the New Jersey–Pennsylvania Experiment*. Santa Monica, CA: Rand.

———. 1998. *The Congressional Response to Social Security Surpluses, 1935–1994*. Stanford, CA: Hoover Press.

———. 2015. *The Impact of Civil War Pensions on Electoral Outcomes: 1888–1912*. Stanford, CA: Hoover Institution.

Coll, Blanche D. 1995. *Safety Net Welfare and Social Security 1929–1979*. New Brunswick, NJ: Rutgers University Press.

Comptroller General of the United States. 1976. *History of the Rising Costs of the Medicare and Medicaid Programs*. Report to Congress. Washington DC: Department of Health Education and Welfare, February 11.

Congressional Budget Office. 1978. "The Administration's Welfare Reform Proposal: An Analysis of the Program for Better Jobs and Income." Budget Issue Paper for Fiscal Year 1979.

Congressional Research Service. 1976. "Report of the Consultant Panel on Social Security to the Congressional Research Service." Prepared for Use of the Committee on Finance of the U.S. Senate and the Committee on Ways and Means of the House of Representatives, 94th Cong., 2nd Sess., August.

Corson, John J. 1937. "Old-Age Insurance: Wage Report for Workers Covered by Federal Old-Age Insurance in 1937." *Social Security Bulletin* 2 (3): 3–8.

Costa, Dora L. 1998. *The Evolution of Retirement: An American Economic History, 1880–1990*. Chicago: University of Chicago Press.

Curtis, Carl T., and Regis Courtemanche. 1986. *Forty Years against the Tide: Congress and the Welfare State*. Washington, DC: Regnery Gateway.

David, Paul A., and Peter Solar. 1986. *A Bicentenary Contribution to the History of the Cost of Living in America*. Greenwich, CT: JAI Press.

Davies, Gareth. 1996. *From Opportunity to Entitlement: The Transformation and Decline of Great Society Liberalism*. Lawrence: University Press of Kansas.

Davies, Wallace Evan. 1955. *Patriotism on Parade—The Story of Veterans' and Hereditary Organizations in America, 1783–1900*. Cambridge, MA: Harvard University Press.

Davis, Kenneth S. 1979. *FDR: The New Deal Years, 1933–1937*. New York: Random House.

Davis, Martha F. 1993. *Brutal Need: Lawyers and the Welfare Rights Movement*. New Haven, CT: Yale University Press.

Dearing, Mary R. 1952. *Veterans in Politics: The Story of the GAR*. Baton Rouge: Louisiana State University Press.

Derthick, Martha. 1979. *Policy Making for Social Security*. Washington, DC: Brookings Institution.

Dewey, Davis Rich. 1931. *The Financial History of the United States*. New York: Longmans, Green.

Dewitt, Larry. 2008. "Financing Social Security, 1939–1949: A Reexamination of the Financing Policies of This Period." *Social Security Bulletin* 67 (4): 51–69.

Diamond, William. 1941. "Urban and Rural Voting in 1896." *American Historical Review* 46:281–305.

Dickson, Paul, and Thomas B. Allen. 2004. *The Bonus Army*. New York: Walker.

Dicey, A. V. 1914. *Lectures on the Relation between Law and Public Opinion in England during the Nineteenth Century*, 2nd ed. London: Macmillan.

Dillingham, William Pyrle. 1952. *Federal Aid to Veterans, 1917–1941*. Gainesville: University of Florida Press.

Douglas, Lewis W. 1935. *The Liberal Tradition: A Free People and a Free Economy*. New York: Van Nostrand.

Douglas, Paul. 1939. *Social Security in the United States: An Analysis and Appraisal of the Federal Social Security Act*. New York: McGraw-Hill.

Douglass, Frederick. 1881. *The Life and Times of Fredrick Douglass*. Hartford Park Publishing Company.

Duggan, Mark. "Testimony before the Joint Economic Committee, United States Congress," November 4, 2015. http://siepr.stanford.edu/sites/default/files/jec-mgd-nov4.pdf.

Duggan, Mark, Robert Gillingham, and John Greenless. 1993. "Returns Paid to Early Social Cohorts." *Contemporary Policy Issues* (October): 1–13.

Duggan, Mark, Melissa S. Kearney, and Stephanie Rennane. 2015. "The Supplemental Security Income (SSI) Program." NBER Working Paper w21209. Cambridge, MA: NBER.

Durbin, Elizabeth. 1973. "Work and Welfare: The Case of Aid to Families with Dependent Children." *Journal of Human Resources* 8:108–125.

Eggert, Gerald G., and Richard Olney. 1974. *Evolution of a Statesman*. University Park: Pennsylvania State University Press,

Eliot, Thomas H. 1992. *Recollections of the New Deal*. Boston: Northeastern University Press.

Epstein, Abraham. 1922. *Facing Old Age: A Study of Old Age Dependency in the United States and Old Age Pensions*. New York: Knopf.

———. 1938. *Insecurity, a Challenge to America: A Study of Social Insurance in the United States and Abroad*. New York: Random House.

Ewing, Oscar R. 1948. *The Nation's Health: A Report to the President*. Washington, DC: U.S. Government Printing Office

Executive Office of the President. Office of Management and Budget. 2010.

"Circular A-11, Preparation, Submission, and Execution of the Budget." July.

Executive Office of the President. Office of Management and Budget. 2015. *Historical Tables: Budget of the United States Government.* Washington, DC: Government Printing Office.

"Federal Health Insurance Urged by Truman, Ewing." 1948. *New York Times,* September 3.

Feenberg, Daniel Richard, and Elizabeth Coutts. 1993. "An Introduction to the TAXSIM Model." *Journal of Policy Analysis and Management* 12 (Winter): 189–194.

Feingold, Eugene. 1966. *Medicare: Policy and Politics: A Case Study and Policy Analysis.* San Francisco: Chandler.

Ferejohn, John. 1986. "Logrolling in an Institutional Context: A Case Study of Food Stamp Legislation." In *Congress and Policy Change,* edited by Gerald C. Wright Jr., Leroy N. Rieselbach, and Lawrence C. Dodd, 223–256. New York: Agathon Press.

Finkelstein, Amy. 2007. "The Aggregate Effects of Health Insurance: Evidence from the Introduction of Medicare." *Quarterly Journal of Economics* 122 (1): 1–37.

Fisher, Kenneth P., and Charles C. Ivie. 1971. *Franchising Justice.* Chicago: American Bar Foundation.

Flynn, John T. 1939. "The Social Security 'Reserve' Swindle." *Harpers Magazine* (February).

Fogel, Robert William. 1960. *The Union Pacific Railroad: A Case in Premature Enterprise.* Baltimore: Johns Hopkins University Press.

Folsom Jr., Burton. 2008. *New Deal or Raw Deal? How FDR's Economic Legacy Has Damaged America.* New York: Simon & Schuster.

Foner, Eric. 1988. *Reconstruction: America's Unfinished Revolution, 1863–1877.* New York: Harper.

Frank, Thomas. 2004. *What's the Matter with Kansas?* New York: Metropolitan Books.

Freidel, Frank. 1973. *Launching the New Deal.* Boston: Little, Brown.

Friedman, Milton, and Rose D. Friedman. 1980. *Free to Choose.* New York: Harcourt.

———. 1989. "The Tide in the Affairs of Men." In *Thinking about America: The United States in the 1990s,* edited by Annelise Anderson and Dennis L. Bark. Stanford, CA: Hoover Institution.

Friedman, Milton, with the assistance of Rose D. Friedman. 2002. *Capitalism and Freedom,* 40th anniversary ed. Chicago: University of Chicago Press.

Frydl, Kathleen J. 2009. *The GI Bill.* Cambridge: Cambridge University Press.

Gebhart, William Franklin. 1918. *Effects of the War upon Insurance, with*

Special Reference to the Substitution of Insurance for Pensions. New York: Oxford University Press.

Geddes, Anne E. 1937. *Trends in Relief Expenditures, 1910–1935.* Washington, DC: Works Progress Administration.

General Accounting Office. 1980. "Legislation Allows Black Lung Benefits to Be Awarded without Adequate Evidence of Disability." Report HRD-80–81. Washington DC: U.S. Government Printing Office.

Gerber, Larry G. 1983. *The Limits of Liberalism.* New York: New York University Press.

Glasson, William H. 1904. "A Costly Pension Law—Act of June 27, 1890." *South Atlantic Quarterly* 3:361–369.

———. 1918. *Federal Military Pensions in the United States.* New York: Oxford University Press.

Gokhale, Jagadeesh. 2014. "SSDI Reform." Washington, DC: Cato Institute.

Goldman, Eric F. 1956. *The Crucial Decade—America, 1945–1955.* New York: Knopf.

Gordon, John Steele. 1998. *Hamilton's Blessing: The Extraordinary Life and Times of Our National Debt.* New York: Penguin Books.

Gould, Lewis L. 1980. *The Presidency of William McKinley.* Lawrence: Regents Press of Kansas.

Graebner, William. 1980. *A History of Retirement: The Meaning and Function of an American Institution, 1885–1978.* New Haven, CT: Yale University Press.

Grant, Margaret. 1939. *Old-Age Security: Social and Financial Trends.* Washington, DC: Committee on Social Security, Social Science Research Council.

Gray, Charles. 1994. *The Freedmen's Bureau: A Missing Chapter in Social Welfare History.* N.p.

Haber, Carole, and Brian Gratton. 1994. *Old Age and the Search for Security: An American Social History.* Bloomington: Indiana University Press.

Hadley, Jack, John Holahan, Teresa Coughlin, and Dawn Miller. 2008. "Covering the Uninsured in 2008: Current Costs, Sources of Payment, and Incremental Costs." *Health Affairs* 27:399–415.

Hahn, Jim. 2014. "Medicare Physician Payment Updates and the Sustainable Growth Rate (SGR) System." Washington, DC: Congressional Research Service.

Handler, Joel F. 1972. *Reforming the Poor: Welfare Policy, Federalism, and Morality.* New York: Basic Books.

Hannan, Michael T., Nancy Brandon Tuma, and Lyle Groeneveld. 1977. "Income and Marital Events: Evidence from an Income-Maintenance Experiment." *American Journal of Sociology* 82:1186–1211.

Harrington, Michael. 1962. *The Other America: Poverty in the United States.* New York: Macmillan.

Harris, Louis. 1980. "A Majority of Americans Support Cuts in Federal Spending." *Chicago Tribune*, June 12.

Harris, Richard. 1966. *A Sacred Trust*. New York: New American Library.

Harris, Seymour E. 1960. *New Economics*. London: Dennis Dobson.

Hart, Albert Bushness. 1907. *The American Nation: A History*, vol. 26: *National Ideals Historically Traced, 1607–1907.* New York: Harper.

Haskins, Ron. 2006. *Work over Welfare: The Inside Story of the 1996 Welfare Reform Law*. Washington, DC: Brookings Institution Press.

Hearne, Jean. 2005. "Medicaid Disproportionate Share Payments." Washington, DC: Congressional Research Service, January 10.

Hibbard, Benjamin Horace. 1965. *A History of Public Land Policies*. Madison: University of Wisconsin Press.

Higgs, Robert. 1987. *Crisis and Leviathan: Critical Episodes in the Growth of American Government*. New York: Oxford University Press.

Hirschfeld, Gerhard. 1944. *Social Security: Past Present Future*. Washington, DC: American Taxpayers Association.

Holcombe, Randall. 1999. "Veterans' Interests and the Transition to Government Growth: 1870–1915." *Public Choice* 99:311–326.

"Hold Health Bill Dead for Session: Sponsors Decide Measure Is Too Controversial." 1946. *New York Times*, July 10.

Honig, Marjorie. 1974. "AFDC Income, Recipient Rates, and Family Dissolution." *Journal of Human Resources* 9 (Summer): 303–322.

———. 1976. "AFDC Income, Recipient Rates, and Family Dissolution: A Reply." *Journal of Human Resources* 11:250–260.

Hormats, Robert D. 2007. *The Price of Liberty: Paying for America's Wars from the Revolution to the War on Terror*. New York: Times Books and Holt.

"Hunger in America." 1968. *Washington Post*, April 24.

Hunt, S. R., and J. Baumohl. 2003. "Drink, Drugs and Disability: An Introduction to the Controversy." *Contemporary Drug Problems* 2003 (1–2): 9–76.

Hutchens, Robert. 1979. "Welfare, Remarriage, and Marital Search." *American Economic Review* 69 (3): 369–379.

Jacob, Meg, and Julian E. Zelizer. 2011. *Conservatives in Power: The Reagan Years, 1981–1989: A Brief History with Documents*. Boston: Bedford Press.

Joe, Tom, and Cheryl Rogers. 1985. *By the Few for the Few: The Reagan Welfare Legacy*. Lexington, MA: Lexington Books.

Johnson, Ronald N., and Gary D. Libecap. 1994. *The Federal Civil Service System and the Problem of Bureaucracy: The Economics and Politics of Institutional Change*. Chicago: University of Chicago Press.

Jones, Jean. 1983. "Chronology of Major Federal Food Assistance Legislation." Washington, DC: Congressional Research Service.

Keeley, Michael C., Philip K. Robins, Robert G. Spiegelman, and Richard W. West. 1977. *The Labor Supply Effects and Cost of Alternative Negative*

Income Tax Programs: Evidence from the Seattle and Denver Income Maintenance Experiments. Part I: The Labor Supply Response Function. Research Memorandum 38. Stanford: Center for the Study of Welfare Policy, Stanford Research Institute.

———. 1978. "The Estimation of Labor Supply Models Using Experimental Data." *American Economic Review* 68 (5): 873–887.

Keller, Morton. 1977. *Affairs of State: Public Life in Late Nineteenth Century America.* Cambridge, MA: Belknap Press of Harvard University Press.

Kelley Jr., Stanley. 1956. *Public Relations and Political Power.* Baltimore: Johns Hopkins University Press.

Kennedy, David, M. 1999. *Freedom from Fear: The American People in Depression and War, 1929–1945.* New York: Oxford University Press.

Kleppner, Paul. 1970. *The Cross of Culture: A Social Analysis of Midwestern Politics, 1850–1890.* New York: Free Press.

Koitz, David. 1980. "Work Disincentives and Disability Insurance." Report 80–160 EPW. Washington, DC: Congressional Research Service.

———. 2000. "The Social Security Lock Box." Washington, DC: Congressional Research Service.

———. 2001. *Seeking Middle Ground on Social Security Reform.* Stanford, CA: Hoover Institution Press.

Kornbluh, Felicia. 2007. *The Battle for Welfare Rights: Politics and Poverty in Modern America.* Philadelphia: University of Pennsylvania Press.

Langlois, Stephen. 2014. "Insuring the Uninsured: Analyzing Aspects of Federal Health Insurance Programs." PhD diss., Stanford University.

Laurence, William L. 1949. "'Delusion' Charged in U. S. Health Plan." *New York Times,* June 6.

Lawrence, Susan E. 1990. *The Poor in Court: The Legal Services Program and Supreme Court Decision Making.* Princeton, NJ: Princeton University Press.

Leiby, James. 1978. *A History of Social Welfare and Social Work in the United States.* New York: Columbia University Press

Leimer, Dean R. 2007. "Cohort-Specific Measures of Lifetime Social Security Taxes and Benefits." Washington, DC: Social Security Administration.

Leip, Dave. 2012. *Dave Leip's Atlas of U.S. Presidential Elections.* http://uselectionatlas.org/.

Letwin, William. 1965. *Law and Economic Policy in America.* New York: Random House.

Levenstein, Lisa. 2000. "From Innocent Children to Unwanted Migrants and Unwed Moms: Two Chapters in the Public Discourse on Welfare in the United States, 1960-1961." *Journal of Women's History* 11(4): 10–33.

Levitan, Sar A. 1969. *The Great Society's Poor Law: A New Approach to Poverty.* Baltimore: John Hopkins University Press.

Levy, Frank. 1979. "The Labor Supply of Female Household Heads, or AFDC Work Incentives Don't Work Too Well." *Journal of Human Resources* 14:76–97.

Levy, Helen, and David Meltzer. 2008. "The Impact of Health Insurance on Health." *American Review of Public Health* 29:399–409.

Levy, Robert A., and William Mellor. 2009. *The Dirty Dozen*. Washington, DC: Cato Institute.

Lewis, Anthony. 1995. "Some Are Less Equal." *New York Times*, November 17.

Linton, Albert. 1936. "Old Age Security for Everybody." *Atlantic Monthly* 157:488–498.

Lodge, Henry Cabot. 1904. *The Works of Alexander Hamilton*. New York: Putnam.

Long, C. D. 1958. *The Labor Force under Changing Income and Employment*. Princeton: Princeton University Press.

"Louisiana Fighting to Stay on Federal Welfare Aid Books." 1960. *Baltimore Afro-American*, November 26.

Lubove, Roy. 1968. *The Struggle for Social Security, 1900–1935*. Cambridge, MA: Harvard University Press.

MacDonald, Maurice. 1977. *Food, Stamps, and Income Maintenance*. New York: Academic Press.

Marmor, Theodore R. 1973. *The Politics of Medicare*. Chicago: Aldine.

Martin, G. 1972. "Emergence and Development of a Social Movement among the Underclass: A Case Study of the NWRO." Ph.D. diss., University of Chicago.

May, Dean L. 1981. *From New Deal to New Economics: The American Liberal Response to the Recession of 1937.* New York: Garland.

Mayer, George, E. 1968. *The Republican Party, 1854–1966.* New York: Oxford University Press.

Medicare Payment Advisory Commission. 2016, 2017. *Report to the Congress.* http://www.medpac.gov/.

McClure, Barbara. 1981. "Federal Black Lung Disability Benefits Program." Congressional Research Service Report 81–239.

McConnell, Stuart. 1992. *Glorious Contentment: The Grand Army of the Republic, 1865–1900.* Chapel Hill: University of North Carolina Press

McElroy, Robert. 1923. *Grover Cleveland: The Man and the Statesman.* New York: Harper.

McMurry, Donald L. 1922. "The Political Significance of the Pension Question, 1885–1897." *Mississippi Valley Historical Review* 9:19–36.

———. 1926. "The Bureau of Pensions during the Administration of President Harrison." *Mississippi Valley Historical Review* 13:343–364.

"Medicare Merry-Go-Round." 1964. *New York Times*, April 28.

"Medicare Shenanigans." 1964. *New York Times*, September 2.

Melnick, R. Shep. 1994. *Between the Lines: Interpreting Welfare Rights.* Washington, DC: Brookings Institution.

Mettler, Suzanne. 2005. *Soldiers to Citizens: The G.I. Bill and the Making of the Greatest Generation.* Oxford: Oxford University Press.

Meyer, Balthasar Henry, and Caroline E. MacGill. 1948. *A History of Transportation in the United States before 1860.* Forge Village, MA: Murray Printing Company.

Miller, David E. 1969. *The Golden Spike.* Salt Lake City: University of Utah Press.

Mills, Ogden. 1937. "The Social Security Hoax." *American Mercury* 42.

Milwaukee County Welfare Rights Organization. 1972. *Welfare Mothers Speak Out, We Ain't Gonna Shuffle Anymore.* New York: Norton.

Minarik, Joseph J., and Robert S. Goldfarb. 1976. "AFDC Income, Recipient Rates, and Family Dissolution: A Comment." *Journal of Human Resources* 11:243–250.

Moffitt, Robert A. 2003. *Means-Tested Transfer Programs in the United States.* Chicago: University of Chicago Press.

Moffitt, R., and W. Nicholson. 1982. "The Effects of Unemployment Insurance on Unemployment: The Case of Federal Supplemental Benefits." *Review of Economics and Statistics* 64:1–11.

Morgan, Paulette. 2001. "Medicare: Prescription Drug Expenditures, 1997." Washington, DC: Congressional Research Service, April.

Morris, Charles R. 1996. *The AARP: America's Most Powerful Lobby and the Clash of Generations.* New York: Times Books.

"Most of U.S. Favors Newburgh Plan." 1961. *Los Angeles Times,* August 11.

Moynihan, Daniel P. 1967. "The President and the Negro: The Moment Lost." *Commentary* February 1, 31.

———. 1969. *Maximum Feasible Misunderstanding: Community Action in the War on Poverty.* New York: Free Press.

———. 1973. *The Politics of a Guaranteed Income.* New York: Random House.

Mugge, Robert. 1963. "Aid to Families with Dependent Children: Initial Findings of the 1961 Report on the Characteristics of Recipients." *Social Security Bulletin* (March): 3–18.

Mulligan, Casey. 2012. *The Redistribution Recession: How Labor Market Distortions Contracted the Economy* and *Parental Priorities and Economic Inequality.* Chicago: University of Chicago Press.

Murray, Charles. 1984. *Losing Ground: American Social Policy, 1950–1980.* New York: Basic Books.

Murray, Robert K. 1969. *The Harding Era: Warren G. Harding and His Administration.* Minneapolis: University of Minnesota Press.

Myers, Jeffrey. 1985. *Hemingway: A Biography.* New York: Harper.

Nadasen, Premilla, Jennifer Mittelstadt, and Marisa Chappell. 2009. *Welfare in the United States: A History with Documents, 1935–96.* New York: Routledge, Taylor, and Francis.

"National Health Insurance Plan." 1970. *New York Times,* July 9.

National Research Council. 1995. *Measuring Poverty: A New Approach,* edited by Constance F. Citro and Robert T. Michael. Washington, DC: National Academy Press.

"Needed Welfare Changes." 1969. *Los Angeles Times,* August 12.

Nevins, Allan. 1933. *Grover Cleveland: A Study in Courage.* New York: Dodd, Mead.

Newhouse, Joseph, and V. D. Taylor. 1970. "Medical Costs, Health Insurance, and Public Policy." Report P-4274. Santa Monica, CA: Rand.

North, Douglass C. 1966. *The Economic Growth of the United States, 1790–1860.* New York: Norton.

Noziak, Robert. 1974. *Anarchy, State and Utopia.* New York: Basic Books.

Oberlander, Jonathan. 2003. *The Political Life of Medicare.* Chicago: University of Chicago Press.

Oliver, John William. 1917. *History of Civil War Pensions, 1861–1885.* Madison: University of Wisconsin.

Oliver, Thomas R., Philip R. Lee, and Helene L. Lipton. 2003. "A Political History of Medicare and Prescription Drug Coverage." *Milbank Quarterly* 82:283–354.

Olson, Keith W. 1974. *The GI Bill, the Veterans, and the Colleges.* Lexington: University Press of Kentucky.

"One FAP Fiasco Is Enough." 1977. *New York Times,* October 7.

"One-Man Veto on Medicare." 1964. *New York Times,* June 26.

Orszag, Peter R., and Ezekiel J. Emanuel. 2010. "Health Care Reform and Cost Control." *New England Journal of Medicine* 363:601–603.

Ortiz, Stephen. 2006. "The 'New Deal' for Veterans: The Economy Act, the Veterans of Foreign Wars, and the Origins of New Deal Dissent." *Journal of Military History* 70:415–438.

O'Sullivan, Jennifer. 2003. "Medicare: Payments to Physicians." Washington, DC: Congressional Research Service.

O'Sullivan, Jennifer, and David Koitz. 1989. "Health Insurance That Supplements Medicare: Background Material and Data." Washington, DC: Congressional Research Service.

Paglin, Morton. 1980. *Poverty and Transfers In-Kind: A Re-Evaluation of Poverty in the United States.* Stanford, CA: Hoover Institution Press, Stanford University.

Palmore, E. 1964. "Retirement Patterns among Aged Men: Findings of the 1963 Survey of the Aged." *Social Security Bulletin* 27(8): 3–10.

Parker, J. S. 1942. *Social Security Reserves.* Washington, DC: American Council on Public Affairs.

Parrott, Thomas M., Lenna D. Kennedy, and Charles G. Scott. 1998. "Non-citizens and the Supplemental Security Income Program." *Social Security Bulletin* 61 (4): 3–31.

Parsons, Donald O. 1980a. "The Decline in Male Labor Force Participation." *Journal of Political Economy* 8 (1): 117–134.

———. 1980b. "Racial Trends in Male Labor Force Participation." *American Economic Review* 70:911–920.

Patterson, James T. 2000. *America's Struggle against Poverty in the Twentieth Century.* Cambridge, MA: Harvard University Press.

Paullin, Charles Oscar. 1906. *Navy of the American Revolution: Its Administration, Its Policy and Its Achievements.* Cedar Rapids, IA: Republican Printing Company.

Pencak, William. 1989. *For God and Country: The American Legion, 1919–1941.* Boston: Northeastern University Press.

Perkins, Frances. 1946. *The Roosevelt I Knew.* New York: Viking Press.

Peters, Gerhard, and John T. Woolley. 1999–2017. *The American Presidency Project.* http://www.presidency.ucsb.edu.

Phelps, Charles. 2003. *Health Economics*, 3rd ed. Reading, MA: Addison-Wesley.

Pierson, Paul. 1994. *Dismantling the Welfare State? Reagan, Thatcher, and the Politics of Retrenchment.* Cambridge: Cambridge University Press

Piven, Frances Fox, and Richard A. Cloward. 1971. *Regulating the Poor: The Functions of Public Welfare.* New York: Random House.

Pope, Jacqueline. 1989. *Biting the Hand That Feeds Them.* New York: Praeger.

Pratt, Henry J. 1976. *The Gray Lobby.* Chicago: University of Chicago Press.

Prucha, Francis Paul. 1984. *The Great Father: The United States Government and the American Indians II.* Lincoln: University of Nebraska Press.

Ransdell, Joseph E. 1916. "The High Social Cost of the Pork Barrel." *American Academy of Political and Social Science* 64 (March): 43–45.

Reinhart C., and K. Rogoff. 2013. *This Time Is Different: Eight Centuries of Financial Folly.* Princeton, NJ: Princeton University Press.

Reisch, Michael, and Janice Andrews. 2002. *The Road Not Taken: A History of Radical Social Work in the United States.* Philadelphia: Brunner-Routledge.

Resch, John Phillips. 1999. *Suffering Soldiers: Revolutionary War Veterans, Moral Sentiment, and Political Culture in the Early Republic.* Amherst: University of Massachusetts Press.

Richardson, James D. 1910. *A Compilation of the Messages and Papers of the Presidents, 1789–1908.* Vol. 7. Washington, DC: Bureau of National Literature and Art.

———. 1911. *A Compilation of the Messages and Papers of the Presidents.* Vols. 8, 11. Washington, DC: Bureau of National Literature and Art.

Rimlinger, Gaston V. 1971. *Welfare Policy and Industrialization in Europe, America, and Russia.* New York: Wiley.

Ripley, Randall B. 1969. "Legislative Bargaining and the Food Stamp Act, 1964." In *Congress and Urban Problems*, edited by Frederic N. Cleaveland. Washington, DC: Brookings Institution.

Ritz, Joseph P. 1966. *The Despised Poor*. Boston: Beacon Press.

Robin, Florence. 1969. *Their Daily Bread: A Study of the National School Lunch Program*. Atlanta, GA: McNelley-Rudd Printing Service.

Rochefort, David A. 1986. *American Social Welfare Policy*. Boulder, CO: Westview Press.

Rosenbaum, David E. 1996. "Gloomy Forecast Touches Off Feud on Medicare Fund." *New York Times*, June 6.

Ross, David R. B. 1969. *Preparing for Ulysses: Politics and Veterans during World War II*. New York: Columbia University Press.

Rubinow, I. M. 1916. *Social Insurance*. Chicago: American Medical Association.

Rumer, Thomas A. 1990. *The American Legion: An Official History 1919–1989*. New York: M. Evans.

Rundquist, Barry S. 1980. *Political Benefits*. Lexington, MA: Lexington Books.

Safire, William. 1995. "Essay: Farewell, Red Ink." *New York Times*, December 7.

Sanders, Heywood T. 1980. "Paying for the 'Bloody Shirt': The Politics of Civil War Pensions." In *Political Benefits: Empirical Studies of American Public Programs*, edited by Barry S. Rundquist. Lexington, MA: Lexington Books.

Sargent, James E. 1981. *Roosevelt and the Hundred Days: Struggle for the Early New Deal*. New York: Garland.

Schick, Allen. 1980. *Congress and Money: Budgeting, Spending, and Taxing*. Washington, DC: Urban Institute.

———. 1986 "Explanation of the Balanced Budget and Emergency Deficit Control Act of 1985." Washington, DC: Congressional Research Service.

Schieber, Sylvester J., and John B. Shoven. 1999. *The Real Deal*. New Haven CT: Yale University Press.

Secretary of the Interior. 1880–1890. *Annual Report of the Commissioner of Pensions*. Washington, DC: Government Printing Office.

Shannon, David A. 1967. *The Socialist Party of America*. Chicago: Quadrangle Paperbacks.

Silberman, Charles. 1968. "The Mixed Up War on Poverty." In *Poverty: Power and Politics*, edited by Chaim Isaac Waxman, 82–83. New York: Grosset and Dunlap.

Skocpol, Theda. 1992. *Protecting Soldiers and Mothers: The Political Origins of Social Policy in the United States*. Cambridge, MA: Belknap Press of Harvard University Press.

Snyder Holly, Walter I. Waskiw, Robert Worden, and Ihor Gawdiak. 1992. *Veterans' Benefits and Judicial Review*. Washington, DC: Federal Research Division, Library of Congress.

Socolofsky, Homer E., and Allan B. Spetter. 1987. *The Presidency of Benjamin Harrison*. Lawrence: University Press of Kansas.

Solomon, Carmen D. 1993. "Disabled and Blind Child Recipients of Supplemental Security Income (SSI): Background and Concerns." 93–897. Washington, DC: Congressional Research Service, October.

Somers, Herman Miles, and Anne Ramsay Somers. 1961. *Doctors, Patients, and Health Insurance: The Organization and Financing of Medical Care*. Washington, DC: Brookings Institution.

Squier, Lee Welling. 1912. *Old Age Dependency in the United States: A Complete Survey of the Pension Movement*. New York: Macmillan.

Starr, Paul. 1982. *The Social Transformation of American Medicine*. New York: Basic Books.

———. 2011. *Remedy and Reaction: The Peculiar American Struggle over Health Care Reform*. New Haven, CT: Yale University Press.

"Starvation in Mississippi." 1968. *New York Times*, March 26.

Stein, Herbert. 1984. *Presidential Economics: The Making of Economic Policy from Roosevelt to Reagan and Beyond*. New York: Simon and Schuster.

Steiner, Gilbert Y. 1966. *Social Insecurity: The Politics of Welfare*. Chicago: Rand McNally.

———. 1971. *The State of Welfare*. Washington, DC: Brookings Institution.

Story, Justice Joseph. 1833. *Commentaries on the Constitution of the United States; With a Preliminary Review of the Constitutional History of the Colonies and States, before the Adoption of the Constitution*. Cambridge, MA: Hilliard, Gray, and Company.

Studenski, Paul, and Herman E. Krooss. 1963. *Financial History of the United State*, 2nd ed. New York: McGraw-Hill.

Taubman, Sarah, Heidi L. Allen, Bill J. Wright, Katherine Baicker, and Amy N. Finkelstein. 2014. "Medicaid Increases Emergency-Department Use: Evidence for Oregon's Health Insurance Experiment." *Science* 343:263–268.

"The Decline of Congress." 1963. *New York Times*, December 21.

"The Health Insurance Debate." 1974. *New York Times*, May 26.

"The Welfare Decision." 1996. *New York Times*, August 1.

Thompson, T. Leigh. 1916. "The Un-American Doctrine of State Compulsory Health Insurance." *Economic World*, March 4.

Tillmon Johnnie. 1972. "Welfare Is a Women's Issue." *Ms. Magazine*.

Trattner, Walter I. 1989. *From Poor Law to Welfare State: A History of Social Welfare in America*, 4th ed. New York: Free Press.

Trent, Logan Douglas. 1981. *The Crédit Mobilier*. New York: Arno Press.

Tynes, Sheryl R. 1996. *Turning Points in Social Security*. Stanford, CA: Stanford University Press.

U.S. Census Bureau. 1975. *Historical Statistics of the United States, Colonial Times to 1970*. Washington, DC: U.S. Government Printing Office.

U.S. Department of Health, Education and Welfare. Social and Rehabilitation Service. 1968. "Medical Assistance Financed under the Public Assistance Titles of the Social Security Act, August 1967."

———. Program Statistics and Data Systems. National Center for Social Statistics. 1973. "Medical Assistance (Medicaid) Financed under Title XIX of the Social Security Act, August 1972." NCSS Report B-1. DHEW Publication (SRS) 73–03150. April.

U.S. General Accountability Office. 1994. *Report to the Chairman, Subcommittee on Oversight and Investigations, Committee on Energy and Commerce, House of Representatives, States Use Illusory Approaches to Shift Program Costs to Federal Government.* August.

U.S. Treasury Department. 1850. *Receipts and Expenditures for the Year Ending June 30, 1850.*

———. 1936. *Combined Statement of the Receipts Various Issues, 1935–49.* Washington, DC: Government Printing Office.

———. 1939. *Combined Statement of the Receipts, 1938–39.* Washington, DC: Government Printing Office.

———. 1980. *Annual Report of the Secretary of the Treasury, Statistical Appendix.* Washington, DC: Government Printing Office.

Van Atta, Dale. 1998. *Trust Betrayed: Inside the AARP.* Washington, DC: Regnery.

Van Gorkom, J. W. 1976. *Social Security: The Long-Term Deficit.* Washington, DC: American Enterprise Institute for Public Policy Research.

Veterans Administration. Various years. *Annual Report.*

Vincent, Cuthbert. 1901. *The Platform Text-Book: Containing the Declaration of Independence, the Constitution of the United States, and All the Platforms of All the Parties.* Book on Demand.

Wainess, Flint. 1999. "The Ways and Means of National Health Care Reform, 1974 and Beyond." *Journal of Health Politics, Policy, and Law* 24:305–333.

Walsh, John Joseph. 1940. *Early Banks in the District of Columbia, 1792–1818.* Washington, DC: Catholic University of America Press.

Warren, Charles. 1923. *The Supreme Court in United States History.* Boston: Little, Brown.

Waters, W. W. (as told to William C. White). 1969. *The Whole Story of the Bonus Army.* New York: Arno Press and New York Times.

Weaver, R. Kent. 2000. *Ending Welfare as We Know It.* Washington, DC: Brookings Institution.

West, Guida. 1981. *The National Welfare Rights Movement: The Social Protest of Poor Women.* New York: Praeger.

West, Guida, and Rhoda Lois Blumberg. 1990. *Women and Social Protest.* New York: Oxford University Press.

White, J., and A. Wildavsky. 1989. *The Deficit and the Public Interest.* Berkeley: University of California Press.

White, Leonard D., with the assistance of Jean Schneider. 1958. *The Republican Era: 1869–1901: A Study in Administrative History.* New York: Macmillan.

Whitman, Kevin, and David Shoffner. 2011. "The Evolution of Social Security's Taxable Maximum." Policy Brief 2011-02. Washington, DC: Social Security Administration, September.

Williams, Charles Richard, and William Henry Smith. 1914. *The Life of Rutherford Birchard Hayes, Nineteenth President of the United States.* Boston: Houghton Mifflin.

Williams, Gertrude. 1944. *The Price of Social Security.* New York: Oxford University Press.

Williams, John Hoyt. 1988. *A Great and Shining Road: The Epic Story of the Transcontinental Railroad.* New York: Times Books.

Witte, Edwin E. 1962a. *Development of the Social Security Act.* Madison: University of Wisconsin Press.

———. 1962b. *Social Security Perspectives.* Madison: University of Wisconsin Press.

Witte, John F. 1985. *The Politics and Development of the Federal Income Tax.* Madison: University of Wisconsin Press.

Woodward, Bob, and Benjamin Weiser. 1994. "Costs Soar for Children's Disability Programs: How 26 Words Cost Taxpayers Billions in New Entitlement Payments." *Washington Post*, February 4,

Wright Jr., Gerald C., Leroy N. Rieselbach, and Lawrence C. Dodd. 1986. *Congress and Policy Change.* New York: Agathon Press.

Wynn, Barbara, Theresa Coughlin, Sehliy Bondarenko, and Brian Bruen. 2002. *Analysis of the Joint Distribution of Disproportionate Share Hospital Payments: Overview of DSH Funding Policies.* Santa Monica, CA: Rand Corporation, September 20.

Young, Jeremiah Simeon. 1902. *Political and Constitutional Study of the Cumberland Road.* Chicago: University of Chicago.

Zelizer, Julian E. 1998. *Taxing America—Wilber D. Mills, Congress and the Senate, 1945–1975.* Cambridge: Cambridge University Press.

Zinn, Howard. 1966. *New Deal Thought.* New York: Bobbs-Merrill.

Index

Page numbers in *italics* indicate tables and figures.